Personal Finance For Canadians

6th Edition

by Eric Tyson, MBA, and
Tony Martin, B.Comm

for **dummies**®
A Wiley Brand

Personal Finance For Canadians For Dummies®, 6th Edition

Published by: **John Wiley & Sons, Inc.**, 111 River Street, Hoboken, NJ 07030-5774, www.wiley.com

Copyright © 2019 by Tony Martin and Eric Tyson

Published simultaneously in Canada

No part of this publication may be reproduced, stored in a retrieval system or transmitted in any form or by any means, electronic, mechanical, photocopying, recording, scanning or otherwise, except as permitted under Sections 107 or 108 of the 1976 United States Copyright Act, without the prior written permission of the Publisher. Requests to the Publisher for permission should be addressed to the Permissions Department, John Wiley & Sons, Inc., 111 River Street, Hoboken, NJ 07030, (201) 748-6011, fax (201) 748-6008, or online at http://www.wiley.com/go/permissions.

Trademarks: Wiley, For Dummies, the Dummies Man logo, Dummies.com, Making Everything Easier, and related trade dress are trademarks or registered trademarks of John Wiley & Sons, Inc. and may not be used without written permission. All other trademarks are the property of their respective owners. John Wiley & Sons, Inc. is not associated with any product or vendor mentioned in this book.

For general information on our other products and services, please contact our Customer Care Department within the U.S. at 877-762-2974, outside the U.S. at 317-572-3993, or fax 317-572-4002. For technical support, please visit https://hub.wiley.com/community/support/dummies.

Wiley publishes in a variety of print and electronic formats and by print-on-demand. Some material included with standard print versions of this book may not be included in e-books or in print-on-demand. If this book refers to media such as a CD or DVD that is not included in the version you purchased, you may download this material at http://booksupport.wiley.com. For more information about Wiley products, visit www.wiley.com.

Library of Congress Control Number: 2018960627

ISBN 978-1-119-52279-9 (pbk); ISBN 978-1-119-52278-2 (ebk); ISBN 978-1-119-52282-9 (ebk)

Manufactured in the United States of America

C10005859_110518

Contents at a Glance

Table of Contents

Introduction

You're probably not a personal finance expert, for good reason. Historically, Personal Finance 101 hasn't been offered in schools — not in high school, university, or even graduate programs. Thankfully, a small but growing number of schools are offering personal-finance-type courses. Of course, every school should.

However, even if you got some financial education and acquired some financial knowledge over the years, you're likely a busy person who doesn't have enough hours in the day to get everything done. So, you want to know how to diagnose your financial situation efficiently (and painlessly) to determine what you should do next. Unfortunately, after figuring out which financial strategies make sense for you, choosing specific financial products in the marketplace is often overwhelming. You have literally thousands of investment, insurance, and loan options to choose from. Talk about information overload!

To further complicate matters, you probably hear about most products through advertising that can be misleading, if not downright false. Of course, some ethical and outstanding firms advertise, but so do those that are more interested in converting your hard-earned income and savings into their short-term profits. And they may not be here tomorrow when you need them.

Perhaps you've ventured online and been attracted to the promise of "free" advice. Unfortunately, discerning the expertise and background (and even identity) of those behind various blogs and websites is too often impossible. And, as we discuss in this book, conflicts of interest (many of which aren't clearly disclosed) abound online.

Despite the development of new media and new financial products and services, folks keep making the same common financial mistakes — procrastinating and lack of planning, wasteful spending, falling prey to financial salespeople and pitches, failing to do sufficient research before making important financial decisions, and so on. This book can keep you from falling into the same traps and get you going on the best paths.

As unfair as it may seem, numerous pitfalls await you when you seek help for your financial problems. The world is filled with biased and bad financial advice. We both constantly see and hear about the consequences of poor advice. All too often, financial advice ignores the big picture and focuses narrowly on investing. Because money is not an end in itself but a part of your whole life, this book helps connect your financial goals and challenges to the rest of your life. You need a broad understanding of personal finance that includes all areas of your financial life: spending, taxes, saving and investing, insurance, and planning for major goals like buying a home, someday running your own business, investing for your future, retiring, and so on.

Even if you understand the financial basics, thinking about your finances in a holistic way can be difficult. Sometimes you're too close to the situation to be objective. Your finances may reflect the history of your life more than they reflect a comprehensive plan for your future.

You want to know the best places to go for your circumstances, so this book contains specific, tried and proven recommendations. We also suggest where to turn next if you need more information and help.

About This Book

The book you hold in your hands reflects hard work and brings you the freshest material for addressing your personal financial quandaries. Here are some of the updates we've made to the book in this edition:

>> Complete coverage of the latest tax laws and rules and how best to take advantage of tax changes in 2018 and beyond affecting individuals, families, investors, and small businesses

>> Expanded and updated coverage of the best ways to shop online (and its changing dangers) and from retail stores

>> The latest changes and rules for Registered Retirement Savings Plans (RRSPs), Registered Education Savings Plans (RESPs), and Tax-Free Savings Accounts (TFSAs), and how best to take advantage of them

>> Updated investment recommendations for exchange-traded funds, mutual funds, international investments, real estate, and more

>> The latest information on government assistance programs, the Canada Pension Plan and Quebec Pension Plan, and Old Age Security, and what all this means in terms of how you should prepare for and live in retirement

>> Revised recommendations for where to get the best insurance deals

>> Coverage of the best personal finance apps

>> Expanded and updated coverage of how to use and make sense of the news and financial resources (especially online)

Aside from being packed with updated information, another great feature of this book is that you can read it from cover to cover if you want, or you can read each chapter and part without having to read what comes before or after. Handy cross-references direct you to other places in the book for more details on a particular subject. If you like, you can skip the sidebars (shaded boxes) and text marked with the Technical Stuff icon; that info is interesting but not essential.

Foolish Assumptions

In writing this book, we made some assumptions about you, dear reader:

>> You want expert advice about important financial topics (such as paying off and reducing the cost of debt, planning for major goals, making wise investments), and you want answers quickly.

>> You want a crash course in personal finance, and you're looking for a book you can read to help solidify major financial concepts and get you thinking about your finances in a more comprehensive way.

This book is basic enough to help novices get their arms around thorny financial issues. But it also challenges advanced readers to think about their finances in a new way and identify areas for improvement.

Icons Used in This Book

The icons in this book help you find particular kinds of information that may be useful to you.

TIP

The Tip icon highlights ways to make the most of your money, as well as the best financial products in the areas of investments, insurance, and so on. When you see this icon, you're sure to find a moneysaving strategy or a product that can help you reach your goals.

REMEMBER

The Remember icon points out information that you'll definitely want to remember.

WARNING

The Warning icon marks things to avoid and points out common mistakes people make when managing their finances. We also use the Warning icon to alert you to scams and scoundrels who prey on the unsuspecting.

TECHNICAL STUFF

The Technical Stuff icon appears beside discussions that aren't critical if you just want to understand basic concepts and get answers to your financial questions. You can safely ignore these paragraphs, but reading them can help deepen and enhance your personal financial knowledge.

Beyond the Book

In addition to what you're reading right now, this product also comes with a free access-anywhere Cheat Sheet that includes debt reduction strategies, more information on RRSPs, and tips for improving your credit score. To get this Cheat Sheet, simply go to www.dummies.com and type **Personal Finance For Canadians For Dummies Cheat Sheet** in the Search box.

Where to Go from Here

This book is organized so you can go wherever you want to find complete information. Want advice on investing strategies, for example? Go to Part 3 for that. You can check out the table of contents to find broad categories of information and a chapter-by-chapter rundown of what this book offers, or you can look up a specific topic in the index.

If you're not sure where you want to go, you may want to start at the beginning with Part 1. It gives you all the basic info you need to assess your financial situation and points to places where you can find more detailed information for improving it.

1
Getting Started with Personal Finance

IN THIS PART . . .

Understand your financial literacy.

Assess your current personal financial health.

Determine where your money is going.

Set and accomplish personal and financial goals.

Chapter **1**

Improving Your Financial Literacy

I n recent years, a continuing stream of studies has indicated that Canadians are, by and large, financially illiterate. Study after study shows that we get a failing grade when it comes to financial literacy.

We know from our many years of work as personal financial teachers, writers, and commentators that many folks do, indeed, have significant gaps in their personal financial knowledge. Though more folks have greater access today to more information than in prior generations, the financial world has grown more complicated, and there are more choices, and pitfalls, than ever before.

Unfortunately, most Canadians don't know how to manage their personal finances because they were never taught how to do so. Their parents may have avoided discussing money in front of them, and most high schools, universities, and colleges lack courses that teach this vital, lifelong-needed skill.

REMEMBER

Some people are fortunate enough to learn the financial keys to success at home, from knowledgeable friends, and from the best expert-written books like this one. Others either never discover important personal finance concepts, or they learn them the hard way — by making lots of costly mistakes. People who lack knowledge make more mistakes, and the more financial errors you commit, the more money passes through your hands and out of your life. In addition to the enormous financial costs, you experience the emotional toll of not feeling in control of your finances. Increased stress and anxiety go hand in hand with not mastering your money.

This chapter examines where people learn about finances and helps you decide whether your current knowledge is helping you or holding you back. You can find out how to improve your financial literacy and take responsibility for your finances, putting you in charge and reducing your anxiety about money. After all, you have more important things to worry about, like what's for dinner.

Talking Money at Home

We were both fortunate — our parents instilled in us the importance of personal financial management. Our moms and dads taught us a lot of things that have been invaluable throughout our lives, and among those things were sound principles for earning, spending, and saving money. Our parents had to know how to do these things, because they were raising large families on (usually) one modest income. They knew the importance of making the most of what you have and of passing that vital skill on to your kids.

WARNING

In many families, money is a taboo subject — parents don't level with their kids about the limitations, realities, and details of their budgets. Some parents we talk with believe that dealing with money is an adult issue and that children should be insulated from it so they can enjoy being kids. In many families, kids hear about money *only* when disagreements and financial crises bubble to the surface. Thus begins the harmful cycle of children having negative associations with money and financial management.

In other cases, parents with the best of intentions pass on their bad money-management habits. You may have learned from a parent, for example, to buy things to cheer yourself up. Or you may have witnessed a family member maniacally chasing get-rich-quick business and investment ideas. Now, we're not saying that you shouldn't listen to your parents. But in the area of personal finance, as in any other area, poor family advice and modeling can be problematic.

Think about where your parents learned about money management and then consider whether they had the time, energy, or inclination to research choices before making their decisions. For example, if they didn't do enough research or had faulty information, your parents may mistakenly have thought that banks were the best places for investing money or that buying stocks was like going to Las Vegas. (You can find the best places to invest your money in Part 3 of this book.)

In still other cases, the parents have the right approach, but the kids do the opposite out of rebellion. For example, if your parents spent money carefully and thoughtfully and often made you feel denied, you may tend to do the opposite, buying yourself gifts the moment any extra money comes your way.

Although you can't change what the educational system and your parents did or didn't teach you about personal finances, you now have the ability to find out what you need to know to manage your finances.

PERSONAL FINANCE AT SCHOOL

In schools, the main problem with personal finance education is the lack of classes, not that kids already know the information or that the skills are too complex for children to understand.

Nancy Donovan teaches personal finance to her fifth-grade math class as a way to illustrate how math can be used in the real world. "Students choose a career, find jobs, and figure out what their taxes and take-home paycheques will be. They also have to rent apartments and figure out a monthly budget," says Donovan. "Students like it, and parents have commented to me how surprised they are by how much financial knowledge their kids can handle." Donovan also has her students invest $10,000 (play money) and then track their investments' performance.

Urging schools to teach the basics of personal finance is just common sense. Children need to be taught how to manage a household budget, the importance of saving money for future goals, and the consequences of overspending. Unfortunately, few schools offer classes like Donovan's. In most cases, the financial basics aren't taught at all.

In the minority of schools that do offer a course remotely related to personal finance, the class is typically in economics (and an elective at that). "Archaic theory is being taught, and it doesn't do anything for the students as far as preparing them for the real world," says one high school principal. Having taken more than our fair share of economics courses in university, we understand the principal's concerns.

Some people argue that teaching children financial basics is their parents' job. However, this well-meant sentiment is what we're relying on now, and for all too many, it isn't working. In some families, financial illiteracy is passed on from generation to generation.

Education takes place in the home, on the streets, and in the schools. Therefore, schools must bear some responsibility for teaching this skill. However, if you're raising children, remember that no one cares as much as you do or has as much ability to teach the important life skill of personal money management.

TIP

If you have children of your own, don't underestimate their potential or send them out into the world without the skills they need to be productive and happy adults. Buy them some good financial books when they head off to university or begin their first job.

Identifying Unreliable Sources of Information

Most folks know that they're not financial geniuses. So they set out to take control of their money matters by reading about personal finance or consulting a financial advisor.

But reading and seeking advice to find out how to manage your money can be dangerous if you're a novice. Misinformation can come from popular and seemingly reliable information sources, as we explain in the following sections. (Because the pitfalls are numerous and the challenges significant when choosing an advisor, we devote Chapter 19 to the financial planning business and tell you what you need to know to avoid being duped and disappointed.)

Understanding the dangers of free financial content online

In addition to being able to quickly access what we want, the other major attraction of the Internet is the abundance of seemingly free websites providing piles of free content. Appearances, however, can be greatly deceiving.

There are exceptions to any rule, but the fact of the matter is that the vast majority of websites purporting to provide a seemingly never-ending array of "free" content are rife with conflicts of interest and quality problems due to the following:

>> **Advertising:** Any publication that accepts advertising has a potential conflict of interest because it may not want to publish articles that would upset its advertisers. Such a mind-set, however, can stand in the way of telling consumers the unvarnished truth about various products and services. For example, auto-leasing companies aren't very interested in advertising someplace that publishes articles highlighting the negatives of leasing. (Check out the section "Publishers pandering to advertisers" later in this chapter for more on the power of advertising to influence the financial information you encounter online, on TV, and elsewhere.)

>> **Advertorials:** Too many website owners are unwilling or unable to pay real writers for quality content and instead publish articles that are written and provided by advertisers. These pieces of "content" are known as *advertorials* and, in the worst cases, aren't even clearly labeled as advertisements, which is precisely what they are.

>> **Affiliate relationships:** Many companies now pay "referral fees" to websites that bring in new customers. Here's how that practise causes major conflicts of interest. On a financial website, you read a glowing review of a particular financial product or service. And the site provides a helpful link to the website of the provider of that product or service. Unbeknownst to you, when you click that link and buy something, the seller kicks money back to the "affiliate" who reeled you in. At a minimum, such relationships should be clearly disclosed and detailed in any review.

>> **Insufficient editorial oversight:** At most established, quality print publications, there are usually several layers of editors who oversee the publication and all its articles. This structure helps ensure the accuracy of what gets into print (although bias, such as political bias, isn't necessarily controlled). Unfortunately, the shoestring budget on which many websites operate precludes these quality-control checks and balances. Thus, sites operated by nonexperts proffering advice place you at great risk.

>> **Lack of accountability:** In part because of a lack of editorial oversight, there's also often a lack of accountability for advice given online. This situation is especially problematic on the numerous sites that are run without disclosure of who is actually in charge of the site and/or who is writing the articles. Although such anonymity may be helpful to the site and its content providers, it's certainly not in your best interests because it prevents you from checking out the background, qualifications, and track record of the providers.

Recognizing fake financial gurus

Before you take financial advice from anyone, examine her background, including professional work experience and education credentials. This is true whether you're getting advice from an advisor, writer, talk-show host, or TV financial reporter.

If you can't easily find such information, that's usually a red flag. People with something to hide or a lack of something redeeming to say about themselves usually don't promote their background.

Of course, just because someone seems to have a relatively impressive-sounding background doesn't mean that he has your best interests in mind or has honestly presented his qualifications. *Forbes* magazine journalist William P. Barrett presented a sobering review of financial author Suze Orman's stated credentials and qualifications:

> Besides books and other royalties, Orman's earned income has come mainly from selling insurance — which gets much more attention in her book than do stocks or bonds. . . . The jacket of her video says she has "18 years of experience at major Wall Street institutions." In fact, she has 7.

When the *Forbes* piece came out, Orman's publicist tried to discredit it and made it sound as if the magazine had falsely criticized Orman. In response, the *San Francisco Chronicle*, which is the nearest major newspaper to Orman's hometown, picked up on the *Forbes* piece and ran a story of its own — written by Mark Veverka in his "Street Smarts" column — which substantiated the *Forbes* story.

Veverka went through the *Forbes* piece point by point and gave Orman's company and the public relations firm numerous opportunities to provide information contrary to the piece, but they did not. Here's some of what Veverka recounts from his contact with them:

> If you want your side told, you have to return reporters' telephone calls. But alas, no callback.

> . . . Orman's publicist said a written response to the *Forbes* piece and the "Street Smarts" column would be sent by facsimile to the *Chronicle.* . . . . However, no fax was ever sent. They blew me off. Twice.

> In what was becoming an extraordinary effort to be fair, I placed more telephone calls over several days to Orman Financial and the publicist, asking for either an interview with Orman or an official response. If Orman didn't fudge about her years on Wall Street or didn't let her commodity-trading advisor license lapse, surely we could straighten all of this out, right?

> Still, no answer. Nada . . . I called yet again. Finally, literally on deadline, a woman who identified herself as Orman's "consultant" called me to talk "off the record" about the column. What she ended up doing was bashing the *Forbes* piece and my column but not for publication. More importantly, she offered no official retort to allegations made by veteran *Forbes* writer William Barrett. I have to say, it was an incredibly unprofessional attempt at spinning. And I've been spun by the worst of them.

You can't always accept stated credentials and qualifications at face value, because some people lie (witness the billions lost to hedge-fund Ponzi-scheme-man

Bernie Madoff). You can't sniff out liars by the way they look, their résumé, their gender, or their age. You can, however, increase your chances of being tipped off by being skeptical (and by regularly reading the "Guru Watch" section of Eric's website at www.erictyson.com).

WARNING

You can see a number of hucksters for what they are by using common sense in reviewing some of their outrageous claims. Some sources of advice, such as Wade Cook's investment seminars, lure you in by promising outrageous returns. The stock market has generated average annual returns of about 9 percent to 10 percent over the long term. However, Cook, a former taxi driver, promoted his seminars as an "alive, hands-on, do the deals, two-day intense course in making huge returns in the stock market. If you aren't getting 20 percent per month, or 300 percent annualized returns on your investments, you need to be there." (We guess we do, as does every investment manager and individual investor we know!)

Cook's get-rich-quick seminars, which cost more than $6,000, were so successful at attracting people that his company went public in the late 1990s and generated annual revenues of more than $100 million. Cook's "techniques" included trading in and out of stocks and options after short holding periods of weeks, days, or even hours. His trading strategies can best be described as techniques that are based upon technical analysis — that is, charting a stock's price movements and volume history, and then making predictions based on those charts.

REMEMBER

The perils of following an approach that advocates short-term trading with the allure of high profits are numerous:

>> You'll rack up enormous brokerage commissions.

>> You won't make big profits — quite the reverse. If you stick with this approach, you'll underperform the market averages.

>> You'll make yourself a nervous wreck. This type of trading is gambling, not investing. Get sucked up in it, and you'll lose more than money — you may also lose the love and respect of your family and friends.

If Cook's followers were able to indeed earn the 300 percent annual returns his seminars claimed to help you achieve, any investor starting with just $10,000 would vault to the top of the list of the world's wealthiest people (ahead of Bill Gates and Warren Buffett) in just 11 years!

HOW SOME GURUS BECOME POPULAR

You may be wondering how Wade Cook became so popular despite the obvious flaws in his advice (see the section "Recognizing fake financial gurus" for the goods on Cook). He promoted his seminars through infomercials and other advertising, including radio ads on respected news stations. The high stock market returns of the 1990s brought greed back into fashion. (Our experience has been that you see more of this greed near market tops.)

The attorneys general of numerous states sued Cook's company and sought millions of dollars in consumer refunds. The suits alleged that the company lied about its investment track record (not a big surprise — this company claimed that you'd make 300 percent per year in stocks).

Cook's company settled the blizzard of state and U.S. Federal Trade Commission (FTC) lawsuits against his firm by agreeing to accurately disclose its trading record in future promotions and give refunds to customers who were misled by past inflated return claims. (That didn't stop Cook, however, from getting into more legal hot water — and serving a seven-year prison term for failing to pay millions in personal income taxes.)

According to a news report by *Bloomberg News,* Cook's firm disclosed that it lost a whopping 89 percent of its own money trading during one year in which the stock market fared well. As Deb Bortner, director of the Washington State Securities Division and president of the North American Securities Administrators Association, observed, "Either Wade is unable to follow his own system, which he claims is simple to follow, or the system doesn't work."

Don't assume that someone with something to sell, who is getting good press and running lots of ads, will take care of you. That "guru" may just be good at press relations and self-promotion. Certainly, talk shows and the media at large can and do provide useful information on a variety of topics, but bad eggs sometimes turn up. These bad eggs may not always smell bad upfront. In fact, they may hoodwink people for years before finally being exposed. Review Part 5 of this book for the details on resources you can trust and those that can cause you to go bust!

Publishers pandering to advertisers

WARNING

Thousands of publications and media outlets — newspapers, magazines, websites, blogs, radio stations, TV networks, and so on — dole out personal financial advice and perspectives. Although some of these "service providers" collect revenue from subscribers, virtually all are dependent — in some cases, fully dependent (especially the Internet, radio, and TV) — on advertising dollars. Although advertising is a necessary part of capitalism, advertisers can taint and, in some cases, dictate the content of what you read, listen to, and view.

Be sure to consider how dependent a publication or media outlet is on advertising. We find that "free" publications, websites, radio stations, and TV networks are the ones that most often create conflicts of interest by pandering to advertisers. (They derive all their revenue from advertising.)

Much of what's on the Internet is also advertiser driven. Many investing websites offer advice about individual stocks. Interestingly, such sites derive much of their revenue from online brokerage firms seeking to recruit customers who are foolish enough to believe that selecting their own stocks is the best way to invest. (See Part 3 of this book for more information about your investment options.)

As you read various publications, watch TV, or listen to the radio, note how consumer oriented these media are. Do you get the feeling that they're looking out for your interests? For example, if lots of auto manufacturers advertise, does the media outlet ever tell you how to save money when shopping for a car or the importance of buying a car within your means? Or is it primarily creating an advertiser-friendly broadcast or publication?

Jumping over Real and Imaginary Hurdles to Financial Success

Perhaps you know that you should live within your means, buy and hold sound investments for the long term, and secure proper insurance coverage; however, you can't bring yourself to do these things. Everyone knows how difficult it is to break habits that have been practised for many years. The temptation to spend money lurks everywhere you turn. Ads show attractive and popular people enjoying the fruits of their labors — a new car, an exotic vacation, and a lavish home.

Maybe you felt deprived by your tightwad parents as a youngster, or maybe you're bored with life and you like the adventure of buying new things. If only you could hit it big on one or two investments, you think, you could get rich quick and do what you really want with your life. As for disasters and catastrophes, well, those things happen to other people, not to you. Besides, you'll probably have advance warning of pending problems, so you can prepare accordingly, right?

Your emotions and temptations can get the better of you. Certainly, part of successfully managing your finances involves coming to terms with your shortcomings and the consequences of your behaviours. If you don't, you may end up enslaved to a dead-end job so you can keep feeding your spending addiction. Or you may spend more time with your investments than you do with your family and friends. Or unexpected events may leave you reeling financially; disasters and catastrophes can happen to anyone at any time.

Discovering what (or who) is holding you back

A variety of personal and emotional hurdles can get in the way of making the best financial moves. As we discuss earlier in this chapter, a lack of financial knowledge (which stems from a lack of personal financial education) can stand in the way of making good decisions.

But we've seen some people caught in the psychological trap of blaming something else for their financial problems. For example, some people believe that adult problems can be traced back to childhood and how they were raised.

We don't want to disregard the negative impact particular backgrounds can have on some people's tendency to make the wrong choices during their lives. Exploring your personal history can certainly yield clues to what makes you tick. That said, adults make choices and engage in behaviours that affect themselves as well as others. They shouldn't blame their parents for their own inability to plan for their financial futures, live within their means, and make sound investments.

Some people also tend to blame their financial shortcomings on not earning more income. Such people believe that if only they earned more, their financial (and personal) problems would melt away. Our experience working and speaking with people from diverse economic backgrounds has taught us that achieving financial success — and more important, personal happiness — has virtually nothing to do with how much income a person makes but rather with what she makes of what she has. We know financially wealthy people who are emotionally poor even though they have all the material goods they want. Likewise, we know people who are quite happy, content, and emotionally wealthy even though they're struggling financially.

Canadians — even those who have not had an "easy" life — ought to be able to come up with numerous things to be happy about and grateful for: a family who loves them; friends who laugh at their stupid jokes; the freedom to catch a movie or play or to read a good book; or a great singing voice, a good sense of humour, or a full head of hair.

Developing good financial habits

After you understand the basic concepts and know where to buy the best financial products when you need them, you'll soon see that managing personal finances well is not much more difficult than other things you do regularly, like tying your shoelaces and getting to work.

REMEMBER

Regardless of your income, you can make your dollars stretch farther if you practise good financial habits and avoid mistakes. In fact, the lower your income, the more important it is that you make the most of your income and savings (because you don't have the luxury of falling back on your next big paycheque to bail you out).

More and more industries are subject to global competition, so you need to be on your financial toes now more than ever. Job security is waning; layoffs and retraining for new jobs are increasing. Putting in 30 years for one company and retiring with the gold watch and lifetime pension are becoming as rare as never having problems with your computer.

Speaking of company pensions, odds are increasing that you work for an employer that has you save toward your own retirement instead of providing a pension for you. Not only do you need to save the money, but you must also decide how to invest it. Chapter 12 can help you get a handle on investing in retirement plans.

Personal finance involves much more than managing and investing money. It also includes making all the pieces of your financial life fit together; it means lifting yourself out of financial illiteracy. Like planning a vacation, managing your personal finances means forming a plan for making the best use of your limited time and dollars.

REMEMBER

Intelligent personal financial strategies have little to do with your gender, ethnicity, or marital status. All people need to manage their finances wisely. Some aspects of financial management become more or less important at different points in your life, but for the most part, the principles remain the same for everyone.

Knowing the right answers isn't enough. You have to practise good financial habits just as you practise other good habits, such as brushing your teeth or eating a healthy diet and getting some exercise. Don't be overwhelmed. As you read this book, make a short list of your financial marching orders and then start working away. Throughout this book, we highlight ways you can overcome temptations and keep control of your money rather than let your emotions and money rule you. (We discuss common financial problems in Chapter 2.)

REMEMBER

What you do with your money is a quite personal and confidential matter. In this book, we try to provide guidance that can keep you in sound financial health. You don't have to take it all — pick what works best for you and understand the pros and cons of your options. But from this day forward, please don't make the easily avoidable mistakes or overlook the sound strategies that we discuss throughout this book.

Throughout your journey, we hope to challenge and even change the way you think about money and about making important personal financial decisions — and sometimes even about the meaning of life. No, we're not philosophers, but we do know that money — for better but more often for worse — is connected to many other parts of our lives.

Chapter **2**

Measuring Your Financial Health

H ow financially healthy are you? When was the last time you reviewed your overall financial situation, including analyzing your spending, savings, future goals, and insurance? If you're like most people, either you've never done this exercise or you did so too long ago.

This chapter guides you through a *financial physical* to help you detect problems with your current financial health. But don't dwell on your "problems." View them for what they are: opportunities to improve your financial situation. In fact, the more areas you can identify that stand to benefit from improvement, the greater the potential you may have to build real wealth and accomplish your financial and personal goals.

Avoiding Common Money Mistakes

Financial problems, like many medical problems, are best detected early. And as with your personal health, the best "problems" are those avoided — clean living is a good thing, right? Here are the common personal financial problems we've seen in our work:

>> **Not planning:** Most of us procrastinate. That's why we have deadlines — and deadline extensions. Unfortunately, you may have no explicit deadlines with your personal finances. You can allow your credit-card debt to accumulate, or you can leave your savings sitting in lousy investments for years. You can pay higher taxes, leave gaps in your retirement and insurance coverage, and overpay for financial products. Of course, planning your finances isn't as much fun as planning a vacation, but doing the former can help you take more of the latter. See Chapter 4 for details on setting financial goals.

>> **Overspending:** Simple arithmetic helps you determine that savings is the difference between what you earn and what you spend — assuming that you're not spending more than you're earning! To increase your savings, you either have to work more, increase your earning power through education or job advancement, get to know a wealthy family who wants to leave its fortune to you, or spend less. For most people, especially over the short term, the thrifty approach is the key to building savings and wealth. (Check out Chapter 3 for a primer on figuring out where your money goes; Chapter 6 gives advice for reducing your spending.)

>> **Buying with consumer credit:** Even with the benefit of today's relatively low interest rates, carrying a balance month to month on your credit card or buying a car on credit means that even more of your future earnings are going to be earmarked for debt repayment. Buying on credit encourages you to spend more than you can really afford. Chapter 5 discusses debt and credit problems.

>> **Delaying saving for retirement:** Most folks say that they want to retire by their mid-60s or sooner. But to accomplish this goal, they need to save a reasonable chunk (around 10 percent) of their incomes starting sooner rather than later. The longer you wait to start saving for retirement, the harder reaching your goal will be. And you'll pay much more in taxes to boot if you don't take advantage of the tax benefits of investing through particular retirement plans, such as a Registered Retirement Savings Plan (RRSP). For information on planning for retirement, see Chapters 4 and 12.

>> **Falling prey to financial sales pitches:** Steer clear of people who pressure you to make decisions, promise you high investment returns, and lack the proper training and experience to help you. Supposed great deals that can't wait for a little reflection or a second opinion are often disasters waiting to happen. A sucker may be born every minute, but a slick salesperson is

pitching something every second! For important investment concepts and what kinds of investments to avoid, turn to Chapter 8.

» **Not doing your homework:** To get the best deal, shop around, read reviews, and get advice from objective third parties. You also need to check references and track records so you don't hire incompetent, self-serving, or fraudulent financial advisors. (For more on hiring financial planners, see Chapter 19.) But with all the different financial products available, making informed financial decisions has become an overwhelming task. We do a lot of the homework for you with the recommendations in this book. We also explain what additional research you need to do and how to do it.

» **Making decisions based on emotion:** You're most vulnerable to making the wrong moves financially after a major life event or change (a job loss, a divorce, or a death in the family, for example), or when you feel under pressure. Maybe your investments plunged in value. Or perhaps a recent divorce has you fearing that you won't be able to afford to retire when you planned, so you pour thousands of dollars into some newfangled financial product. Take your time and keep your emotions out of the picture. In Chapter 22, we discuss how to approach major life changes and determine what changes you may need to make to your financial picture.

» **Not separating the wheat from the chaff:** In any field in which you're not an expert, you're at risk of following the advice of someone you think is an expert but really isn't. This book shows you how to separate the financial fluff from the financial facts. (Flip to Chapters 20 and 21 for information on how to evaluate financial advice online and how to evaluate financial coverage in the mass media.) You're the person who is best able to manage your personal finances. Educate and trust yourself!

» **Exposing yourself to catastrophic risk:** You're vulnerable if you and your family don't have insurance to pay for financially devastating losses. In the worst cases, folks without a savings reserve and a support network can end up homeless. Many people lack sufficient insurance coverage to replace their income. Don't wait for a tragedy to strike to find out whether you have the right insurance coverage. Check out Part 4 for more on insurance.

» **Focusing too much on money:** Placing too much emphasis on making and saving money can warp your perspective on what's important in life. Money is not the first — or even second — priority in happy people's lives. Your health, relationships with family and friends, career satisfaction, and fulfilling interests are more significant. That's not to say that it's okay to ignore or give insufficient attention to your personal finances and associated decisions.

REMEMBER

Money problems can be fixed over time with changes in your behaviour. That's what the rest of this book is all about.

Determining Your Financial Net Worth

Your financial net worth is an important barometer of your monetary health. Your net worth indicates your capacity to accomplish major financial goals, such as buying a home, retiring, and withstanding unexpected expenses or loss of income.

Your *net worth* is your financial assets minus your financial liabilities:

Financial Assets – Financial Liabilities = Net Worth

The following sections explain how to determine those numbers.

Adding up your financial assets

A *financial asset* is real money or an investment you can convert into your favourite currency that you can use to buy things now or in the future. Financial assets generally include the money you have in bank accounts, stocks, bonds, mutual funds, and exchange-traded funds (see Part 3, which deals with investments). Money that you have in retirement plans (including those with your employer) and the value of any businesses or real estate that you own are also counted.

TIP

We generally recommend that you exclude your personal residence when figuring your financial assets. Include your home only if you expect to sell it someday or otherwise live off the money you now have tied up in it (perhaps by taking out a reverse mortgage, which we discuss in Chapter 15). If you plan on eventually tapping into the *equity* (the difference between the market value and any debt owed on the property), add that portion of the equity that you expect to use to your list of assets.

Assets can also include your future expected Canada Pension Plan (CPP) or Quebec Pension Plan (QPP) benefits, Old Age Security (OAS), and other government social security income, as well as any pension payments (if your employer has such a plan). These assets are usually quoted in dollars per month rather than as a lump-sum value. In Table 2-1, we explain how to account for these monthly benefits when tallying your financial assets.

REMEMBER

Consumer items — such as your car, clothing, stereo, and so forth — do *not* count as financial assets. We understand that adding these things to your assets makes your assets *look* larger (and some financial software and publications encourage you to list these items as assets), but you can't live off them unless you sell them. And if you do sell them, you likely won't get anywhere near what you'd like to think you would get.

TABLE 2-1   ## Your Financial Assets

Account	Value
Savings and investment accounts (including RRSPs and other retirement plans):	
Example: Bank savings account	*$5,000*
_____	$_____
_____	$_____
_____	$_____
_____	$_____
_____	$_____
_____	$_____
Subtotal =	$_____
Benefits earned that pay a monthly retirement income:	
Employer's pensions	$_____ per month
CPP or QPP	$_____ per month
OAS and other government income support programs	
	× 240 *
Subtotal =	$_____
Total financial assets (add the two subtotals) =	$_____

To convert benefits that will be paid to you monthly into a total dollar amount, and for purposes of simplification, assume that you'll spend 20 years in retirement. Inflation may reduce the value of your employer's pension if it doesn't contain a cost-of-living increase each year in the same way that CPP/QPP does. Don't sweat this now — you can take care of that concern in the section on retirement planning in Chapter 4.

Subtracting your financial liabilities

To arrive at your financial net worth, you must subtract your *financial liabilities* from your assets. Liabilities include loans and debts outstanding, such as credit-card and car-loan debts. When figuring your liabilities, include money you borrowed from family and friends — unless you're not expected to pay it back!

Include mortgage debt on your home as a liability *only* if you include the value of your home in your asset list. Be sure to also include debt owed on other real estate — no matter what (because you count the value of investment real estate as an asset).

Crunching your numbers

Table 2-1 provides a place for you to figure your financial assets. Go ahead and write in the spaces provided, unless you plan to lend this book to someone and don't want to put your money situation on display. *Note:* See Table 4-1 in Chapter 4 to estimate your CPP/QPP, OAS, and other government benefits.

Now comes the potentially depressing part — figuring out your debts and loans in Table 2-2.

TABLE 2-2

Your Financial Liabilities

Loan	Balance
Example: Bank credit card	*$4,000*
_____	$_____
_____	$_____
_____	$_____
_____	$_____
_____	$_____
_____	$_____
Total financial liabilities =	**$_____**

Now you can subtract your liabilities from your assets to figure your net worth in Table 2-3.

TABLE 2-3

Your Net Worth

Find	Write It Here
Total financial assets (from Table 2-1)	$_____
Total financial liabilities (from Table 2-2)	– $_____
Net worth =	**$_____**

Interpreting your net worth

Your net worth is important and useful only to you and your unique situation and goals. What seems like a lot of money to a person with a simple lifestyle may seem like a pittance to a person with high expectations and a desire for an opulent lifestyle.

In Chapter 4, you can crunch numbers to determine your financial status more precisely for goals such as retirement planning. We also discuss saving toward other important goals in that chapter. In the meantime, if your net worth (excluding expected monthly retirement benefits such as those from CPP or QPP, OAS, and pensions) is negative or less than half your annual income, take notice. If you're in your 20s and you're just starting to work, a low net worth is less concerning and not unusual. Focus on turning this number positive over the next several years. However, if you're in your 30s or older, consider this a wakeup call to aggressively address your financial situation.

Getting rid of your debts — beginning with the ones with the highest interest rates — is the most important thing. Then you want to build a safety reserve equal to three to six months of living expenses. Your overall plan should involve getting out of debt (Chapter 5), reducing your spending (Chapter 6), and developing tax-wise ways to save and invest your future earnings (Part 3).

Examining Your Credit Score and Reports

You may not know or care, but you probably have a personal credit report and a credit score. Lenders examine your credit report and score before granting you a loan or credit line. This section highlights what you need to know about your credit score and reports, including how to obtain them and how to improve them.

Understanding what your credit data includes and means

A *credit report* contains information such as

>> **Personal identifying information:** Includes your name, address, Social Insurance Number, and so on

>> **Record of credit accounts:** Details when each account was opened, the latest balance, your payment history, and so on

>> **Bankruptcy filings:** Indicates whether you've filed bankruptcy in recent years

>> **Inquiries:** Lists who has accessed your credit report because you applied for credit

Your *credit score*, which is not the same as your credit report, is a three-digit score based on the report. Lenders use your credit score as a predictor of your likelihood of defaulting on repaying your borrowings. As such, your credit score has a major impact on whether a lender is willing to extend you a particular loan and at what interest rate.

FICO is the leading credit score in the industry. FICO scores range from a low of 300 to a high of 850. Most scores fall in the 600s and 700s. As with university entrance examinations, higher scores are better. (In recent years, the major credit bureaus — Equifax, Experian, and TransUnion — have developed their own credit scoring systems, but many lenders still use FICO the most.)

The higher your credit score, the lower your predicted likelihood of defaulting on a loan (see Figure 2-1). The *rate of credit delinquency* refers to the percentage of consumers who will become 90 days late or later in repaying a creditor within the next two years. As you can see in the chart, consumers with low credit scores have dramatically higher rates of falling behind on their loans. Thus, low credit scorers are considered much riskier borrowers, and fewer lenders are willing to offer them a given loan; those who do offer loans charge relatively high interest rates.

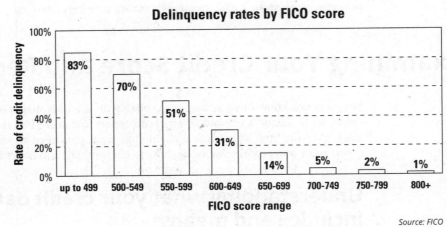

FIGURE 2-1:
Lenders use credit scores to estimate how likely people are to default on a loan.

Source: FICO

The median FICO score is around 720. You generally qualify for the best lending rates if your credit score is in the mid-700s or higher.

Obtaining your credit reports and score

Given the importance of your personal credit report, you may be pleased to know that federal law entitles you to receive a free copy of your credit report annually from the two main credit bureaus in Canada (Equifax and TransUnion).

WARNING

Both the Equifax and TransUnion websites promote their online services, encouraging you to pay for quick online access to your credit report. However, you can obtain a credit report for free by requesting it by mail. You need to submit a form (which you can print online) along with photocopies of two government-issued pieces of identification. You can contact Equifax and TransUnion here:

Equifax Canada National Consumer Relations
P.O. Box 190, Station Jean-Talon
Montreal, QC H1S 2Z2
800-465-7166
www.equifax.com

TransUnion Consumer Relations Department
P.O. Box 338, LCD1
Hamilton, ON L8L 7W2
800-663-9980
www.transunion.ca

x avoil

Residents of Quebec can use the following information to contact TransUnion:

Centre De Relations Aux Consommateurs TransUnion
1 Place Laval Ouest, Bureau 370
Laval, QC H7N 1A1
877-713-3393
www.transunion.ca

When you receive your reports, the best first step is to examine them for possible mistakes (see the upcoming section "Getting credit report errors corrected" to find out how to fix problems in your reports).

You may be surprised to find that your credit reports do *not* include your credit score. The reason for this is quite simple: Although the credit agencies must provide a free credit report annually to those who request a copy, they aren't mandated to provide a credit score. So, if you want to obtain your credit score, it's going to cost you.

TIP

You can pay Equifax and TransUnion for your credit score. Save your money. There are lower-cost ways to get your credit score. In fact, you can get your current credit score without paying anything! You can start with the FICO score simulator at www.myfico.com/free-credit-score-range-estimator, which provides you with an estimated range for your FICO score based upon your answers to a short list of questions about your history with and usage of credit.

WARNING

If you do choose to pay for your current credit score, be crystal clear about what you're buying. You may not realize that you're agreeing to some sort of ongoing credit monitoring service for $200 or more per year, an expenditure we don't generally feel is worthwhile. And the credit bureaus' websites seem designed to send you down the wrong — and much more expensive — path. Consider TransUnion's particularly devious online form for obtaining your credit report and score. It begins by asking you for a lot of personal information — even your Social Insurance Number, which it then notes in much smaller letters is "optional."

Worse, it doesn't make it clear what exactly you're purchasing or the price. It's only over on the right-hand side of the page, under a bright banner saying "You have chosen:" accompanied by yet another stock photo of a woman beaming a smile of sheer joy, that you find out the truth: Not only is the cost $19.95, but you're actually signing up for TransUnion's ongoing credit monitoring service . . . for $19.95 *every month!*

Improving your credit reports and score

Instead of simply throwing money into buying your credit scores or paying for some ongoing monitoring service to which you may not give much attention, take an interest in improving your credit standing and score. Working to boost your credit rating is especially worthwhile if you know that your credit report contains detrimental information.

Here are the most important actions that you can take to boost your attractiveness to lenders:

>> **Get both of your credit reports, and be sure each is accurate.** Correct errors (as we explain in the next section), and be especially sure to get accounts removed from your credit report if they aren't yours and show late payments or are in collection.

>> **Ask to have any late or missed payments that are more than seven years old removed.** Ditto for a bankruptcy that occurred more than ten years ago.

>> **Pay all your bills on time.** To ensure on-time payments, sign up for automatic bill payment, a service that most companies (like phone and utility providers) offer. You can also arrange to have your credit-card bill automatically paid off in full every month. Just be sure to take the time to review your statements before the payment date.

>> **Be loyal if it doesn't cost you.** The older your open loan accounts are, the better your credit rating will be. Closing old accounts and opening a bunch of new ones generally lowers your credit score. But don't be loyal if it costs you! For example, if you can refinance your mortgage and save some money, by all means do so. The same logic applies if you're carrying credit-card debt at a high interest rate and you want to transfer that balance to a lower-rate card. If your current credit-card provider refuses to match a lower rate you find elsewhere, move your balance and save yourself some money (see Chapter 5 for details).

>> **Limit your debt and debt accounts.** The more loans, especially consumer loans, that you hold, and the higher the balances, the lower your credit score will be.

>> **Work to pay down consumer revolving debt (such as credit-card debt).** Turn to Chapters 5 and 6 for suggestions.

Getting credit report errors corrected

If you obtain your credit report and find a blemish on it that you don't recognize as being your mistake or fault, do *not* assume that the information is correct. Credit reporting bureaus and the creditors who report credit information to these bureaus often make errors.

You hope and expect that, if a credit bureau has negative and incorrect information in your credit report and you bring the mistake to their attention, they'll graciously and expeditiously fix the error. If you believe that, you're the world's greatest optimist; perhaps you also think you won't have to wait in line to renew your passport or dispute a parking ticket.

You're going to have to fill out a form on a website, make some phone calls, or write a letter or two to fix the problems on your credit report. Here's how to correct most errors that aren't your fault:

>> **If the credit problem is someone else's:** A surprising number of personal credit report glitches are the result of someone else's negative information getting on your credit report. If the bad information on your report is completely foreign looking to you, contact the credit bureau (by phone or online) and explain that you need more information because you don't recognize the creditor.

>> **If the creditor made a mistake:** Creditors make mistakes, too. You need to write or call the creditor to get it to correct the erroneous information that it sent to the credit bureau. Phoning the creditor first usually works best. (The credit bureau should be able to tell you how to reach the creditor if you don't know how.) If necessary, follow up with a letter or email to document and provide a record of your request.

TIP

Whether you speak with a credit bureau or an actual lender, make note of your conversations. If representatives say that they can fix the problem, get their names, email addresses, and phone extensions, and follow up with them if they don't deliver as promised. If you're ensnared in bureaucratic red tape, escalate the situation by speaking with a department manager.

Telling your side of the story

With a minor credit infraction, some lenders may simply ask for an explanation. Years ago, Eric had a credit-report blemish that was the result of being away for several weeks and missing the payment due date for a couple of small bills. When his proposed mortgage lender saw his late payments, the lender asked for a simple written explanation.

You and a creditor may not see eye to eye on a problem, and the creditor may refuse to budge. If that's the case, credit bureaus are generally required to allow you to add a 100-word explanation to your credit file.

Sidestepping credit-repair firms

Online and in various publications, you may see ads for credit-repair companies that claim to fix your credit-report problems. In the worst cases we've seen, these firms charge outrageous amounts of money and don't come close to fulfilling their marketing hype.

If you have legitimate glitches on your credit report, credit-repair firms can't make the glitches disappear. Hope springs eternal, however — some people would like to believe that their credit problems can be magically fixed and expunged.

REMEMBER

If your credit-report problems are fixable, you can fix them yourself. You don't need to pay a credit-repair company big bucks to do it.

Knowing the Difference between Bad Debt and Good Debt

Why do you borrow money? Usually, you borrow money because you don't have enough to buy something you want or need — like a university or college education. A four-year university education can easily cost $30,000 to $60,000, and double that if you include residence, room and board, or renting an apartment. Most people don't have that kind of spare cash. So, borrowing money to finance part of that cost enables you to buy the education.

How about a new car? A trip to your friendly local car dealer shows you that a new set of wheels can set you back $25,000 or more. Although more people may have the money to pay for that than, say, the university education, what if you don't? Should you finance the car the way you finance the education?

The auto dealers and bankers who are eager to give you an auto loan say that you deserve and can afford to drive a nice, new car, and they tell you to borrow away (or lease, which we don't love either — see Chapter 6). We say, "No! No! No!" Why do we disagree with the auto dealers and lenders? For starters, we're not trying to sell you a car or loan from which we derive a profit! More important, there's a *big* difference between borrowing for something that represents a long-term investment and borrowing for short-term consumption.

If you spend, say, $1,500 on a vacation, the money is gone. *Poof!* You may have fond memories and photos, but you have nothing of financial value to show for it. "But," you say, "vacations replenish my soul and make me more productive when I return — the vacation more than pays for itself!"

We're not saying that you shouldn't take a vacation. By all means, take one, two, three, or as many vacations and trips as you can afford every year. But the point is to take what you can afford. If you have to borrow money in the form of an outstanding balance on your credit card for many months in order to take the vacation, then you can't afford it.

Consuming your way to bad debt

We coined the term *bad debt* to refer to debt incurred for consumption, because such debt is harmful to your long-term financial health. (We used this term back in the early 1990s when the first edition of this book was published, and we're flattered that others have since used the same terminology.)

You'll be able to take many more vacations during your lifetime if you save the cash in advance. If you get into the habit of borrowing and paying all the associated interest for vacations, cars, clothing, and other consumer items, you'll spend more of your future income paying back the debt and interest, leaving you with less money for your other goals.

The relatively high interest rates that banks and other lenders charge for bad (consumer) debt is one of the reasons you're less able to save money when using such debt. Not only does money borrowed through credit cards, auto loans, and other types of consumer loans carry a relatively high interest rate, but it also isn't tax-deductible.

We're not saying that you should never borrow money and that all debt is bad. Good debt, such as that used to buy real estate and small businesses, is generally available at lower interest rates than bad debt and is usually tax-deductible. If well managed, these investments may also increase in value. Borrowing to pay for educational expenses can also make sense. Education is generally a good long-term investment because it can increase your earning potential. And the interest on student loans generally is tax-deductible (see Chapter 7). Taking out good debt, however, should be done in proper moderation and for acquiring quality assets. See the section later in this chapter, "Assessing good debt: Can you get too much?"

Recognizing bad debt overload

Calculating how much debt you have relative to your annual income is a useful way to size up your debt load. Ignore, for now, good debt — the loans you may owe on real estate, a business, an education, and so on (we get to that in the next section). We're focusing on bad debt, the higher-interest debt used to buy items that depreciate in value.

To calculate your bad-debt danger ratio, divide your bad debt by your annual income. For example, suppose you earn $40,000 per year. Between your credit cards and an auto loan, you have $20,000 of debt. In this case, your bad debt represents 50 percent of your annual income.

$$\$20,000 \div \$40,000 = 0.5, \text{ or } 50 \text{ percent}$$

REMEMBER

The financially healthy amount of bad debt is zero. While enjoying the convenience of credit cards, *never* buy anything with your credit cards that you can't afford to pay off in full when the bill comes at the end of the month. Not everyone agrees with us. One major credit-card company says — in its "educational" materials, which it "donates" to schools to teach students about supposedly sound financial management — that carrying consumer debt amounting to 10 percent to 20 percent of your annual income is just fine.

WARNING

When your bad-debt danger ratio starts to push beyond 25 percent, it can spell real trouble. Such high levels of high-interest consumer debt on credit cards and auto loans grow like cancer. The growth of the debt can snowball and get out of control unless something significant intervenes. If you have consumer debt beyond 25 percent of your annual income, see Chapter 5 to find out how to get out of debt.

How much good debt is acceptable? The answer varies. The key question is: *Are you able to save sufficiently to accomplish your goals?* In the "Analyzing Your Savings" section later in this chapter, we help you figure out how much you're actually saving, and in Chapter 4, we help you determine how much you need to save to accomplish your goals. (See Chapter 15 to find out how much mortgage debt is appropriate to take on when buying a home.)

THE LURE OF EASY CREDIT

We've both worked as consultants, and we've done a lot of work with companies in the financial-services industry, including some of the major credit-card companies. Their game then, as it is now, was to push cards into the hands of as many people as possible who have a tendency and propensity to carry debt from month to month at high interest rates. Their direct-marketing campaigns are quite effective. Ditto for the auto manufacturers who successfully entice many people who can't really afford to spend $20,000, $30,000, $40,000, or more on a brand-new car to buy new autos financed with an auto loan or lease.

And just as alcoholic beverage companies and tobacco companies target young people with their advertising, credit-card companies are recruiting and grooming the next generation of over-spenders on university and college campuses. Unbelievably, our institutions of higher learning receive substantial fees from credit-card companies for allowing them to promote their cards on campuses!

As widely available as credit is today, so, too, are suggestions for how to spend it. We're bombarded with ads 24/7 on radio, TV, websites, blogs, cellphones, the sides of buses and trains and the tops of taxicabs, people's clothing, and cars. You couldn't go a day without being exposed to advertising if you wanted to — you're surrounded!

REMEMBER

Borrow money only for investments (good debt) — for purchasing things that retain and hopefully increase in value over the long term, such as an education, real estate, or your own business. Don't borrow money for consumption (bad debt) — for spending on things that decrease in value and eventually become financially worthless, such as cars, clothing, vacations, and so on.

Assessing good debt: Can you get too much?

As with good food, you can get too much of a good thing, including good debt! When you incur debt for investment purposes — to buy real estate, for small business, even your education — you hope to see a positive return on your invested dollars.

But some real-estate investments don't work out. Some small businesses crash and burn, and some educational degrees and programs don't help in the way that some people hope they will.

There's no magic formula for determining when you have too much "good debt." In extreme cases, we've seen entrepreneurs, for example, borrow up to their eye-balls to get a business off the ground. Sometimes this works, and they end up financially rewarded, but in most cases, extreme borrowing doesn't.

Here are three important questions to ponder and discuss with your loved ones about the seemingly "good debt" you're taking on:

>> Are you and your loved ones able to sleep well at night and function well during the day, free from great worry about how you're going to meet next month's expenses?

>> Are the likely rewards worth the risk that the borrowing entails?

>> Are you and your loved ones financially able to save what you'd like to work toward your goals (see Chapter 4)?

If you answer "no" to these questions, see the debt-reduction strategies in Chapter 5 for more information.

Playing the credit-card float

Given what we have to say about the vagaries of consumer debt, you may think that we're always against using credit cards. Actually, used properly, besides the convenience credit cards offer, there's another benefit: free use of the bank's money until the time the bill is due. (Some cards offer other benefits, such as frequent-flyer miles or other rewards — for more details on reward cards, see Chapter 6.) Also, purchases made on credit cards may be contested if the sellers of products or services don't stand behind what they sell.

When you charge on a credit card that does *not* have an outstanding balance car-ried over from the prior month, you typically have several weeks (known as the *grace period*) from the date of the charge to the time when you must pay your bill. This is called *playing the float.* Had you paid for this purchase by cash or cheque, you would've had to shell out your money sooner.

WARNING

If you have difficulty saving money and plastic tends to break your budget, forget the float and rewards games. You're better off not using credit cards. The same applies to those who pay their bills in full but spend more because it's so easy to do so with a piece of plastic. (For information on alternatives to using credit cards, see Chapter 5.)

Bordereau date de retour/Due date slip

Bibliothèque de Beaconsfield Library
514-428-4460
13 Feb 2021 03:03PM

Usager / Patron . 23872000339999

Date de retour/Date due: 06 Mar 2021
Personal finance for Canadians for dummi

Total : 1

Horaire / Opening Hours
Lun-mar / Mon-Tues 10:00 - 17:00
Mer-jeu / Wed Thurs 13:00 - 19:30
Vendredi / Friday: 10:00 - 17:00
Samedi / Saturday: 10:00 - 17:00
Dimanche / Sunday: 10:00 - 17:00

beaconsfieldbiblio.ca

Analyzing Your Savings

How much money have you actually saved in the past year? By that we mean the amount of new money you've added to your nest egg, stash, or whatever you like to call it.

Most people don't know or have only a vague idea of the rate at which they're saving money. The answer may sober, terrify, or pleasantly surprise you. In order to calculate your savings over the past year, you need to calculate your net worth as of today *and* as of one year ago.

The amount you actually saved over the past year is equal to the change in your net worth over the past year — in other words, your net worth today minus your net worth from one year ago. We know it may be a pain to find statements showing what your investments were worth a year ago, but bear with us — it's a useful exercise.

If you own your home, ignore it in the calculations. (However, you can consider the extra payments you make to pay off your mortgage principal faster as new savings.) And don't include personal property and consumer goods, such as your car, computer, clothing, and so on, with your assets. (See the earlier section "Determining Your Financial Net Worth" if you need more help with this task.)

When you have your net worth figures from both years, plug them into Step 1 of Table 2-4. If you're anticipating the exercise and you're already subtracting your net worth of a year ago from what it is today in order to determine your rate of savings, your instincts are correct, but the exercise isn't quite that simple. You need to do a few more calculations in Step 2 of Table 2-4. Why? Well, counting the appreciation of the investments you've owned over the past year as savings wouldn't be fair. Suppose you bought 100 shares of a stock a year ago at $17 per share, and now the value is at $34 per share. Your investment increased in value by $1,700 during the past year. Although that may have increased your net worth, and made you the envy of your friends, the $1,700 of increased value is not "savings." Instead, it represents appreciation on your investments, so you must remove this appreciation from the calculations. (Just so you know, we're not unfairly penalizing you for your shrewd investments — you also get to add back the decline in value of your less-successful investments.)

TIP

If all this calculating gives you a headache, you get stuck, or you just hate crunching numbers, try the intuitive, seat-of-the-pants approach: Save a regular portion of your monthly income. You can save it in a separate savings — ideally a Tax-Free Savings Account (TFSA) or retirement plan, such as an RRSP.

TABLE 2-4   **Your Savings Rate over the Past Year**

Step 1: Figuring Your Savings				
Today			One Year Ago	
Savings and investments	$ _____		Savings and investments	$ _____
– Loans and debts	$ _____		– Loans and debts	$ _____
= Net worth today	$ _____		= Net worth 1 year ago	$ _____
Step 2: Correcting for Changes in Value of Investments You Owned during the Year				
Net worth today				$ _____
– Net worth 1 year ago				$ _____
– Appreciation of investments (over past year)				$ _____
+ Depreciation of investments (over past year)				$ _____
= Savings rate				$ _____

How much do you save in a typical month? Get out the statements for accounts and plans you contribute to or save money in monthly. It doesn't matter if you're saving money in a retirement plan that you can't access — money is money.

Note: If you save, say, $200 per month for a few months, and then you spend it all on auto repairs, you're not really saving. If you contributed $5,000 to an RRSP, for example, but you depleted money that you had from long ago (in other words, money that wasn't saved during the past year), don't count the $5,000 RRSP contribution as new savings. All you've done is move the same money from one place to another, even if it's a better vehicle for your savings.

Save at least 5 percent to 10 percent of your annual income for longer-term financial goals such as retirement (Chapter 4 helps you to fine-tune your savings goals). If you're not saving that much, be sure to read Chapter 6 to find out how to reduce your spending and increase your savings.

Evaluating Your Investment Knowledge

Congratulations! If you've stuck with us from the beginning of this chapter, you've completed the hardest part of your financial physical. The physical is much easier from here!

Regardless of how much or how little money you have invested in banks, mutual funds, brokerage accounts, or other types of accounts, you want to invest your money in the wisest way possible. Knowing the rights and wrongs of investing is vital to your long-term financial well-being. Few people have so much extra money that they can afford major or frequent investing mistakes.

Answering "yes" or "no" to the following questions can help you determine how much time you need to spend with our Investing Crash Course in Part 3, which focuses on investing. *Note:* The more "no" answers you reluctantly scribble, the more you need to find out about investing, and the faster you should turn to Part 3.

» _____ Do you understand the investments you currently hold?

» _____ Is the money that you'd need to tap in the event of a short-term emergency in an investment where the principal does not fluctuate in value?

» _____ Do you know what marginal income-tax bracket (combined federal and provincial) you're in, and do you factor that in when choosing investments?

» _____ For money outside of retirement plans, do you understand how these investments produce income and gains and whether these types of investments make the most sense from the standpoint of your tax situation?

» _____ Do you have your money in different, diversified investments that aren't dependent on one or a few securities or one type of investment (that is, bonds, stocks, real estate, and so on)?

» _____ Is the money that you're going to need for a major expenditure in the next few years invested in conservative investments rather than in riskier investments such as stocks or pork bellies?

» _____ Is the money that you've earmarked for longer-term purposes (more than five years) invested to produce returns that are likely to stay ahead of inflation?

» _____ If you currently invest in or plan to invest in individual stocks, do you understand how to evaluate a stock, including reviewing the company's balance sheet, income statement, competitive position, price–earnings ratio versus its peer group, and so on?

» _____ If you work with a financial advisor, do you understand what he or she is recommending that you do, are you comfortable with those actions and that advisor, and is your advisor compensated in a way that minimizes potential conflicts of interest in the strategies and investments he or she recommends?

REMEMBER

Making and saving money are not guarantees of financial success; they're prerequisites. If you don't know how to choose sound investments that meet your needs, you'll likely end up throwing money away, which leads to the same end result as never having earned and saved it in the first place. Worse still, you won't be able to derive any enjoyment from spending the lost money on things that you perhaps need or want. Turn to Part 3 to discover the best ways to invest; otherwise, you may wind up spinning your wheels working and saving.

Assessing Your Insurance Savvy

In this section, you have to deal with the prickly subject of protecting your assets and yourself with insurance. The following questions help you get started. Answer "yes" or "no" for each question.

>> _____ Do you understand what's covered, the types of protection, and amounts of each insurance policy you have?

>> _____ Does your current insurance protection make sense given your current financial situation (as opposed to your situation when you bought the policies)?

>> _____ If you wouldn't be able to make it financially without your income, do you have adequate long-term disability insurance coverage?

>> _____ If you have family members who are dependent on your continued income, do you have adequate life insurance coverage to replace your income if you die?

>> _____ Do you know when it makes sense to buy insurance through fee-for-service advisors, and companies that sell directly to the public (bypassing agents) and when it doesn't?

>> _____ Do you carry enough liability insurance on your home, car (including umbrella/excess liability), and business to protect all your assets?

>> _____ Have you recently (in the last year or two) shopped around for the best price on your insurance policies?

>> _____ Do you know whether your insurance companies have good track records when it comes to paying claims and keeping customers satisfied?

That wasn't so bad, was it? If you answered "no" more than once or twice, don't feel bad — nine out of ten people make significant mistakes when buying insurance. Find your insurance salvation in Part 4. If you answered "yes" to all the preceding questions, you can spare yourself from reading Part 4, but keep in mind that many people need as much help in this area as they do in other aspects of personal finance.

Chapter **3**

Managing Where Your Money Goes

O ver the years, both of us have spoken in depth with hundreds of people about their finances, people who have small incomes, people who have six-figure and even seven-figure incomes, and everyone in between. At every income level, people fall into one of the following three categories:

» People who spend more than they earn (accumulating debt)

» People who spend all that they earn (saving nothing)

» People who save 2 percent, 5 percent, 10 percent, or even 20 percent or more

We've seen $40,000 earners who save 20 percent of their income ($8,000), $80,000 earners who save just 5 percent ($4,000), and people earning well into six figures annually who save nothing or accumulate debt.

Suppose that you currently earn $50,000 per year and spend all of it. You may wonder, "How can I save money?" Good question! Rather than knock yourself out at a second job, you may want to try living below your income — in other words, spending less than you earn. Consider that for every discontented person earning and spending $50,000 per year, someone else is out there making do on $45,000.

A great many people live on less than you make. If you spend as they do, you can save and invest the difference. In this chapter, we examine why people overspend and help you look at your own spending habits. When you know where your money goes, you can find ways to spend less and save more (see Chapter 6) so that someday, you, too, can live richly and achieve your life's goals.

Examining Overspending

If you're like most people, you must live within your means to accomplish your financial goals. Doing so requires spending less than you earn and then investing your savings intelligently (unless you plan on winning the lottery or receiving a large inheritance). To put yourself in a position that allows you to start saving, take a close look at your spending habits.

Many folks earn just enough to make ends meet. And some can't even do that; they simply spend more than they make. The result of such spending habits is, of course, an accumulation of debt.

Most of the influences in society encourage you to spend. Think about it: More often than not, you're referred to as a *consumer* in the media and in the hallowed halls of the Canadian government. You're not referred to as a person, a citizen, or a human being. This section looks at some of the adversaries you're up against as you attempt to control your spending.

Having access to credit

As you probably already know, spending money is easy. Thanks to innovations like ATMs, credit cards, PayPal, and so on, your money is always available, 24/7.

Sometimes it may seem as though lenders are trying to give away money by making credit so easily available. But this free money is a dangerous illusion. Credit is most perilous when you make consumption purchases you can't afford in the first place. When it comes to consumer debt (credit cards, auto loans, and the like), lenders aren't giving away anything except the misfortune of getting in over your head, racking up high interest charges, and delaying your progress toward your financial and personal goals.

Misusing credit cards

The modern-day bank credit card was invented by Bank of America near the end of the baby boom. The credit industry has been generally growing along with the boomers ever since.

If you pay your bill in full every month, credit cards offer a convenient way to buy things with an interest-free, short-term loan. But if you carry your debt over from month to month at high interest rates, credit cards encourage you to live beyond your means. Credit cards make it easy and tempting to spend money that you don't have.

WARNING

You'll never pay off your credit-card debt if you keep charging on your card and make only the minimum monthly payments. Interest continues to pile up on your outstanding debt. Paying only the minimum monthly payment can lead to your carrying high-interest debt on your card for decades (not just months or years)!

Some credit cards are now trying to sell cardholders "insurance" at a cost of 10 percent or more annually to pay the minimum payments due on credit-card balances for those months that the debtor is unable to pay because of some life transition (such as a job layoff). One such card normally charges a 13 percent annual interest rate on credit-card balances, so with the insurance charges, the annual interest rate is more than 25 percent!

TIP

If you have a knack for charging up a storm and spending more than you should with those little pieces of plastic, only one solution exists: Get rid of your credit cards. Put scissors to the plastic. Go cold turkey. You can function without them. (See Chapter 5 for details on how to live without credit cards.)

Taking out car loans

Walking onto a car lot and going home with a new car that you can never afford if you had to pay cash is easy. The dealer gets you thinking in terms of monthly, biweekly, or even weekly payments that sound small when compared to what that four-wheeler is *really* gonna cost you. Auto loans are easy for just about anyone to get (except maybe a recently paroled felon).

Suppose you're tired of driving around in your old clunker. The car is battle scarred and boring, and you don't like being seen in it. Plus, the car is likely to need more repairs in the months ahead and perhaps doesn't have all the safety features of newer models. So, off you go to your friendly local car dealer.

You start looking around at all the shiny, new cars, and then — like the feeling you experience when spotting a water fountain on a scorching hot day — there it is: your new car. It's sleek and clean, and has air conditioning, an amazing stereo, a rear-view camera, Bluetooth, and heated seats. Before you can read the fine print on the sticker page on the side window, the salesperson moseys on up next to you. He gets you talking about how nice the car is, the weather, what sports teams you follow . . . anything *but* the sticker price of that car.

"How can this guy afford to spend time with me without knowing if I can afford this thing?," you think. After a test drive and more talk about the car, the weather, and your love life (or lack thereof) comes your moment of truth. The salesperson, it seems, doesn't care about how much money you have. Whether you have lots of money or very little doesn't matter. The car is only $399 a month!

"That price isn't bad," you think. Heck, you were expecting to hear that the car would cost you at least $25,000. Before you know it, the dealer runs a credit report on you and has you sign a few papers, and minutes later you're driving home with your new car.

WARNING

The dealer wants you to think in terms of monthly payments because the cost *sounds* so cheap: $399 for a car. But, of course, that's $399 per month for many, many months. You're gonna be payin' forever — after all, you just bought a car that cost a huge chunk of your yearly take-home pay.

But it gets worse. What does the total sticker price come to when interest charges are added in? (Even if interest charges are low, you may still be buying a car with a sticker price you can't afford.) And what about the cost of insurance, registration, and maintenance over the seven or so years that you'll probably own the car? Now you're probably up to more than a year's worth of your income. Ouch! (See Chapter 6 for information on how to spend what you can afford on a car.)

Bending to outside influences and agendas

You go out with some friends to dinner, a sporting event, or a show. Try to remember the last time one of you said, "Let's go someplace (or do something) less costly. I can't afford to spend this much." On the one hand, you don't want to be a stick in the mud. But on the other hand, some of your friends may have more money than you do — and the ones who don't may be running up debt fast.

Some people just have to see the latest hit movie, wear the latest designer clothes, or get the newest smartphone or tablet. They don't want to feel left out or behind the times.

When was the last time you heard someone say that she decided to forgo a purchase because she was saving for retirement or a home purchase? It doesn't happen often, does it? Just dealing with the here and now and forgetting your long-term needs and goals is tempting. This mind-set leads people to toil away for too many years in jobs they dislike.

Living for today has its virtues: Tomorrow *may* not come. But odds are good that it will. Will you still feel the same way about today's spending decisions tomorrow? Or will you feel guilty that you again failed to stick to your goals?

Your spending habits should be driven by *your* desires and plans, not those of others. If you haven't set any goals yet, you may not know how much you should be saving. Chapter 4 helps you kickstart the planning and saving process.

Spending to feel good

Life is full of stress, obligations, and demands. "I work hard," you may say, "and darn it, I deserve to indulge!" — especially after your boss took the credit for your last great idea or blamed you for his last major screwup. So, you buy something expensive or go to a fancy restaurant. Feel better? You won't when the bill arrives. And the more you spend, the less you save, and the longer you'll be stuck working for jerks like your boss!

Just as people can become addicted to alcohol, tobacco, food, or gambling, some people also become addicted to the high they get from spending. Researchers can identify a number of psychological causes for a spending addiction, with some relating to how your parents handled money and spending. (And you thought you'd identified all the problems you can blame on Mom and Dad!)

If your spending and debt problems are chronic, or even if you'd simply like to be a better consumer and saver, see Chapter 5 for more information.

Analyzing Your Spending

Brushing your teeth, eating a diverse diet including plenty of fruits and vegetables, and exercising regularly are good habits. Spending less than you earn and saving enough to meet your future financial objectives are the financial equivalents of these habits.

Despite having relatively high incomes compared with the rest of the world, some Canadians have a hard time saving a good percentage of their incomes. Why? Often it's because they spend too much — sometimes far more than necessary.

The first step to saving more of the income that you work so hard for is to figure out where that income typically gets spent. The spending analysis in the next section helps you determine where your cash is flowing. Do the spending analysis if any of the following applies to you:

>> You aren't saving enough money to meet your financial goals. (If you're not sure whether this is the case, see Chapter 4.)

>> You feel as though your spending is out of control, or you don't really know where all your income goes.

>> You're anticipating a significant life change (for example, marriage, leaving your job to start a business, having children, retiring, and so on).

If you're already a good saver, you may not need to complete the spending analysis. After you save enough to accomplish your goals, we don't see as much value in continually tracking your spending. You've already established the good habit — saving. Tracking exactly where you spend your money month after month is *not* the good habit. (You may still benefit from perusing our smarter spending recommendations in Chapter 6.)

The immediate goal of a spending analysis is to figure out where you typically spend your money. The long-range goal is to establish a good habit: maintaining a regular, automatic savings routine.

Notice the first four letters in the word *analysis.* Knowing where your money is going each month is useful, and making changes in your spending behavior and cutting out the fat so you can save more money and meet your financial goals is terrific. However, you may make yourself and those around you miserable if you're anal about documenting precisely where you spend every single dollar and cent.

Saving what you need to achieve your goals is what matters most.

Tracking spending the low-tech way

Analyzing your spending is a little bit like being a detective. Your goal is to reconstruct the spending. You probably have some major clues at your fingertips or somewhere on the desk or computer where you handle your finances.

Unless you keep meticulous records that detail every dollar you spend, you won't have perfect information. Don't sweat it! A number of sources can enable you to detail where you've been spending your money. To get started, get out or access the following:

- >> Recent pay stubs
- >> Tax returns
- >> Online banking/bill payment record
- >> Log of cheques paid and monthly debit-card transactions
- >> Credit-card bills

Ideally, you want to assemble the information needed to track 12 months of spending. But if your spending patterns don't fluctuate greatly from month to month (or you won't complete the exercise if it means compiling a year's worth of data), you can reduce your data gathering to one six-month period, or to every second or third month for the past year. If you take a major vacation or spend a large amount on gifts during certain months of the year, make sure that you include these months in your analysis. Also account for insurance or other financial payments that you may choose not to pay monthly and instead pay quarterly, semi-annually, or annually.

TIP

Purchases made with cash are the hardest to track because they don't leave a paper trail. Over the course of a week or perhaps even a month, you *could* keep a record of everything you buy with cash. Tracking cash can be an enlightening exercise, but it can also be tedious. (See the section "Tracking your spending on 'free' websites and apps" later in this chapter.) If you lack the time and patience, you can try *estimating*. Think about a typical week or month — how often do you buy things with cash? For example, if you eat lunch out four days a week, paying around $8 per meal, that's about $130 a month. You may also want to try adding up all the cash withdrawals from your chequing-account statement and then working backward to try to remember where you spent the cash.

Separate your expenditures into as many useful and detailed categories as possible. Table 3-1 gives you a suggested format; you can tailor it to fit your needs. Remember, if you lump too much of your spending into broad, meaningless categories like "Other," you'll end up right back where you started — wondering where all the money went. (*Note:* When completing the tax section in Table 3-1, report the total tax you paid for the year as tabulated on your annual income tax return — and take the total Canada Pension Plan [CPP] or Quebec Pension Plan [QPP] and Employment Insurance deductions paid from your end-of-year tax slips rather than the tax withheld or paid during the year.)

TABLE 3-1 **Detailing Your Spending**

Category	Monthly Average ($)	Percent of Total Gross Income (%)
Taxes, taxes, taxes (income)		_____
Federal	_____	
Provincial	_____	
CPP or QPP	_____	
Employment Insurance premiums	_____	
The roof over your head		_____
Rent	_____	
Mortgage	_____	
Property taxes	_____	
Gas, electric, oil	_____	
Water, garbage	_____	
Phones	_____	
Cable TV and Internet	_____	
Gardener, housekeeper	_____	
Furniture, appliances	_____	
Maintenance, repairs	_____	
Food, glorious food		_____
Supermarket	_____	
Restaurants and takeout	_____	
Getting around		_____
Gasoline	_____	
Maintenance, repairs	_____	
Provincial registration fees	_____	
Tolls and parking	_____	
Bus or subway fares or passes	_____	
Style		_____
Clothing	_____	
Shoes	_____	

Category	Monthly Average ($)	Percent of Total Gross Income (%)
Jewellery (watches, earrings)	_____	
Dry cleaning	_____	
Debt repayments (excluding mortgage)		_____
Credit cards	_____	
Auto loans	_____	
Student loans	_____	
Other	_____	
Fun stuff		_____
Entertainment (movies, concerts)	_____	
Vacation and travel	_____	
Gifts	_____	
Hobbies	_____	
Subscriptions, memberships	_____	
Pets	_____	
Other	_____	
Personal care		_____
Haircuts	_____	
Health club or gym membership	_____	
Makeup	_____	
Other	_____	
Personal business		_____
Accountant, lawyer, financial advisor	_____	
Other	_____	
Healthcare		_____
Physicians and hospitals	_____	
Drugs	_____	

(continued)

TABLE 3-1 *(continued)*

Category	Monthly Average ($)	Percent of Total Gross Income (%)
Dental and vision	_____	
Therapy	_____	
Insurance		_____
Homeowner's or renter's	_____	
Auto	_____	
Health	_____	
Life	_____	
Disability	_____	
Long-term care	_____	
Umbrella liability	_____	
Educational expenses		_____
Tuition	_____	
Books	_____	
Supplies	_____	
Housing costs (room and board)	_____	
Living expenses	_____	
Children		_____
Daycare	_____	
Toys	_____	
Activities	_____	
Child support	_____	
Charitable donations	_____	_____
Other		_____
_____	_____	
_____	_____	
_____	_____	

Tracking your spending on "free" websites and apps

Software programs and websites can assist you with paying bills and tracking your spending. The main advantage of using software or websites is that you can continually track your spending as long as you keep entering the information. Software packages and websites can even help speed up the cheque-writing process (after you figure out how to use them, which isn't always an easy thing to do).

But you don't need a computer and fancy software to pay your bills and figure out where you're spending money. Many people we know stop entering data after a few months. If tracking your spending is what you're after, you need to enter information from the bills you pay by cheque and the expenses you pay by credit card and cash. Like home exercise equipment and exotic kitchen appliances, such software often ends up in the consumer graveyard.

Plenty of folks have trouble saving money and reducing their spending. So, it's no surprise that in the increasingly crowded universe of free websites, plenty are devoted to supposedly helping you to reduce your spending.

More of these sites keep springing up, but among those you may have heard of and stumbled upon are BudgetTracker, Geezeo, Mint, and Wally. We've kicked the tires and checked out these sites, and frankly, we have mixed-to-negative feelings about them. The biggest problem that we have with these "free" sites is that they're loaded with advertising and/or have *affiliate relationships* with companies. This simply means that the site gets paid if you click a link to one of their recommended service providers and buy what they're selling.

This compensation, of course, creates an enormous conflict of interest and thoroughly taints any recommendation made by "free" sites that profit from affiliate referrals. For starters, they have no incentive or reason to recommend companies that won't pay them an affiliate fee. And, there's little — if any — screening of companies for quality, service level, and other criteria important to you as a consumer.

Also, be forewarned that after registering you as a site user, the first thing most of these sites want you to do is connect directly to your financial institutions (banks, brokerages, investment companies) and download your investment account and spending data. If your intuition tells you this may not be a good idea, trust your instincts. Yes, there are security concerns, but they pale in comparison to privacy concerns and apprehension about the endless pitching to you of products and services.

Another problem we have with these websites is the incredibly simplistic calculators that they have. One that purports to help with retirement planning doesn't allow users to choose a retirement age younger than 62 and has no provisions for part-time work. When it asks about your assets, it makes no distinction between equity in your home and financial assets (stocks, bonds, mutual funds, and so on). Finally, these sites generally offer no phone support, so if you encounter a problem using them, you're relegated to ping-ponging emails in the hope of getting your questions answered.

We noticed over time that many "free" financial websites were singing the praises of the software You Need A Budget (YNAB). We test-drove the product (which is like a slimmed-down version of Quicken) and found it to be a decent, but not exceptional, product. Our research uncovered the fact that the makers of YNAB pay a whopping 35 percent commission to website affiliates who pitch to users and direct them to buy the product. The owner of a website promoting YNAB pockets about $21 of the software's price ($60) for each customer it refers who buys a copy. Does that taint a site's recommendation of YNAB? Of course, it does.

REMEMBER

Paper, pencil, and a calculator can work just fine for tracking your spending. For those who want to use technology to track bill payments and expenses, we recommend the best software packages and discuss websites and apps in detail in Chapter 20.

DON'T WASTE TIME ON FINANCIAL ADMINISTRATION

Tom is the model of financial organization. His financial documents are neatly organized into colour-coded folders. Every month, he reviews all his spending information on his computer. He even carries a notebook to detail his cash spending so that every penny is accounted for. Tom also balances his chequebook "to make sure that everything is in order." He can't remember the last time his bank made a mistake, but he knows someone who once found a $50 error.

If you spend seven hours per month balancing your chequebook and detailing all your spending (as Tom does), you may be wasting about two weeks' worth of time per year — the equivalent of two-thirds of your vacation time if you take three weeks annually.

Suppose that, every other year, you're "lucky" enough to find a $100 error the bank made in its favour. If you spend just three hours per month tracking your spending and balancing your chequebook to discover this glitch, you're spending 72 hours over two years to find a $100 mistake. Your hourly pay: a wafer-thin $1.39 per hour. (*Note:* If you make significant-sized deposits or withdrawals, make sure you capture them on your statement.)

To add insult to injury, you may not have the desire and energy to do the more important stuff after working a full week and doing all your financial and other chores. Your big personal financial picture — establishing goals, choosing wise investments, securing proper insurance coverage — may continue to be shoved to the back burner. As a result, you may lose thousands of dollars annually. Over the course of your adult life, this amount can translate into tens or even hundreds of thousands of lost dollars.

Tom, for example, doesn't know how much he should be saving to meet his retirement goals. He doesn't review his employer's benefit materials, so he doesn't understand his insurance and retirement-plan options. He knows that he pays a lot in taxes, but he isn't sure how to reduce his taxes.

You want to make the most of your money. Unless you truly enjoy dealing with dollars and cents, you need to prioritize the money activities you work on. Time is limited, and life is short. Working harder on financial administration doesn't earn you bonus points. The more time you spend dealing with your personal finances, the less time you have available to gab with friends, watch a good movie, read a good book, and do other things you really enjoy.

Don't get us wrong — nothing is inherently wrong with balancing your chequebook. In fact, if you regularly bounce cheques because you don't know how low your balance is, the exercise may save you a lot in returned-cheque fees. However, if you keep enough money in your chequing account so you don't have to worry about the balance reaching $0 or if you have overdraft protection, balancing your chequebook is probably a waste of time, even if your hourly wages aren't lofty. If you're busy, consider ways to reduce the amount of time you spend on mundane financial tasks like bill paying. Many companies, for example, allow you to pay your monthly bills electronically via your bank or credit union chequing account or your credit card. (Don't use the latter option unless you pay your credit-card bill in full each month.) The fewer bills you have to pay, the fewer separate cheques and envelopes you must process each month. That translates into more free time and fewer paper cuts!

Chapter **4**

Establishing and Achieving Goals

In our work in the personal-finance world, we regularly ask people what their short- and long-term personal and financial goals are. Most people report that reflecting on this question was incredibly valuable, because they hadn't considered it for a long time — if ever.

In this chapter, we help you dream about what you want to get out of life. Although our expertise is largely in personal finance, we wouldn't be doing our job if we didn't get you to consider your nonfinancial goals and how money fits into the rest of your life goals. So, before we jump into how to establish and save toward common financial goals, we discuss how to think about making and saving money, as well as how to best fit your financial goals into the rest of your life.

Creating Your Own Definition of Wealth

Peruse any major financial magazine, newspaper, or website, and you'll quickly see our culture's obsession with financial wealth. The more money financial executives, movie stars, or professional athletes have, the more publicity and attention they seem to get. In fact, many publications go as far as ranking those people who earn the most or have amassed the greatest wealth!

We can tell you from our decades of working as personal financial writers and observers, and interacting with folks from varied backgrounds, that there's surprisingly little correlation between financial wealth and emotional wealth. That's why in your pursuit of financial wealth and security, you should always remember the emotional side. The following sections can help you gain some perspective.

Acknowledging what money can't buy

Recall the handful of best moments in your life. Odds are, these times don't include the time you bought a car or found a designer sweater that you liked. The old saying is true: The most enjoyable and precious things of value in your life can't be bought.

The following statement should go without saying, but we must say it, because too many people act as if it isn't so: Money can't buy happiness. It's tempting to think that if you could only make 20 percent more or twice as much money, you'd be happier because you'd have more money to travel, eat out, and buy that new car you've been eyeing, right? Not so. A great deal of thoughtful research suggests that little relationship exists between money and happiness.

"Wealth is like health: Although its absence can breed misery, having it is no guarantee of happiness," says psychology professor Dr. David G. Myers, who has written and researched happiness across cultures for decades. Despite myriad technological gadgets and communication devices, cheap air travel, microwaves, personal computers, voicemail, smartphones, and all the other stuff that's supposed to make life easier and more enjoyable, people aren't any happier than they were five decades ago, according to research conducted by the National Opinion Research Center. These results occur even though incomes, after being adjusted for inflation, have more than doubled during that time.

Managing the balancing act

Believe it or not, some people save *too* much. In our work, we've seen plenty of people who fall into that category. If making and saving money are good things, then the more the better, right? Well, take the admittedly extreme case of Anne Scheiber, who, on a modest income, started saving at a young age, allowing her money to compound in wealth-building investments such as stocks over many years. As a result, she was able to amass $20 million before she passed away at the age of 101.

Scheiber lived in a cramped studio apartment and never used her investments. She didn't even use the interest or dividends — she lived solely on her government benefits and a small pension from her employer. Scheiber was extreme in her frugality and obsessed with her savings. As reported by James Glassman in *The Washington Post,* "She had few friends . . . she was an unhappy person, totally consumed by her securities accounts and her money." Most people, probably you included, wouldn't choose to live and save the way that Scheiber did.

Even those who are saving for an ultimate goal can become consumed by their saving habits. We see some people pursuing higher-paying jobs and pinching pennies in order to retire early. But sometimes they make too many personal sacrifices today while chasing after some vision of their expected lives tomorrow. Others get consumed by work and then don't understand why their family and friends feel neglected — or don't even notice that they do.

Another problem with seeking to amass wealth is that tomorrow may not come. Even if all goes according to plan, will you know how to be happy when you're not working if you spend your entire life making money? More important, who will be around to share your leisure time? One of the costs of an intense career is time spent away from friends and family. You may realize your goal of retiring early, but you may be putting off too much living today in expectation of living tomorrow. As Charles, Duke of Orléans, said in 1465, "It's very well to be thrifty, but don't amass a hoard of regrets."

Of course, at the other extreme are spendthrifts who live only for today. As an acquaintance once remarked, "I'm not into delayed gratification." "Shop 'til you drop" seems to be the motto of this personality type. "Why save when I might not be here tomorrow?" reasons this type of person.

The danger of this approach is that tomorrow may come after all, and most people don't want to spend all their tomorrows working for a living. The earlier neglect of saving, however, may make it necessary for you to work when you're much older. And if for some reason you can't work and you have little money to live on, much less live enjoyably, the situation can be tragic. The only difference between a person without any savings or access to credit and some homeless people is a few months of unemployment.

Making and saving money are like eating food. If you don't eat enough, you may suffer. If you eat too much, the extra calories may go to waste or make you overweight. The right amount, perhaps with some extra to spare, affords you a healthy, balanced, peaceful existence. Money should be treated with respect and acknowledged for what it is — a means to an end and a precious resource that shouldn't be thoughtlessly squandered and wasted.

REMEMBER

As Dr. David Myers, whom we introduce earlier in this chapter, says, "Satisfaction isn't so much getting what you want as wanting what you have. There are two ways to be rich: One is to have great wealth; the other is to have few wants."

Find ways to make the most of the money that does pass through your hands, and never lose sight of all that is far more important than money.

Prioritizing Your Savings Goals

Most people we know have financial goals. The rest of this chapter discusses the most common financial goals and how to work toward them. See whether any of the following reflect your ambitions:

>> **Owning your home:** Renting and dealing with landlords can be a financial and emotional drag, so most folks want to buy into the Canadian dream and own some real estate — the most basic of which is your own home. (Despite the slide in property prices in some regions in the late 2000s, real estate has a solid track record as a long-term investment.)

>> **Making major purchases:** Most folks need to plan ahead for major purchases such as a car, living room furniture, vacations, and so on.

>> **Retiring:** No, retiring doesn't imply sitting on a rocking chair watching the world go by while hoping that some long-lost friend, your son's or daughter's family, or the neighbourhood dog comes by to visit. *Retiring* is a catchall term for discontinuing full-time work or perhaps not even working for pay at all.

>> **Educating the kids:** All those diaper changes, late-night feedings, and trips to the zoo aren't enough to get your kids out of your house and into the real world as productive, self-sufficient adults. You may want to help your children get a university or college education. Unfortunately, that can cost a truckload of dough.

>> **Owning your own business:** Many employees want to take on the challenges and rewards that come with being the boss. The primary reason that most people continue just to dream is that they lack the money to leave their primary jobs. Although many businesses don't require gobs of start-up cash, almost all require that you withstand a substantial reduction in your income during the early years.

Because everyone is different, you can have goals (other than those in the preceding list) that are unique to your own situation. Accomplishing such goals almost always requires saving money. As one of our favourite Chinese proverbs says, "Do not wait until you are thirsty to dig a well," so don't wait to save money until you're ready to accomplish a personal or financial goal!

Knowing what's most important to you

Unless you earn really big bucks or have a large family inheritance to fall back on, your personal and financial desires will probably outstrip your resources. This means that you must prioritize your goals.

One of the biggest mistakes we see people make is rushing into a financial decision without considering what's really important to them. Because many people get caught up in the responsibilities of their daily lives, they often don't have time for reflection.

TIP

As a result of our experience teaching people — and talking with them — about better personal financial management, we can tell you that the folks who accomplish their goals aren't necessarily smarter or higher-income earners than those who don't. People who identify their goals and then work toward them, which often requires changing some habits, are the ones who accomplish their goals.

Valuing retirement plans

Where possible, try to save and invest in plans that give you a tax advantage — precisely what registered retirement plans offer. These accounts, known by such enlightening acronyms and names as RRSP (Registered Retirement Savings Plan), RPP (Registered Pension Plan), and TFSA (Tax-Free Savings Account) offer tax breaks to people of all economic means.

Consider the following advantages to investing in registered retirement plans:

>> **Contributions are usually tax-deductible.** By putting money in an RRSP or RPP, not only do you plan wisely for your future, but you also get an immediate financial reward: lower taxes, which means more money available for saving and investing. Contributions to registered retirement plans generally aren't taxed until you withdraw the money. If you're paying, say, 35 percent between federal and provincial taxes (see Chapter 7 to determine your tax bracket), a $5,000 contribution to a retirement account lowers your taxes by $1,750.

>> **In some company retirement plans, companies match a portion of your own contributions.** Thus, in addition to tax breaks, you get free extra money courtesy of your employer!

TECHNICAL STUFF

>> **Returns on your investment compound over time without taxation.** After you put money into an RRSP, RPP, or TFSA, any interest, dividends, and appreciation add to your plan without being taxed. Of course, there's no such thing as a free lunch — these plans (with the exception of TFSAs) don't allow for complete tax avoidance. Yet you can get a really great lunch at a discount: You get to defer taxes on all the accumulating gains and profits until you withdraw the money down the road. Thus, more money is working for you over a longer period of time.

The tax rates on stock dividends and *capital gains* are lower than the tax rates levied on ordinary income (such as that earned through working). This fact makes some people think that investing through RRSPs or RPPs may not be worthwhile because all investment earnings are taxed at the relatively high ordinary income tax rates when money is withdrawn from registered retirement plans. We'll cut to the chase: The vast majority of people are better off contributing to an RRSP or RPP (see Chapter 7 for more details).

Dealing with competing goals

Unless you enjoy paying higher taxes, why would you save money outside of an RRSP or company pension plan, which shelter your money from taxation? The reason is that some financial goals are not easily achieved by saving in registered retirement plans. Also, such plans have caps on the amount you can contribute annually.

If you're accumulating money for a down payment on a home or to start or buy a business, for example, you'll probably need to save that money outside of a registered retirement plan. Why? Because if you withdraw funds from a registered retirement plan, you have to include that money in your income and pay tax on it. Because you're constrained by your financial resources, you need to prioritize your goals. Before funding your registered retirement plans and racking up those tax breaks, read on to consider your other goals.

Building Emergency Reserves

Because you don't know what the future holds, preparing for the unexpected is financially wise. Even if you're the lucky sort who sometimes finds $5 bills on street corners, you can't control the sometimes chaotic world in which we live.

Conventional wisdom says that you should have approximately six months of living expenses put away for an emergency. This particular amount may or may not be right for you, because it depends, of course, on how expensive the emergency is. Why six months, anyway? And where should you put it?

TIP

How much of an emergency stash you need depends on your situation. We recommend saving the following emergency amounts under differing circumstances (in Chapter 13, we recommend preferred places to invest this money):

>> **Three months' living expenses:** Choose this option if you have other accounts, such as an RRSP or TFSA, or family members and close friends whom you can tap for a short-term loan. This minimalist approach makes sense when you're trying to maximize investments elsewhere (for example, in retirement plans) or you have stable sources of income (employment or otherwise).

>> **Six months' living expenses:** This amount is appropriate if you don't have other places to turn for a loan or you have some instability in your employment situation or source of income.

>> **Up to one year's living expenses:** Set aside this much if your income fluctuates wildly from year to year or if your profession involves a high risk of job loss, finding another job can take you a long time, and you don't have other places to turn for a loan.

TIP

In the event that your only current source of emergency funds is a high-interest credit card, first save at least three months' worth of living expenses in an accessible account before funding a retirement plan or saving for other goals.

Saving to Buy a Home or Business

When you're starting out financially, deciding whether to save money to buy a home or to put money into a retirement plan presents a dilemma. In the long run, owning your own home is generally a wise financial move. On the other hand, saving sooner for retirement makes achieving your goals easier.

Presuming both goals are important to you, save toward both buying a home *and* retiring. If you're eager to own a home, you can throw all your savings toward achieving that goal and temporarily put your retirement savings on hold. Save for both purposes simultaneously if you're not in a rush.

TIP

If you're saving for a home, it can be a good idea to save at least some of that money inside an RRSP. Why? You can generally withdraw up to $25,000 from your RRSP to buy or build a home under the Home Buyers' Plan (HBP). Unlike regular withdrawals from an RRSP, money taken out under the HBP isn't treated as income, and you don't have to pay tax on it. (However, you do have to repay the money to your RRSP over the next 15 years.) For more on the HBP, see Chapter 15.

When saving money for starting or buying a business, most people encounter the same dilemma they face when deciding to save to buy a house: If you fund your retirement plans to the exclusion of earmarking money for your small-business dreams, your entrepreneurial aspirations may never become a reality. Generally, we advocate hedging your bets by saving money in your tax-sheltered retirement plans as well as toward your business venture. As we discuss in Part 3, an investment in your own small business can produce great rewards, so you may feel comfortable focusing your savings on your own business.

Funding Kids' Educational Expenses

WARNING

Wanting to provide for your children's future is perfectly natural, but doing so before you've saved adequately toward your own goals can be a major financial mistake. This concept may sound selfish, but you need to take care of *your* future first. Take advantage of saving through your tax-sheltered retirement plans before you set aside money in a Registered Education Savings Plan (RESP) or other educational savings plan for your kids. This practise isn't selfish: Do you really want to have to leech off your kids when you're old and frail because you didn't save any money for yourself? (See Chapter 14 for a complete explanation of how to save for educational expenses.)

Saving for Big Purchases

If you want to buy a car, a canoe, and a plane ticket to Thailand, do not, we repeat, do *not* buy such things with *consumer credit* (that is, carry debt month to month to finance the purchase on a credit card or auto loan). As we explain in Chapter 5, cars, boats, vacations, and the like are consumer items, not wealth-building investments, such as real estate or small businesses. A car begins to depreciate the moment you drive it off the sales lot. A plane ticket is worthless the moment you arrive back home. (We know your memories will be priceless, but they won't pay the bills.)

TIP

Don't deny yourself gratification; just learn how to delay it. Get into the habit of saving for your larger consumer purchases to avoid paying for them over time with high-interest consumer credit. When saving up for a consumer purchase such as a car, a TFSA (see Chapter 13) is a good place to store your short-term savings.

Paying the huge cost of high-interest consumer debt can cripple your ability not only to save for long-term goals but also to make major purchases in the future. Interest on consumer debt is exorbitantly expensive — upwards of 20 percent on credit cards. When contemplating the purchase of a consumer item on credit, add up the total interest you'd end up paying on your debt and call it the price of instant gratification.

Preparing for Retirement

Many people toil away at work, dreaming about a future in which they can stop the daily commute and grind; get out from under that daily deluge of voicemails, emails, and other never-ending technological intrusions; and do what they want, when they want. People often assume that this magical day will arrive when they retire or win the lottery — whichever comes first.

We've never cared much for the term *retire*, which seems to imply idleness or the end of usefulness to society. But if retirement means not having to work at a job (especially one you don't enjoy) and having financial flexibility and independence, then we're all for it.

Many folks aspire to retire sooner rather than later. But this idea has some obvious problems. First, you set yourself up for disappointment. If you want to retire by your mid-60s (when the Canada Pension Plan or Quebec Pension Plan normally kicks in), you need to save enough money to support yourself for 20 to 30 years, maybe longer. Two to three decades is a long time to live off your savings. You're going to need a good-size chunk of money — more than most people realize.

The earlier you hope to retire, the more money you need to set aside and the sooner you have to start saving — unless you plan to work part-time in retirement to earn more income! See Chapter 12 for more information about how to save and invest that money for retirement.

WARNING

Many of the people we speak to say that they do want to retire, and most say "the sooner, the better." Yet one survey found that just 36 percent of Canadians have planned or are planning for retirement. And almost one-third haven't even begun to save for retirement. When Eric asked one of his middle-aged counselling clients, who had saved little for retirement, when he would like to retire, he deadpanned, "Sometime before I die." If you're in this group (and even if you're not), determine where you stand financially regarding retirement. If you're like most working people, you need to increase your savings rate for retirement.

DON'T NEGLECT NONFINANCIAL PREPARATIONS FOR RETIREMENT

Investing your money is just one (and not even the most important) aspect of preparing for your retirement. In order to enjoy the lifestyle that your retirement savings will provide, you need to invest energy into other areas of your life as well.

Few things are more important than your physical health. Without your health, enjoying the good things in life can be hard. Unfortunately, many people aren't motivated to care about their health until *after* they discover problems. By then, it may be too late.

Although exercising regularly, eating a balanced and nutritious diet, driving safely, and avoiding substance abuse can't guarantee you a healthful future, these good habits go a long way toward preventing many of the most common causes of death and debilitating disease. Regular medical exams also are important in detecting problems early.

In addition to your physical health, be sure to invest in your psychological health. People live longer and have happier and healthier lives when they have a circle of family and friends around them for support.

Unfortunately, many people become more isolated and lose regular contact with business associates, friends, and family members as they grow older.

Happy retirees tend to stay active, getting involved in volunteer organizations and new social circles. They may travel to see old friends or younger relatives who may be too busy to visit them.

Treat retirement life like a bubbly, inviting hot tub set at 39°C. You want to ease yourself in nice and slow; jumping in hastily can take most of the pleasantness out of the experience. Abruptly leaving your job without a plan for spending all that free time is an invitation to boredom and depression. Everyone needs a sense of purpose and a sense of routine. Establishing hobbies, volunteer work, or a sideline business while gradually cutting back your regular work schedule can be a terrific way to ease into retirement.

Figuring out what you need for retirement

If you hope to someday reduce the time you spend working or cease working altogether, you'll need sufficient savings to support yourself. Many people — particularly young people and those who don't work well with numbers — underestimate the amount of money needed to retire. To figure out how much you should save per month to achieve your retirement goals, you need to crunch a few numbers. (Don't worry — this number crunching is usually easier than doing your taxes.)

Lucky for you, you don't have to start cold. Studies show how people typically spend money before and during retirement. Most people need about 70 percent to 80 percent of their preretirement income throughout retirement to maintain their standard of living. For example, if your household earns $50,000 per year before retirement, you're likely to need $35,000 to $40,000 (70 percent to 80 percent of $50,000) per year during retirement to live the way you're accustomed to living. The 70 percent to 80 percent is an average. Some people may need more simply because they have more time on their hands to spend their money. Others adjust their standard of living and live on less.

TIP

So, how do you figure out what you're going to need? The following three profiles provide a rough estimate of the percentage of your preretirement income you're going to need during retirement. Pick the one that most accurately describes your situation. If you fall between two descriptions, pick a percentage in between those two.

To maintain your standard of living in retirement, you may need about

>> **Sixty-five percent of your preretirement income if you**

- Save a large amount (15 percent or more) of your annual earnings

- Are a high-income earner

- Will own your home free of debt by the time you retire

- Do not anticipate leading a lifestyle in retirement that reflects your current high income

If you're an especially high-income earner who lives well beneath your means, you may be able to do just fine with even less than 65 percent. Pick an annual dollar amount or percentage of your current income that will allow the kind of retirement lifestyle you desire.

>> **Seventy-five percent of your preretirement income if you**

- Save a reasonable amount (5 percent to 14 percent) of your annual earnings

- Will still have some mortgage debt or a modest rent to pay by the time you retire

- Anticipate having a standard of living in retirement that's comparable to what you have today

>> **Eighty-five percent of your preretirement income if you**

- Save little or none of your annual earnings (less than 5 percent)
- Will have a relatively significant mortgage payment or sizable rent to pay in retirement
- Anticipate wanting or needing to maintain your current lifestyle throughout retirement

Of course, you can use a more precise approach to figure out how much you need per year in retirement. Be forewarned, though, that using a more personalized method is far more time-consuming, and because you're making projections into an uncertain future, it may not be any more accurate than the simple method we explain here. If you're data oriented, you may feel comfortable tackling this method: Figure out where you're spending your money today (worksheets are available in Chapter 3) and then work up some projections for your expected spending needs in retirement (the information in Chapter 20 may help you as well).

Understanding retirement building blocks

Did you play with LEGO blocks or Tinkertoy construction sets when you were a child? You start by building a foundation on the ground, and then you build up. Before you know it, you're creating bridges, castles, and animal figures. Although preparing financially for retirement isn't exactly like playing with blocks, the concept is the same: You need a basic foundation so your necessary retirement reserves can grow.

If you've been working steadily, you may already have a good foundation, even if you haven't been actively saving toward retirement. In the pages ahead, we walk you through the probable components of your future retirement income and show you how to figure how much you should be saving to reach particular retirement goals.

Considering government benefits

If you think that you can never retire because you don't have any money saved, we're happy to inform you that you're probably wrong. You likely have some government benefits. Although they'll likely be bare-bones, some form of various government programs should be around to provide you with some income when you retire, no matter how old you are today. The Canada Pension Plan (CPP), Quebec Pension Plan (QPP), and Old Age Security (OAS) are sacred-cow political programs. Imagine what would happen to the group of politicians who voted not to pay any more benefits!

WARNING

Social security programs generally don't provide enough to live on comfortably. Federal government retirement benefits are only intended to provide you with a subsistence level of retirement income for the basic necessities: food, shelter, and clothing. They're not intended to be your sole source of income. The CPP or QPP, for example, is designed to replace about a quarter of your preretirement income — but only up to a certain limit. Few people could maintain their current lifestyles without supplementing their CPP or QPP with personal savings and company retirement plans.

In the following sections, we provide more detail on the government retirement benefits you're entitled to.

THE CANADA PENSION PLAN AND QUEBEC PENSION PLAN

The CPP is the mainstay of government benefit programs that provide retirement income to Canadians. The CPP also replaces some of the income lost when a contributor becomes disabled, or in the event of his death. The CPP is in operation in all of Canada, except for Quebec. There, the role of the CPP is taken by the QPP. CPP and QPP payments are made monthly and are included in your taxable income.

All workers over the age of 18, including the self-employed, are required to contribute to the CPP or QPP. Two factors determine the amount of retirement pension you'll receive:

» **The number of years you contribute to the plan:** The more years you contribute, the higher your payments will be.

» **How much you contribute to the plan over those years:** When you're working, you're required to contribute. For a number of years, the contribution rate has been set at 9.9 percent. If you're employed, your required contributions are split evenly between you and your employer, each contributing 4.95 percent. If you're self-employed, you have to pay the full amount yourself. The actual amount is a percentage of your *pensionable earnings* (your gross earnings, plus any taxable benefits). However, there is an exemption on your first earnings each year, currently $3,500. In addition, you only contribute on earnings up to a set maximum, which for 2018 was $55,900. (This ceiling — the *yearly maximum pensionable earnings* — is regularly adjusted for inflation.)

Take the example of an employee with pensionable earnings of $60,000 in 2018. Her contributions for the year would be 4.95 percent of $52,400 (the 2018 maximum of $55,900, less the $3,500 exemption), or $2,593.80. Her employer would also contribute the same amount. If she was self-employed, she would pay the entire 9.9 percent, or $5,187.60, herself.

The rates are slightly different in Quebec for those contributing to the QPP. The QPP contribution rate is 10.8 percent, and the maximum annual contribution for employees for 2018 was $2,829.60; for the self-employed, $5,659.20.

For 2018, the maximum CPP benefit was $1,134.17 per month, or $13,610 per year. However, only a small minority of Canadians actually receive the maximum. To do so, you must have both paid into the plan for a full 40 years *and* contributed the maximum each year. In contrast, the *average* in 2018 was about $690. The payments are set for life. They're also adjusted annually every January for inflation. (You don't make CPP or QPP contributions when you're receiving disability payments from the CPP or QPP.)

You can elect to begin receiving CPP or QPP monthly pension benefits as early as age 60, even if you're still working. You're still required to make regular CPP or QPP contributions up to age 65. However, if you're still working between ages 65 and 70, it's up to you whether you want to continue making contributions. Also, when you turn 70, you stop paying into the plan even if you're still working and you haven't yet started receiving your CPP or QPP retirement benefits.

You can start collecting as early as age 60 or as late as age 70. The amount of your monthly benefits will be permanently reduced by 0.6 percent for every month before age 65 that you start drawing your pension. This works out to 7.2 percent a year; the reduction continues for the rest of your life. On the other hand, if you choose to delay receiving your CPP or QPP, your benefits will be increased by 0.7 percent per month, or 8.4 percent a year beyond your 65th birthday. This means that if you delay receiving your benefits until age 70, you'll receive 42 percent more than if you had started at age 65.

Beyond a retirement pension, CPP pays out a monthly benefit to eligible contributors to the plan (and their dependent children) with a qualifying disability. There is also a survivor's pension, which is paid to someone who is the legal spouse or common-law partner of a contributor at the time of the person's death. (Even if separated, the legal spouse of a contributor may still qualify for this benefit if, at the time of the person's death, he or she was not cohabiting with a common-law partner.) A number of factors determines the amount of these payments, including the age of the survivor, whether the survivor is raising a dependent child, and whether the survivor is receiving CPP benefits.

TIP

Aside from the post-retirement beneficiaries, everyone must apply to receive CPP benefits. They aren't paid out automatically.

THE NEW "ENHANCED" CANADA PENSION PLAN AND QUEBEC PENSION PLAN

The federal and provincial governments have agreed to revamp the CPP, with changes beginning in January 2019. The goal now is to have CPP eventually replace one-third of your preretirement income, up to certain limits. (The QPP is being enhanced in the same way as the CPP is.)

The changes are significant. The net result is that the maximum retirement pension will be some 50 percent higher than it is currently. For example, someone with an annual income of $50,000 who would have been eligible for around $12,000 a year in CPP benefits would receive approximately $16,000 after the changes have fully come into effect.

Note that although the legislation had been approved at the time of writing, the numbers may change from what we lay out here. One big reason may be that the *actuaries* (the number-crunching wizards) decide that the contribution rates may not be sufficient to pay for the planned benefits. This may require the contribution rates to be raised, because the CPP and QPP are intended to be self-funding.

REMEMBER

Before you start getting excited, don't forget that governments love to loudly announce the dollar amount of any financial good news for Canadians. But they typically use a much quieter voice to tell folks when exactly those benefits can be expected. In the case of the increased CPP benefits, your kids — assuming they're still teenagers, or only just hitting their 20s — will be much happier about the changes. The full 50 percent increase in retirement benefits won't actually be seen until 2065.

In particular, if you've already retired, you won't see any change to your CPP benefits. However, if you're working in retirement, you may see an improvement to any postretirement benefits you earn.

If you're planning to start your benefits in the next few years, you'll see little if any increase from the enhancements, because you won't have had much of a chance to make increased contributions. Indeed, one estimate was that you won't see any benefit from these rules if you apply for CPP up to 2024. However, every year from 2025 onward, you can anticipate betting about 1.3 percent more than you would currently.

To support the increased payouts, the amount both individuals and employers have to contribute will also rise. Both the percentage used to calculate contributions, as well as the maximum amount of income subject to CPP, will be increased.

Based on the supporting legislation, Bill C-26, the CPP contributions that had been in place for many years will be replaced by three levels of CPP contributions that can, very generally, be described as follows:

>> **Base CPP contribution:** This is the 2018 contribution rate (4.95 percent for employees and employers, and 9.9 percent for self-employed persons). The percentage is multiplied by the employee's income for the year (less the basic exemption) up to the yearly maximum pensionable earnings (YMPE).

- » **First additional CPP contribution:** For 2019 onward, the first additional contribution rate for a specific year (one rate for both employees and employers; double that for the self-employed), multiplied by your earnings for the year in excess of a basic exemption, up to the maximum for the year, the YMPE.

- » **Second additional CPP contribution:** For 2024 and subsequent years, there is a second additional contribution rate for the year (again for employees/employers, or the self-employed). This is multiplied by the amount your earnings exceed the YMPE for that year, up to a second, higher earnings limit.

The increases to the CPP contribution rates will be implemented over seven years, beginning in January 2019. This will be done in two basic stages:

- » **Stage 1:** Contribution rates will increase by 0.15 percent in each of 2019 and 2020, by 0.2 percent in 2021, and by 0.25 percent in each of 2022 and 2023. By 2023 — and for every year thereafter — each employee and employer will be contributing 5.95 percent annually (an increase of 1 percent) for a combined total of 11.9 percent. If you're self-employed, you'll have to contribute the full 11.9 percent yourself. This increase will be applied to pensionable income above the basic exemption of $3,500 (as of mid-2018) and the ceiling, or YMPE.

- » **Stage 2:** Beginning in 2024, a second additional mandatory contribution to CPP comes into effect. However, it will only affect people whose pensionable earnings are higher than the regular earnings ceiling, or maximum pensionable earnings. (Traditionally, no CPP contributions have been required on any income above this level.) When stage 2 comes into effect, however, you'll have to contribute an anticipated extra 4 percent on all your earnings above this level and up to a new, second earnings ceiling. This means that if your salary stays under the first maximum earnings ceiling, you don't have to make this extra layer of contributions. (These contribution rates can change if government number crunchers determine they aren't sufficient to fund the enhanced benefits.)

This extra contribution may cut into your ability to contribute to an RRSP. To make up for this, those employees who have to make this new, second level of CPP contributions will be able to claim it as a tax deduction, as opposed to a tax credit, which will generally reduce their overall tax bill further.

Table 4-1 shows just how much extra both employees and the self-employed will have to contribute to CPP as a result of the enhanced payouts.

To get a projection of how much you can expect to receive from the CPP or QPP, as well as the optimal time to start receiving your benefits, use the handy calculator on Tony's website, www.moneygrower.ca.

TABLE 4-1 ## Additional Contribution Requirements for Enhanced CPP

Stage 1 Additional Contribution Rates			
Year	Employee's Contribution	Employer's Contribution	Self-Employed Contribution
2019	0.15%	0.15%	0.3%
2020	0.3%	0.3%	0.6%
2021	0.5%	0.5%	1%
2022	0.75%	0.75%	1.5%
2023	1%	1%	2%
2024 and future years	1%	1%	2%

Stage 2 Additional Contribution Rates			
Year	Employee's Contribution	Employer's Contribution	Self-Employed Contribution
2024 and future years	4%	4%	8%

To help low-income workers with the higher contributions that come with an enhanced CPP, increased financial benefits will be provided under the new Canada Workers Benefit, a refundable tax credit that will replace the existing Working Income Tax Benefit as of 2019. The purpose of this benefit is, in part, to provide financial support to encourage low-income individuals to join — or remain in — the workforce. For more information on the Canada Workers Benefit, visit www.canada.ca and search for "Canada Workers Benefit."

In addition to the increased CPP pension payments that will eventually arrive, thanks to the increase in contribution rates, the enhanced CPP rules also contain several other beneficial changes. Here are some of the more helpful new regulations:

>> **Parents who have raised or are raising children:** Many parents see their income greatly reduced or disappear altogether when they stop working — or cut down on their hours — to raise their children. Without any adjustments, this would reduce their lifetime earnings and, thus, their CPP payments. The Child Rearing Dropout Provision works to counteract that. As long as you received Family Allowance payments, or were eligible for the Canada Child Tax Benefit (even if you didn't receive it because your family income was too high), if you stopped working or took a lower-paying job to be the primary caregiver of a child under 7, you can drop out the period from the time your child was 1 month old until he or she turned 7. However, this still resulted in drop-in retirement benefits. As a result, the new rules swap the "drop-out" option for a "drop-in"

provision. This will involve assigning a higher income — based on your average earnings for the five-year period immediately prior to the child-rearing period — for those years, thus boosting your CPP retirement payments.

>> **Disabled contributors:** Similar to the childcare situation, if a contributor had years of low or no income due to a disability, he or she could drop those years when it came to calculating the lifetime earnings. This would somewhat counteract the resulting decrease in CPP benefits. Under the new rules, though, if a contributor becomes disabled from 2019 onward and receives a disability pension, when he is eligible for a CPP retirement pension, he'll be credited with a *dropped-in* income amount of 70 percent of his average earnings for the six years leading up to his becoming disabled.

>> **Survivor's pension for younger recipients:** As of 2018, CPP survivor's pensions are reduced for those who are under the age of 45, except for those who are disabled or have dependent children. And unless they meet either of those two conditions, those under the age of 35 don't get any survivor pension whatsoever.

These restrictions will be eliminated by the proposed changes. In addition, anyone who is currently receiving a reduced under-age-45 survivor's pension will have it automatically increased in 2019. In addition, anyone who did not get a survivor's pension because she was under age 35 when her spouse or common-law partner died can apply for a survivor's pension to start in 2019.

>> **Retirement pension recipients under age 65:** Strangely, the pre-enhancement rules are that if you become disabled before age 65 but after you started receiving your CPP retirement pension, you're ineligible for a CPP disability pension. At the time we were writing this edition of the book, this was going to be changed effective 2019. But the only details available were that those in this specific situation would "receive an additional payment."

>> **Death benefit:** A $2,500 lump-sum payment will be paid to a CPP contributor's estate when he or she dies. Pre-enhancement, the CPP death benefit was determined by a contributor's earnings, set at six times a contributor's "calculated retirement pension" at 65, up to a maximum of $2,500. (The Liberal government says this will help people with lower incomes who, as a result, hadn't been receiving the maximum benefit. But the value of this benefit, if it had been increased with the cost of living, would actually be somewhere above $5,000, had it not been frozen at $2,500 in 1998.)

OLD AGE SECURITY PENSIONS

The OAS pension is the companion to the CPP and QPP. Like the CPP and QPP, the OAS is nowhere big enough (nor is it intended to be) to support you in your retirement years. But like the CPP and QPP, it will likely be a helpful — if not critical — addition to your income when you retire. OAS payments typically begin at age 65.

OAS benefits are determined each July based on your previous year's net income. The OAS pension payment amounts and benefits are adjusted quarterly if the cost of living has risen. OAS pension payments are taxed as regular income.

You should receive a letter from Service Canada the month after you turn 64. The letter may tell you that you've been automatically enrolled in OAS and your payments will start when you turn 65. You only need to reply if the information is incorrect or if you want to defer your payments.

If you don't get a letter, you'll need to apply for OAS yourself. You have to do this in writing, using the Application for the Old Age Security Pension form (ISP-3000). For details, contact Service Canada at 800-277-9914 or go to www.canada.ca.

Unlike CPP and QPP payments, which are based on your mandatory contributions, eligibility for OAS is a function of your income level, your age, and how long you've lived in Canada. In addition, your annual income cannot be more than a set maximum, which for the period of July to September 2018 was $123,302.

You'll generally qualify for OAS benefits if you're 65 or older and living in Canada, a Canadian citizen, or a legal resident at the time your OAS pension application is approved, and you've resided in Canada for at least ten years since the age of 18.

If you're living outside of Canada, you may still be eligible to receive OAS. You must be 65 years old or older and have been a resident of Canada for a minimum of 20 years since the age of 18. Additionally, on the day you left Canada, you must have been a Canadian citizen or a legal resident of Canada.

TECHNICAL STUFF

Even if neither of the two above scenarios applies to you, you may still be able to receive an OAS pension, a pension from another country, or even a pension from both countries. To be eligible, you must have lived in a country with which Canada has a social security agreement in place and contributed to the social security system of one of those countries.

The amount you'll receive from OAS is determined by the number of years you've lived in Canada past the age of 18. In addition to the basic OAS pension, you may also qualify for the three supplementary benefits, depending on your income and marital status. These benefits are not considered taxable income.

In order to be eligible for the full OAS pension, one of the following must apply to you:

>> You resided in Canada for a minimum of 40 years after turning 18.

>> You were born before July 1, 1952, and you resided in Canada on July 1, 1977.

>> After turning 18, you resided in Canada for a period of time before, but not on, July 1, 1977.

>> On July 1, 1977, you possessed a valid Canadian immigration visa.

Plus, you must have resided continuously in Canada for the ten years immediately before the approval of your OAS pension. If you lived outside Canada at some point in that ten-year period, you may still be eligible for the full OAS pension if *both* of the following apply to you:

>> You lived in Canada for at least one year immediately before being approved for an OAS pension.

>> There were earlier periods when you resided in Canada, and, when totaled together, these periods were at least three times the length of your absence from Canada during the ten-year period. (In other words, you need to have at least three years of residing in Canada for every year of absence.) For example, an absence of three years between the ages of 60 and 63 can be offset by nine years of residence in Canada after age 18 and before age 55.

THE OAS CLAW-BACK

If your net income in a year exceeds a set amount, your OAS payments are hit by a special tax, or *clawed back*. This is done by reducing or eliminating your monthly OAS pension payments. The income used to assess whether you've exceed the threshold amount lags behind when any OAS payments are clawed back. For example, if your 2017 income exceeds the threshold, the OAS recovery tax is applied on OAS pension benefits received from July 2018 through June 2019. The recovery tax rate is 15 percent of any income beyond the threshold amount. This means that when your income exceeds a further ceiling, you end up having to repay your entire OAS pension for those 12 months. The income at which you end up having to repay all that year's OAS pension is known as the *maximum income recovery threshold*.

Here's an illustration using your 2018 income: The minimum income recovery threshold for 2018 was $75,910. So, for every dollar your income exceeded that amount, 15 percent would be clawed back. If your 2018 income was $80,000, you would have to pay back 15 percent of $4,090 (the difference between the $75,910 threshold and $80,000), or $613.50. That amount would then be divided by 12 and deducted from your monthly payments from July 2019 through June 2020. (For the 2018 income-tax year, if your income exceeded $123,302, the maximum income recovery threshold, your OAS payment for this period would be reduced to zero.)

If you don't qualify for the full OAS pension, either because you don't (and won't ever) meet the basic requirements, or because you will meet the basic requirements but you don't currently, you may still be able to get some money from OAS.

If you've lived in Canada for at least ten years, you may be eligible for partial payments. For the purposes of determining your OAS benefits, you may be able to add the years you lived in another country — assuming you contributed to its social security system — to the years you've resided in Canada. This is a result of social security agreements Canada has with a number of other countries.

ADDITIONAL OLD AGE SECURITY BENEFITS

Beyond the OAS monthly pension, there are three additional benefits: A Guaranteed Income Supplement (GIS), an OAS Allowance, and an Allowance for the Survivor. None of these benefits is taxed. Your income in any year, as well as your marital status, determines your eligibility for the OAS pension and the three OAS supplements for the 12-month period running from the following July to the next June.

Here are the details on the three supplemental OAS benefits:

>> **Guaranteed Income Supplement:** If you live in Canada and you have a low income, this monthly nontaxable benefit can be added to your OAS pension. You're eligible for this nontaxable benefit if you're receiving an OAS pension and your income (or for couples, your combined income) doesn't exceed a ceiling called the *GIS maximum annual threshold*. Eligibility is assessed each July using your previous year's net income.

>> **OAS Allowance:** If your spouse or common-law partner receives an OAS pension and is eligible for the GIS, you may be eligible to receive this benefit. To qualify, you must

- Be 60 to 64 years old (including the month of your 65th birthday)

- Be a Canadian citizen or legal resident

- Reside in Canada and have resided in Canada for at least ten years since the age of 18

- Have a combined income that is less than the maximum allowable annual threshold

>> **Allowance for the Survivor:** Somewhat similar to the regular OAS Allowance describe earlier, you may qualify for this benefit if you're 60 to 64 years of age and widowed. (This includes the death of a common-law partner.) As with the Allowance, to be eligible to receive the Allowance for the Survivor, you must

- Be a Canadian citizen or a legal resident

- Reside in Canada and have resided in Canada for at least ten years since the age of 18

- Not have remarried or entered into a common-law relationship

- Have an annual income that is less than the maximum annual threshold

To help you estimate how much you might receive while planning your retirement income, Tables 4-2 and 4-3 shows the maximum amounts available from OAS for mid-2018.

OAS payments begin at age 65 and are paid monthly. You can, however, choose to defer receiving your OAS benefits for up to five years, in exchange for higher payments. (For every month you delay receiving OAS, your monthly benefit will be increased by 0.6 percent. If you hold off on receiving OAS until 70, the maximum, your payments will be 36 percent higher.) Only the OAS pension, and not the OAS income-tested benefits (GIS, Allowance, and Allowance for the Survivor), is increased.

TABLE 4-2   **OAS Pension and Guaranteed Income Supplement Payments (July–September 2018)**

Your Marital Situation	Maximum Monthly Payment	Maximum Allowable Annual Income for Eligibility
OAS Pension		
Regardless of your marital status	$596.67	$123,302 (individual income)
GIS Amounts for Individuals Receiving a Full OAS Pension		
If you're a single, widowed or divorced pensioner	$891.18	$18,096 (individual income)
If your spouse or common-law partner receives the full OAS pension	$536.48	$23,904 (combined income)
If your spouse or common-law partner does not receive an OAS pension	$891.18	$43,392 (combined income)
If your spouse or common-law partner receives the Allowance	$536.48	$43,392 (combined income)

TABLE 4-3 **OAS Allowance/Allowance for the Survivor Payments (July–September, 2018)**

Your Marital Situation	Maximum Monthly Payment	Maximum Allowable Annual Income for Eligibility
OAS Allowance		
If your spouse or common-law partner receives the GIS and the full OAS pension	$1,133.15	$33,456 (combined income)
OAS Allowance for the Survivor		
If you're a surviving spouse or common-law partner	$1,350.74	$24,360 (individual income)

Deferring your OAS pension has two costs:

>> For the period you're eligible to receive OAS payments but choose not to, you're ineligible for the GIS.

>> Your spouse (or common-law partner) will be ineligible for the Allowance benefit for the period you're delaying your OAS pension.

TIP

To get a projection of how much you can expect to receive in CPP or QPP benefits, as well as the optimal time to begin, use the handy calculator on Tony's website, www.moneygrower.ca.

TIP

To get a more precise handle on your CPP or QPP and OAS benefits, contact Service Canada at 800-277-9914 or go to www.canada.ca. Check your income and other details, because occasional errors do arise and — surprise! — they usually aren't in your favour.

Planning your personal savings and investment strategy

Money you're saving toward retirement can include money under the mattress as well as money in a retirement plan such as an RRSP (see Chapter 11) or RPP. You can also personally earmark investments that are not in registered retirement plans for your retirement.

Equity (the difference between the market value and any mortgage balances owed) in rental or investment real estate can be counted toward your retirement as well. Deciding whether to include the equity in your primary residence (your home) is trickier. If you don't want to count on using this money in retirement, don't include it when you tally your stash.

You may want to consider counting a portion of your home equity in your total assets for retirement. Some people sell their homes when they retire and move to a lower-cost area, move closer to family, or downsize to a more manageable-size home. And increasing numbers of older retirees are tapping their homes' equity through reverse mortgages (see Chapter 15 for information on mortgages).

Making the most of pensions

Pension plans are a benefit offered by some employers — mostly larger organizations and government agencies. Even if your current employer doesn't offer a pension, you may have earned pension benefits through a previous job.

The plans we're referring to are known as *defined-benefit plans.* With these plans, you qualify for a monthly benefit amount to be paid to you in retirement based on your years of service for a specific employer.

Although each company's plan differs, all plans calculate and pay benefits based on a formula. A typical formula may credit you with 1.5 percent of your salary for each year of service (full-time employment). For example, if you work ten years, you earn a monthly retirement benefit worth 15 percent of your monthly salary.

TIP

Pension benefits can be quite valuable. In the better plans, employers put away the equivalent of 5 percent to 10 percent of your salary to pay your future pension. This money is in addition to your salary — you never see it in your paycheque, and it isn't taxed. The employer puts this money away in its plan for your retirement.

To qualify for pension benefits, you don't have to stay with an employer long enough to receive the 25-year gold watch. Depending on your province or territory, employees must be fully *vested* (entitled to receive full benefits based on years of service upon reaching retirement age) after either two or five years of full-time service.

Defined-benefit pension plans are becoming rarer for two major reasons:

>> They're costly for employers to fund and maintain. Many employees don't understand how these plans work and why they're so valuable, so companies don't get mileage out of their pension expenditures — employees don't see the money, so they don't appreciate the company's generosity.

>> Many of the new jobs being generated are with smaller companies that typically don't offer these types of plans.

More employers offer plans that, instead of specifying how much you'll receive when you retire, only lay out how much you can put into the plan in your name. Known as *defined-contribution plans,* these plans allow you to save toward your retirement at your own expense rather than at your employer's expense. (To encourage participation in defined-contribution plans, some employers "match" a portion of their employees' contributions.) More of the burden and responsibility of investing for retirement falls on your shoulders with defined-contribution plans, so understanding how these plans work is important. Most people are ill-equipped to know how much to save and how to invest the money. The retirement planning worksheet in the next section can help you get started with figuring out the amount you need to save. (Part 3 shows you how to invest.)

Crunching numbers for your retirement

Now that you've toured the components of your future retirement income, take a shot at tallying where you stand in terms of retirement preparations. Don't be afraid to do this exercise — it's not difficult, and you may find that you're not in such bad shape. We even explain how to catch up if you find that you're behind in saving for retirement.

Note: The Retirement Planning Worksheet (Table 4-4) and the Growth Multiplier (Table 4-5) assume that you're going to retire at age 66 and that your investments will produce an annual rate of return that is 4 percent higher than the rate of inflation. (For example, if inflation averages 3 percent, this table assumes that you'll earn 7 percent per year on your investments.)

TABLE 4-4   **Retirement Planning Worksheet**

Retirement Income or Needs	Amount
1. Annual retirement income needed in today's dollars (see earlier in this chapter)	$ _____ per year
2. Annual government benefits and pensions	– $ _____ per year
3. Annual employer pension benefits (ask your benefits department); multiply by 60% if your pension won't increase with inflation during retirement	– $ _____ per year
4. Annual retirement income needed from personal savings (subtract lines 2 and 3 from line 1)	= $ _____ per year
5. Savings needed to retire at age 66 (multiply line 4 by 15)	$ _____
6. Value of current retirement savings	$ _____
7. Value of current retirement savings at retirement (multiply line 6 by Growth Multiplier in Table 4-5)	$ _____
8. Amount you still need to save (line 5 minus line 7)	$ _____
9. Amount you need to save per month (multiply line 8 by Savings Factor in Table 4-5)	$ _____ per month

TABLE 4-5

Growth Multiplier

Your Current Age	Growth Multiplier	Savings Factor
26	4.8	0.001
28	4.4	0.001
30	4.1	0.001
32	3.8	0.001
34	3.5	0.001
36	3.2	0.001
38	3	0.002
40	2.8	0.002
42	2.6	0.002
44	2.4	0.002
46	2.2	0.003
48	2	0.003
50	1.9	0.004
52	1.7	0.005
54	1.6	0.006
56	1.5	0.007
58	1.4	0.009
60	1.3	0.013
62	1.2	0.02
64	1.1	0.041

TIP

To get a more precise handle on where you stand in terms of retirement planning (especially if you'd like to retire earlier than your mid-60s), turn to Chapter 20, where we recommend retirement-planning software and websites that can ease your number-crunching burdens. Also, visit Tony's website at www.moneygrower.ca. In addition to helpful advice, you'll find a number of easy-to-use calculators to help you work through the numbers, how much you can expect from various government programs, as well as a tool to work out your expected income in retirement.

Making up for lost time

If the amount you need to save per month to reach your retirement goals seems daunting, all is not lost. *Remember:* Winners never quit, and quitters never win. Here are our top recommendations for making up for lost time:

>> **Question your spending.** You have two basic ways to boost your savings: Earn more money, or cut your spending. (Of course, you can — and may want or need to — do both.) Most people don't spend their money nearly as thoughtfully as they earn it. See Chapter 6 for suggestions and strategies for reducing your spending.

>> **Be more realistic about your retirement age.** If you extend the age at which you plan to retire, you get a double benefit: You earn and save money for more years, and you spend your nest egg over fewer years. Of course, if your job is making you crazy, this option may not be too appealing. Try to find work that makes you happy, and consider working, at least part-time, during your "early" retirement years.

>> **Use your home equity.** The prospect of tapping the cash in your home can be troubling. You're delighted not to have to mail a mortgage payment to the bank anymore. After getting together the down payment, you probably worked for many years to pay off that sucker. But what's the use of owning a house free of mortgage debt when you lack sufficient retirement reserves? All the money that's tied up in the house can be used to help increase your standard of living in retirement.

You have a number of ways to tap your home's equity:

- **Sell your home and either move to a lower-cost property or rent an apartment.** In general, any money you make when you sell your home is not taxed. (The home must qualify as what the tax authorities call your *principal residence*. A rental property, for instance, doesn't qualify.)

- **Take out a reverse mortgage.** In a reverse mortgage, you get a monthly income cheque as you build a loan balance against the value of your home. The loan is paid when your home is finally sold. (See Chapter 15 for more information about reverse mortgages.)

>> **Get your investments growing.** The faster the rate at which your money grows and compounds, the less you need to save each year to reach your goals. (Make sure, however, that you're not reckless; don't take huge risks in the hopes of big returns.) Earning just a few extra percentage points per year on your investments can dramatically slash the amount you need to save. The younger you are, the more powerful the effect of compounding interest. For

example, if you're in your mid-30s and your investments appreciate 6 percent per year (rather than 4 percent) faster than the rate of inflation, the amount you need to save each month to reach your retirement goals drops by about 40 percent! (See Part 3 for more on investing.)

>> **Turn a hobby into supplemental retirement income.** Even if you earn a living in the same career over many decades, you have skills that are portable and can be put to profitable use. Pick something you enjoy and are good at, develop a business plan, and get smart about how to market your services and wares. *Remember:* As people get busier, more specialized services are created to support their hectic lives. A demand for quality, homemade goods — and services — of all varieties also exists. Be creative! You never know — you may wind up profiled in a business publication!

>> **Invest to gain tax-free and other free money.** By investing in a tax-wise fashion, you can boost the effective rate of return on your investments without taking on additional risk.

    In addition to the tax benefits you gain from funding most types of retirement plans in this chapter (see the earlier section "Valuing retirement plans"), some employers offer free matching money. Also, you can invest money in a TFSA. Unlike an RRSP, your contributions have to be made with after-tax dollars, but when it's inside, the money can grow tax-free, and you also don't pay any tax when you withdraw money from these accounts. (See Chapter 7 for more on TFSAs.)

    As for money outside of tax-sheltered retirement plans, if you're in a relatively high tax bracket, you may earn more by investing in tax-free investments, dividend-paying investments, and other vehicles that minimize highly taxed distributions.

>> **Think about inheritances.** Although you should never count on an inheritance to support your retirement, you may inherit money someday. If you want to see what impact an inheritance has on your retirement calculations, add a conservative estimate of the amount you expect to inherit to your current total savings in Table 4-4.

2
Spending Less, Saving More

Chapter **5**

Dealing with Debt

ccumulating *bad debt* (consumer debt) by buying things like new living room furniture or a new car that you really can't afford is like living on a diet of sugar and caffeine: a quick fix with little nutritional value. Borrowing on your credit card to afford an extravagant vacation is detrimental to your long-term financial health.

When you use debt for investing in your future, we call it *good debt* (see Chapter 2). Borrowing money to pay for an education, to buy real estate, or to invest in a small business is like eating a well-balanced and healthy diet. That's not to say that you can't get yourself into trouble when using good debt. Just as you can gorge yourself on too much good food, you can develop financial indigestion from too much good debt.

In this chapter, we mainly help you battle the pervasive problem of consumer debt. Getting rid of your bad debts may be even more difficult than giving up the junk foods you love. But in the long run, you'll be glad you did; you'll be financially healthier and emotionally happier. And after you get rid of your high-cost consumer debts, make sure you practise the best way to avoid future credit problems: *Don't borrow with bad debt.*

Before you decide which debt-reduction strategies make sense for you, you must first consider your overall financial situation (see Chapter 2) and assess your alternatives. (We discuss strategies for reducing your current spending — which help you free up more cash to pay down your debts — in the next chapter.)

Using Savings to Reduce Your Consumer Debt

Many people build a mental brick wall between their savings and investment accounts and their consumer debt accounts. By failing to view their finances holistically, they simply fall into the habit of looking at these accounts individually. The thought of putting a door in that big brick wall doesn't occur to them. This section helps you see how your savings can be used to lower your consumer debt.

Understanding how you gain

If you have the savings to pay off consumer debt, like high-interest credit card and auto loans, consider doing so. (Make sure you pay off the loans with the highest interest rates first.) Sure, you diminish your savings, but you also reduce your debts. Although your savings and investments may be earning decent returns, the interest you're paying on your consumer debts is likely higher.

REMEMBER

Paying off consumer loans on a credit card at, say, 12 percent is like finding an investment with a guaranteed return of 12 percent — *tax-free.* You would actually need to find an investment that yielded even more — anywhere from 16 percent to 24 percent, depending on your marginal tax rate — to net 12 percent after paying taxes on those investment returns in order to justify not paying off your 12 percent loans. The higher your tax bracket (see Chapter 7), the higher the return you need on your investments to justify keeping high-interest consumer debt.

Even if you think that you're an investing genius and you can earn more on your investments, swallow your ego and pay down your consumer debts anyway. In order to chase that higher potential return from investments, you need to take substantial risk. You *may* earn more investing in that hot stock tip or that bargain real estate, but you probably won't.

WARNING

If you use your savings to pay down consumer debts, be careful to leave yourself enough of an emergency cushion. (In Chapter 4, we tell you how to determine what size emergency reserve you should have.) You want to be in a position to withstand an unexpected large expense or temporary loss of income. On the other hand, if you use savings to pay down credit card debt, you can run your credit card balances back up in a financial pinch (unless your card gets cancelled), or you can turn to a family member or wealthy friend for a low-interest loan.

Finding the funds to pay down consumer debts

TIP

Have you ever reached into the pocket of an old jacket and found a rolled-up $20 bill you forgot you had? Stumbling across some forgotten funds is always a pleasant experience. But before you root through all your closets in search of stray cash to help you pay down that nagging credit card debt, check out some of these financial jacket pockets you may have overlooked:

>> **Borrow against your cash-value life-insurance policy.** If you did business with a life-insurance agent, she probably sold you a cash-value policy because it pays high commissions to insurance agents. Or perhaps your parents bought one of these policies for you when you were a child. Borrow against the cash value to pay down your debts. (**Note:** You may want to consider discontinuing your cash-value policy altogether and simply withdraw the cash balance — see Chapter 17 for details.)

>> **Sell investments held outside of registered retirement plans.** Maybe you have some shares of stock or a Canada Savings Bond gathering dust in your safety deposit box. Consider cashing in these investments to pay down your consumer loans. Just be sure to consider the tax consequences of selling these investments. If possible, sell investments that won't generate a big tax bill.

>> **Tap the equity in your home.** If you're a homeowner, you may be able to tap in to your home's *equity,* which is the difference between the property's market value and the outstanding loan balance. You can generally borrow against real estate at a lower interest rate. However, you must take care to ensure that you don't overborrow on your home and risk losing it to your lender.

>> **Lean on family.** They know you, love you, realize your shortcomings, and probably won't be as cold-hearted as some bankers. Money borrowed from family members can have strings attached, of course. Treating the obligation seriously is important. To avoid misunderstandings, write up a simple agreement listing the terms and conditions of the loan. Unless your family members are the worst bankers we know, you'll probably get a fair interest rate, and your family will have the satisfaction of helping you out. Just don't forget to pay them back.

Decreasing Debt When You Lack Savings

If you lack savings to throw at your consumer debts, not surprisingly, you have some work to do. If you're currently spending all your income (and more!), you need to figure out how you can decrease your spending (see Chapter 6 for lots of great ideas) and/or increase your income. In the meantime, you need to slow the growth of your debt.

Reducing your credit card's interest rate

Different credit cards charge different interest rates. So why pay 14 percent, 16 percent, 18 percent, or more, when you can pay less? The credit card business is highly competitive. Until you get your debt paid off, slow the growth of your debt by reducing the interest rate you're paying. Here are some sound ways to do that:

WARNING

>> **Apply for a lower-rate credit card.** If you're earning a decent income, you're not too burdened with debt, and you have a clean credit record, qualifying for lower-rate cards is relatively painless. Some persistence (and cleanup work) may be required if you have income and debt problems or nicks in your credit report. After you're approved for a new, lower-interest card, you can simply transfer your outstanding balance from your higher-interest card.

 You can find a list of the best low-interest and no-annual-fee cards (among others, including secured cards) on Tony's website, www.moneygrower.ca. It also has a useful tool that allows you to use your current credit-card-spending — and bill-paying — habits to find the card that will cost you the least, and, if they're important to you, provide the most rewards.

>> **Call the bank(s) that issued your current high-interest credit card(s) and say that you want to cancel your card(s) because you found a competitor that offers no annual fee and a lower interest rate.** Your bank may choose to match the terms of the "competitor" rather than lose you as a customer. But be careful with this strategy and consider just paying off or transferring the balance. Cancelling the credit card, especially if it's one you've had for a number of years, may lower your credit score in the short term.

>> **While you're paying down your credit card balance(s), stop making new charges on cards that have outstanding balances.** Many people don't realize that interest starts to accumulate *immediately* when they carry a balance. *You have no grace period* — the 20 or so days you normally have to pay your balance in full without incurring interest charges — if you carry a credit card balance from month to month.

Understanding all credit-card terms and conditions

WARNING

Avoid getting lured into applying for a credit card that hypes an extremely low interest rate. One such card advertised a 1.9 percent rate, but you had to dig into the fine print for the rest of the story.

First, any card that offers such a low interest rate will honour that rate only for a short period of time — in this case, six months. After six months, the interest rate skyrocketed to nearly 15 percent.

But wait, there's more: Make just one late payment or exceed your credit limit, and the company raises your interest rate to 19.8 percent (or even 24 percent, 29 percent, or more) and slaps you with a $29 fee — $39 thereafter. If you want a cash advance on your card, you get socked with a fee equal to 3 percent of the amount advanced. (Some banks have even advertised 0 percent interest rates — although that rate generally has applied only to balances transferred from another card, and such cards have been subject to all the other vagaries discussed in this section.)

We're not saying that everyone should avoid this type of card. Such a card may make sense for you if you want to transfer an outstanding balance and then pay off that balance within a matter of months and cancel the card to avoid getting socked with the card's high fees.

TIP

If you hunt around for a low-interest credit card, be sure to check out all the terms and conditions. Start by reviewing the uniform rates and terms disclosure, which details the myriad fees and conditions (especially how much your interest rate can increase for missed or late payments). Also, be sure you understand how the future interest rate is determined on cards that charge variable interest rates.

Cutting up your credit cards

TIP

If you have a tendency to live beyond your means by buying on credit, get rid of the culprit — the credit card (and other consumer credit). To kick the habit, a smoker needs to toss *all* the cigarettes, and an alcoholic needs to get rid of *all* the booze. Cut up *all* your credit cards and call the card issuers to cancel your accounts. And when you buy consumer items such as cars and furniture, do not apply for credit.

The world worked fine back in the years B.C. (Before Credit). Think about it: Just a couple generations ago, credit cards didn't even exist. People paid with cash and cheques — imagine that! You *can* function without buying anything on a credit card. In certain cases, you may need a card as collateral — such as when renting a car. When you bring back the rental car, however, you can pay with cash or a debit card. Leave the card at home in the back of your sock drawer or freezer, and pull (or thaw) it out only for the occasional car rental.

If you can trust yourself, keep a separate credit card *only* for new purchases that you know you can absolutely pay in full each month. No one needs three, five, or ten credit cards! You can live with just one, given the wide acceptance of most cards.

Retailers such as department stores and gas stations just love to issue cards. Not only do these cards charge outrageously high interest rates, but they're also not widely accepted like Visa and MasterCard. Virtually all retailers accept Visa and MasterCard. More credit lines means more temptation to spend what you can't afford.

If you decide to keep one widely accepted credit card instead of getting rid of them all, be careful. You may be tempted to let debt accumulate and roll over for a month or two, starting up the whole horrible process of running up your consumer debt again. Consider making all your purchases on a debit card, only using your credit card when a debit card isn't accepted.

Discovering debit cards: The best of both worlds

Credit cards are the main reason today's consumers are buying more than they can afford. So logic says that one way you can keep your spending in check is to stop using your credit cards. But in a society that's used to the widely accepted Visa and MasterCard plastic for purchases, changing habits is hard.

TIP

Debit cards truly offer the best of both worlds. The beauty of the debit card is that it offers you the convenience of making purchases with a piece of plastic without the temptation or ability to run up credit card debt. Debit cards keep you from spending money you don't have and help you live within your means.

The big difference between debit cards and credit cards is that debit card purchase amounts are deducted electronically from your account the moment your purchase is approved.

WARNING

If you switch to a debit card and you keep your chequing account balance low and don't ordinarily balance your chequebook, you may need to start balancing it. Otherwise, you may face charges for overdrawing your account.

Here are some other differences between debit and credit cards:

>> If you pay your credit-card bill in full and on time each month, your credit card gives you free use of the money you owe until it's time to pay the bill. Debit cards take the money out of your account essentially immediately.

WHAT IF YOUR DEBIT CARD IS LOST OR STOLEN?

Personal credit cards and debit cards offer you similar so-called "zero liability" if someone illegally uses your card. If your debit card is lost or stolen and someone makes fraudulent charges on your debit card, you simply sign statements with your bank stating that the charges aren't yours. If money is deducted from your account for unauthorized purchases, you'll be reimbursed typically in a matter of days. (You should report your card as lost or stolen as soon as you notice it's missing.)

However, cards designated and listed as business (commercial) cards may not have the same zero liability as consumer cards. Generally speaking, banks view businesses as riskier and more prone to internal fraud. Suppose, for example, that your business issued debit cards to its employees, and one of them gave his card to a friend to use, and then that the card was lost and those purchases were fraudulent.

Given this background, therefore, we recommend getting a separate consumer debit card for your small business (simply keep your name, not the business's, on the account) or use a bank that offers the same protections on its business debit cards as on its consumer debit cards. Otherwise, you can get socked with a hefty bill that you didn't bargain for. And don't provide debit cards to your small business's employees.

>> Credit cards make it easier for you to dispute charges for problematic merchandise through the issuing bank. Most banks allow you to dispute charges for up to 60 days after purchase and may credit the disputed amount to your account pending resolution. Most debit cards offer a much shorter window, typically less than one week, for making disputes.

Turning to Credit-Counselling Agencies

If your debt load is troubling you, consider contacting a not-for-profit credit-counselling agency. Two umbrella organizations can help you find an approved agency in your area:

>> **Canadian Association of Credit Counselling Services:** 800-263-0260; info@ccacs.cas; www.caccs.ca

>> **Credit Counselling Canada:** 866-398-5999; info@creditcounselling canada.ca; www.creditcounsellingcanada.ca

Some credit-counselling agencies are licenced by government departments, some are attached to Family Services departments, and some are independent. Their funding comes from a variety of different sources, including provincial governments, the United Way, local government, and creditors. Different offices have different funding arrangements.

The goal of nonprofit credit-counselling agencies is to offer no-cost (or low-cost) credit counselling. Depending on your situation, you may simply be given some ideas for free about how to manage your savings better, and assistance in budgeting. The agencies also put a strong emphasis on education to assist people in not continuing with debt-happy habits. A member organization can also contact creditors for you, set you up with a third-party mediator, or assist you in obtaining a consolidation loan.

Beware biased advice at credit-counselling agencies

Leona Davis, whose family racked up significant debt due largely to unexpected medical expenses and a reduction in her income, found herself in trouble with too much debt. So, she turned to one of the large, nationally promoted credit-counselling services, which she heard about through its advertising and marketing materials.

The credit-counselling agency Davis went to markets itself as a "nonprofit community service." Davis, like many others we know, found that the "service" was not objective. After her experience, Davis feels that a more appropriate name for the organization she worked with would be the Credit Card Collection Agency.

Unbeknownst to Davis — and many others — credit-counselling agencies in the United States or based in the United States tend to get the vast majority of their funding from the fees that creditors pay them. These credit-counselling agencies collect fees on a commission basis — just as collection agencies do! Their strategy is to place those who come in for help on their "debt-management program." Under this program, counselees like Davis agree to pay a certain amount per month to the agency, which in turn parcels out the money to the various creditors.

Because of Davis's tremendous outstanding consumer debt (it exceeded her annual income), her repayment plan was doomed to failure. Davis managed to make ten months' worth of payments, largely because she raided a retirement account for $28,000. Had Davis filed bankruptcy (which she ultimately needed to do), she would've been able to keep her retirement money. But Davis's counsellor never discussed the bankruptcy option. "I received no counselling," says Davis. "Real counsellors take the time to understand your situation and offer options. I was offered one solution: a forced payment plan."

Others who have consulted various credit-counselling agencies, including one of Eric's research assistants who, undercover, visited an office to seek advice, confirm that some agencies use a cookie-cutter approach to dealing with debt. Such agencies typically recommend that debtors go on a repayment plan that has the consumer pay, say, 3 percent of each outstanding loan balance to the agency, which in turn pays the money to creditors.

Unable to keep up with the enormous monthly payments, Davis finally turned to a lawyer and filed for bankruptcy — but not before she had unnecessarily lost thousands of dollars because of the biased recommendations.

Although such credit-counselling agencies' promotional materials and counsellors aren't shy about highlighting the drawbacks to bankruptcy, counsellors are reluctant to discuss the negative impact of signing up for a debt payment plan. Davis's counsellor never told her that restructuring her credit-card payments would tarnish her credit reports and scores. The counsellor Eric's researcher met with also neglected to mention this important fact. When asked, the counsellor was evasive about the debt-management program's impact on his credit report.

TIP

If you're considering bankruptcy or you're otherwise unable to meet your current debt obligations, first be sure to read the rest of this chapter. Also, interview any counselling agency you may be considering working with. Remember that you're the customer and you should do your homework first and be in control. Don't allow anyone or any agency to make you feel that they're in a position of power simply because of your financial troubles.

Ask questions and avoid debt-management programs

Probably the most important question to ask a credit-counselling agency is whether it offers *debt-management programs* (DMPs), whereby you're put on a repayment plan with your creditors and the agency gets a monthly fee for handling the payments. You do *not* want to work with an agency offering DMPs because of conflicts of interest. An agency can't offer objective advice about all your options for dealing with debt, including bankruptcy, if it has a financial incentive to put you on a DMP.

TIP

Here are some additional questions that the U.S. Federal Trade Commission (FTC) suggests you ask prospective counselling agencies you may hire:

>> **What are your fees? Are there setup and/or monthly fees?** Get a specific price quote in writing.

>> **What if I can't afford to pay your fees or make contributions?** If an organization won't help you because you can't afford to pay, look elsewhere for help.

>> **Will I have a formal written agreement or contract with you?** Don't sign anything without reading it first. Make sure all verbal promises are in writing.

>> **Are you licenced to offer your services in my province or territory?** You should work only with a licenced agency.

>> **What are the qualifications of your counsellors? Are they accredited or certified by an outside organization? If so, by whom? If not, how are they trained?** Try to use an organization whose counsellors are trained by a non-affiliated party.

>> **What assurance do I have that information about me (including my address, phone number, and financial information) will be kept confidential and secure?** A reputable agency can provide you with a clearly written privacy policy.

>> **How are your employees compensated? Are they paid more if I sign up for certain services, if I pay a fee, or if I make a contribution to your organization?** Employees who work on an incentive basis are less likely to have your best interests in mind than those who earn a straight salary that isn't influenced by your choices.

Filing Bankruptcy

For consumers in over their heads, the realization that their monthly income is increasingly exceeded by their bill payments is usually a traumatic one. In many cases, years can pass before people consider a drastic measure like filing bankruptcy. Both financial and emotional issues come into play in one of the most difficult and painful, yet potentially beneficial, decisions.

When Helen, a mother of two and a sales representative, contacted a bankruptcy attorney, her total credit-card debt equaled her annual gross income. As a result of her crushing debt load, she couldn't meet her minimum monthly credit-card payments. Rent and food gobbled up most of her earnings. What little was left over went to the squeakiest wheel.

Creditors were breathing down Helen's neck. "I started getting calls from collection departments at home and work — it was embarrassing," she said. Helen's case is typical in that credit-card debt was the prime cause of her bankruptcy.

As the debt load grew (partly exacerbated by the high interest rates on the cards), more and more purchases got charged — from the kids' clothing to repairs for the car. Finally, after running out of cash, she had to take a large cash advance on her credit cards to pay for rent and food.

Despite trying to work out lower monthly payments to keep everyone happy, most of the banks to which Helen owed money were inflexible. "When I asked one bank's Visa department if it preferred that I declare bankruptcy because it was unwilling to lower my monthly payment, the representative said yes," Helen says. After running out of options, Helen filed personal bankruptcy.

Understanding bankruptcy benefits

The point of bankruptcy is to give someone who is buried in debt a fresh start. When you declare bankruptcy, you *assign* (surrender) everything you own to someone who is licenced by the Superintendent of Bankruptcy to administer proposals and bankruptcies and to manage assets held in trust (called a *trustee in bankruptcy*) in exchange for the elimination of your debts. Annually, about 50,000 Canadian households (that's about 1 in every 200 households) file for personal bankruptcy.

With bankruptcy, certain types of debts can be completely eliminated, or *discharged.* Debts that typically can be discharged include credit card, medical, auto, utilities, and rent. Debts that may *not* be cancelled generally include child support, alimony, taxes, and court-ordered damages. Helen was an ideal candidate for bankruptcy because her debts (credit cards) were dischargeable.

Also, because bankruptcy is a legal process, a *stay of proceedings* can prevent anybody from garnishing your income and stops your creditors from calling.

Student loans

Student loans are generally not cancelled if bankruptcy is filed within seven years of completing your studies. (Prior to July 7, 2008, the limit was ten years.) You can, however, apply to be released from your student loans on the basis of financial hardship five years after you cease being a full- or part-time student. The court will likely discharge your student loans at that point if it's satisfied that you acted in good faith with respect to your student loan obligation and that financial difficulty prevents you from repaying these debts. The court will also look at other factors, including how you used your student loans and your efforts to complete your studies.

Income-tax debt

Income-tax debt is treated like other unsecured debt, such as money owed to a credit-card company. However, if you have more than $200,000 in personal income-tax debt, and this is 75 percent or more of your total unsecured debts, you aren't eligible for an automatic discharge. (This new regulation came into effect September 18, 2009.) Instead, you have to request a court order to have your debts discharged.

Secured loans

Declaring personal bankruptcy deals only with unsecured creditors. A secured loan is money you've borrowed using an asset — a car or a house, for example — as a type of guarantee. If you don't repay the money you've borrowed, the lender can take possession of the asset. If you have a secured loan, the lender can simply repossess the asset.

In the case of car loans, the person going bankrupt can generally claim a provincial exemption and keep the vehicle. However, this requires continuing to make payments on the loan.

The roof over your head may also not be as secure as it first seems. Utilities are prevented from shutting your service off typically only during the winter months, and you may be required to pay a security deposit before they turn things back on. If you're a renter, bankruptcy can eliminate owed rent, but it doesn't prevent your landlord from evicting you.

One significant change brought in with the 2009 bankruptcy laws is that a secured lender can't terminate a contract simply because you've filed bankruptcy. If you have a car loan, for example, and your payments are up to date, you can generally keep the car and continue to make your loan payments.

Eliminating your debt also allows you to start working toward your financial goals. Depending on the amount of debt you have outstanding relative to your income, you may need a decade or more to pay it all off. In Helen's case, at the age of 48, she had no money saved for retirement, and she was increasingly unable to spend money on her children.

Filing bankruptcy offers not only financial benefits, but also emotional benefits. "I was horrified at filing, but it is good to be rid of the debts and collection calls — I should have filed six months earlier. I was constantly worried. When I saw homeless families come to the soup kitchen where I sometimes volunteer, I thought that someday that could be me and my kids," says Helen.

WHAT YOU CAN KEEP IF YOU FILE BANKRUPTCY

You can retain certain property and assets even though you're filing for bankruptcy. (The provinces and territories all have different amounts that are exempt, and they sometimes revise these limits.) In most provinces, you're allowed to keep a few thousand dollars' worth of personal effects. This generally includes clothing, jewellery, sports equipment, and so on. You can also hang on to furniture worth up to a total of $10,000 or so. You likely will also be able to keep a few thousand dollars' worth of the tools of your trade if such items are necessary for you to earn a living.

In addition, depending on the province that you live in, you may also be able to hang on to a vehicle worth no more than $5,000 or $6,000, assuming that you don't owe any money on a car loan and you own the vehicle outright. You may also possibly retain a small amount of equity in your home. (One major exception is Alberta, which allows you to keep $40,000 worth of equity in your home.)

Thanks to the new bankruptcy rules, all Registered Retirement Savings Plans (RRSPs) are protected and can't be seized (as of July 7, 2008). In addition to RRSPs, this includes Registered Retirement Income Funds (RRIFs) and deferred profit-sharing plans (DPSPs). However, any contributions made to an RRSP in the 12 months leading up to bankruptcy are not exempt.

Coming to terms with bankruptcy drawbacks

Filing bankruptcy, needless to say, has a number of drawbacks. First, bankruptcy appears on your credit report for up to ten years, so you'll have difficulty obtaining credit, especially in the years immediately following your filing. However, if you already have problems on your credit report (because of late payments or a failure to pay previous debts), damage has already been done. And without savings, you're probably not going to be making major purchases (such as a home) in the next several years anyway.

REMEMBER

If you do file bankruptcy, getting credit in the future is still possible. You may be able to obtain a *secured credit card,* which requires you to deposit money in a bank account equal to the credit limit on your credit card. Of course, you'll be better off without the temptation of any credit cards and better served with a debit card. Also, know that if you can hold down a stable job, most creditors will be willing to give you loans within a few years of your filing bankruptcy. Almost all lenders ignore bankruptcy after five to seven years.

Another drawback of bankruptcy is that it costs money, and those expenses have jumped higher due to the requirements of bankruptcy laws (more on that in a moment). We know this expense seems terribly unfair. You're already in financial trouble — that's why you're filing bankruptcy! Court filing and legal fees can easily exceed $1,000, especially in areas with a higher cost of living.

And finally, most people find that filing bankruptcy causes emotional stress. Admitting that your personal income can't keep pace with your debt obligations is painful. Although filing bankruptcy clears the decks of debt and gives you a fresh financial start, feeling a profound sense of failure (and sometimes shame) is common. Despite the increasing incidence of bankruptcy, bankruptcy filers are reluctant to talk about it with others, including family and friends.

Another part of the emotional side of filing bankruptcy is that you must open your personal financial affairs to court scrutiny and court control during the several months it takes to administer a bankruptcy. A court-appointed bankruptcy trustee oversees your case and tries to recover as much of your property as possible to satisfy the *creditors* — those to whom you owe money.

Some people also feel that they're shirking responsibility by filing for bankruptcy. One client Eric worked with should have filed, but she couldn't bring herself to do it. She said, "I spent that money, and it's my responsibility to pay it back."

If you file for bankruptcy, don't feel bad about not paying back the bank. Credit cards are one of the most profitable lines of business for banks. (Now you know why your mailbox and email inbox are always stuffed with solicitations for more cards.) The nice merchants from whom you bought the merchandise have already been paid. *Charge-offs* (the bankers' term for taking the loss on debt that you discharge through bankruptcy) are the bankers' cost, which is another reason why the interest rate is so high on credit cards and why borrowing on them is a bad idea.

Seeking bankruptcy advice

Be careful where you get advice about whether to file for bankruptcy. Trustees in bankruptcy who earn a fee from doing bankruptcy filings, for example, have a conflict of interest. All things being equal, their bias is to — you guessed it — *recommend bankruptcy,* which generates their fees.

TIP

If you want to learn more about the pros, cons, and details of filing for bankruptcy, pick up a copy of the *Bankruptcy Guide* by Earl Sands (Self-Counsel Press). Another good source of information is the website of the Office of the Superintendent of Bankruptcy Canada at www.ic.gc.ca/eic/site/bsf-osb.nsf/intro. The site includes a directory of trustees, as well as a helpful section called "Alternatives to Bankruptcy."

Considering a Consumer Proposal: An Alternative to Bankruptcy

If your debts total $250,000 or less — not including debts such as a mortgage secured by your principal residence — a *consumer proposal* can be a good alternative to filing bankruptcy. With a consumer proposal, you can negotiate to repay only a portion of the money you owe. At the time you file your proposal, the debts covered by the proposal are frozen, and no more interest can be charged on them from that point on. In addition, your creditors are restricted from taking further legal action against you, and any garnishing of your wages is stopped (except for support and alimony payments).

A consumer proposal is similar to a debt-repayment plan that a credit-counselling agency may work out for you. It's an option when you have money coming in that will allow you to pay off a good portion of your debts, but you need more time to do so. Typically, a trustee assists you in assessing your assets and income, organizes a budget for you, and provides a few counselling sessions. Your trustee will present a plan to your creditors, detailing how much and when you'll pay them, to which the creditors have 45 days to respond. If a majority of your creditors accept the proposal, it's deemed to have been accepted by all of them. The agreement is legally binding.

A consumer proposal covers common unsecured debts, such as credit cards, lines of credit, and personal loans, as well as income taxes. In general, secured debt isn't covered under a consumer proposal. (*Secured debt* is money borrowed with an agreement that the lender can take possession of some of your property and sell it to recover its money if you fail to repay the loan.) In addition, alimony, child support, and legal fines aren't covered by the proposal; they remain payable in full.

TIP

A consumer proposal is often a sensible route to take, especially if you have a lot of assets and a regular income. In a regular bankruptcy, almost all your assets are sold. Under a consumer proposal, that may not be necessary if your creditors are willing to settle for a piece of your paycheque.

A consumer proposal is likely to be accepted only if your unsecured lenders foresee getting paid more than they would if you file bankruptcy. Also, some lenders may prefer you to file bankruptcy because it's a much more short-term, finite process for them. In contrast, under a consumer proposal, you can arrange to spread your payments out over as much as five years. After you've completed your payments under the proposal, a record of the agreement remains in your credit history for two years.

Stopping the Spending/Consumer Debt Cycle

Regardless of how you deal with paying off your debt, you're in real danger of falling back into old habits. Backsliding happens not only to people who file bankruptcy but also to those who use savings or home equity to eliminate their debt. This section speaks to that risk and tells you what to do about it.

Resisting the credit temptation

TIP

Getting out of debt can be challenging, but we have confidence that you can do it with this book by your side. In addition to the ideas we discuss earlier in this chapter (such as eliminating all your credit cards and getting a debit card), the following list provides some additional tactics you can use to limit the influence credit cards hold over your life. (If you're concerned about the impact that any of these tactics may have on your credit rating, turn to Chapter 2.)

» **Reduce your credit limit.** If you choose not to take our advice and get rid of all your credit cards or get a debit card, be sure to keep a lid on your credit card's *credit limit* (the maximum balance allowed on your card). You don't have to accept the increase just because your bank keeps raising your credit limit to reward you for being such a profitable customer. Call your credit card's toll-free phone number and lower your credit limit to a level you're comfortable with.

» **Replace your credit card with a charge card.** A *charge card* (such as the American Express card) requires you to pay your balance in full each billing period. You have no credit line or interest charges. Of course, spending more than you can afford to pay when the bill comes due is possible. But you'll be much less likely to overspend if you know you have to pay in full monthly.

» **Never buy anything on credit that depreciates in value.** Meals out, cars, clothing, and shoes all depreciate in value. Don't buy these things on credit. Borrow money only for sound investments — education, real estate, or your own business, for example.

» **Think in terms of total cost.** Everything sounds cheaper in terms of monthly payments — that's how salespeople entice you into buying things you can't afford. Take a calculator along, if necessary, to tally up the sticker price, interest charges, and upkeep. The total cost will scare you. *It should.*

>> **Stop the junk-mail avalanche.** Look at your daily mail — we bet half of it is solicitations and mail-order catalogues. You can save some trees and time sorting junk mail by removing yourself from most mailing lists.

To remove your name from mailing lists, register with the Canadian Marketing Association's Do Not Contact service. Call 416-391-2362 or go to www.the-cma.org.

>> **Stop telemarketing calls.** To reduce unwanted telemarketing calls, register your phone number with Canada's National Do Not Call List operated by the Canadian government. For more information, call 866-580-3625 or go to www.lnnte-dncl.gc.ca.

>> **Stop getting credit-card offers.** To remove your name from the major credit-reporting agency lists that are used by credit-card solicitation companies, call 888-567-8688. Also, tell any credit-card companies you keep cards with that you want your account marked to indicate that you don't want any of your personal information shared with telemarketing firms.

>> **Limit what you can spend.** Go shopping with a small amount of cash and no plastic or cheques. That way, you can spend only what little cash you have with you.

Identifying and treating a compulsion

No matter how hard they try to break the habit, some people become addicted to spending and accumulating debt. It becomes a chronic problem that starts to interfere with other aspects of their lives and can lead to problems at work and with family and friends.

Debtors Anonymous (DA) is a nonprofit organization that provides support (primarily through group meetings) to people trying to break their debt accumulation and spending habits. DA is modeled after the 12-step Alcoholics Anonymous (AA) program.

Like AA, DA works with people from all walks of life and socioeconomic backgrounds. You can find people who are financially on the edge, $100,000-plus income earners, and everybody in between at DA meetings. Even former millionaires join the program.

DA has a simple questionnaire that helps determine whether you're a problem debtor. If you answer "yes" to at least 8 of the following 15 questions, you may be developing or already have a compulsive spending and debt accumulation habit:

>> Are your debts making your home life unhappy?

>> Does the pressure of your debts distract you from your daily work?

- ≫ Are your debts affecting your reputation?

- ≫ Do your debts cause you to think less of yourself?

- ≫ Have you ever given false information in order to obtain credit?

- ≫ Have you ever made unrealistic promises to your creditors?

- ≫ Does the pressure of your debts make you careless when it comes to the welfare of your family?

- ≫ Do you ever fear that your employer, family, or friends will learn the extent of your total indebtedness?

- ≫ When faced with a difficult financial situation, does the prospect of borrowing give you an inordinate feeling of relief?

- ≫ Does the pressure of your debts cause you to have difficulty sleeping?

- ≫ Has the pressure of your debts ever caused you to consider getting drunk?

- ≫ Have you ever borrowed money without giving adequate consideration to the rate of interest you're required to pay?

- ≫ Do you usually expect a negative response when you're subject to a credit investigation?

- ≫ Have you ever developed a strict regimen for paying off your debts, only to break it under pressure?

- ≫ Do you justify your debts by telling yourself that you are superior to the "other" people, and when you get your "break," you'll be out of debt?

TIP

To find a DA support group in your area, call 800-421-2383 or 781-453-2743 or go to www.debtorsanonymous.org.

Chapter **6**

Reducing Your Spending

Telling people how and where to spend their money is a risky undertaking, because most people like to spend money and hate to be told what to do. So, in this chapter, we detail numerous strategies that we have seen work for other people. (We also can personally vouch for having used many of these strategies ourselves.) The final decision for what to cut rests solely on you. Only you can decide what's important to you and what's dispensable (should you cut out your weekly poker games or cut back on your growing designer shoe collection?).

With these recommendations, we assume that you value your time. Therefore, we don't tell you to scrimp and save by doing things like cutting open a tube of toothpaste so that you can use every last bit of it. And we don't tell you to ask your spouse to do your ironing to reduce your dry-cleaning bills — no point in having extra money in the bank if your significant other walks out on you!

The fact that you're busy all the time may be part of the reason you spend money as you do. Therefore, the recommendations in this chapter focus on methods that produce significant savings but don't involve a lot of time. In other words, these strategies provide bang for the buck.

Unlocking the Keys to Successful Spending

For most people, spending money is a whole lot easier and more fun than earning it. Far be it from us to tell you to stop having fun and turn into a penny-pinching, stay-at-home miser. Of course, you can spend money. But there's a world of difference between spending money carelessly and spending money *wisely*.

If you spend too much and spend unwisely, you put pressure on your income and your future need to continue working. Savings dwindle, debts may accumulate, and you can't achieve your financial (and perhaps personal) goals.

If you dive into details too quickly, you may miss the big picture. So, before we jump into the specific areas where you may be able to trim your budget, we give you our four overall keys to successful spending:

>> Living within your means

>> Looking for the best values

>> Cutting excess spending

>> Shunning consumer credit

These four principles run through our recommendations in this chapter.

Living within your means

Spending too much is a *relative* problem. Two people can each spend $40,000 per year (including their taxes) yet still have drastically different financial circumstances. How? Suppose that one of them earns $50,000 annually, while the other earns $35,000. The $50,000 earner saves $10,000 each year. The $35,000 earner, on the other hand, accumulates $5,000 of new debt (or spends that amount from prior savings). So, spend within your means. If you do nothing else in this chapter, be sure to do this!

TIP

Don't let the spending habits of others dictate yours. Certain people — and you know who they are — bring out the big spender in you. Do something else with them besides shopping and spending. If you can't find any other activity to share with them, try shopping with limited cash and no credit cards. That way, you can't overspend on impulse.

How much you can safely spend while working toward your financial goals depends on what your goals are and where you are financially. Save first for your goals, and then live on what's left over. Chapter 4 helps you figure out how much you should be saving and what you can afford to spend while still accomplishing your financial goals.

Looking for the best values

You can find high quality and low cost in the same product. Conversely, paying a high price is no guarantee that you're getting high quality. Cars are a good example. Whether you're buying a subcompact, a sports car, or a luxury four-door sedan, some cars are more fuel efficient and cheaper to maintain than rivals that carry the same sticker price.

When you evaluate the cost of a product or service, think in terms of total, long-term costs. Suppose that you're comparing the purchase of two used cars: the Solid Sedan, which costs $11,995, and the Clunker Convertible, which weighs in at $9,995. On the surface, the convertible appears to be cheaper. However, the price that you pay for a car is but a small portion of what that car ultimately costs you. If the convertible is costly to operate, maintain, and insure over the years, it could end up costing you much more than the sedan would (later in this chapter, we detail where to find such information). Sometimes, paying a reasonable amount more upfront for a higher-quality product or service ends up saving you money in the long run.

WARNING

People who sell particular products and services may initially appear to have your best interests at heart when they steer you toward something that isn't costly. However, you may be in for a rude awakening when you discover the ongoing service, maintenance, and other fees you face in the years ahead. Salespeople are generally trained to pitch you a lower-cost product if you indicate that's what you're after.

Don't waste money on brand names

TIP

You don't want to compromise on quality, especially in the areas where quality is important to you. But you also don't want to be duped into believing that brand-name products are better or worth a substantially higher price. Be suspicious of companies that spend gobs on image-oriented advertising. Why? Because heavy advertising costs many dollars, and as a consumer of those companies' products and services, you pay for all that advertising.

All successful companies advertise their products. Advertising is cost effective *and* good business (if it brings in enough new business). But you need to consider the products and services and the claims that companies make. In grocery stores, for example, you can often find name brands and store brands for the same product sitting in close proximity to one another. Upon reading the label, you can see that the products may, in fact, be identical, and the only difference between the two products is that the name-brand product costs more (because of the branding and associated advertising and marketing).

Branding is used in many fields to sell overpriced, mediocre products and services to consumers. Does a cola beverage really taste better if it's "the real thing" or "the choice of a new generation"? Consider all the silly labels and fluffy marketing of beers. Blind taste testing demonstrates little if any difference between the more expensive brand-name products and the cheaper, less heavily advertised ones.

Now, if you can't live without your Coca-Cola or Stella Artois, and you think that these products are head and shoulders above the rest, drink them to your heart's content. But question the importance of the name and image of the products you buy. Companies spend a lot of money creating and cultivating an image, which has zero impact on how their products taste or perform.

Tread carefully online

Online shopping has grown in popularity for some good reasons. It's reasonably fast and convenient, and you can quickly research different products and services before buying.

Over the years, we've warmed to shopping online, especially when we know what we want already. Without much time or effort, you can quickly determine what a competitive price is for a product and get it ordered and delivered in short order. No need to get in your car and waste gasoline and have to navigate traffic, possible accidents, and salespeople.

WARNING

If this all sounds too good to be true, it's because it is. Online shopping has plenty of pitfalls, some minor, some possibly major. Here is a summary of the potential downsides to shopping online and what can and cannot be done about each of them:

>> **The low price isn't really so low with hidden costs.** You can't simply go by the sticker price of products as listed on websites. Be especially careful when ordering from smaller and/or newer websites that may not stand behind what they sell. Shipping costs are often hard to discern and, in the worst cases, not disclosed until after you've invested plenty of your time going through an online checkout process that involves entering lots of personal information. You may also find that the particular colour or style of a product you want is more expensive. Also, be aware that provinces are forcing online retailers to collect provincial sales tax so that cost advantage is disappearing.

>> **Online shopping encourages overspending.** Shopping online is easy — too easy. In addition to not even using real cash to buy, you don't even have the sense that you're buying something because when the transaction is complete, all you have is your online receipt. So, for folks with a propensity to overspend, online shopping may be especially problematic.

>> **Connection of shopping to social media exposes you to even more advertising and problems.** The online-shopping experience is very much intertwined on many sites with social media.

>> **On less-than-secure websites, as well as on sites set up for the sole purpose of tricking you into revealing your personal and financial details, identity theft is a concern.** See Chapter 23 for tips and advice on this important topic.

>> **Bogus and biased online reviews can lead you astray.** Unfortunately, too many online reviews are posted by folks with a vested interest and/or who have never even actually bought and used the product. This is not to say that you can't learn from reading online reviews, but be careful and suspicious, especially with overly flattering reviews. Combat this problem by using Fakespot (www.fakespot.com) to determine how authentic or bogus reviews are posted for particular products and services online.

>> **If you like to shop for the best prices you can find online for specific products you want to buy, you greatly increase the odds of being led to sites that are actually selling fake merchandise.** Even if what you're buying is the real thing, if you have problems with it, the manufacturer may not stand behind the product in the way that it normally would if you had bought from a so called "authorized retailer."

See the next section for more shopping advice.

Get your money back

TIP

Take a look around your home for items you never use. Odds are you have some (maybe even many). Returning such items to where you bought them can be cathartic; it also reduces your home's clutter and puts more money in your pocket.

Also, think about the last several times you bought a product or service and didn't get what was promised. What did you do about it? Most people do nothing and let the derelict company off the hook. Why? Here are some common explanations for this type of behavior:

>> **Low standards:** Consumers have come to expect shoddy service and merchandise because of the common lousy experiences they've had.

>> **Conflict avoidance:** Most people shun confrontation. It makes them tense and anxious, and it churns their stomachs.

>> **Hassle aversion:** Some companies don't make it easy for complainers to get their money back or obtain satisfaction. To get restitution from some companies, you need the tenacity and determination of a pit bull.

You can increase your odds of getting what you expect for your money by doing business with companies that

>> **Have fair return policies:** Don't purchase any product or service until you understand the company's return policy. Be especially wary of buying from companies that charge hefty "restocking" fees for returned merchandise or simply don't allow returns at all. Reputable companies offer full refunds and don't make you take store credit (although taking credit is fine if you're sure that you'll use it soon and that the company will still be around).

>> **Can provide good references:** Suppose that you're going to install a fence on your property, and, as a result, you're going to be speaking with fencing contractors for the first time. You can sift out many inferior firms by asking each contractor that you interview for at least three references from people in your local area who have had a fence installed in the past year or two.

>> **Are committed to the type of product or service they provide:** Suppose that your chosen fencing contractor does a great job, and now that you're in the market for new gutters on your home, the contractor says that he does gutters, too. Although the path of least resistance would be to simply hire the same contractor for your gutters, you should inquire about how many gutters the contractor has installed and also interview some other firms that specialize in such work. Because your fencing contractor may have done only a handful of gutter jobs, he may not know as much about that type of work.

Following these guidelines can greatly diminish your chances of having unhappy outcomes with products or services you buy. And here's another important tip: Whenever possible and as long as you can pay the balance in full when due, buy with a credit card if your credit's in good standing. Doing so enables you to dispute a charge within 60 days and gives you leverage for getting your money back.

If you find that you're unable to make progress when trying to get compensation for a lousy product or service, here's what we recommend you do:

>> **Document:** Taking notes whenever you talk to someone at a company can help you validate your case down the road, should problems develop. Obviously, the bigger the purchase and the more you have at stake, the more carefully you should document what you've been promised. Try to get into the habit of writing down the name of the person you're speaking with and the time and date of your call. Keep copies of companies' marketing literature, because such documents often make promises or claims that companies fail to live up to in practise.

RECOGNIZING THE BETTER BUSINESS BUREAU'S CONFLICTS OF INTEREST

The Better Business Bureau (BBB) states that its mission is "to promote and foster the highest ethical relationship between businesses and the public." Unfortunately, the reality of the typical consumer's experience of dealing with the BBB doesn't live up to the BBB's marketing. BBBs are nonprofits and are not agencies of any governmental body.

"It's a business trade organization, and each local BBB is basically independent, like a franchise," says John Bear, an author of consumer advocacy books. "By and large, when somebody has a problem with a company and they fill out a complaint form with the BBB, if the company is a member of the BBB, there's ample evidence that consumers often end up not being satisfied. The BBB protects their members."

Particularly problematic among the BBB's pro-business practises are the company reports that the BBB keeps on file. The BBB often considers a legitimate complaint satisfactorily resolved even when you're quite unhappy and the company is clearly not working to satisfy the problems for which it's responsible.

Bear also cites examples of some truly troubling BBB episodes. In one case, he says that a *diploma mill* (a company that sells degrees but provides little, if any, education) in the southern states was a member of the local BBB. "When complaints started coming in," says Bear, "the BBB's response was always that the company met their standards and that the complaints were resolved. The reality was that the complaints weren't satisfactorily resolved, and it took about two years until complaints reached into the hundreds for the BBB to finally cancel the diploma mill's membership and give out a bland statement about complaints. Two months later, the FBI raided the company. Millions of consumers' dollars were lost because the BBB didn't do its job."

The Toronto office of the BBB also has had its share of troubles. In the late 1990s, the branch was engulfed in a spending scandal, including the finding of a forensic audit that the then-president had been given a $1 million "termination" package and immediately rehired. In 2000, a former director and chair of the Toronto BBB was found guilty of securities violations. The office had its licence revoked by the governing body in 2001. The truth about some BBBs is unfortunate, because as consumer protection agencies are being hit by cutbacks, and dissatisfied consumers are being shunted to the BBB, more people are in for unsatisfactory experiences with an organization that doesn't go to bat for them.

» **Escalate:** Some frontline employees either aren't capable of resolving disputes or lack the authority to do so. No matter what the cause, speak with a department supervisor and continue escalating from there. If you're still not making progress, lodge a complaint to whatever regulatory agency (if any) oversees such companies. Consider posting your beefs on some of the numerous consumer complaint-compiling websites and possibly social media outlets, but be careful to stick to the facts and avoid saying something false or incendiary that can lead to your being sued. Tell your friends and colleagues not to do business with the company (and let the company know that you're doing so until your complaint is resolved to your satisfaction). Also consider contacting a consumer help group — these groups are typically sponsored by broadcast or print media in metropolitan areas. They can be helpful in resolving disputes or shining a light on disreputable companies or products.

» **Litigate:** If all else fails, consider taking the matter to small-claims court if the company continues to be unresponsive. (Depending on the amount of money at stake, this tactic may be worth your time.) The maximum dollar limit that you may recover in most provinces is $25,000. For larger amounts than those allowed in small-claims court in your province, you can, of course, hire a lawyer and pursue your claim through the traditional legal channels — although you may end up throwing away more of your time and money. Mediation and arbitration are generally a better option than following through on a lawsuit.

Cutting excess spending

If you want to reduce your overall spending by, say, 10 percent, you can just cut all your current expenditures by 10 percent. Or, you can reach your 10 percent goal by cutting some categories a lot and others not at all. You need to set priorities and make choices about where you want (and don't want) to spend your money.

TIP

What you spend your money on is sometimes a matter of habit rather than a matter of what you really want or value. For example, some people shop at whatever stores are close to them. These days, some people order many things online, but that can lead to overspending as well. But eliminating fat doesn't necessarily mean cutting back on your purchases: You can save money by buying in bulk. Some stores specialize in selling larger packages or quantities of a product at a lower price because they save money on the packaging and handling. If you're single, shop with a friend and split the bulk purchases. You can also do some comparison shopping online, but be sure you're surveying reputable websites that stand behind what they sell and that provide high-quality customer service.

Shunning consumer credit

As we discuss in Chapters 3 and 5, buying items that depreciate — such as cars, clothing, and vacations — on credit is hazardous to your long-term financial health. Buy only what you can afford today. If you'll be forced to carry a debt for months or years on end, you can't really afford what you're buying on credit.

WARNING

Without a doubt, *renting to own* is the most expensive way to buy. Here's how it works: You see a huge ad blaring "$39.99 for a 65-inch smart TV!" Well, the ad has a big hitch: That's $39.99 per week, for many weeks. When all is said and done (and paid), buying a $998 65-inch smart TV through a rent-to-own store costs a typical buyer more than $3,639! Welcome to the world of rent-to-own stores, which offer cash-poor consumers the ability to lease consumer items and, at the end of the lease, an option to buy.

If you think that paying a 20 percent interest rate on a credit card is expensive, consider this: The effective interest rate charged on many rent-to-own purchases exceeds 100 percent; in some cases, it may be 200 percent or more! Renting to own makes buying on a credit card look like a great deal. We're not sharing this information to encourage you to buy on credit cards, but to point out what a rip-off renting to own is. Such stores prey on cashless consumers who either can't get credit cards or don't understand how expensive renting to own really is. Forget the instant gratification and save a set amount each week until you can afford what you want.

REMEMBER

Consumer credit is expensive, and it reinforces a bad financial habit: spending more than you can afford.

Budgeting to Boost Your Savings

When most people hear the word *budgeting,* they think unpleasant thoughts — like those associated with *dieting* — and rightfully so. But budgeting can help you move from knowing how much you spend on various things to successfully reducing your spending.

The first step in the process of *budgeting,* or planning your future spending, is to analyze where your current spending is going (refer to Chapter 3). After you do that, calculate how much more you'd like to save each month. Then comes the hard part: deciding where to make cuts in your spending.

Suppose that you're currently not saving any of your monthly income and you want to save 10 percent for retirement. If you can save and invest through a tax-sheltered retirement savings plan, you don't actually need to cut your spending by

10 percent to reach a savings goal of 10 percent (of your gross income). When you contribute money to a tax-deductible Registered Retirement Savings Plan (RRSP), you reduce your federal and provincial taxes. If you're a moderate-income earner paying, say, 35 percent in taxes on your marginal income, you actually need to reduce your spending by only 6.5 percent to save 10 percent. The other 3.5 percent of the savings comes from the lowering of your taxes. (The higher your tax bracket, the less you need to cut your spending to reach a particular savings goal.)

So, to boost your savings rate to 10 percent, go through your current spending category by category until you come up with enough proposed cuts to reduce your spending by 7 percent. Make your cuts in the areas that will be the least painful and where you're getting the least value from your current level of spending. Another method of budgeting involves starting completely from scratch rather than examining your current expenses and making cuts from that starting point. Ask yourself how much you'd like to spend on different categories. The advantage of this approach is that it doesn't allow your current spending levels to constrain your thinking. You'll likely be amazed at the discrepancies between what you think you should be spending and what you actually are spending in certain categories.

Reducing Your Spending

As you read through the following strategies for reducing your spending, please keep in mind that some of these strategies will make sense for you and some of them won't. Start your spending reduction plan with the strategies that come easily and seem most appealing. Work your way through them. Keep a list of the options that are more challenging for you — ones that may require more of a sacrifice but may be workable if necessary to achieve your spending and savings goals.

No matter which of the ideas in this chapter you choose, rest assured that keeping your budget lean and mean pays enormous dividends. After you implement a spending reduction strategy, you'll reap the benefits for years to come. Take a look at Figure 6-1: For every $1,000 that you shave from your annual spending (that's just $83 per month), check out how much more money you'll have down the road. (This chart assumes that you invest your newfound savings in an RRSP, you average returns of 8 percent per year on your investments, and you're in a combined federal and provincial tax bracket of 35 percent — see Chapter 7 for information on tax brackets.)

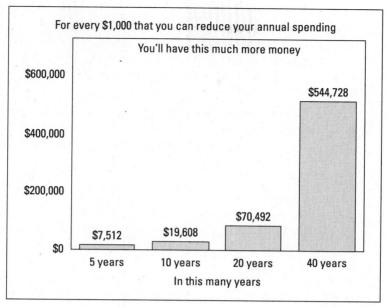

For every $1,000 that you can reduce your annual spending

You'll have this much more money

$544,728

$70,492

$19,608

$7,512

In this many years

5 years   10 years   20 years   40 years

FIGURE 6-1:
Reducing your spending can yield large investment sums.

© John Wiley & Sons

Managing food costs

Not eating is one way to reduce food expenditures; however, this method tends to make you weak and dizzy, so it's probably not a viable long-term strategy. The following culinary cutbacks can keep you on your feet — perhaps even improve your health — and help you save money.

Eating out frugally

Eating meals out and getting takeout can be time-savers, but they rack up big bills if done too often and too lavishly. Eating out is a luxury — think of it as hiring someone to shop, cook, and clean up for you. Of course, some people either hate to cook or don't have the time, space, or energy to do much in the kitchen. If this sounds like you, choose restaurants carefully and order from the menu selectively.

TIP

Here are some tips for eating out:

>> **Avoid beverages, especially alcohol.** Most restaurants make big profits on beverages. Drink water instead. (Water is healthy, and it reduces the likelihood that you'll want a nap after a big meal.)

>> **Favour fast casual restaurants.** Examples include Chipotle, Panera, and Qdoba. Ordering at the counter saves you from having to tip the usual 15 percent on your bill. You can also save at these types of restaurants by not having a waiter encouraging you to order more (for example, appetizers, beverages, dessert, and so on).

>> **Consider buying prepared food and taking it home or eating it outside someplace nice.** The abundance of premium grocery stores provides access to an unbelievable array of prepared foods. That's not to say that you can ignore prices, because if you do, you can end up spending plenty on these purchases.

>> **Order vegetarian.** Vegetarian dishes generally cost less than meat-based entrées (and they're generally better for you). We're not suggesting that you only order vegetarian, especially if you're sharing with a number of other people, but that you consider some vegetarian dishes.

We don't want to be killjoys. We're not saying that you should live on bread and water. You can have dessert — heck, have some wine, too, for special occasions! Just try not to eat dessert with every meal, or try eating appetizers and dessert at home, where they're a lot less expensive.

Eating healthy at home without spending a fortune

TIP

If you aren't skilled in the kitchen, consider learning how to cook. Folks who eat out a lot do so in part because they don't really know how to cook. Ask your family and friends who know how to cook to show you the basics, take a cooking class, and read some good books on the topic.

Even if you have rudimentary cooking skills, there is one simple key to keep in mind if you want to minimize your food costs and eat well. Be sure to maintain a good inventory of food that you like, that is reasonably priced, and that is nutritious. When you go grocery shopping, buy enough to make it worthwhile. Of course, you don't want food to spoil, but, for example, if you like eating yogurt for breakfast every day, get enough to last you at least a couple of weeks. Always check the freshness dates on perishable items you're buying. If you find getting to the store and hauling groceries home to be a big obstacle, check out grocery delivery services in your areas. Minimize delivery fees by placing larger orders. And try to avoid going grocery shopping when you're hungry. You'll often end up over-buying, and loading your grocery cart with a lot of high-calorie, sugar-rich foods designed and packaged to appeal to an empty stomach.

As evidenced by the number of diet and weight-loss books on bookstore shelves — and the growth of the natural and organic grocery stores like Whole Foods and Farm Boy — Canadians are trying to eat healthier. Consumers are concerned about all the pesticides, antibiotics, and hormones that end up in the food supply, so organic food purchases are growing at a fast rate.

Problem is, financially speaking, better-quality food, especially organic foods, can cost more, sometimes much more — but not always. A number of studies we've seen demonstrate that highly processed foods, which are less nutritious and worse for your health, can be as costly as (or even more expensive than) fresh, so-called "whole" foods. The key to not overspending on fresher, healthier, and organic foods is to be flexible when you're at the grocery store. Buy more of what is seasonal and, therefore, currently less expensive; stock up on sale items that aren't perishable; and buy more at stores that have competitive pricing. Many larger grocery chains carry some organic foods — just be sure to comparison price. Local food co-ops, which source food locally, are another great source for competitively priced food and sometimes pay dividends annually to members.

TIP

According to various studies, spending the money to buy organic food makes the most sense when buying the following foods:

>> **Meat, poultry, eggs, and dairy:** By going organic, you avoid supplemental hormones and antibiotics. You also greatly reduce the risk of exposure to the agent believed to cause mad cow disease, and you minimize your exposure to other potential toxins in nonorganic feed.

>> **Produce:** Apples, bell peppers, celery, cherries, garlic, hot peppers, imported grapes, nectarines, peaches, pears, potatoes, red raspberries, spinach, and strawberries have historically been found to carry the greatest amount of pesticides, even after washing.

>> **Baby food:** Baby food is typically loaded with condensed fruits and vegetables, which contain concentrated pesticide residues. Also, children's small and developing bodies are especially vulnerable to toxins.

One area where many folks are wasting money is in buying bottled water. Although tap water often does leave something to be desired, bottled water is typically not as pure as some folks think. You can save hundreds of dollars annually and drink cleaner water by installing a water filtration system at home and improving your tap (or well) water. According to a recent *Consumer Reports* review of the topic, "Water filters have become simpler to install and more convenient to maintain. Several under-sink and reverse-osmosis models use simple screw-on plumbing connections instead of saddle valves, which require drilling into the cold water supply line, and can leak."

The simplest and lowest-cost approach is a carafe-style system (such as a Brita or Clear2O), which you fill at your sink and can keep in your refrigerator. Such systems generally have filters that require periodic replacement. Among *Consumer Reports* recommended "Best Buy" water filtration systems deemed ". . . effective at removing common contaminants and off-tastes" are countertop-type and under-sink systems, which go for about $200 to $400. For more serious water problems, *Consumer Reports* recommends reverse-osmosis filtration systems, which begin in that same price range but can be much more expensive.

Even if you hire someone to do the installation, these systems should easily pay for themselves within the first year, and then you'll enjoy a more than 100 percent annual return on your investment by being able to eliminate those costly bottled-water purchases. How's that for a low-risk, super-high-return investment?

To dispense your own bottled water for use outside your home, get a small supply of dishwasher-safe, stainless-steel containers such as those made by MEC, Klean Kanteen, and SIGG. Or there's the innovative Tap Water Bottle (www.tapwater-bottle.com), a glass bottle with one of those rubber tops that seals by flipping down the metal attachment.

Joining a wholesale superstore

TIP

Superstores such as Costco enable you to buy groceries in bulk at wholesale prices. And contrary to popular perception, you don't have to buy 1,000 rolls of toilet paper at once — just 24.

We've performed price comparisons between wholesale superstores and retail grocery stores and found that wholesalers charge about 30 percent less for the exact same stuff — all without the hassle of clipping coupons or hunting for the store that has the best price on paper towels this month! (At these discount prices, you only need to spend about $150 per year to recoup membership fees to stores like Costco, which start at around $60.) In addition to saving you lots of money, buying in bulk requires fewer shopping trips. You'll have more supplies around your humble abode, so you'll have less need to eat out (which is costly) or make trips (which wastes time and gasoline) to the local grocer, who may be really nice but charges the most.

WARNING

Perishables run the risk of living up to their name, so only buy what you can reasonably use. Repackage bulk packs into smaller quantities and store them in the freezer if possible. If you're single, shop with a friend and split the order. Also, be careful when you shop at the warehouse clubs — you may be tempted to buy things you don't really need. These stores carry all sorts of items, including the newest TVs, computers, furniture, clothing, complete sets of baseball cards, and giant canisters of biscotti — so wallet and waistline beware! Try not to make impulse purchases, and be especially careful when you have kids in tow.

To find a Costco store near you, call 800-463-3783 or go to www.costco.ca.

Saving on shelter

Housing and all the costs associated with it (utilities, furniture, appliances, and, if you're a homeowner, maintenance, repairs, and home insurance) can gobble a large chunk of your monthly income. We're not suggesting that you live in an igloo or tent (though they're probably less costly), but people often overlook opportunities to save money in this category.

Reducing rental costs

TIP

Rent can take up a sizable chunk of your monthly take-home pay. Many people consider rent to be a fixed and inflexible part of their expenses, but it's not. Here's what you can do to cut down your rental costs:

>> **Move to a lower-cost rental.** Of course, a lower-cost rental may not be as nice — it may be smaller, lack a private parking spot, or be located in a less popular area. Remember that the less you spend renting, the more you can save toward buying your own place. Just be sure to factor in all the costs of a new location, including the possible higher commuting costs.

>> **Share a rental.** Living alone has some benefits, but financially speaking, it's a luxury. If you rent a larger place with roommates, your rental costs should be a good deal less, and you'll get more home for your rental dollars. You have to be in a sharing mood, though. Roommates can be a hassle at times, but they can also be a plus — you get to meet all sorts of new people, and you have someone else to blame when the kitchen's a mess.

>> **Negotiate your rental increases.** Every year, like clockwork, your landlord bumps up your rent by a certain percentage. If your local rental market is soft or your living quarters are deteriorating, stand up for yourself! You have more leverage and power than you probably realize. A smart landlord doesn't want to lose good tenants who pay rent on time. Filling vacancies takes time and money. State your case: You've been a responsible tenant, and your research shows comparable rentals going for less. Crying "poor" may help, too. At the very least, if you can't stave off the rent increase, maybe you can wrangle some improvements to the place.

>> **Buy rather than rent.** Purchasing your own place may seem costly, but in the long run, owning is cheaper than renting, and you have something to show for it in the end. If you purchase real estate, your mortgage payment (which is your biggest ownership expense) remains constant for the term of your mortgage. Only your property taxes, maintenance, and insurance costs are exposed to the vagaries of inflation. As a renter, your entire monthly housing cost can rise with increases in the cost of living (unless you're the beneficiary of a rent-controlled apartment). See Chapter 15 to find out the smart way to buy real estate and determine if buying in your local area makes financial sense.

Reducing homeowner expenses

WARNING

As every homeowner knows, houses suck up money. You should be especially careful to watch your money in this area of your budget.

» **Know what you can afford.** Whether you're on the verge of buying your first home or trading up to a more costly property, crunch some realistic numbers before you commit. Calculate how much you can afford to spend monthly on a home. Do the exercises in Chapter 3, on where you're spending your money, and Chapter 4, on saving for retirement, to help you calculate the amount you can afford.

Although real estate can be a good long-term investment, you can end up pouring a large portion of your discretionary dollars into your home. In addition to decorating and remodelling, some people feel the need to trade up to a bigger home every few years. Of course, after they're in their new home, the remodelling and renovation cycle simply begins again, which costs even more money. The cost of most home renovations or remodelling will never come close to being recouped. In addition, a major renovation may result in higher property taxes, as well as higher homeowner's insurance costs. Appreciate what you have, and remember that homes are for living in, not museums for display. If you have children, why waste a lot of money on expensive furnishings that take up valuable space and require you to constantly nag your kids to tread carefully? And don't covet — the world will always have people with bigger houses and more toys than you.

» **Rent out a room.** Because selling your home to buy a less expensive place can be a big hassle, consider taking in a tenant (or charge those adult "children" still living at home!) to reduce your housing expenses. Check out the renter thoroughly: Get references, run a credit report, research civil and criminal databases online, and talk about ground rules and expectations before sharing your space. Don't forget to check with your insurance company to see whether your homeowner's policy needs adjustments to cover potential liability from renting.

» **Appeal your property-tax assessment.** If you bought your property when housing prices were higher in your area than they are now, you may be able to save money by appealing your assessment. Also, if you live in an area where your assessment is based on how the local assessor valued the property (rather than what you paid for your home), your home may be over-assessed. Check with your local assessor's office for the appeals procedure you need to follow. An appraiser's recent evaluation of your property may help. Also, review how the assessor valued your property compared with similar ones nearby — mistakes happen.

>> **Reduce utility costs.** Sometimes you have to spend money to save money. Old refrigerators, for example, can waste a lot of electricity. Insulate to save on heating and air-conditioning bills. Install water flow regulators in shower-heads. When planting your yard, don't select water-guzzling plants, and keep your lawn area reasonable. Even if you don't live in an area susceptible to droughts, why waste water (which isn't free) and lawn fertilizer unnecessarily? Recycle — recycling means less garbage, which translates into lower trash bills (because you won't be charged for using larger garbage containers) and benefits the environment by reducing landfill. Consider installing solar and other newer energy alternatives, but run the numbers and be sure you'll get your expenditures back within a reasonable number of years.

Cutting transportation costs

Canada is a car-driven society. In most other countries, cars are a luxury. If more people in Canada thought of cars as a luxury, Canadians might have far fewer financial problems. Not only do cars pollute the air and clog the highways, but they also cost you a bundle.

Purchasing a quality car and using it wisely can reduce the cost of car ownership. Using alternative modes of transportation can also help you save.

Contrary to advertising slogans, cars aren't built to last; manufacturers don't want you to stick with the same car forever. New models are constantly introduced with new features and styling changes. But getting a new set of wheels every few years is an expensive luxury. Don't try to keep up with the Joneses as they show off their new cars every year — for all you know, they're running themselves into financial ruin trying to impress others. Let your neighbours admire you for your thriftiness and wisdom instead.

Research before you buy a car

When you buy a car, you don't just pay the initial sticker price: You also have to pay for gas, insurance, registration fees, maintenance, and repairs. And then there's the sales tax. Don't simply compare sticker prices; think about the total, long-term costs of car ownership, and see whether they fit into your budget while still allowing you to save toward your goals.

Speaking of total costs, remember that you're also trusting your life to the car. With about 2,000 Canadians killed in road collisions annually (more than half of which it's estimated are caused by drunk drivers), safety should be an important consideration as well. (If you take care of your health, probably the most danger-ous thing you'll ever do is get behind the wheel.) Air bags, for example, may save your life. The U.S. National Highway Traffic Safety Administration's website (www.safercar.gov) has lots of crash-test data, as well as information on other car-safety issues.

TIP

Check out the annual Canadian *Lemon-Aid* books put out by Phil Edmonston for a detailed assessment of defects, repair costs, and safety ratings. He has different titles dealing with new cars, used cars, new trucks and vans, and used trucks and vans (including minivans). The books also detail average resale prices by model and year. *Consumer Reports* (www.consumerreports.org) publishes a number of useful buying guides for new and used cars.

IntelliChoice (www.motortrend.com/intellichoice) provides information about all categories of ownership costs, warranties, and dealer costs for new cars, which are rated based on total ownership costs. Edmunds (www.edmunds.com) provides more general information about different makes and models of both new and used cars. Be aware that these two sites have advertising and may receive referral fees if you buy a car through a dealer the website refers you to.

Don't lease, don't borrow: Buy your car with cash

The main reason people end up spending more than they can afford on a car is that they finance the purchase. As we discuss in Part 1, you should avoid borrowing money for consumption purchases, especially for items that depreciate in value (like cars). A car is most definitely *not* an investment.

WARNING

Leasing is generally more expensive than borrowing money to buy a car. Leasing is like a long-term car rental. Everyone knows how well rental cars get treated — leased cars are treated just as well, which is one of the reasons leasing is so costly.

"But I can't buy a new car with cash," you may be thinking. Some people feel that it's unreasonable of us to expect them to use cash to buy a new car, but we're trying to look out for your best long-term financial interests. Consider the following:

>> **If you lack sufficient cash to buy a new car, don't buy a new car!** Most of the world's population can't even afford a car, let alone a new one! Buy a car that you can afford — which for most people is a used one.

>> **Don't fall for the rationale that says buying a used car means lots of maintenance, repair expenses, and problems.** Do your homework and buy a good-quality used car (see the preceding section). That way, you can have the best of both worlds. A good used car costs less to buy and, thanks to lower insurance costs, less to operate.

>> **You don't need a fancy car to impress people for business purposes.** Some people we know say that they absolutely must drive a nice, brand-spanking-new high-end car to set the right impression for business purposes. We're not going to tell you how to manage your career, but we will ask you to consider that if clients and others see you driving an expensive new car, they may think that you spend money wastefully or that you're getting rich off of them!

If you absolutely must finance some or all of your new car purchase price, and you're a homeowner, consider using a home-equity line of credit. Interest rates on these loans are very reasonable.

Replace high-cost cars

Maybe you realize by now that your car is too expensive to operate because of insurance, gas, and maintenance costs. Or maybe you bought too much car — people who lease or borrow money for a car frequently buy a far more expensive car than they can realistically afford.

TIP

Sell your expensive car and get something more financially manageable. The sooner you switch, the more money you'll save. Getting rid of a car on a lease is a challenge, but it can be done. We know of one person who, when he lost his job and needed to slash expenses, convinced the dealer (by writing a letter to the owner) to take the leased car back.

Keep cars to a minimum

For most households, maintaining two or more cars is an expensive extravagance. Try to find ways to make do with fewer cars. You can move beyond the confines of owning a car by carpooling or riding transit or commuter trains to work. Some employers give incentives for taking public transit to work, and some cities and municipalities offer assistance for setting up vanpools or carpools along popular routes. By leaving the driving to someone else, you can catch up on reading or just relax on the way to and from work. You also help reduce pollution. And if you just occasionally need a car — or an extra one — look at signing up with one of the many car-share services.

When you're considering the cost of living in different areas, don't forget to factor in commuting costs. One advantage of living close to work, or at least close to public-transit systems, is that you may be able to make do with fewer cars (or no car at all) in your household.

Buy commuter passes

TIP

In many areas, you can purchase train, bus, or subway passes to help reduce the cost of commuting. Many toll bridges also have booklets of tickets or passes that you can buy at a discount. Electronic passes help you keep moving, and eliminate sitting in toll-collection lines that waste your time and gas. Unfortunately, the federal government short-sightedly eliminated the public-transit credit in 2017. Some provinces may offer a similar credit, but it may be available only to seniors.

Use regular unleaded gas

A number of studies have shown that "premium" gasoline isn't worth the extra expense. But make sure that you buy gasoline that has the minimum octane rating recommended for your vehicle by consulting your owner's manual. Paying more for higher-octane gasoline just wastes money. Your car doesn't run better; you just pay more for gas. Also, don't use credit cards to buy your gas if you have to pay a higher price to do so.

Service your car regularly

Sure, servicing your car (for example, changing the oil every 12,000 to 16,000 kilometres) costs money, but it saves you dough in the long run by extending the operating life of your car. Servicing your car also reduces the chance that your car will conk out in the middle of nowhere, which requires a hefty towing charge to a service station. Stalling on the freeway during peak rush hour and having thousands of angry commuters delayed because of you is even worse.

Lowering your energy costs

Escalating energy prices remind all of us how much we depend upon and use oil, electricity, and natural gas in our daily lives. A number of terrific websites are packed with suggestions and tips for how to lower your energy costs. Before we present those to you, however, here are the basics:

>> **Drive fuel-efficient cars and drive efficiently.** If you're safety minded, you know how dangerous driving can be and aren't willing to risk your life driving a pint-size vehicle just to get a car with super-low gas consumption. That said, you can drive safe cars that are fuel-efficient (see the earlier section "Research before you buy a car"). Also, take it easy on the gas pedal and brakes; do both gradually and don't speed on the highway because doing so gobbles more gas. Although it varies based upon the type of car you drive and your driving habits, each 8 kilometres per hour you drive over 100 kilometres per hour can reduce your fuel economy by about 7 percent.

>> **Be thrifty at home.** Ask all family members to turn off lights they don't need. Turn down the heat at night, which saves money and helps you sleep better, and turn it down when no one is home. *Hint:* If people are walking around your home during the winter with shorts on (as happens in too many college dormitories) instead of wearing sweaters, turn the heat down!

>> **Service and maintain what you have.** Anything that uses energy — from your cars to your furnace — should be regularly serviced. For instance, make sure you clean your filters.

>> **Investigate energy efficiency before you buy.** This advice applies not only to appliances but also to an entire home. Some builders are building energy efficiency into their new homes.

TIP

Our favourite energy information and tip websites are Natural Resources Canada's Office of Energy Efficiency (go to `www.nrcan.gc.ca` and search for "Office of Energy Efficiency") and the U.S. Department of Energy's Energy Efficiency and Renewable Energy (`www.energy.gov/energysaver/energy-saver`).

Controlling clothing costs

TIP

Given the amount of money that some people spend on clothing and related accessories, we've come to believe that people in nudist colonies must be great savers! But you probably live among the clothed mainstream of society, so here's a short list of economical ideas:

>> **Avoid clothing that requires dry cleaning.** When you buy clothing, try to stick with cottons and machine-washable synthetics rather than wools or silks that require dry cleaning. Check labels before you buy clothing.

>> **Don't chase the latest fashions.** Fashion designers and retailers are constantly working to tempt you to buy. Don't do it. Ignore publications that pronounce this season's look. In most cases, you simply don't need to buy racks of new clothes or an entire new wardrobe every year. True fashion, as defined by what people wear, changes quite slowly. In fact, the classics never go out of style. If you want the effect of a new wardrobe every year, store last year's purchases away next year and then bring them out the year after. Or rotate your clothing inventory every third year. Set your own fashion standards. Buy basic and buy classic — if you let fashion gurus be your guide, you'll end up with the biggest wardrobe in the poorhouse!

>> **Minimize accessories.** Shoes, jewellery, handbags, and the like can gobble large amounts of money. Again, how many of these accessory items do you really need? The answer is probably very few, because each one should last many years.

TIP

Go to your closet or jewellery box and tally up the loot. What else could you have done with all that cash? Do you see things you regret buying or forgot you even had? Don't make the same mistake again. Have a garage sale if you have a lot of stuff that you don't want. Return recent unused purchases to stores. For older items you have no intention of using anymore, try donating to one of the several charities that run clothing drives.

Repaying your debt

In Chapter 5, we discuss strategies for reducing the cost of carrying consumer debt. The *best* way to reduce the costs of such debt is to avoid it in the first place when you're making consumption purchases.

REMEMBER

You can avoid consumer debt by eliminating your access to credit or by limiting your purchase of consumer items to what you can pay off each month. Borrow only for long-term investments (see Chapter 2 for more information).

Don't keep a credit card that charges you an annual fee, especially if you pay your balance in full each month. Many no-fee credit cards exist — and some even offer you a benefit for using them. You can find a helpful up-to-date list of recommended no-fee credit cards on Tony's website, www.moneygrower.ca.

Consider the cards in the preceding list only if you pay your balance in full each month, because no-fee cards typically don't offer the lowest interest rates for balances carried month to month. The small rewards that you earn really won't do you much good if they're negated by high interest charges.

TIP

If you have a credit card that charges an annual fee, try calling the company and saying that you want to cancel the card because you can get a competitor's card without an annual fee. Many banks will agree to waive the fee on the spot. Some require you to call back yearly to cancel the fee — a hassle that can be avoided by getting a true no-fee card.

Some cards that charge an annual fee and offer credits toward the purchase of a specific item, such as a car or airline ticket or hotel stay, may be worth your while if you pay your bill in full each month and charge $10,000 or more annually. *Note:* Be careful — you may be tempted to charge more on a card that rewards you for more purchases. Spending more in order to rack up bonuses defeats the purpose of the credits.

Indulging responsibly in fun and recreation

Having fun and taking time out for R&R can be money well spent. But when it comes to fun and recreation, financial extravagance can wreck an otherwise good budget.

Look at low-cost entertainment

If you adjust your plans and expectations, entertainment doesn't have to cost a great deal of money. Many movies, theatres, museums, and restaurants offer discount prices on certain days and/or at certain times. Many library systems have passes you can borrow for free access to museums, art galleries, zoos, and science centres.

Cultivate some interests and hobbies that are free or low-cost. Visiting with friends, hiking, reading, and playing sports can be good for your finances as well as your health.

Vacation for less

WARNING

For many people, vacations are a luxury. For others, regular vacations are essential parts of their routine. Regardless of how you recharge your batteries, remember that vacations aren't investments, so you shouldn't borrow through credit cards to finance your travels. After all, how relaxed will you feel when you have to pay all those bills?

Try taking shorter vacations that are closer to home. Have you been to a state or national park recently? Great places that you've always wanted to see but haven't visited for one reason or another are probably located within 200 to 300 kilometres of you. Folks from other countries flock to Canada to visit and enjoy our huge range of parks and natural attractions. There are probably many such spots you haven't gotten around to visiting within just a few hours' drive of where you live. Or you may want to just block out some time and do what family pets do: Relax around your home and enjoy some naps.

TIP

If you do travel a long way to a popular destination, travel during the off-season for the best deals on airfares and hotels. Keep an eye out for discounts. The *Consumer Reports Travel* newsletter and numerous Canadian websites — including Cheapflights (www.cheapflights.ca), Flight Centre (www.flightcentre.ca), itravel2000.com (www.itravel2000.com), redtag.ca (www.redtag.ca), and SellOff Vacations (www.selloffvacations.com) — can help you find low-cost travel options as well. Also check out the big U.S.-based online companies, including Expedia (www.expedia.ca), Priceline (www.priceline.com), and Travelocity (www.travelocity.ca). Senior citizens generally qualify for special fares at most airlines — ask the airline what programs it offers.

REMEMBER

Be sure to shop around, even when working with a travel agent. Travel agents work on commission, so they may not work hard to find you the best deals. Tour packages, when they meet your interests and needs, can also save you money.

Be thrifty with gifts

Think about how you approach buying gifts throughout the year — especially during the holidays. We know people who spend so much on their credit cards during the year-end holidays that it takes them until late spring or summer to pay off their debts! Some people forget their thrifty shopping habits when gift buying, perhaps because they don't like to feel cheap when buying a gift. As with other purchases you make, paying careful attention to where and what you buy can save you significant dollars. Don't make the mistake of equating the value of a gift with its dollar cost.

Although we don't want to deny your loved ones gifts from the heart — or deny you the pleasure of giving them — spend wisely. Homemade gifts are less costly to the giver and may be dearer to recipients. Many children actually love durable, classic, basic toys. If the TV commercials and web ads dictate your kids' desires, it may be time to limit the TV and Internet usage or set better rules for what the kids are allowed to watch. Use DVR services to record desired shows so you can zap through the ubiquitous commercials.

And here's a good suggestion for getting rid of those old, unwanted gifts: a white elephant gift exchange. Everyone brings a wrapped, unwanted gift from the past and exchanges it with someone else. After the gifts are opened, trading is allowed. (Just be sure not to bring a gift that was given to you by any of the exchange participants!)

Lowering your phone bills

Thanks to increased competition and technology, phone costs continue to fall. If you haven't looked for lower rates in recent years, you're probably paying more than you need to for quality phone service. Unfortunately, shopping among the many service providers is difficult. Plans come with different restrictions, minimums, and bells and whistles.

TIP

You may have to switch companies to reduce your bill, but we find that many people can save significantly with their current phone company simply by getting onto a better calling plan. So, before you spend hours shopping around, contact your current local and long-distance providers and ask them which of their calling plans offer the lowest cost for you based on the patterns of your calls.

Cellphones are ubiquitous. And although being able to make calls from wherever you are can be enormously convenient, you can spend a lot of money for service given the myriad extra charges, and put yourself in harm's way if you use your phone while driving and even walking if you're not paying attention to your surroundings. On the other hand, if you take advantage of the included minutes many plans offer, a good cellphone service can save you money.

WARNING

CELLPHONES AND KIDS CAN BE A DANGEROUS MIX

Everywhere you look these days, it seems as if every teen (and just as often, every adult) has a cellphone. Cellphones are a great way for parents to keep in contact with their children, especially in emergencies. But important safety issues come up when teens get caught up in using cellphones.

A number of studies have raised concerns about the impact of repeated cellphone usage on the brain and the possible linkage between brain tumours and usage of cellphones held near the side of one's head. Getting teens who talk on the phone to use earpieces connected to the cellphone is easier said than done.

A second health concern with cellphone usage is the common occurrence of older teens being on their phones while driving. Horrible accidents have happened with teens fiddling with their phones not only while placing and receiving calls, but also while typing out text messages or surfing online. Distracted-driving laws, which typically include a ban on the use of handheld devices, are in now in place across the country.

However, Canadians still face some of the highest bills in the world thanks to our long-standing tradition of limiting new players and allowing ruses like the recently abandoned "system access fee," which phone companies positioned as a required regulatory fee. It actually was nothing of the kind (despite the strange fact that many different phone companies charged their customers exactly the same amount each month!), and when consumer pressure grew to be too much, the fictitious "fee" was quietly abandoned.

The primary reason that some parents elect to provide cellphones to their teenage children is for safety, the ability to call home for a ride, and so on. If you're getting phones for your kids, you don't necessarily need all the costly bells and whistles.

In addition to downloads, text messaging, web surfing, and other services, kids (and adults) can find all sorts of entertaining ways to run up huge cellphone bills each month. Also, we hear a lot of complaints from parents about kids racking up data charges.

To deal with exceeding what your plan allows, you have a few options:

>> **Examine family-plan options that don't limit usage in the categories most important to you.** Shop around and make sure you sign up with the best plan and carrier given your typical usage. Reputable carriers let you test out their services. They also offer full refunds if you're not satisfied after a week or two of service.

>> **Set and enforce limits.** If you provide a cellphone to a child, keep in mind that kids don't need to use their phones for hours daily. This point is especially important with data usage, which you can block so that your kids can only use Wi-Fi when available. With teens, why not tie having good grades to being able to have some of the extra features?

>> **Check out prepaid or no-contract plans.** In addition to the big cellphone companies, research the impressively low-cost offerings of often-overlooked suppliers such as 7-Eleven's SpeakOut, and Petro-Canada Mobility.

Technology: Spending wisely

Canadians today have email, cellphones, smartphones, voicemail, tablets, satellite TV, the Internet, and too many other ways to stay in touch and entertained 24/7. Visit a store that sells electronics, and you'll find no end to new gadgets.

Although we enjoy choices and convenience as much as the next person, we also see the detrimental impact these technologies have on people's lives. As it is, most families struggle to find quality time together given their work obligations, long school days, and various other activities. At home, all these technology choices and options compete for attention and often pull families apart. The cost for all these services and gadgets adds up, leading to continued enslavement to your job. Err on the side of keeping your life simple. Doing so costs less, reduces stress, and allows more time for the things that really do matter in life.

REMEMBER

The worst way to shop for electronics and technology–based products is to wander around stores selling lots of these goods while a salesperson pitches you things. These folks are trained in what buttons to push to get you to whip out your Visa card and be on your way with things you don't know how you ever could've lived without. Educate yourself. Check out *Consumer Reports* and CNET (www.cnet.com), and determine what you really need instead of going to a store and being seduced by a salesperson.

Curtailing personal-care costs

TIP

You have to take care of yourself, but as with anything else, you can find ways to do it that are expensive, and you can find ways that save you money. Try this moneysaving advice:

>> **Hair care:** Going bald is one way to save money in this category. In the meantime, if you have hair to be trimmed, a number of no-frills, low-cost, hair-cutting joints can do the job. Topcuts and Supercuts are some of the larger hair-care chains. You may insist that your stylist is the only one who can

manage your hair the way you like it. At the prices charged by some of the trendy hair places, you have to really adore what she does to justify the price. Consider going periodically to a no-frills stylist for maintenance after getting a fabulous cut at a more expensive place. If you're daring, you can try getting your hair cut at a local training school.

For parents of young children, buying simple-to-use home haircutting electric clippers (such as Wahl's) can be a great time- and money-saver — no more agonizing trips with little ones to have their hair cut by a "stranger." The kit pays for itself after just two haircuts!

» **Other personal-care services:** As long as we're on the subject of outward beauty, we have to say that, in our personal opinion, the billions spent annually on cosmetics are largely a waste of money (not to mention all the wasted time spent applying and removing them). Women look fine without makeup — in many cases, they look better — and having regular facials, pedicures, and manicures can add up quickly. And, as detailed in the book *There's Lead in Your Lipstick* by Gillian Deacon (Penguin Canada), of the 127 or so different chemicals we expose our bodies to when we apply makeup, as well as take a bubble bath, use shaving cream, or apply deodorant, many of them are toxic.

» **Health-club expenses:** Money spent on exercise is almost always money well spent. But you don't have to belong to a trendy club to receive the benefits of exercise. Local schools, colleges, and universities often have tennis courts, running tracks, swimming pools, basketball courts, and exercise rooms, and they may provide instruction as well. Community centres offer fitness programs and classes, too. Metropolitan areas that have lots of health clubs undoubtedly have the widest range of options and prices. *Note:* When figuring the cost of membership, be sure to factor in the cost of travel to and from the club, as well as any parking costs (and the realistic likelihood of going there regularly to work out).

Don't forget that healthy exercise can be done indoors or out, free of charge. Isn't hiking in the park more fun than pedaling away on a stationary bike, anyway? You may want to buy some basic gym equipment for use at home. Be careful, though: Lots of exercise equipment gathers dust in people's basements.

Paring down professional expenses

Accountants, lawyers, and financial advisors can be worth their expense if they're good. But be wary of professionals who create or perpetuate work and have conflicts of interest with their recommendations.

Make sure that you get organized before meeting with professionals for tax, legal, or financial advice. Do some background research to evaluate their strengths and biases. Set goals and estimate fees in advance so you know what you're getting yourself into.

Computer-based and printed resources (see Chapters 20 and 21) can be useful, low-cost alternatives and supplements to hiring professionals.

Managing medical expenses

The cost of healthcare continues going up fast. Your health insurance — if you have health insurance, that is — probably covers most of your healthcare needs. (Chapter 17 explains how to shop for health insurance.) But many plans require you to pay for certain expenses out of your own pocket.

WARNING

Medical care and supplies are like any other services and products — prices and quality vary. And medicine in the United States, like any other profession, is a business. A conflict of interest exists whenever the person recommending treatment benefits financially from providing that treatment. Many studies have documented some of the unnecessary surgeries and medical procedures that have resulted from this conflict of interest.

Remember to shop around when seeking health insurance. Don't take any one physician's advice as gospel. Always get a second opinion for any major surgery. Most health-insurance plans, out of economic self-interest, require a second opinion, anyway.

Therapy can be useful and even lifesaving. Have a frank talk with your therapist about how much total time and money you can expect to spend and what kind of results you can expect to receive. As with any professional service, a competent therapist gives you a straight answer if he's looking out for your psychological *and* financial well-being.

TIP

Alternative medicine (holistic, for example) is gaining attention because of its focus on preventive care and the treatment of the whole body or person. Although alternative medicine can be dangerous if you're in critical condition, alternative treatment for some forms of chronic pain or disease may be worth investigating. Alternative medicine may lead to better *and* lower-cost healthcare.

TIP

If you have to take certain drugs on an ongoing basis and pay for them out of pocket, ordering through a mail-order company can bring down your costs and help make refilling your prescriptions more convenient. Ask your health-plan provider for more information about this option. Also, inquire about generic versions of drugs.

Examine your employer's benefit plans. Take advantage of being able to put away a portion of your income before taxes to pay for out-of-pocket healthcare expenses.

Make sure that you pay close attention to the "use it or lose it" provisions of some plans. (Uncover more about health savings accounts in Chapter 17.)

Eliminating costly addictions

TIP

Human beings are creatures of habit. Everybody has habits he wishes he didn't have, and breaking those habits can be very difficult. Costly habits are the worst. The following tidbits may nudge you in the right direction toward breaking your own financially draining habits:

» **Kick the smoking habit.** Check with local hospitals for smoking-cessation programs. If you want to quit, the Canadian Cancer Society (888-939-3333; www.cancer.ca) offers a self-help program, along with a hotline. The Society can also refer you to local programs. The Canadian Lung Association (888-566-5864; www.lung.ca) offers tips on how to quit and can refer you to provincial associations, many of which offer programs to help you stop smoking.

The American Lung Association (800-586-4872; www.lung.org) also offers Freedom from Smoking clinics around the United States. The National Cancer Institute (800-422-6237; www.cancer.gov) and the Office on Smoking and Health at the U.S. Centers for Disease Control and Prevention (800-784-8669; www.cdc.gov/tobacco/about/osh) also offer free information online and in guides that contain effective methods for stopping smoking.

» **Stop abusing alcohol and other drugs.** Thousands of Canadians seek treatment annually for alcoholism or drug abuse. These addictive behaviours, like spending, transcend all educational and socioeconomic lines in our society. Even so, studies have demonstrated that only one in seven alcohol or drug abusers seeks help. Three of the ten leading causes of death — cirrhosis of the liver, accidents, and suicides — are associated with excessive alcohol consumption.

The Canadian Centre on Substance Use and Addiction (833-235-4048; www.ccdus.ca) can refer you to local treatment programs such as Alcoholics Anonymous. It also has an excellent publication, "Finding Quality Addiction Care in Canada: Drug and Alcohol Treatment Guide," that outlines the different treatment options that are available, along with key questions you should ask when considering a treatment program or speaking with an addiction or healthcare provider. The publication includes a useful listing of crisis and helplines for the provinces and territories. You can find it online at www.ccsa.ca/Resource%20Library/CCSA-Addiction-Care-in-Canada-Treatment-Guide-2017-en.pdf.

For drug addiction, start by contacting your provincial ministry of health. You can also dig up lists of sources for help online. One good example is ConnexOntario, a very helpful and welcome service that provides free information and referrals as well as a 24/7 phone line answered by real humans (866-531-2600; www.connexontario.ca) Another starting point is the Centre for Addiction and Mental Health (800-463-2338; www.camh.ca). Drug Rehab Services is also a good, free addiction resource (877-254-3348; www.drugrehab.ca). It's operated by what it calls ". . . a fellowship of recovered addicts or families who dedicate their lives to providing direction and support for families in need of advice on recovery options."

>> **Don't gamble.** The house *always* comes out ahead in the long run. Why do you think so many governments run lotteries? Because governments make money on people who gamble, that's why. Casinos, horse and dog racetracks, and other gambling establishments are sure long-term losers for you. So, too, is the short-term trading of stocks, which isn't investing but gambling. Getting hooked on the dream of winning is easy. And sure, occasionally you win a little bit (just enough to keep you coming back). Every now and then, a few folks win a lot. But your hard-earned capital mostly winds up in the pockets of the casino owners.

If you gamble just for entertainment, take only what you can afford to lose. Gamblers Anonymous (626-960-3500; www.gamblersanonymous.org) helps those for whom gambling has become an addiction.

Keeping an eye on insurance premiums

TIP

Insurance is a vast minefield. In Part 4, we explain the different types of coverage, suggest what to buy and avoid, and detail how to save on policies. The following list explains the most common ways people waste money on insurance:

>> **Keeping low deductibles.** The *deductible* is the amount of a loss that must come out of your pocket. For example, if you have an auto-insurance policy with a $100 collision deductible and you get into an accident, you pay for the first $100 of damage, and your insurance company picks up the rest. Low deductibles, however, translate into much higher premiums for you. In the long run, you save money with a higher deductible, even when factoring in the potential for greater out-of-pocket costs to you when you do have a claim. Insurance should protect you from economic disaster. Don't get carried away with a really high deductible, which can cause financial hardship if you have a claim and lack savings.

If you have a lot of claims, you won't come out ahead with lower deductibles, because your insurance premiums will escalate. Plus, low deductibles means more claim forms to file for small losses (creating more hassle). Filing an insurance claim usually isn't an enjoyable or quick experience.

>> **Covering small potential losses.** You shouldn't buy insurance for anything that won't be a financial catastrophe if you have to pay for it out of your own pocket. Although the postal service isn't perfect, insuring inexpensive gifts sent in the mail isn't worth the price. Buying dental or home-warranty plans, which also cover relatively small potential expenditures, doesn't make financial sense for the same reason. And if no one's dependent on your income, you don't need life insurance either. (Who will be around to collect when you're gone?)

>> **Failing to shop around.** Rates vary *tremendously* from insurer to insurer. In Part 4, we recommend the best companies to call for quotes and other cost-saving strategies.

Trimming your taxes

Taxes are probably one of your largest expenditures, if not *the* largest. So, why is it last here? Read on to find out.

Registered Retirement Savings Plans (RRSPs) are one of the best and simplest ways to reduce your tax burden. (We explain more about RRSPs in Chapter 11.) Unfortunately, most people can't take full advantage of these plans because they spend everything they make. So, not only do they have less savings, but they also pay higher income taxes — a double whammy.

We've attended many presentations where a fast-talking investment guy in an expensive suit lectures about the importance of saving for retirement and explains how to invest your savings. Yet details and tips about finding the money to save (the hard part for most people) are left to the imagination.

REMEMBER

In order to take advantage of the tax savings that come through RRSPs, you must first spend less than you earn. Only then can you afford to contribute to these plans. That's why the majority of this chapter is about strategies to reduce your spending.

Reduced sales tax is another benefit of spending less and saving more. When you buy most consumer products, you pay sales tax. Therefore, when you spend less money and save more in retirement accounts, you reduce your income and sales taxes. (See Chapter 7 for detailed tax-reduction strategies.)

IN THIS CHAPTER

» Getting the lowdown on taxes and tax rates

» Lowering your income taxes on employment and investment income

» Tapping into education tax breaks

» Finding helpful tax resources

» Making an audit as painless as possible

Chapter **7**

Trimming Your Taxes

You pay a lot of money in taxes — probably more than you realize. Few people know just how much they pay in taxes each year. Most people remember whether they received a refund or owed money on their return. But when you file your tax return, all you're doing is settling up with the tax authorities over the amount of taxes you paid during the year versus the total tax you owe based on your income and deductions.

Understanding the Taxes You Pay

Some people feel lucky when they get an income-tax refund, but all such a refund really indicates is that you overpaid your income taxes during the year. You should have had this money in your own account all along. If you're consistently getting big income-tax refunds, you should be paying less tax throughout the year.

TIP

Instead of focusing on whether you're going to get a refund when you complete your annual tax return, concentrate on the *total* taxes you pay, which we discuss in this section.

Focusing on your total taxes

To find out the *total* income taxes you pay, you need to get out your income tax return. On the federal T1 General form, there is a line called "Total payable." (On recent returns, this is line 435.) Subtract all credits — including your provincial tax credits — that are deducted from your total tax payable, except for tax that you've already had deducted (line 437) or tax that you have paid in installments (line 476). The number you'll end up with is probably one of your single largest annual expenses.

The goal of this chapter is to help you legally and permanently reduce your total taxes. Understanding the tax system is the key to reducing your tax burden — if you don't, you'll surely pay more taxes than necessary. Your tax ignorance can lead to mistakes, which can be costly if the Canada Revenue Agency (CRA) catches your underpayment errors. With the proliferation of computerized information and data tracking, discovering mistakes has never been easier.

The tax system, like other public policy, is built around incentives to encourage desirable behavior and activity. For example, saving for retirement is considered desirable because it encourages people to prepare for a time in their lives when they may be less able or interested in working so much and when they may have additional healthcare expenses. Therefore, the tax code offers all sorts of tax perks, which we discuss later in this chapter (and in Chapter 11), to encourage people to save in Registered Retirement Savings Plans (RRSPs), registered retirement plans, and other tax-deferred or tax-sheltered plans. This includes Tax-Free Savings Accounts (TFSAs), Registered Education Savings Plans (RESPs), and Registered Disability Savings Plans (RDSPs).

Now, it's a free country, and you should make the choices that work best for your life and situation. However, keep in mind that the *fewer* desirable activities you engage in, the more you'll generally pay in taxes. If you understand the options, you can choose the ones that meet your needs as you approach different stages of your financial life.

Recognizing the importance of your marginal tax rate

When it comes to taxes, *not all income is treated equally.* This fact is far from self-evident. If you work for an employer and earn a constant salary during the course of a year, a steady and equal amount of taxes (federal and provincial combined) is deducted before you get paid, whether it's by direct deposit or you receive an actual physical paycheque. So, it appears as though all that earned income is being taxed equally.

In reality, however, you pay less tax on your *first* dollars of earnings each year, and more tax on your *last* dollars of earnings. For example, if you're single and your taxable income (see the next section) totals $56,000 during 2018, you don't pay any tax on the first $12,000 because of a tax credit that offsets tax on that income each year. Your combined federal and provincial tax rate would be approximately 25 percent on income from $12,000 to $46,000. Your tax rate would be 34 percent on income between $46,000 up to $56,000.

TECHNICAL STUFF

These percentages are approximate. Your tax rate is a combination of federal and provincial taxes. And each province has different marginal rates, tax brackets, and surtaxes. The result is a great variance in how different levels of income are taxed in different provinces and territories.

Table 7-1 gives the approximate combined federal and provincial tax rates. (Your actual marginal bracket may be somewhat higher or lower, depending on the tax rate in your province.)

TABLE 7-1

Approximate Combined Federal and Provincial Income Tax Brackets and Rates for 2018

Taxable Income	Tax Rate (Bracket)
$0–$12,000	0%
$12,000–$46,000	25%
$46,000–$92,000	34%
$92,000–$142,000	42%
$142,000–$203,000	46%
More than $203,000	50%

REMEMBER

Your *marginal tax rate* is the rate of tax you pay on your *last*, or so-called *highest*, dollars of income in the year. A person with taxable income of $56,000 has a federal marginal tax rate of 34 percent. In other words, she effectively pays 34 percent federal tax on her last dollars of income — those dollars in excess of $46,000.

Marginal tax rates are a powerful concept. Your marginal tax rate allows you to quickly calculate the additional taxes you'd have to pay on additional income. Conversely, you can enjoy quantifying the amount of taxes you save by reducing your taxable income, either by decreasing your income or by increasing your deductions.

Defining taxable income

Taxable income is the amount of income on which you actually pay income taxes. (In the sections that follow, we explain strategies for reducing your taxable income.) Here's why you don't pay taxes on your total income:

>> **Not all income is taxable.** For example, any profit you make when you sell the home you live in — your principal residence — generally isn't taxable. Neither is the profit you earn on money invested inside tax-favoured plans such as RRSPs and TFSAs. (As we discuss later in this chapter, if you earn interest on money outside such accounts, it's taxed at the same rate as your regular employment income. Other income, such as that from stock dividends and long-term capital gains, is taxed at lower rates.)

>> **You get to subtract deductions from your income.** Some deductions are available just for being a living, breathing human being. In 2018, every taxpayer got an automatic exemption — known as the *basic personal amount* — on her first $12,000 of income. When you contribute to a qualified retirement plan, such as an RRSP, you also effectively get a deduction.

Being mindful of the second tax system: Alternative minimum tax

You may find this hard to believe, but a second tax system actually exists (as if the first tax system weren't already complicated enough). This second system may raise your taxes even higher than they would normally be.

Over the years, as the government grew hungry for more revenue, taxpayers who slashed their taxes by claiming lots of deductions or exclusions from taxable income came under greater scrutiny. So the government created a second tax system — the alternative minimum tax (AMT) — to ensure that those with high deductions or exclusions pay at least a certain percentage of taxes on their incomes. (The minimum tax does not apply in the year of someone's death.)

WARNING

If you have a lot of deductions or exclusions from income taxes, you may fall prey to AMT. Even if you're not claiming a lot of deductions or using tax-sheltered investments such as limited partnerships, you may also get tripped up by AMT. For instance, someone who receives a substantial capital gain — say, a farmer who sells off a large plot of land — may find that the AMT kicks in.

AMT restricts you from claiming certain deductions and requires you to add back in some so-called *tainted shelter deductions*. These include tax shelters and resource write-offs. You also have to add back 60 percent of the untaxed one-half of any capital gains. You then take a $40,000 exemption, and calculate your federal tax at 15 percent (for 2017). You can use most personal tax credits, except for the dividend tax and the investment tax credits, just as you would when calculating your regular tax.

You're not done yet. You need to carry out a similar calculation for your provincial taxes. The minimum provincial tax rate will range from around 34 percent to 57 percent of the federal minimum tax with adjustments for your province's credits and surtaxes. (If you live in Quebec, the minimum tax essentially follows the federal approach, but there are specific rules and calculations. The minimum tax rate in Quebec was 16 percent for the 2017 tax year.)

When all the number crunching is done, you have to compare your tax payable under the AMT system and under the regular system, and pay the higher amount.

TIP

If you do have to pay the higher amount prescribed by the minimum tax calculation, the money may not be gone forever. In the following seven years, you can recover it by the amount your regular tax owing exceeds what you would pay using the minimum tax calculation.

Trimming Employment Income Taxes

You're supposed to pay taxes on income you earn from work. Countless illegal methods can reduce your taxable employment income — for example, not reporting it — but if you use them, you can very well end up paying a heap of penalties and extra interest charges on top of the taxes you owe. And you may even get tossed in jail. Because we don't want you to serve jail time or lose even more money by paying unnecessary penalties and interest, this section focuses on the best *legal* ways to reduce your income taxes on your earnings from work.

Contributing to registered retirement plans

An RRSP or employer's pension plan is one of the few painless and authorized ways to reduce your taxable employment income. Besides reducing your taxes, registered retirement plans help you build up a nest egg so that you don't have to work for the rest of your life.

You can exclude money from your taxable income by tucking it away in an RRSP or employer-based retirement plan. If your marginal tax rate is 34 percent, and you contribute $1,000 to one of these plans, you reduce your taxes by $340. Do you like the sound of that? How about this: Contribute another $1,000, and your taxes drop another $340 (as long as you're still in the same marginal tax rate). And when it's inside a retirement plan, your money can compound and grow without taxation.

Many people miss this great opportunity to reduce their taxes because they *spend* all (or too much) of their current employment income and, therefore, have nothing (or little) left to put into a retirement plan. If you're in this predicament, you first need to reduce your spending before you can contribute money to a retirement plan. (Chapter 6 explains how to decrease your spending.)

If your employer doesn't offer the option of saving money through a retirement plan, lobby the benefits and human resources departments. If they resist, you may want to add this to your list of reasons for considering another employer. Many employers offer this valuable benefit, but some don't. Some company decision makers either don't understand the value of these plans or feel that they're too costly to set up and administer.

If your employer doesn't offer a retirement or pension plan, an RRSP is your best bet. (You may also be able to contribute to an RRSP after contributing the maximum to your employer's pension plan.) Chapter 11 can help you determine whether you should contribute to an RRSP and how to make the most of registered retirement plans.

Shifting some income

Income shifting, which has nothing to do with money laundering, is a more esoteric tax-reduction technique that's an option only to those who can control *when* they receive their income.

For example, suppose your employer tells you in late December that you're eligible for a bonus. You're offered the option to receive your bonus in either December or January. If you're pretty certain that you'll be in a higher tax bracket next year, you should choose to receive your bonus in December.

Or, suppose you run your own business and you think that you'll be in a lower tax bracket next year. Perhaps you plan to take time off to be with a newborn or take an extended trip. You may be able to push a big contract off until January, so the income is earned and, therefore, taxed in the next year.

Organizing your taxes

Locating all the scraps of paper you need when completing your tax return can be a hassle. Setting up a filing system can be a big time-saver:

>> **Folder or shoebox:** If you have limited patience for setting up neat file folders, and you lead an uncomplicated financial life (that is, you haven't saved receipts throughout the year), you can confine your filing to January and February. During those months, you should receive tax summary statements on wages

paid by your employer (T4), taxable dividend income from Canadian corporations (T5), income from profit-sharing plans (T4PS), and interest income (T5 for bank account and regular interest Canada Savings Bond "R" bonds; T5008 for T-bills). If you're older, you may also get a slip for Old Age Security (OAS) income (T4AOAS) and the Canada Pension Plan (CPP) or Quebec Pension Plan (QPP) (T4A[P]). You may also have received a T3 for income from a mutual fund trust.

Set up a folder that's labeled with something easy to remember (something like "2019 Taxes" would be a brilliant choice), and dump these papers as well as your tax booklet into it. When you're ready to crunch numbers, you should have everything you need to complete the form.

» **Accordion-type file:** Organizing the bills you pay into individual folders during the entire year is a more thorough approach. This method is essential if you own your own business and need to tabulate your expenditures for office supplies each year. No one is going to send you a form totaling your office expenditures for the year — you're on your own.

» **Software:** Software programs can help organize your tax information during the year and save you time and accounting fees come tax-prep time. See Chapter 20 for more information about tax and financial software.

Increasing Your Deductions

Deductions are amounts you subtract from your adjusted gross income before calculating the tax you owe. To determine just what a deduction is worth, multiply it by your marginal tax rate.

In the following sections, we detail some of the more common deductions you may be able to take advantage of. The dollar figures we use are for the 2017 tax year, meaning the return you would complete and file in the spring of 2018 — many of the numbers will likely have been revised for subsequent years.

Childcare expenses

Many of the costs of having others take care of your children can be deducted from your income. Babysitters, day nurseries, day care, day camps, and boarding-school expenses all qualify. However, the expenses must be incurred to enable you either to work or to take an occupational training course.

You can deduct up to $8,000 of expenses for each child who is under age 7 at the end of the year, and up to $5,000 for each child ages 7 to 16. Your total deduction can't be greater than two-thirds of the salary or net business income (technically, *earned income*) of the lower-earning spouse or the single parent. (For Quebec residents, childcare expenses give you a refundable credit, not a deduction, and different limits apply.) The limit for a child eligible for the disability tax credit — up to and including 17 — is $11,000.

Alimony and maintenance payments

Alimony or maintenance payments you make to a former spouse can be deducted as long as they're made following a decree, order, judgment, or written agreement. To be deductible, they must be an allowance that is paid out in regular, predetermined payments. You can't deduct any transfers of property or one-time payments you make as part of a settlement.

Child support

If you receive child-support payments, they aren't taxed as income. And if you pay child support, you can't deduct it from your taxable income. Like alimony payments, the amounts must be predetermined; paid under a written agreement or under a decree, order, or judgment of a competent tribunal; and paid on a periodic basis. You also must be living apart from your spouse or former spouse because of a marriage breakdown at the time the payments are made.

TIP

The rules are notably different for child-support payments that are made according to an agreement that was reached before May 1, 1997. In that case — if they're established in advance as an allowance that involves recurring payments — they are deductible from the taxable income of the payer and are included in the taxable income of the recipient.

Annual union and professional fees

Regular annual dues (often taken off automatically from your paycheque) are deductible, but you can't claim initial fees or special assessments. Fees paid to professional organizations are deductible, but only if they must be paid to maintain a professional standing recognizable by law, such as a registered nurse. This applies even if maintaining that status isn't required by your current job. If you're self-employed, you can generally deduct dues you pay to voluntarily belong to work-related organizations.

MARRIED VERSUS COMMON-LAW PARTNERS

Although your parents may not agree, you're as good as married in the eyes of the tax authorities if you've been living in a common-law relationship for more than a year. You're considered to be common-law spouses if you and your partner "cohabit in a conjugal relationship" and either have had a child together or have been living together continuously for at least 12 months. (Since 2001, same-sex couples who have lived together for at least one year have been treated by the tax authorities in the same way as opposite-sex common-law couples.) You're deemed to have "separated" — or lost your common-law status — only if you're separated for more than 90 days due to the relationship breaking down.

This means you can take advantage of planning opportunities, including setting up a spousal RRSP and pooling some expenses to take the most advantage of various credits. However, if you're living in common law, you can't claim the eligible dependant (formerly the "equivalent-to-married") credit for a child.

Business losses

You can use losses from an unincorporated business or professional practise to reduce your employment or professional income. Say that you have a salaried job in a car plant, and you start up a contracting business. If your business expenses are greater than the income it brings in, you can subtract your losses from your other income.

Interest on investment loans

If you borrow money to buy investments or to earn income from a business, the interest can be deducted. (This rule doesn't apply to money borrowed to make an RRSP contribution.) You'll need to keep a record of any money you borrow and use to invest and the interest you pay during the year.

Moving expenses

Not only is moving a major hassle, but it can be very costly, so eligible moving expenses can be a very valuable deduction. If you start a business or start working at a new location and move to a home that is at least 40 kilometres closer by road to your new business or job location than your old home, the associated costs can be claimed as a deduction. Moving to Canada from another country — or moving from Canada *to* another country — doesn't qualify.

Eligible expenses include the travelling costs to move you and your family (including food and lodging along the way) and your household belongings, as well as any related storage costs. In addition, you can deduct the cost of selling your old home, including the real estate commissions, and the legal bills on purchasing your new home.

Expenses can be deducted only against income that is earned in the new location. If you're unable to deduct all the expenses in the year of the move, the remainder can be deducted in future years. So, don't forget to carry that deduction forward.

Students who move so they can attend university or another postsecondary institution full-time can also deduct moving expenses. The expenses must be deducted against taxable scholarships, bursaries, research grants, or fellowships. Students can also claim moving expenses if the move is in order to take a job — including a summer job — or to start a business.

Making the Most of Tax Credits

Tax credits are different from deductions in one fundamental way: Deductions are subtracted from your income before your tax bill is calculated. After your tax bill has been calculated from your taxable income, credits are applied against your tax bill as though you've already paid that amount in taxes. As a result, your taxes are reduced by the full amount of the credit. A $500 credit is worth the same amount to everybody — it reduces the tax you have to pay by $500.

TIP

Most credits are *nonrefundable,* which means that they can't be used to make your tax liability less than zero. If you have $1,200 in credits left over after wiping out your federal tax payable, that's as good as it gets. The government won't send you a cheque for $1,200.

Understanding how the federal and provincial tax systems work together

All the provinces (except Quebec) calculate their piece of your tax bill by applying their marginal rates directly to your taxable income. This is known as the tax-on-net-income (TONI) method. With the TONI method, both the federal and provincial governments calculate your tax by multiplying your income by their respective tax rate. You then separately deduct your federal and provincial tax credits from the corresponding gross tax payable to arrive at what's called your basic federal and basic provincial tax.

**TECHNICAL
STUFF**

Previously, provincial taxes were calculated as a percentage of your basic federal tax bill; this was known as the *tax-on-tax method*. Credits were generally deducted from your federal tax bill before your provincial taxes and surtaxes were calculated. With the old tax-on-tax system, tax credits were worth from 50 percent to 70 percent more than the straight federal credit. By cutting your federal taxes, you also reduced your provincial taxes and surtaxes. When they moved to the TONI method, the provinces were required to maintain the basic credits that are offered at the federal level. The value of a federal credit will be about 40 percent to 70 percent more when the provincial tax credit is factored in.

Maximizing your tax credits

In the following sections, we outline some common credits that may be available to you and your family, and some tips on how to maximize them. *Note:* Most of the dollar figures are from the 2017 tax year. Check your tax guide for the specific amounts for the year you're filing for.

Basic personal tax credit

Everyone gets a basic federal credit, which for the 2017 tax year was $1,745. (Going through the form, you claim a "basic personal amount" — $11,635 for 2017 — which is then multiplied by 15 percent.)

Spousal credit

You can claim a federal spousal credit of up to $1,745 if your spouse (including a common-law spouse) earned less than $11,635. If your spouse makes more than the cutoff amount, the lower-earning partner may be able to get under the threshold by making an RRSP contribution.

Wholly dependent person credit

You can claim this credit if you're single, separated, divorced, or widowed and you support a relative who lives with you. (This used to be known as the *equivalent-to-married credit.*) The most common example of this is a single parent. You can claim this credit if you're financially responsible for supporting a child, parent, or other relative. The only conditions are that the dependent must be related to you, completely financially dependent on you, living in Canada, and, except in the case of a parent or grandparent, under 18 years old at some point in the tax year. (The age limit doesn't apply if the person is dependent on you because of a mental or physical disability.) You can't claim this credit if you have a common-law or same-sex spouse. The amounts are the same as the spousal credit.

Credits for contributing to charities

As long as you get an official tax receipt, you can earn credits from most contributions made to charities. In addition to cash contributions, you can often gain tax credits when you donate items of significant value, such as a used computer. The amount of the receipt must reflect the item's fair market value. However, you can't get a receipt for your time or the expenses you ring up while doing charitable work.

The first $200 you donate earns you a 15 percent federal tax credit. After your savings on provincial taxes are accounted for, this works out to be worth about 25 percent. For donations beyond the $200 level, though, your donations give you a 29 percent federal tax credit, worth about 46 percent after the savings on provincial taxes are counted. (This makes your donations above $200 worth almost as much as a deduction if you're in the top tax bracket.)

Finally, if your income is over $203,000, your donation gives you a 33 percent federal tax credit. When the provincial credit is factored in, this translates to a 50 percent value. (This rate only applies to any donations above $200 up to the amount your income exceeds $203,000. The 46 percent credit applies to the remainder.) Also, this third level of tax credit applies only for donations made in 2016 and onward; it cannot be used for donations carried forward from 2015 or earlier.

TIP

If you donate only small amounts each year, try to pool several years' contributions to put you over the $200 donation level. You can also combine your spouse's and your own contributions on one return. This prevents both of you from having to get the lower credit on the first $200. Note that you don't have to claim a charitable deduction in the year that it's made. Unclaimed contributions can be carried forward and claimed on your return in any of the five years after the year in which you make the charitable contribution. Also, if you're already over $200 in donations and you plan to make further donations in the new year, instead of waiting, make them in December if possible. This will allow you to receive the tax savings a year earlier.

Medical expenses credit

A surprisingly wide range of medical costs and health-related expenditures are eligible for a nonrefundable credit, but you generally have to submit all your receipts.

After totaling your expenses, you can claim only the amount that exceeds 3 percent of your net income, up to a set amount. For 2017, the 3 percent threshold was capped if your income exceeded $75,600. If you made more than that, you can claim medical expenses in excess of a flat $2,268.

To maximize the benefit of this credit, one spouse can and should claim the entire family's medical expenses. The spouse with the lowest income generally should make the claim, to get over the 3 percent floor as quickly as possible. Plus, in any tax year, you can claim your expenses for any 12 months ending in that particular year. If you have a lot of bills in the fall and spring, for example, it may pay to make your claim run from August 1 to July 31.

You can include a broad range of medical costs in calculating this credit. Add up any payments to doctors, nurses, dentists, and public or licenced private hospitals for medical or dental care. In addition, you can include payments for any prescription drugs and medications, eyeglasses, and therapy for speech or hearing problems. You can also include any premiums for private health-insurance plans. (That includes the cost of travel insurance for your vacations out of the country; see Chapter 17 for more information.) You can't claim any expenses that you're reimbursed for from, say, a company dental plan, but any deductibles you pay do qualify.

Low-income earners who have high medical bills may also be able to take advantage of the *medical expense supplement.* For 2017, the supplement credit was worth up to $1,203.

WARNING

If you live in Quebec, the 3 percent mark your medical expenses have to exceed in order to be claimable is based not on your individual income, but on your family income. Quebec defines your family income as the combined net income of both you and your spouse. And, unlike the federal 3 percent, there is no limit on the 3 percent threshold in Quebec.

Pension income credit

You can claim a federal credit of 15 percent for a small amount of certain types of pension income, called *qualifying pension income.* This generally means payments that are received from a private pension. If you're 65 or older, or you're receiving benefits due to your spouse's death, payments from a Registered Retirement Income Fund (RRIF), the income portion of a regular annuity, and payments from annuities from an RRSP or deferred profit-sharing plan also qualify. CPP, OAS, or Guaranteed Income Supplement (GIS) payments do not qualify. For the 2017 tax year, the federal tax credit was 15 percent on the first $2,000 of qualifying pension income. If you're unable to use the credit, it may be transferred to your spouse. To make use of this credit, try to have at least $2,000 of qualifying pension income each year if possible, as well as an additional $2,000 for your spouse.

Age 65 or older

If you're 65 or older by the end of the year, you can claim a federal tax credit — the *age credit.* In 2017, the maximum was $7,225, making it worth up to around $1,085. However, this credit is reduced by 15 percent of your net income over a certain amount (in 2017, this amount was $36,430) and is completely eliminated if your income exceeds a set level, which in 2017 was $84,597.

Disability credit

You're eligible for a nonrefundable federal credit if you have a severe and prolonged mental or physical impairment. In 2017, the credit was $8,113, worth $1,217. Depending on the type of disability, it must be certified by the relevant professional (medical doctor, optometrist, audiologist, occupational therapist, or psychologist).

If a dependent relative doesn't earn enough income to use all his disability credit, a supporting relative can use any unused amount. The eligible dependant can be a spouse, child, grandchild, parent, grandparent, sibling, aunt, uncle, niece, or nephew. In addition, lower-income families caring for a child eligible for the disability tax credit may also qualify for Child Disability Benefit payments.

Families that care for children with severe disabilities can also receive a supplementary credit of up to $4,732, worth $710 (in 2017). This is usually reduced by childcare expenses, the medical-expense tax credit, and the disability support deduction.

If a parent supports a disabled child who is over 18 years old, the parent is allowed an additional federal credit. This credit was $630 for the 2017 tax year. However, the credit is reduced if the infirm dependant earns more than $5,956, and is zero if the dependant's income exceeds $10,154.

Canada caregiver credit

The Canada caregiver credit came into being in 2017. It replaced three longstanding credits: the infirm dependant credit, the caregiver credit (for in-home care of a relative), and the family caregiver credit.

You can claim the caregiver credit if, at any time during the year, your spouse or common-law partner, a minor child, other eligible relative, or a dependent of your partner is dependent on you because of a physical or mental infirmity.

Unlike the old credit rules, it's not required that your dependant lives with you, but the person has to be dependent upon you for "support," which includes basic necessities including food, shelter, and clothing.

TIP Obtain a Disability Tax Certificate from a doctor or nurse practitioner.

Previously, you were generally eligible for the credit for supporting a parent who lived with you and was at least 65, but who did not have a medical condition. However, there is no longer a credit for non-infirm parents over 65 who live with you.

The caregiver credit is nonrefundable, meaning it can reduce your taxes all the way to zero, but it won't get you a refund. (You might end up with a refund, but that's only because you've paid too much tax during the year.)

The maximum credit amount for 2017 was $6,883. However, the credit is reduced dollar for dollar for the parent's income above a set point, which for 2017 was $16,163, meaning it's reduced to zero if the parent's net income is $23,046 or higher.

However, there is a second lower maximum credit (previously, the family caregiver amount) of $2,150 that may apply. This lower level applies if, for the disabled dependent, you've also claimed the credit for

>> A spouse or common-law partner

>> An eligible dependent

>> A disabled child under age 18

TIP

If claiming this second, lower maximum leaves you paying more taxes than you would have if the first, higher amount had been claimed, you get a top-up amount that offsets any difference.

British Columbia, Ontario, and Yukon have corresponding credits. The other provinces, however, have stuck with the older caregiver amount, which provides a credit if your parent lives with you and is 65 or older, or if you're caring for an infirm adult relative.

Trading consumer debt for mortgage debt

If you've run up high-interest consumer debt, and you own a home or other real estate and you haven't borrowed the maximum, you may be able to take on some low-cost debt to pay off some high-cost debt. You can save on interest charges by refinancing your mortgage or taking out a home-equity loan at a lower rate, and putting the cash toward paying off your credit card, auto loan, or other costly credit lines.

WARNING

This strategy involves some danger. Borrowing against the equity in your home can be an addictive habit. We've seen cases where people run up significant consumer debt three or four times and then refinance their home the same number of times over the years to bail themselves out.

An appreciating home creates the illusion that excess spending isn't really costing you. But debt is debt, and all borrowed money ultimately has to be repaid (unless you file bankruptcy). In the long run, you wind up with greater mortgage debt, and paying it off takes a bigger bite out of your monthly income. Refinancing and establishing home-equity lines of credit costs you more in terms of loan application fees and other charges (points, appraisals, credit reports, and so on).

At a minimum, the continued expansion of your mortgage debt handicaps your ability to work toward other financial goals. In the worst case, easy access to borrowing encourages bad spending habits that can lead to bankruptcy or foreclosure on your debt-ridden home.

Deducting self-employment expenses

TIP

When you're self-employed, you can deduct a multitude of expenses from your income before calculating the tax you owe. If you buy a computer or office furniture, you can deduct those expenses. (Sometimes they need to be gradually deducted, or *depreciated*, over time.) Salaries for your employees, payments to casual or contract help, office supplies, rent or mortgage interest for your office space, and phone/communications expenses are also generally deductible.

Many self-employed folks don't take all the deductions they're eligible for. In some cases, people simply aren't aware of the wonderful world of deductions. Others are worried that large deductions will increase the risk of an audit. Spend some time finding out more about tax deductions; you'll be convinced that taking full advantage of your eligible deductions makes sense and saves you money.

The following are common mistakes made by people who are their own bosses:

>> **Being an island unto yourself:** When you're self-employed, going it alone is usually a mistake when it comes to taxes. You must educate yourself to make the tax laws work for rather than against you. Hiring tax help is well worth your while. (See "Hiring professional help" later in this chapter for information on hiring tax advisors.)

>> **Making administrative tax screwups:** As a self-employed individual, you're responsible for the correct and timely filing of all taxes owed on your income and employment taxes on your employees. You need to make estimated tax payments on a quarterly basis. And if you have employees, you also need to withhold taxes from each paycheque they receive and make timely payments to the CRA. In addition to federal and provincial income taxes, you also need to withhold and send in CPP or QPP contributions and Employment Insurance premiums.

>> **Failing to document expenses:** When you pay with cash, following the paper trail for all the money you spent can be hard for you to do (and for the CRA to do, in the event you're ever audited). At the end of the year, how are you going to remember how much you spent for parking or client meals if you fail to keep a record? How will you survive a CRA audit without proper documentation?

Debit cards are accepted most places and provide a convenient paper trail. (Be careful about getting a debit card in your business's name, because some banks don't offer protection against fraudulent use of business debit cards.) Otherwise, you need a record of your daily petty cash purchases. Most pocket calendars or daily organizers include ledgers that allow you to track these small purchases. (Some apps can help with this as well.) If you aren't that organized, at least get receipts for cash transactions and write on each receipt what the purchase was for. Then stash the receipts in a file folder in your desk or keep the receipts in envelopes labeled with the month and year. You can also keep a record of your receipts by taking a picture with your smartphone; just be sure to back up your photos regularly.

>> **Failing to fund a retirement plan:** You should be saving money toward retirement anyway, and you can't beat the tax break. People who are self-employed are allowed to contribute up to 18 percent of their net income to an RRSP. (This amount is capped each year at a set dollar amount, which for 2018 was $26,230.) If they also belong to a registered pension plan, the maximum amount they're allowed to contribute is decreased by a pension adjustment. To find out more about RRSPs, see Chapter 11.

>> **Failing to use numbers to help manage business:** If you're a small-business owner who doesn't track her income, expenses, staff performance, and customer data on a regular basis, your tax return may be the one and only time during the year when you take a financial snapshot of your business. After you go through all the time, trouble, and expense to file your tax return, make sure you reap the rewards of all your work; use those numbers to help analyze and manage your business.

Some bookkeepers and tax preparers can provide you with management information reports on your business from the tax data they compile for you. Just ask! See "Using software and websites" later in this chapter for our recommendations.

>> **Failing to pay family help:** If your children, spouse, or other relatives help with some aspect of your business, consider paying them for the work. Besides showing them that you value their work, this practise may reduce your family's tax liability. For example, children are usually in a lower tax bracket. By shifting some of your income to family members, you not only cut your tax bill, but also can make them eligible for attractive savings options like an RRSP.

Reducing Investment Income Taxes

The distributions and profits on investments that you hold outside of RRSPs and other tax-sheltered retirement plans are exposed to taxation when you receive them. Interest, dividends, and *capital gains* (profits from the sale of an investment at a price that's higher than the purchase price) are all taxed.

Although this section explains some of the best methods for reducing the taxes on investments exposed to taxation, Chapter 13 discusses how and where to invest money held outside of tax-sheltered retirement plans.

Selecting other tax-friendly investments

Too often, when selecting investments, people mistakenly focus on past rates of return. Everyone knows that the past is no guarantee of the future. But choosing an investment with a reportedly high rate of return without considering tax consequences is an even worse mistake. What you get to keep — after taxes — is what matters in the long run.

For example, when comparing two similar funds, most people prefer a fund that averages returns of 14 percent per year to one that earns 12 percent per year. But what if the 14-percent-per-year fund, because of greater taxable distributions, causes you to pay a lot more in taxes? What if, after factoring in taxes, the 14-percent-per-year fund nets just 9 percent, while the 12-percent-per-year fund nets an effective return of 10 percent? In such a case, you'd be unwise to choose a fund solely on the basis of the higher (pretax) reported rate of return.

We call investments that appreciate in value and don't distribute much in the way of highly taxed income *tax-friendly.* (Some in the investment business use the term *tax-efficient.*) See Chapter 10 for more information on tax-friendly stocks and stock mutual funds.

Stocks that pay dividends are one of the most tax-friendly investments. Typically, the after-tax yield of these investments is better than that on interest-paying guaranteed investment certificates (GICs) or bonds. The yield is not guaranteed, but major companies try to maintain their dividends, especially for preferred shares. If you're in the 34 percent tax bracket, you'll pay exactly the same rate on any interest income. However, the effective tax rate on qualifying dividends is just 14 percent.

Making your profits long term

As we discuss in Part 3, when you buy growth investments such as stocks and real estate, you should do so for the long term — ideally, ten or more years. The tax system rewards your patience with lower tax rates on your profits.

TIP

When you sell an investment (outside of a registered retirement plan) such as a stock, bond, mutual fund, or rental property for more than you paid, that profit is called a *capital gain*, and you get a significant tax break. Specifically, only 50 percent of any capital gain is taxable and gets included in your income. So your marginal tax rate on capital gains is half what you pay on your regular income. The approximate effective tax rates on capital gains are shown in Table 7-2.

TABLE 7-2

Approximate Effective Tax Rates on Capital Gains for 2018

Taxable Income	Tax Rate (Bracket)
$0–$12,000	0%
$12,000–$46,000	12.5%
$46,000–$92,000	17%
$92,000–$142,000	21%
$142,000–$203,000	23%
More than $203,000	25%

Enlisting Education Tax Breaks

The government offers several tax reduction opportunities for those with educational expenses. Knowing that you don't want to read the dreadful tax code, here's a summary of key provisions you should know about for yourself and your kids if you have them. There are several credits — two now retired, but still claimable — are available to students and their families:

>> **Tuition tax credit:** Students receive a credit worth 15 percent of tuition fees (as long as they total more than $100 per institution) paid to a Canadian university, college, or other postsecondary institution during the year. Fees paid to an institution certified by Employment and Immigration Canada are also eligible. Tuition paid to universities outside Canada may be eligible as well, but fees paid to private elementary schools or high schools don't earn you a tax credit.

A lot more than just the standard admission charges or tuition can be included here. You can also claim library and lab costs, exam fees, and mandatory computer service fees. Plus, you can include mandatory associated fees such as those for health services and athletics.

In Quebec, the credit is 8 percent, and a $100 threshold applies to total expenses. In New Brunswick, the tuition and education tax credit was eliminated beginning in 2017. In Ontario, the tuition tax credit has also been eliminated and can't be claimed for courses starting after September 4, 2017.

>> **Credit for interest paid on student loans:** A taxpayer may claim a 15 percent federal nonrefundable tax credit on interest paid in the year — or any of the five preceding years — on a student loan granted under a federal or provincial program. The credit is not transferable, but it can be carried forward for up to five years. In New Brunswick and Ontario, this credit also applies to interest paid on Canadian loans to apprentices.

>> **Federal education tax credit:** Prior to 2017, students also got a federal education tax credit worth about $60 for each month they were attending a postsecondary educational institution full-time. Students with qualifying disabilities could also generally claim this amount even if they were studying only part time.

Those studying part time could claim an education tax credit of $18 for every month they attended an eligible program for at least three consecutive weeks and which involved at least 12 hours of course work per month. The education tax credit could also be claimed for postsecondary education that's related to a job, as long as none of the costs are paid for by the employer.

TIP

Although ended, this credit still warrants looking into. Any unused education credits from the years before 2017 can be carried forward and claimed on your current return or used in the future.

>> **Textbook tax credit:** Similar to the education tax credit, prior to 2017 students also benefited from a nonrefundable tax credit to help cover the cost of textbooks. The credit was $65 for each month the student qualified for the full-time education tax credit amount, worth about $10 per month. For those who qualified for the part-time education tax credit amount, the textbook credit was $20 per month, only worth about $3. As with the education amount, this credit was eliminated beginning January 1, 2017. However, any unused textbook credits from prior to 2017 can be carried forward and used in the current year or in the future.

TIP

If the student in your family doesn't need to use all — or any — of the tuition-fee tax credit or the education credit to bring her federal tax bill to zero, the credits don't go to waste. Up to $5,000 (worth about $750) of the unused portion of either — or both — credits generally can be transferred to a parent, grandparent, or spouse. Unused tuition and education amounts can also be carried forward and claimed against your income in future years. However, be forewarned that any amounts carried forward can only be claimed in a later year by the student and aren't transferable.

>> **Additional childcare expense credits:** Students who are single parents or part of a two-parent family where both parents attend school full-time can usually deduct childcare expenses above the normal limits on childcare-expense deductions. The limit is usually two-thirds of your actual net income, as opposed to your earned income. For each week the parent(s) are attending school full-time, the limits are

- $200 per child under 7

- $125 per child 7 to 16

- $275 per child eligible for the disability tax credit

- $125 per week per child over 16, infirm, but ineligible for the disability tax credit

Be sure to read Chapter 14 for the best ways and strategies to pay for educational expenses.

Getting Help from Tax Resources

There are all sorts of ways to prepare your tax return. Which approach makes sense for you depends on the complexity of your situation and your knowledge of taxes.

Regardless of which approach you use, you should be taking financial steps during the year to reduce your taxes. By the time you actually file your return in the following year, it's often too late for you to take advantage of many tax-reduction strategies.

Obtaining CRA assistance

If you have a simple, straightforward tax return, filing it on your own using only the CRA instructions is fine. This approach is as cheap as you can get. The main costs are time, patience, photocopying expenses (always keep a copy for your files), and, if you're not filing electronically, postage for mailing the completed tax return.

WARNING

The CRA has been known to give incorrect information from time to time. When you call the CRA with a question, be sure to take notes about your conversation to protect yourself in the event of an audit. Date your notes and include the name and identification number of the tax employee you talked to, the questions you asked, and the employee's responses. File your notes in a folder with a copy of your completed return. To reach the CRA with your questions, call 800-959-8281.

TIP

In addition to the standard instructions that come with your tax return, the CRA offers a number of free and helpful tax guides that you can pick up at your nearest taxation centre (or call to request them). These guides serve as useful references and provide more detail and insight than the basic CRA publications. For the self-employed, many booklets are available depending on your occupation, including *Business and Professional Income, Farming Income, Fishing Income,* and *Rental Income.* Other guides deal with specific circumstances. To inquire about and request these documents, call 800-959-2221 (905-712-5813 in the Toronto area) or go to www.cra-arc.gc.ca.

Consulting preparation and advice guides

Books about tax preparation and tax planning that highlight common problem areas and are written in clear, simple English are invaluable. They supplement the official instructions not only by helping you complete your return correctly but also by showing you how to save as much money as possible.

Check out *Tax Planning For You and Your Family* prepared by KPMG and published by Thomson Carswell for easy-to-understand, digestible explanations and advice. Another accounting firm, Raymond Chabot Grant Thornton, also has a helpful *Tax Planning Guide,* which you can download at http://en.planiguide.ca.

Using software and websites

TIP

If you have access to a computer, good tax-preparation software can be helpful. StudioTax, available at www.studiotax.com for free, regardless of your income level, is a great, easy-to-use program. TurboTax and H&R Block Tax Software are also programs that we've reviewed and rated as very good. If you go the software route, we highly recommend having a good tax-advice book by your side.

For you web surfers, the CRA's website (www.cra-arc.gc.ca) is among the better tax websites, believe it or not.

Hiring professional help

Competent tax preparers and advisors can save you money — sometimes more than enough to pay their fees — by identifying tax-reduction strategies you may overlook. They can also help reduce the likelihood of an audit, which can be triggered by blunders. Mediocre and lousy tax preparers, on the other hand, may make mistakes and be unaware of sound ways to reduce your tax bill.

Tax practitioners come with varying backgrounds, training, and credentials. The three main types of tax practitioners are preparers, Chartered Professional

Accountants (CPAs), and tax lawyers. The more training and specialization a tax practitioner has (and the more affluent her clients), the higher her hourly fee usually is. Fees and competence vary greatly. If you hire a tax advisor and you're not sure of the quality of the work performed or the soundness of the advice, try getting a second opinion.

Preparers

Preparers generally have the least amount of training of all the tax practitioners, and a greater proportion of them work part-time. As with financial planners, no national regulations apply to preparers, and no licensing is required.

Preparers are appealing because they're relatively inexpensive — they can do most basic returns for around $100 or so. The drawback of using a preparer is that you may hire someone who doesn't know much more than you do.

TIP

Preparers make the most sense for folks who have relatively simple financial lives, who are budget-minded, and who hate doing their own taxes. If you're not good about hanging on to receipts or you don't want to keep your own files with background details about your taxes, you should definitely shop around for a tax preparer who's committed to the business. You may need all that stuff someday for an audit, and many tax preparers keep and organize their clients' documentation rather than return everything each year. Also, going with a firm that's open year-round may be a safer option (some small shops are open only during tax season) in case tax questions or problems arise.

Chartered Professional Accountants

If you have a more complex return, a CPA is often a better choice. Many CPAs have large personal income-tax practises and may also have expertise in preparing returns for small businesses. A professional who is familiar with the peculiarities of your industry may be able to give you more complete advice on opportunities for saving and how to organize your business to minimize your tax bill. What's more, she'll likely be able to do your return more quickly, meaning a lower bill.

CPAs don't close down when the tax season ends. That means you can go to them for advice and help on your schedule, and you'll be able to get help if you have problems after filing your return.

Fees for CPA vary tremendously. Many charge around $125 to $200 per hour, but CPAs at large companies and in areas with a high cost of living tend to charge somewhat more (sometimes significantly more). Fees for a straightforward return should be about $100 to $200, while more complex situations (for example, a part-time business or investment income) may mean a bill of anywhere from several hundred to several thousand dollars.

TIP

If you're self-employed and/or you file lots of other schedules, you may want to hire a CPA. But you don't need to do so every year. If your situation grows complex one year and then stabilizes, consider getting help for the perplexing year and then using preparation guides, software, or a lower-cost preparer in the future.

Tax lawyers

Tax lawyers deal with complicated tax problems and issues that usually have some legal angle. Unless you're a super-high-income earner with a complex financial life, hiring a tax lawyer to prepare your annual return is prohibitively expensive. In fact, many tax lawyers don't prepare returns, but they may offer tax preparation as an ancillary service through others in their office.

Because of their level of specialization and training, tax lawyers tend to have the highest hourly billing rates — $200 to $300 or more per hour is not unusual.

Dealing with an Audit

On a list of real-life nightmares, most people would rank tax audits right up there with root canals and court appearances. Many people are traumatized by audits because they feel like they're on trial and being accused of a crime. Take a deep breath and don't panic.

You may be getting audited simply because someone at the CRA or a business that reports tax information on you made an error regarding the data on your return. In the vast majority of cases, the CRA conducts its audit by corresponding with you through the mail.

Audits that require you to schlep to the local CRA office are the most feared type of audit. In these cases, a minority of such audited returns are left unchanged by the audit — in other words, the taxpayer doesn't end up owing more money. In fact, if you're the lucky sort, you may be one of the few people who actually gets a refund because the audit finds a mistake in your favor!

Unfortunately, you'll most likely be in the majority of audit survivors who end up owing more tax money. The amount of additional tax that you owe in interest and penalties hinges on how your audit goes.

Getting your act together

Preparing for an audit is sort of like preparing for a test at school. The CRA lets you know which sections of your tax return it wants to examine.

The first decision you face when you get an audit notice is whether to handle it yourself or hire a tax advisor to represent you. Hiring representation may help you save time, stress, and money.

TIP

If you normally prepare your own return and you're comfortable with your understanding of the areas being audited, handle the audit yourself. When the amount of tax money in question is small compared to the fee you'd pay the tax advisor to represent you, self-representation is probably your best option. However, if you're likely to turn into a babbling, intimidated fool and you're unsure of how to present your situation, hire a tax advisor to represent you. (See "Hiring professional help," earlier in this chapter, for information about whom to hire.)

If you decide to handle the audit yourself, get your act together sooner rather than later. Don't wait until the night before to start gathering receipts and other documentation. You may need to contact others to get copies of documents you can't find.

You need to document and be ready to speak about only the areas the audit notice says are being investigated. Organize the various documents and receipts into folders. You want to make it as easy as possible for the auditor to review your materials. Don't show up, dump shopping bags full of receipts and paperwork on the auditor's desk, and say, "Here it is — *you* figure it out."

WARNING

Whatever you do, don't ignore your audit request letter. The CRA is the ultimate bill-collection agency. And if you end up owing more money (the unhappy result of most audits), the sooner you pay, the less interest and penalties you'll owe.

Surviving the day of reckoning

Two people with identical situations can walk into an audit and come out with very different results. The loser can end up owing much more in taxes and have the audit expanded to include other parts of the return. The winner can end up owing no additional tax or even owing less.

TIP

Here's how to be a winner in your tax audit:

>> **Treat the auditor as a human being.** This advice may be obvious, but it isn't practised by taxpayers very often. You may be resentful or angry about being audited. You may be tempted to gnash your teeth and tell the auditor how unfair it is that an honest taxpayer like yourself had to spend hours getting ready for this ordeal. You may feel like ranting and raving about how the government wastes too much of your tax money, or how the party in power is out to get you. Bite your tongue.

Believe it or not, most auditors are decent people just trying to do their jobs. They're well aware that taxpayers don't like seeing them. Don't suck up, either — just relax and be yourself. Behave as you would around a boss you like — with respect and congeniality.

>> **Stick to the knitting.** Your audit is for discussing *only* the sections of your tax return that are in question. The more you talk about other areas or things that you're doing, the more likely the auditor is to probe into other items. Don't bring documentation for parts of your return that aren't being audited. Besides creating more work for yourself, you may be opening up a can of worms that doesn't need to be opened. If the auditor asks about areas that aren't covered by the audit notice, politely say that you're not prepared to discuss those other issues and that another meeting should be scheduled.

>> **Don't argue when you disagree.** State your case. When the auditor wants to disallow a deduction or otherwise increase the taxes you owe and you disagree, state once why you don't agree with his assessment. If the auditor won't budge, don't get into a knock-down, drag-out confrontation. He may not want to lose face and is inclined to find additional tax money — that's the auditor's job.

REMEMBER

When necessary, you can plead your case with several people who work above your auditor. If this method fails and you still feel wronged, you can take your case to tax court.

>> **Don't be intimidated.** Most auditors are not tax geniuses. The work is stressful — being in a job where people dislike seeing you isn't easy. Turnover is quite high. So, many auditors are fairly young, just-out-of-school types who majored in something like English, history, or sociology. They may know less about tax and financial matters than you do. The basic CRA tax boot camp that auditors go through doesn't come close to covering all the technical details and nuances in the tax code. So, you may not be at such a disadvantage in your tax knowledge after all, especially if you work with a tax advisor (most tax advisors know more about the tax system than the average CRA auditor).

3

Building Wealth through Investing

Master critical investment concepts such as major types of investments, expected returns, risks, and diversification.

Understand the specific types of investments to choose among.

Discover how to use mutual funds and exchange-traded funds.

Find out how to invest inside and outside of Registered Retirement Savings Plans and other registered plans and for future educational expenses.

Master the fundamentals of investing in real estate through your own home and beyond.

Chapter **8**

Considering Important Investment Concepts

M aking wise investments doesn't have to be complicated. However, many investors get bogged down in the morass of the thousands of investment choices out there and the often-conflicting perspectives on how to invest. This chapter helps you grasp the important bigger-picture issues that can help you ensure that your investment plan meshes with your needs and the realities of the investment marketplace.

Establishing Your Goals

TIP

Before you select a specific investment, first determine your investment needs and goals. Why are you saving money? What are you going to use it for? You don't need to earmark every dollar, but you should set some major objectives. Establishing objectives is important because the expected use of the money helps you determine how long to invest it. And that, in turn, helps you determine which investments to choose.

The risk level of your investments should factor in your time frame and your comfort level. Investing in high-risk vehicles doesn't make sense if you'll need to spend the funds within the next few years or if you'll have to spend all your profits on stress-induced medical bills. For example, suppose you've been accumulating money for a down payment on a home you want to buy in a few years. You can't afford much risk with that money because you're going to need it sooner rather than later. Putting that money in the stock market, then, is foolish. As we discuss later in this chapter, the stock market can drop a lot in a year or over several years, so stocks are probably too risky a place to invest money you plan to use soon.

Perhaps you're saving toward a longer-term goal, such as retirement, that's 20 or 30 years away. In this case, you're in a position to make riskier investments, because your holdings have more time to bounce back from temporary losses or setbacks. You may want to consider investing in growth investments, such as stocks, within a retirement plan that you leave alone for 20 years or longer. (If stocks aren't to your liking, we discuss other growth investments throughout Part 3.) You can tolerate year-to-year volatility in the market — you have time on your side. If you haven't yet done so, take a tour through Chapter 4, which helps you contemplate and set your financial goals.

Understanding the Primary Investments

For a moment, forget all the buzzwords, jargon, and product names you've heard tossed around in the investment world — in many cases, they obscure, sometimes intentionally, what an investment really is and hide the hefty fees and commissions.

Imagine a world with only two investment flavours — think of chocolate and vanilla ice cream (or low-fat frozen yogurt for you health-minded folks). The investment world is really just as simple. You have only two major investment choices: You can be a lender or an owner.

Looking at lending investments

You're a lender when you invest your money in a guaranteed investment certificate (GIC), a Treasury bill, a term deposit, or a bond issued by a company like Bombardier. In each case, you lend your money to an organization — a bank, the federal government, or Bombardier. You're paid an agreed-upon rate of interest for lending your money. The organization also promises to have your original investment (the *principal*) returned to you on a specific date.

Getting paid all the interest in addition to your original investment (as promised) is the best that can happen with a lending investment. Given that the investment landscape is littered with carcasses of failed investments, this is not a result to take for granted.

The worst that can happen with a lending investment is that you don't get everything you were promised. Promises can be broken under extenuating circumstances. When a company goes bankrupt, for example, you can lose all or part of your original investment.

WARNING

Another risk associated with lending investments is that even if you get what you were promised, the ravages of inflation may reduce the purchasing power of your money. Also, the value of a bond may drop below what you paid for it if interest rates rise or the quality or risk of the issuing company declines.

Table 8-1 shows the reduction in the purchasing power of your money at varying rates of inflation after just ten years.

TABLE 8-1

Reduction in Purchasing Power Due to Inflation

Inflation Rate	Reduction in Purchasing Power after Ten Years
2%	–18%
4%	–32%
6%	–44%
8%	–54%
10%	–61%

Some investors make the common mistake of thinking that they're diversifying their long-term investment money by buying several bonds, some GICs, and an annuity. The problem, however, is that all these investments pay a relatively low fixed rate of return that's exposed to the vagaries of inflation.

REMEMBER

A final drawback to lending investments is that you don't share in the success of the organization to which you lend your money. If the company doubles or triples in size and profits, your principal and interest rate don't double or triple in size along with it; they stay the same. Of course, such success does ensure that you'll get your promised interest and principal.

Exploring ownership investments

You're an *owner* when you invest your money in an asset, such as a company or real estate, that can generate earnings or profits. Suppose that you own 100 shares of Canadian National Railway (CNR) stock. With hundreds of millions of shares of stock outstanding, CNR is a mighty big company — your 100 shares represent a tiny piece of it. What do you get for your small slice of CNR? As a stockholder, although you don't get free train tickets, you do share in the profits of the company in the form of annual dividends and an increase (you hope) in the stock price if the company grows and becomes more profitable. Of course, you receive these benefits if things are going well. If CNR's business declines, your stock may be worth less (or even worthless!).

Real estate is another one of our favourite financially rewarding and time-honoured ownership investments. Real estate can produce profits when it's rented out for more than the expense of owning the property or sold at a price higher than what you paid for it. We know numerous successful real-estate investors who have earned excellent long-term profits.

The value of real estate depends not only on the particulars of the individual property but also on the health and performance of the local economy. When companies in the community are growing and more jobs are being produced at higher wages, real estate often does well. When local employers are laying people off and excess housing is sitting vacant because of previous overbuilding, rent and property values fall, as they did in the late 2000s.

Finally, many Canadians have also built substantial wealth through small business. According to *Forbes* magazine, more of the world's wealthiest individuals have built their wealth through their stakes in small businesses (that became bigger) than through any other vehicle. Small business is the engine that drives much of the country's economic growth. You can participate in small business in a variety of ways. You can start your own business, buy and operate an existing business, or simply invest in promising small businesses. In the chapters ahead, we explain each of these major investment types in detail.

Shunning Gambling Instruments and Behaviors

Although investing is often risky, it's not gambling. *Gambling* is putting your money into schemes that are sure to lose you money over time. That's not to say that everyone loses or that you lose every time you gamble. However, the deck is stacked against you. The house wins most of the time.

WARNING

Horse-racing tracks, gambling casinos, and lotteries are set up to pay out 50 cents to 60 cents on the dollar. The rest goes to profits and covering the costs of those businesses — don't forget that they *are* businesses. Sure, your chosen horse may win a race or two, but in the long run, you're almost guaranteed to lose about 40 percent to 50 percent of what you bet. Would you put your money in an "investment" where your expected return over the long term was *negative* 40 percent?

Forsaking futures, options, and other derivatives

Futures, options, and commodity futures are *derivatives*, or financial investments whose value is derived from the performance of another security, such as a stock or bond.

Suppose you hear a radio ad from the firm Fleecem, Cheatem, and Leavem advocating that you buy heating oil futures because of conflicts in the Middle East and the upcoming rise in heating oil usage due to the cold-weather months. You call the firm and are impressed by the smooth-talking vice president. His logic makes sense, and he spends a lot of time with little ol' you, so you send him $10,000.

Buying futures isn't much different from blowing $10,000 at the craps tables in Vegas. Futures prices depend on short-term, highly volatile price movements. As with gambling, you occasionally win when the market moves the right way at the right time. But in the long run, you're gonna lose. In fact, you can lose it all.

Options are as risky as futures. With options, you're betting on the short-term movements of a specific security. If you have inside information (such as knowing in advance when a major corporate development is going to occur), you can get rich. But insider trading is illegal and will land you in jail.

Honest brokers who help their clients invest in stocks, bonds, and mutual funds tell them the truth about commodities, futures, and options. Here's how one former broker who worked for various major brokerage firms for 12 years put it, "I had just one client who made money in options, futures, or commodities, but the only reason he came out ahead was because he was forced to pull money out to close on a home purchase just when he happened to be ahead. The commissions were great for me, but there's no way a customer will make money in them." Remember these words if you're tempted to gamble with futures, options, and the like.

Futures and options are not always used for speculation and gambling. Some sophisticated professional investors use them to *hedge*, or actually reduce the risk of, their broad investment holdings. When futures and options are used in this fashion, things don't often work out the way that the pros hoped. You, the individual investor, should steer clear of futures and options.

Ditching day trading

WARNING

Day trading (the rapid buying and selling of securities online) is an equally foolish vehicle for individual investors to pursue. This is speculation and gambling, not investing. Placing trades via the Internet is far cheaper than the older methods of trading (such as calling a broker), but the more you trade, the more trading costs eat into your investment capital.

You can certainly make some profits when day trading. However, over an extended period of time, you'll inevitably underperform the broad market averages. In those rare instances where you may do a little better than the market averages, the profits are rarely worth the time and personal sacrifices that you, your family, and your friendships endure.

Understanding Investment Returns

The previous sections describe the difference between ownership and lending investments, and they help you distinguish gambling and speculation from investing. "That's all well and good," you say, "but how do I choose which type of investments to put my money into? How much can I make, and what are the risks?"

Good questions. We'll start with the returns you *might* make. We say "might" because this requires looking at history, and history is a record of the past. Using history to predict the future — especially the near future — is dangerous. History may repeat itself, but not always in exactly the same fashion and not necessarily when you expect it to.

During this past century, ownership investments such as stocks and investment real estate returned around 9 percent per year, handily beating lending investments such as bonds (around 5 percent) and savings accounts (roughly 2 percent to 3 percent) in the investment performance race. Inflation has averaged about 3 percent per year.

If you already know that the stock market can be risky, you may be wondering why investing in stocks is worth the anxiety and potential losses. Why bother for a few extra percent per year? Well, over many years, a few extra percent per year can really magnify the growth of your money (see Table 8-2). The more years you have to invest, the greater the difference a few percent makes in your returns.

TABLE 8-2 **The Difference a Few Percent Makes**

At This Rate of Return on $10,000 Invested	You'll Have This Much in 25 Years	You'll Have This Much in 40 Years
3% (savings account)	$20,938	$32,620
5% (bond)	$33,864	$70,400
9% (stocks and investment real estate)	$86,231	$314,094

REMEMBER

Investing is not a spectator sport. You can't earn good returns on stocks and real estate if you keep your money in cash on the sidelines. If you invest in growth investments such as stocks and real estate, don't chase one new investment after another trying to beat the market average returns. The biggest value comes from being in the market, not from beating it.

Sizing Investment Risks

Many investors have a simplistic understanding of what risk means and how to apply it to their investment decisions. For example, when compared to the yo-yo motions of the stock market, a bank savings account may seem like a less risky place to put your money. Over the long term, however, the stock market usually beats the rate of inflation, while the interest rate on a savings account does not, especially when factoring in taxes. Thus, if you're saving your money for a long-term goal like retirement, a savings account can be a "riskier" place to put your money if you're concerned about the future purchasing power of your investments.

TIP

Before you invest, ask yourself these questions:

>> **What am I saving and investing this money for?** In other words, what's my goal?

>> **What is my timeline for this investment?** When will I use this money?

>> **What is the historical volatility of the investment I'm considering?** Does that suit my comfort level and timeline for this investment?

After you answer these questions, you'll have a better understanding of risk and you'll be able to match your savings goals to their most appropriate investment vehicles. In Chapter 4, we help you consider your savings goals and timeline. We address investment risk and returns in the sections that follow.

Comparing the risks of stocks and bonds

Given the relatively higher historic returns we mention for ownership investments in the previous section, some people think they should put all their money in stocks and real estate. So, what's the catch?

WARNING

The risk with ownership investments is the short-term fluctuations in their value. During the last century, stocks declined, on average, by more than 10 percent once every five years. Drops in stock prices of more than 20 percent occurred, on average, once every ten years. Real-estate prices suffer similar periodic setbacks.

Therefore, in order to earn those generous long-term returns from ownership investments like stocks and real estate, you must be willing to tolerate volatility. You absolutely should *not* put all your money in the stock or real estate market. Investing your emergency money or money you expect to use within the next five years in such volatile investments is not a good idea.

The shorter the time period that you have for holding your money in an investment, the less likely growth-oriented investments like stocks are to beat out lending-type investments like bonds. Table 8-3 illustrates the historical relationship between stock and bond returns based on number of years held.

TABLE 8-3

Stocks versus Bonds

Number of Years Investment Held	Likelihood of Stocks Beating Bonds
1	60%
5	70%
10	80%
20	91%
30	99%

Some types of bonds have higher yields than others, but the risk–reward relationship remains intact (see Chapter 9 for more on bonds). A bond generally pays you a higher rate of interest when it has a

>> **Lower credit rating:** To compensate for the higher risk of default and the higher likelihood of losing your investment

>> **Longer-term maturity:** To compensate for the risk that you'll be unhappy with the bond's set interest rate if the market level of interest rates moves up

Focusing on the risks you can control

When Eric taught a personal finance class at the University of California, he always asked students to write down what they'd like to learn. Here's what one student had to say: "I want to learn what to invest my money in now, as the stock market is overvalued and interest rates are about to go up, so bonds are dicey and banks give lousy interest — HELP!"

This student recognized the risk of price fluctuations in her investments, but she also seemed to believe, like too many people, that you actually can predict what's going to happen. How did she know that the stock market was overvalued, and why hadn't the rest of the world figured it out? How did she know that interest rates were about to go up, and why hadn't the rest of the world figured that out either?

TIP

When you invest in stocks and other growth-oriented investments, you must accept the volatility of these investments. That said, you can take several actions, which we discuss in this chapter and the remainder of Part 3, to greatly reduce your risk when investing in these higher-potential-return investments. Invest the money that you've earmarked for the longer term in these vehicles. Minimize the risk of these investments through diversification. Don't buy just one or two stocks; buy a number of stocks. Later in this chapter, we discuss what you need to know about diversification.

Discovering low-risk, high-return investments

TIP

Despite what professors teach in the nation's leading business and finance graduate-school programs, low-risk investments that almost certainly lead to high returns are available. We can think of at least four such investments:

>> **Paying off consumer debt:** If you're paying 10 percent, 14 percent, 18 percent, or higher interest on an outstanding credit-card debt or other consumer loan, pay it off before investing. To get a comparable return through other investment vehicles (after the government takes its share of your profits), you'd have to start a new career as a loan shark. If, between federal and provincial taxes, you're in a 30 percent combined income-tax bracket and you're paying 14 percent interest on consumer debt, you need to annually earn a whopping pretax return of 20 percent on your investments to justify not paying off the debt. Good luck with that!

When your only source of funds for paying off debt is a small emergency reserve equal to a few months' living expenses, paying off your debt may involve some risk. Tap into your emergency reserves only if you have a backup source — for example, the ability to borrow from a willing family member or against a retirement account balance.

>> **Investing in your health:** Eat healthy, exercise, and relax.

>> **Investing in friends and family:** Invest time and effort in improving your relationships with loved ones.

>> **Investing in personal and career development:** Pick up a new hobby or reinvigorate your interest in an old one, improve your communication skills, or read widely. Take an adult-education course or go back to school for a degree. Your investment will most likely lead to greater happiness and perhaps even higher paycheques.

Diversifying Your Investments

Diversification is one of the most powerful investment concepts. It refers to saving your eggs (or investments) in different baskets. Diversification requires you to place your money in different investments with returns that are not completely correlated, which is a fancy way of saying that when some of your investments are down in value, odds are that others are up in value.

TIP

To decrease the chances of all your investments getting clobbered at the same time, you must put your money in different types of investments, such as bonds, stocks, real estate, and small business. (We cover all these investments and more in Chapter 9.) You can further diversify your investments by investing in domestic as well as international markets.

Within a given class of investments, such as stocks, investing in different types of that class (such as different types of stocks) that perform well under various economic conditions is important. For this reason, *mutual funds,* which are diversified portfolios of securities such as stocks or bonds, are a highly useful investment vehicle. The same is true of exchange-traded funds (ETFs), which are like mutual funds but trade on a stock exchange. When you buy into a mutual fund or ETF, your money is pooled with the money of many other people and invested in a vast array of stocks or bonds.

You can look at the benefits of diversification in two ways:

>> Diversification reduces the volatility in the value of your whole portfolio. In other words, your portfolio can achieve the same rate of return that a single investment can provide with less fluctuation in value.

>> Diversification allows you to obtain a higher rate of return for a given level of risk.

Keep in mind that no one, no matter whom he works for or what credentials he has, can guarantee returns on an investment. You can do good research and get lucky, but no one is free from the risk of losing money. Diversification allows you to hedge the risk of your investments. See Figures 8-1, 8-2, and 8-3 to get an idea of how diversifying can reduce your risk. (The figures in these charts are adjusted for inflation.) Notice that different investments did better during different economic environments and time periods.

Recent decades have shown fluctuations as well. In the 1990s, stocks appreciated greatly, and bonds did pretty well, too, while gold and silver did poorly. In the 2000s, stocks treaded water (except those in emerging markets) while bonds and precious metals did well. Since the end of the severe recession in 2009, stocks have soared while precious metals have greatly lagged. Because the future can't be predicted, diversifying your money into different investments is safer.

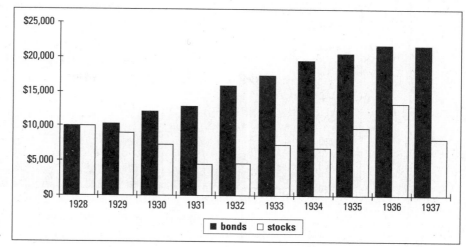

FIGURE 8-1:
Value of $10,000
invested from
1928 to 1937.

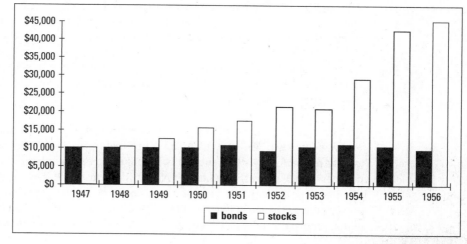

FIGURE 8-2:
Value of $10,000
invested from
1947 to 1956.

Spreading the wealth: Asset allocation

Asset allocation refers to how you spread your investing dollars among different investment options (stocks, bonds, money-market accounts, and so on). Before you can intelligently decide how to allocate your assets, you need to ponder a number of issues, including your present financial situation, your goals and priorities, and the pros and cons of various investment options.

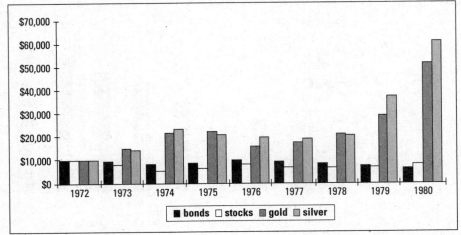

FIGURE 8-3:
Value of $10,000
invested from
1972 to 1980.

Although stocks and real estate offer attractive long-term returns, they can sometimes suffer significant declines. Thus, these investments are not suitable for money that you think you may want or need to use within, say, the next five years.

TIP

Everyone should have a reserve of money — about three to six months' worth of living expenses — that's accessible in an emergency. (Refer to Chapter 4 for more on emergency reserves.)

The best place to keep money that you expect to use soon is inside a Tax-Free Savings Account (TFSA), which came into being in 2009. The name is unfortunately misleading — you could easily make the costly mistake of assuming that you can only have cash in your TFSA, just like you would in a regular bank savings or chequing account. In fact, you can hold any investment that's eligible for a Registered Retirement Savings Plan (RRSP) inside a TFSA. This includes, stocks, bonds, mutual funds, ETFs, annuities, and real-estate investment trusts.

Given that you plan on withdrawing the money in the near future, don't put it into stocks or other investments that can and do take regular drops in value. Your best bet is a high-interest account, money-market fund, or short-term bond fund.

When you put money into a TFSA, you don't get a tax deduction. But like an RRSP, any gains on the money inside your TFSA can grow and compound tax-free. What's more, unlike withdrawals from an RRSP, which are taxed, there is no tax due on withdrawals from a TFSA. This includes not only your original contributions, but also any profits you've made.

In 2018, the maximum you could put into a TFSA for the year was capped at $5,500. This maximum is indexed to inflation and is rounded off to the nearest $500. And there's more good news: If you don't contribute the maximum in any given year, that unused amount is carried forward and added to the amount you're allowed to contribute in the current year.

Allocating money for the long term

Investing money for retirement is a classic long-term goal that most people have. Your current age and the number of years until you retire are the biggest factors to consider when allocating money for long-term purposes. The younger you are and the more years you have before retirement, the more comfortable you can afford to be with growth-oriented (and more volatile) investments, such as stocks and real estate.

TIP

One useful guideline for dividing or allocating your money between longer-term growth investments, such as stocks, and more-conservative lending investments, such as bonds, is to subtract your age from 110 (120 if you want to be aggressive; 100 to be more conservative) and invest the resulting percentage in stocks. You then invest the remaining amount in bonds. For example, if you're 30 years old, you invest from 70 percent (100 – 30) to 90 percent (120 – 30) in stocks. You invest the remaining 10 percent to 30 percent in bonds.

Table 8-4 lists some guidelines for allocating long-term money based on your age and the level of risk you desire.

TABLE 8-4

Allocating Long-Term Money

Your Investment Attitude	Bond Allocation (%)	Stock Allocation (%)
Play it safer	Your age	100 – your age
Middle-of-the-road	Your age – 10	110 – your age
Aggressive	Your age – 20	120 – your age

For example, if you're the conservative sort who doesn't like a lot of risk but recognizes the value of striving for some growth and making your money work harder, you're a middle-of-the-road type. Using Table 8-4, if you're 40 years old, you may consider putting 30 percent (40 – 10) in bonds and 70 percent (110 – 40) in stocks.

In most employer retirement plans, mutual funds are the typical investment vehicle. If your employer's retirement plan includes more than one stock mutual fund as an option, you may want to try discerning which options are best by using the criteria we discuss in Chapter 10. In the event that all your retirement plan's stock-fund options are good, you can simply divide your stock allocation among the choices.

When one or more of the choices is an international stock fund, consider allocating a percentage of your stock-fund money to overseas investments — at least 20 percent for play-it-safe investors, 25 percent to 35 percent for middle-of-the-road investors, and as much as 35 percent to 50 percent for aggressive investors.

If the 40-year-old middle-of-the-roader from the previous example is investing 70 percent in stocks, about 25 percent to 35 percent of the stock-fund investments (which works out to be about 18 percent to 24 percent of the total) can be invested in a combination of U.S. and international stock funds.

In generations past, most employees didn't have to make their own investing decisions with their retirement money. That's because pension plans in which the company directs the investments were much more common. It's interesting to note that in a typical pension plan, companies choose to allocate the majority of money to stocks (about 60 percent), with a bit less placed in bonds (about 35 percent) and other investments. (For more information on investing in RRSPs and retirement plans, see Chapters 11 and 12.)

Sticking with your allocations: Don't trade

Your goals and desire to take risk should drive the allocation of your investment dollars. As you get older, gradually scaling back on the riskiness (and, therefore, growth potential and volatility) of your portfolio generally makes sense.

Don't tinker with your portfolio daily, weekly, monthly, or even annually. (Every two to three years or so, you may want to rebalance your holdings to get your mix to a desired asset allocation, as discussed in the preceding section.) Don't engage in trading with the hopes of buying into a hot investment and selling your losers. Jumping onto a "winner" and dumping a "loser" may provide some short-term psychological comfort, but in the long term, such an investment strategy often produces below-average returns.

When an investment gets front-page coverage and everyone is talking about its stunning rise, it's definitely time to take a reality check. The higher an investment's price rises, the greater the danger that it's overpriced. Its next move may be downward. Don't follow the herd.

During the late 1990s, many technology (especially Internet) stocks had spectacular rises and attracted a huge amount of attention. However, the fact that the economy was increasingly becoming technology based didn't mean that any price you paid for a technology stock was fine. Some investors who neglected to do basic research and bought into the attention-grabbing, high-flying technology stocks lost 80 percent to 90 percent or more of their investments in the early 2000s. Ouch!

Conversely, when things look bleak (as when stocks in general suffered significant losses in the early 2000s and then again in the late 2000s), giving up hope is easy — who wants to be associated with a loser? The more the markets fall, it seems, the more people become fearful that further drops are imminent. However, the opposite is typically what happens: The market rebounds, often offering patient investors double-digit returns in the year or two following a large sell-off. But investors who forget about their overall asset allocation plan and panic and sell *after* a major decline miss out on what turn out to be tremendous buying opportunities.

Many people like buying everything from clothing to cars to ketchup on sale — yet whenever the stock market has a clearance sale, most investors stampede for the exits instead of snatching up great buys. Demonstrate your courage; don't follow the herd.

Investing lump sums via dollar-cost averaging

When you have a large chunk of cash to invest — whether you received it from an accumulation of funds over the years, an inheritance, or a recent windfall from work you've done — you may have a problem deciding what to do with it. Many people, of course, would like to have your problem. (You're not complaining, right?) You want to invest your money, but you're a bit skittish — if not outright terrified — at the prospect of investing the lump of money all at once.

REMEMBER

If the money is residing in a savings or money-market account, you may feel like it's wasting away. You want to put it to work! Our first words of advice are "Don't rush." Nothing is wrong with earning a small return in a money-market account. Just be sure to put the maximum you're allowed to into a TFSA. As noted earlier in this chapter, you're allowed to put money that's inside a TFSA into a variety of investments, including money-market funds. (See Chapter 13 for our recommendations of the best money-market funds.) Remember that a money-market fund beats the heck out of rushing into an investment in which you may lose 20 percent or more. And money inside a TSFA can grow tax-free. We sometimes speak with people in a state of near-panic. Typically, these folks have GICs coming due, and they feel it's absolutely imperative that they decide exactly where they want to invest the money before the GIC matures.

TIP

Take a deep breath. You have absolutely no reason to rush into an important decision. Tell your friendly banker that when the GIC matures, you want to put the proceeds into the bank's highest-yielding savings or money-market account, preferably inside a TFSA wrapper. That way, your money continues to earn interest while you buy yourself some breathing room. (And if it's inside a TFSA, it grows tax-free.)

One approach to investing is called *dollar-cost averaging* (DCA). With DCA, you invest your money in equal chunks on a set, regular schedule — such as once a month — into a diversified group of longer-term investments. For example, if you have $60,000 to invest, you can invest $2,500 per month until it's all invested, which will take a couple of years. The money awaiting future investment isn't lying fallow; you keep it in a money-market account or high-interest savings account so it can earn a bit of interest while waiting its turn.

The attraction of DCA is that it allows you to ease into riskier investments instead of jumping in all at once. If the price of the investment drops after some of your initial purchases, you can buy some later at a lower price. If you dump your entire chunk of money into an investment all at once and then it drops like a stone, you'll be kicking yourself for not waiting.

The flip side of DCA is that when your investment of choice appreciates in value, you may wish that you had invested your money faster. Another drawback of DCA is that it requires some discipline to stay the course. You may get cold feet as you continue to pour money into an investment that's dropping in value. Many people who are attracted to DCA because they fear that they may buy before a price drop end up bailing out of what feels like a sinking ship.

DCA can also cause headaches with your taxes when the time comes to sell investments held outside retirement plans. When you buy an investment at many different times and prices, the accounting becomes muddied as you sell blocks of the investment.

TIP

DCA is most valuable when the money you want to invest represents a large portion of your total assets and you can stick to a schedule. Make DCA automatic so you're less likely to chicken out if the investment falls after your initial purchases. Most of the investment firms we recommend in the next few chapters provide such automatic services.

Acknowledging Differences among Investment Firms

Thousands of firms sell investments and manage money. Banks, mutual-fund companies, securities brokerage firms, and even insurance companies all vie for your dollars.

Just to make matters more complicated, each industry plays in the others' backyards. You can find mutual-fund companies that offer securities brokerage, insurance firms that are in the mutual-fund business, and mutual-fund companies that offer banklike accounts and services. You may benefit from this competition and one-stop shopping convenience. On the other hand, some firms are novices at particular businesses and count on folks shopping by brand-name recognition.

Focusing on the best firms

TIP

Make sure you do business with a firm that

>> **Offers the best value investments in comparison to its competitors:** Value is the combination of performance (including service) and cost. Given the level of risk that you're comfortable with, you want investments that offer higher rates of return, but you don't want to have to pay a small fortune for them. Commissions, management fees, maintenance fees, and other charges can turn a high-performance investment into a mediocre or poor one.

>> **Employs representatives who don't have an inherent self-interest in steering you into a particular type of investment:** This criterion has nothing to do with whether an investment firm hires polite, well-educated, or well-dressed people. The most important factor is the way the company compensates its employees. If the investment firm's personnel are paid on commission, be wary. Give preference to investing firms that don't tempt their employees to push one investment over another in order to generate more fees.

No-load (commission-free) mutual-fund companies

Mutual funds are an ideal investment vehicle for most investors. *No-load mutual-fund companies* are firms through which you can invest in mutual funds without paying sales commissions. In other words, every dollar you invest goes to work in the mutual funds you choose — nothing is siphoned off to pay sales commissions. Many of these firms also offer ETFs, which are similar to mutual funds in many ways, are (in the best cases) lower cost, and trade on a major stock exchange and, thus, can be bought and sold during the trading day. (See Chapter 10 for details on investing in mutual funds and ETFs.)

Discount brokers

In one of the most beneficial changes for investors in the past century, the U.S. Securities and Exchange Commission (SEC) deregulated the retail brokerage industry on May 1, 1975. (In 1983, the Toronto and Montreal stock exchanges followed suit.) Prior to this date, investors were charged fixed commissions when they bought or sold stocks, bonds, and other securities. In other words, no matter which brokerage firm an investor did business with, the cost of the firm's services was set (and the level of commissions was high). After deregulation, brokerage firms could charge people whatever their little hearts desired.

Competition inevitably resulted in more and better choices. Many new brokerage firms (that didn't do business the old way) opened. They were dubbed *discount brokers* because the fees they charged customers were substantially lower than what brokers charged under the old fixed–fee system.

ROBINHOOD: A "FREE" STOCK TRADING APP

Thanks to deregulation decades ago, and now technology, brokerage trading fees have dropped dramatically. Many leading investment companies that we highlight offer broad menus of the best investments (for example, mutual funds, ETFs, stocks, bonds, and so on). We've explained in our books how to buy many of the funds without any trading fees at all, and when fees are levied, they're typically quite low.

But that hasn't stopped some folks from trying to offer even better deals. Hence, the rise of some brokerage firms claiming "free" trading. Of course, there is a catch: A brokerage firm can't possibly exist, survive, and continue to stay in business if it doesn't charge any fees at all for any of its services!

One such typical company offering "free" stock trading, Robinhood, had many, many catches that turned up with a little digging:

- It only exists as an app, so there's no way for you to access the company through a traditional desktop (or laptop) computer or through a web-based platform.

- If you need customer service or help resolving a problem with your account, you have limited access to phone assistance and only during normal business hours. After hours, including on weekends, you're stuck using email.

- You can only use the app for taxable accounts. Robinhood doesn't offer registered retirement accounts.

- It doesn't offer mutual funds.

- There are no tools or research to tap into.

- If you want a paper statement of your account, that will cost you $5 each time you request it.

- If you decide to close your account and have it transferred to another broker, Robinhood charges you $75 for the privilege of leaving.

Even more important than saving customers money, discount brokers established a vastly improved compensation system that greatly reduced conflicts of interest. Discount brokers generally pay the salaries of their brokers. The term *discount broker* is actually not an enlightening one. Certainly, this new breed of brokerage firm saves you lots of money when you invest; you can easily save 50 percent to 80 percent through the major discount brokers. But these firms' investments are not "on sale" or "second rate." Discount brokers are simply brokers without major conflicts of interest. Of course, like any other for-profit enterprise, they're in business to make money, but they're much less likely to steer you in the wrong direction for their own benefit.

WARNING

Be wary of discount brokers selling load mutual funds. (We discuss the reasons you should shun these brokers in Chapter 10.)

Places to consider avoiding

The worst places to invest are those that charge you a lot, have mediocre- or poor-performing investments, and have major conflicts of interest. The prime conflict of interest arises when investment firms pay their brokers commissions on the basis of what and how much they sell. The result: The investment firms sell lots of stuff that pay fat commissions, and they *churn*, or cause a rapid turnover of, your account. (Because each transaction has a fee, the more you buy and sell, the more money they make.)

WARNING

Some folks who call themselves *financial planners* or *financial consultants* work on commission. In addition to working at the bigger brokerage firms, many of them belong to so-called *broker-dealer networks,* which provide back-office support and investment products to sell. When a person claiming to be a financial planner or advisor is part of a broker-dealer network, odds are quite high that you're dealing with an investment salesperson. (See Chapter 19 for more background on the financial planning industry and questions to ask an advisor you're thinking about hiring.)

Commissions and their impact on human behaviour

Investment products bring in widely varying commissions. The products that bring in the highest commissions tend to be the ones that money-hungry brokers push the hardest.

Table 8-5 lists the commissions that you pay — and that come out of your investment dollars — when you work with brokers, financial consultants, and financial planners who work on commission.

TABLE 8-5 Investment Sales Commissions

Investment Type	Average Commission on a $20,000 Investment	Average Commission on a $100,000 Investment
Annuities	$1,400	$7,000
Initial public offerings (new stock issue)	$1,000	$5,000
Limited partnerships	$1,800	$9,000
Load mutual funds	$1,000	$5,000
Options and futures	$2,000+	$10,000+

Besides the fact that you can never be sure that you're getting an unbiased recommendation from a salesperson working on commission, you're wasting money unnecessarily. The best investments can be bought on a *no-load* (commission-free) basis.

TIP

When you're unsure about an investment product that's being pitched to you (and even when you *are* sure), ask for a copy of the prospectus. In the first few pages, check out whether the investment includes a commission (also known as a *load*). Although salespeople can hide behind obscure titles such as vice president or financial consultant, a prospectus must detail whether the investment carries a commission.

Investment salespeople's conflicts of interest

Financial consultants (also known as stockbrokers), financial planners, and others who sell investment products can have enormous conflicts of interest when recommending strategies and specific investment products. Commissions and other financial incentives can't help but skew the advice of even the most earnest and otherwise well-intentioned salespeople.

WARNING

Numerous conflicts of interest can damage your investment portfolio. The following are the most common conflicts to watch out for:

>> **Pushing higher-commission products:** As we discuss earlier in this chapter, commissions on investment products vary tremendously. Products like limited partnerships, commodities, options, and futures are at the worst end of the spectrum for you (and the best end of the spectrum for a salesperson). Investments such as no-load mutual funds, ETFs, and Treasury bills that are 100 percent commission free are at the best end of the spectrum for you (and, therefore, the worst end of the spectrum for a salesperson).

Surprisingly, commission-based brokers and financial planners don't have to give you the *prospectus* (where commissions are detailed) before you buy a financial product that carries commissions (as with a load mutual fund). In contrast, commission-free investment companies, such as no-load mutual-fund companies, must send a prospectus before taking a mutual-fund order. (Commission-based investment salespeople should also be required to provide a prospectus and disclose any commissions upfront and in writing before making a sale.) However, dealers and other mutual-fund salespeople must provide you with a three- to four-page document inelegantly called "Fund Facts" before accepting a mutual-fund purchase order. Written in straightforward language, a Fund Facts document details the costs of buying and holding the fund; how much of the fees you pay go to your advisor; and the fund's level of risk, its holdings, and up to ten years of annual returns.

» **Recommending active trading:** Investment salespeople often advise you to trade frequently into and out of different securities. They usually base their advice on current news events or an analyst's comments on the security. Sometimes these moves are valid, but more often they're not. In extreme cases, brokers trade on a monthly basis. By the end of the year, they've churned through your entire portfolio. Needless to say, all these transactions cost you big money in trading fees.

Diversified mutual funds and ETFs (see Chapter 10) make more sense for most people. You can invest in funds free of sales commissions. Besides saving money on commissions, you earn better long-term returns by having an expert money manager work for you.

» **Failing to recommend investing through a company retirement plan:** An investment salesperson is not likely to recommend that you contribute to your employer's retirement plan. Such contributions cut into the money you have available to invest with your friendly salesperson.

» **Pushing high-fee products:** Many of the brokerage firms that used to sell investment products only on commission moved into fee-based investment management. This change is an improvement for investors because it reduces some of the conflicts of interest caused by commissions.

On the other hand, these brokers may charge extraordinarily high fees, which are usually quoted as a percentage of assets under management on their managed-investment (or wrap) accounts (see the sidebar "Wrap [or managed] accounts" for more info).

Valuing brokerage research

Brokerage firms and the brokers who work for them frequently argue that their research is better. With their insights and recommendations, they say, you'll do better and "beat the market averages."

WHAT TO DO WHEN YOU'RE FLEECED BY A BROKER

You can't sue a broker just because you lose money on that person's investment recommendations. However, if you have been the victim of one of the following cardinal financial sins, you may have some legal recourse:

- **Misrepresentation and omission:** If you were told, for example, that a particular investment guaranteed returns of 15 percent per year and then the investment ended up plunging in value by 50 percent, you were misled. Misrepresentation can also be charged if you're sold an investment with hefty commissions after you were originally told that it was commission free.

- **Unsuitable investments:** Retirees who need access to their capital are often advised to invest in limited partnerships (LPs, discussed in Chapter 9) for safe, high yields. The yields on most LPs end up being anything but safe. LP investors have also discovered how *illiquid* (not readily converted into cash) their investments are — some can't be liquidated for up to ten years or more.

- **Churning:** If your broker or financial planner is constantly trading your investments, odds are that his weekly commission cheque is getting boosted at your expense.

- **Rogue elephant salespeople:** When your planner or broker buys or sells without your approval or ignores your request to make a change, you may be able to collect for losses caused by these actions.

Two major types of practitioners — securities lawyers and arbitration consultants — stand ready to help you recover your lost money. You can find securities lawyers by searching for "securities lawyers" online or calling your local bar association for referrals. Arbitration consultants can be found in phone directories under "Arbitrators." If you come up dry, try contacting business writers at a major newspaper in your area or at your favourite personal-finance magazine. These sources may be able to give you names and numbers of folks they know.

Many such lawyers and consultants work on a *contingency-fee* basis — they get a percentage (about 20 percent to 40 percent) of the amount collected. They also often ask for an upfront fee, ranging from several hundred to several thousand dollars, to help them cover their expenses and time. If they take your case and lose, they generally keep the upfront money. Securities lawyers are usually a more expensive option.

You may want to go to *arbitration* — in fact, you likely agreed to do just that (probably without realizing it) when you set up an account to work with the broker or planner. Arbitration is usually much quicker, cheaper, and easier than going to court. You can even choose to represent yourself. The arbitrators then make a decision that neither side can squabble over or appeal. If you decide to prepare for arbitration by yourself, the nonprofit American Arbitration Association can send you a package of background materials to help with your case. Contact the association's headquarters (800-778-7879; www.adr.org). The website is for Americans, but it offers a lot of useful general information and tips about arbitration. Although similar Canadian organizations exist, they're largely professional development bodies.

Bay Street and Wall Street analysts are often simply overly optimistic when it comes to predicting corporate profits. If analysts were simply inaccurate or bad estimators, you'd expect that they'd sometimes underestimate and, at other times, overestimate companies' earnings. The discrepancy identifies yet another conflict of interest among many of the brokerage firms.

Brokerage-firm analysts are reluctant to write a negative report about a company because the firms these analysts work for also solicit companies to issue new stock to the public. What better way to show businesses your potential for selling shares to the public at a high price than by showing how much you believe in certain companies and writing glowing reports about their future prospects?

Seeing through Experts Who Predict the Future

Hoping that you can increase your investment returns by following the prognostications of certain gurus is a common mistake that some investors make, especially during more trying and uncertain times. Many people may want to believe that some experts can predict the future of the investment world and keep them out of harm's way. Trusting in gurus makes it easier to accept the risk you know you're taking when trying to make your money grow. The sage predictions that you read in an investment newsletter or hear from an "expert" who is repeatedly quoted in financial publications make you feel protected — sort of like Linus and his security blanket.

Investment newsletter subscribers and guru followers would be better off buying a warm blanket instead — it has a lot more value and costs a whole lot less! No one can predict the future. If people could, they'd be so busy investing their own money and getting rich that they wouldn't have the time and desire to share their secrets with you.

Investment newsletters

Many investment newsletters purport to time the markets, telling you exactly the right time to get into and out of certain stocks or mutual funds (or the financial markets in general). Such an approach is doomed to failure in the long run. By failure, we mean that this approach won't beat the tried-and-true strategy of buying and holding.

We see people paying hundreds of dollars annually to subscribe to all sorts of market-timing and stock-picking newsletters. One such investor, a lawyer, subscribed to several newsletters. When asked why, he said that their marketing materials claimed that if you followed their advice, you would make a return of 20 percent per year. But in the four years that he'd followed their advice, he'd actually *lost* money, despite appreciating financial markets overall.

The marketing materials for most investment newsletters typically hype the supposed returns that the publication's recommendations have produced. Sadly, newsletters seem to be able to make lots of bogus claims without suffering the timely wrath of securities regulators.

Consider the observations of Mark Hulbert. Hulbert began publishing his *Hulbert Financial Digest* in 1980, tracking the results investors could expect if they followed the advice of some 28 different newsletters. Hulbert eventually added more than 100 others to those he monitored. Although he closed the enterprise down in 2016, his overall conclusions led him to the same advice offered by legendary — and sound — experienced investors including John Bogle, who helped pioneer index funds through the firm he founded in 1975, Vanguard Group, and Warren Buffett: Most investors will fare the best by focusing on index funds.

TIP

Don't get predictive advice from newsletters. If newsletter writers were so smart about the future of financial markets, they'd be making lots more money as money managers. The only types of investment newsletters and periodicals that you should consider subscribing to are those that offer research and information rather than predictions. We discuss the investment newsletters that fill the bill in the subsequent investment chapters. Eric's website (www.erictyson.com) provides excerpts and updates from some of the better newsletters. Also, check out the "Guru Watch" section of his site, in which he evaluates the advice and recommendations of commonly quoted gurus.

Investment gurus

Investment gurus come and go. Some of them get their 15 minutes of fame on the basis of one or two successful predictions that someone in the press remembers (and makes famous).

During the financial crisis of 2008 and 2009, all sorts of pundits were coming out of the woodwork claiming that they had predicted what was unfolding. Chief among them was an economist named Nouriel Roubini, whom few people had previously heard of. Many news services credited Roubini for supposedly predicting the recession. And research did show that Roubini had, indeed, predicted a recession. The only problem, however, is that Roubini also predicted a recession in 2004. And in 2005, 2006, and 2007. So he was wrong for four long years in a row. In 2008, his prediction of a recession finally came true. Calling this "great insight" is somewhat akin to saying a broken clock is highly accurate because, twice every 24 hours, it nails the time to the exact second.

When the stock market dropped sharply and the recession worsened in late 2008, Roubini maintained a breakneck schedule with the news media. So, he made even more predictions. For example, in late October 2008, Roubini predicted that ". . . hundreds of hedge funds are poised to fail as frantic investors rush to redeem their assets and force managers into a fire sale of assets. . . . We've reached a situation of sheer panic. Don't be surprised if policy makers need to close down markets for a week or two in coming days." This prediction sounded absurd to us at the time and, of course, never happened. Roubini was wrong.

In January 2009, Roubini predicted oil prices would stay below US$40 per barrel for all of 2009. It didn't take long for that prediction to be proven wrong: Oil jumped above US$50 per barrel by April and US$70 by June.

When the Dow Jones Industrial Average fell to 6,500 in early 2009, Roubini said the market was likely to fall much farther, and he described any rally from that level as a "sucker's rally." Those people who panicked and sold in early 2009 because of Roubini's dire prediction were soon disappointed again as the stock market rebounded sharply.

The sad part about hyped articles with hyped predictions is that they cause some individual investors to panic and do the wrong thing — selling good assets like stocks at depressed prices. The media shouldn't irresponsibly publicize hyped predictions, especially without clearly and accurately disclosing the predictor's track record. Don't fall victim to such hype.

REMEMBER

Commentators and experts who publish predictive commentaries and newsletters and who are interviewed in the media can't predict the future. Ignore the predictions and speculations of self-proclaimed gurus and investment soothsayers. The few people who have a slight leg up on everyone else aren't going to share their investment secrets — they're too busy investing their own money! If you have to believe in something to offset your fears, believe in good information and proven investment managers. And don't forget the value of optimism, faith, and hope — regardless of what or whom you believe in!

Leaving You with Some Final Advice

TIP

We cover a lot of ground in this chapter. In the remaining chapters in Part 3, we detail different investment choices and accounts and how to build a champion portfolio! Before you move on, here are several other issues to keep in mind as you make important investing choices:

>> **Don't invest based on sales solicitations.** Companies that advertise and solicit prospective customers aggressively with tactics such as telemarketing offer some of the worst financial products with the highest fees. All companies have to do some promotion, but the companies with the best investment offerings don't have to use the hard-sell approach; they get plenty of new business through the word-of-mouth recommendations of satisfied customers.

>> **Don't invest in what you don't understand.** When you don't understand an investment, odds are good that it won't be right for you. Slick-tongued brokers (who may call themselves "financial consultants," "financial advisors," or "financial planners") who earn commissions based on what they sell can talk you into inappropriate investments. Before you invest in anything, you need to know its track record, its true costs, and how *liquid* (easily convertible to cash) it is.

>> **Minimize fees.** Avoid investments that carry high sales commissions and management expenses (usually disclosed in a prospectus). Virtually all investments today can be purchased without a salesperson. Besides paying unnecessary commissions, the bigger danger in investing through a salesperson is that you may be directed along a path that's not in your best interests. Management fees create a real drag on investment returns. Not surprisingly, higher-fee investments, on average, perform worse than alternatives with lower fees. High ongoing management fees often go toward lavish offices, glossy brochures, and skyscraper salaries, or toward propping up small, inefficient operations. Do you want your hard-earned dollars to support these types of businesses?

>> **Pay attention to tax consequences.** Even if you never become an investment expert, you're smart enough to know that the more money you pay in taxes, the less you have for investing and playing with. (See Chapter 12 for info on how RRSPs can help boost your investment returns.) For investments outside registered retirement plans, you need to match the types of investments to your tax situation (see Chapter 13).

WRAP (OR MANAGED) ACCOUNTS

Wrap accounts (also called managed accounts) are all the rage among commission-based brokerage firms. These accounts go by a variety of names, but they're all similar in that they charge a fixed percentage of the assets under management to invest your money through money managers.

Wrap accounts can be poor investments because their management expenses may be extraordinarily high — up to 2 percent per year (some even higher) of assets under management. Remember that in the long haul, stocks can return about 9 percent per year before taxes. So, if you're paying 2 percent per year to have your money managed in stocks, 22 percent of your return (before taxes) is siphoned off. But don't forget — because the government sure won't — that you pay a good chunk of money in taxes on your 9 percent return as well. So, the 2 percent wrap fee can end up depleting a third or more of your after-tax profits!

The best no-load (commission-free) mutual funds and ETFs offer investors access to the nation's best investment managers for a fraction of the cost of wrap accounts. You can invest in dozens of top-performing funds for an annual expense of 2 percent per year or less. Some of the best fund companies offer excellent funds for a cost as low as 0.3 percent to 1.5 percent (see Chapter 10).

You may be told, in the marketing of wrap accounts, that you're getting access to investment managers who don't normally take money from small-fry investors like you. Not a single study shows that the performance of money managers has anything to do with the minimum account they handle. Besides, no-load funds hire many of the same managers who work at other money-management firms. You also may be told that you'll earn a higher rate of return, so the extra cost is worth it. "You could have earned 18 percent to 25 percent per year," they say, "had you invested with the 'Star of Yesterday' investment management company." The key word here is *had*. History is history. Many of yesterday's winners become tomorrow's losers or mediocre performers.

You also need to remember that, unlike mutual funds and ETFs, wrap-account performance records may include marketing hype. Showing only the performance of selected accounts — those that performed the best — is the most common ploy.

Chapter **9**

Understanding Your Investment Choices

Which vehicle you choose for your investment journey depends on where you're hoping to go, how fast you want to get there, and what risks you're willing to take. If you haven't yet read Chapter 8, you may want to do so now. In it, we cover a number of investment concepts, such as the difference between lending and ownership investments, which will enhance your ability to choose among the common investment vehicles we discuss in this chapter.

Slow and Steady Investments

Everyone should have some money in stable, safe investment vehicles, including money that you've earmarked for your near-term expenses, both expected and unexpected. Likewise, if you're saving money for a home purchase within the next few years, you certainly don't want to risk that money on the roller coaster of the stock market.

The investment options that follow are appropriate for money you don't want to put at great risk.

Transaction/chequing accounts

Transaction/chequing accounts are best used for depositing your monthly income and paying your bills. If you want to have unlimited bill-paying and cheque-writing privileges and access to your money with an ATM card, chequing accounts at local banks are often your best bet.

TIP

Here's how not to waste money on banks:

>> **Consider credit unions and online banks.** You may get a better chequing-account deal at a credit union or at a bank that operates online only. Because you can easily get cash through the cash-back option when you make purchases at many supermarkets and other retail stores (the amount of cash you want is simply added to the cost of your purchase to come up with the total deducted from your account), you may not need to do business with Big City Bank, which has ATMs and branch offices at every intersection. Whatever institution you use, make sure your deposits are fully insured by the Canada Deposit Insurance Corporation (CDIC) or a similar provincial agency, which typically provide deposit insurance for credit unions.

>> **Shop around.** Some banks don't require you to maintain a minimum balance to avoid a monthly service charge when you have your paycheque directly deposited to your account. Make sure that you shop around for accounts that don't ding you $2 or $3 here for the use of an ATM and $15 there for a low balance. Those seemingly small fees can quickly add up to hundreds of dollars a year.

>> **Limit the amount you keep in chequing.** Keep only enough money in the account for your monthly bill-payment needs. If you consistently keep more than a few thousand dollars in a chequing account, get the excess out. You can generally earn more in a savings, high-interest, or money-market account, which we describe in the following section. And, if you're a high roller, be sure to limit the total amount you invest at any one institution to avoid having more on deposit than is covered by insurance.

Savings accounts and money-market funds

Savings accounts are available through banks, credit unions, and a number of other institutions such as Simplii Financial and Tangerine, as well as some of the newer online-only banks, such as Implicity Financial and EQ Bank; money-market funds are available through mutual-fund companies. Savings accounts and money-market funds are nearly identical, except that high-interest accounts and money-market funds generally pay a better rate of interest. The interest rate paid to you, also known as the *yield*, fluctuates over time, depending on the level of interest rates in the overall economy. (Note that some banks offer money-market accounts, which are basically like savings accounts and shouldn't be confused with money-market mutual *funds*.)

The CDIC insures most bank savings accounts, while provincial agencies generally insure deposits at credit unions. Money-market funds are not insured. But don't give preference to a bank or credit union account just because your investment (principal) is insured. In fact, your preference should lean toward money-market funds, because the better ones are higher yielding than the better bank savings accounts. Money-market funds are not covered by CDIC or provincial deposit insurance, but we haven't heard of the industry causing an individual to lose even a penny of principal. The risk difference versus a bank account is nil.

General-purpose money-market funds invest in safe, short-term guaranteed investment certificates (GICs), Government of Canada Treasury bills, provincial Treasury bills, and corporate commercial paper (short-term debt), which is issued by the largest and most creditworthy companies. Money-market-fund investments generally must have an average maturity of less than 90 days. In the unlikely event that an investment in a money-market fund's portfolio goes sour, the mutual-fund company that stands behind the money-market fund would almost certainly cover the loss.

TIP

If you still find yourself uneasy about the lack of insurance on money-market funds, here's a way to get the best of both worlds: Select a money-market fund that invests exclusively in Canadian government securities, which are virtually risk-free because they're backed by the full strength and credit of the federal government. However, these types of accounts typically pay around a quarter of a percent less interest than other money-market funds.

Bonds

When you invest in a bond, you effectively lend your money to an organization. When a bond is issued, it includes a specified maturity date at which time the principal will be repaid. Bonds are also issued at a particular interest rate, or what's known as a *coupon*. This rate is fixed on most bonds. So, for example, if you buy a five-year, 5 percent bond issued by Bombardier, you're lending your money to Bombardier for five years at an interest rate of 5 percent per year. (Bond interest is usually paid in two equal, semi-annual installments.)

The value of a bond generally moves in the opposite direction of the change in interest rates. For example, if you're holding a bond issued at 5 percent and rates on similar bonds increase to 7 percent, your 5 percent bond will decrease in value. (Why would anyone want to buy your bond at the price you paid if it yields just 5 percent and 7 percent can be obtained elsewhere?)

THE OVERUSED GUARANTEED INVESTMENT CERTIFICATE

A GIC is another type of bond that's issued by banks and credit unions. With a GIC, as with a real bond, you agree to lend your money to an organization (in this case, a bank or credit union) for a predetermined number of months or years. Generally, the longer you agree to lock up your money, the higher the interest rate you receive.

With most GICs, you pay a penalty for early withdrawal. If you want your money back before the end of the GIC's term, you get whacked with the loss of a number of months' worth of interest. Some GICs don't let you cash out early, period. Others may offer you the option of getting your money back before the GIC matures, but at the cost of a lower interest rate. GICs also don't tend to pay very competitive interest rates. You can usually beat the interest rate on shorter-term GICs (those that mature within a year or so) with the best high-interest savings accounts or money-market funds, which offer complete liquidity without any penalty.

Some bonds are tied to variable interest rates. For example, you can buy bonds that are adjustable-rate mortgages, on which the interest rate can fluctuate. As an investor, you're actually lending your money to a mortgage borrower — indirectly, you're the banker making a loan to someone buying a home.

Bonds differ from one another in the following major ways:

>> **The type of institution to which you're lending your money:** With municipal bonds, you lend your money to local governments; with Treasury bills, you lend your money to the federal government; with mortgage-backed securities, you lend your money to a mortgage holder; with corporate bonds, you lend your money to a corporation.

>> **The credit quality of the borrower to whom you lend your money:** Credit quality refers to the probability that the borrower will pay you the interest and return your principal as agreed.

>> **The length of maturity of the bond:** Short-term bonds mature within a few years, intermediate bonds within 7 to 10 years, and long-term bonds within 30 years. Longer-term bonds generally pay higher yields, but their value fluctuates more with changes in interest rates.

TECHNICAL STUFF

Bonds are rated on their degree of safety by major credit-rating agencies, usually on a scale where AAA is the highest possible rating. For example, high-grade corporate bonds (AAA or AA) are considered the safest (that is, most likely to pay you back). Next in safety are general bonds (A or BBB), which are still safe but just a little less so. Junk bonds rated BB or B are actually not all that junky; they're just lower in quality and have a slight (1 percent or 2 percent) probability of default over long periods of time. Junk bonds with even lower ratings — such as C or lower — carry higher default rates.

Some bonds are *callable,* which means that the bond's issuer can decide to pay you back earlier than the previously agreed-upon date. This event usually occurs when interest rates fall and the lender wants to issue new, lower-interest-rate bonds to replace the higher-interest-rate, outstanding bonds. To compensate you for early repayment, the lender typically gives you a small premium over what the bond is currently valued at.

Building Wealth with Ownership Vehicles

The three best legal ways to build wealth are to invest in stocks, real estate, and small business. We've found this to be true from observing many investors and from our own personal experiences and interactions with entrepreneurs. Check out the following sections for more details about these three options.

Socking your money away in stocks

Stocks, which represent shares of ownership in a company, are the most common ownership investment vehicle. When companies "go public," they issue shares of stock that people like you can purchase on the major stock exchanges, such as the Toronto Stock Exchange, the New York Stock Exchange, and NASDAQ (short for *National Association of Securities Dealers Automated Quotation*).

As the economy grows and companies grow with it, earning greater profits, stock prices (and dividend payouts on those stocks) generally follow suit. Stock prices and dividends don't move in lockstep with earnings, but over the years, the relationship is pretty close. In fact, the *price/earnings ratio* — which measures the level of stock prices relative to (or divided by) company earnings — of stocks has averaged approximately 15 (although it has tended to be higher during periods of low inflation and interest rates). A price-earnings ratio of 15 simply means that stock prices per share, on average, are selling at about 15 times those companies' earnings per share.

Companies that issue stock (called *publicly held* companies) include automobile manufacturers, computer-software producers, fast-food restaurants, hotels, publishers, supermarkets, technology companies, wineries, and everything in between! (You can also invest overseas — see the "International stocks" section.)

By contrast, some companies are *privately held,* which means that they've elected to have senior management and a small number of affluent investors own their stock. Privately held companies' stocks do not trade on a stock exchange, so folks like you can't buy stock in such firms.

TECHNICAL STUFF

Companies differ in what industry or line of business they're in and also in size. In the financial press, you often hear companies referred to by their *market capitalization,* which is the value of their outstanding stock (the number of total shares multiplied by the market price per share). When describing the sizes of companies, Bay Street and Wall Street have done away with such practical adjectives as *big* and *small* and replaced them with expressions like *large cap* and *small cap* (where *cap* is shorthand for *market capitalization*). Such is the language of financial geekiness.

REMEMBER

Investing in the stock market involves occasional setbacks and difficult moments (just like raising children or going mountain climbing), but the overall journey is almost certainly worth the effort. Over the past two centuries, the U.S. stock market (for which decades more data exist than for the Canadian stock market) has produced an annual average rate of return of about 9 percent to 10 percent. However, the market, as measured by the Dow Jones Industrial Average (DJIA), fell more than 20 percent during 16 different periods in the 20th century. On average, these periods of decline lasted less than two years. So, if you can withstand a temporary setback over a few years, the stock market is a proven place to invest for long-term growth.

You can invest in stocks by making your own selection of individual stocks or by letting mutual funds or exchange-traded funds (ETFs) do it for you. (Turn to Chapter 10 for more on mutual funds and ETFs.)

Investing internationally in stocks

Not only can you invest in company stocks that trade on the Canadian stock exchanges, but you can also invest in stocks in the United States and around the world. If you're in Canada, you might ask why you would want to invest in international stocks.

We can give you two very good reasons:

>> **Many investing opportunities exist beyond our borders.** If you look at the total value of all stocks outstanding worldwide, the value of Canadian stocks is less than 3 percent of the total. Investing in international stocks allows you to take advantage of business growth in other countries.

>> **You're diversifying your portfolio even further.** International securities markets don't move in tandem with Canadian markets. During various Canadian stock-market drops, some international stock markets drop less, while others may sometimes *rise* in value.

Some people hesitate to invest in international securities out of concern that overseas investing hurts the Canadian economy and contributes to a loss of Canadian jobs. We have counterarguments:

>> **If you don't profit from the growth of economies in the United States and overseas, someone else will.** If there's money to be made, Canadians may as well be there to participate. Profits from a foreign company are distributed to all stockholders, no matter where they live. Dividends and stock-price appreciation know no national boundaries.

>> **You already live in a global economy.** Making a distinction between Canadian and non-Canadian companies is no longer appropriate. Many companies that are headquartered in Canada also have U.S. and overseas operations. Some Canadian firms derive a large portion of their revenue from their international divisions. Conversely, many firms based in the United States or overseas also have Canadian operations. An increasing number of companies are worldwide operations.

So, where are the major investing opportunities outside Canada? International investing managers generally look at opportunities in four major geographic regions:

>> The United States

>> Latin America (including countries such as Argentina, Brazil, Chile, Colombia, Costa Rica, Mexico, Panama, and Peru)

>> Europe (including countries such as Belgium, Denmark, France, Germany, Ireland, Italy, Netherlands, Norway, Spain, Sweden, Switzerland, and the United Kingdom)

>> Asia-Pacific (including countries such as Australia, China, Hong Kong, India, Japan, New Zealand, Singapore, South Korea, Taiwan, Thailand, and Vietnam)

Companies in Canada are generally a very small investment portion held by many international and global stock funds. Canadian holdings may be listed separately or as a part of "North America" holdings.

GLOBALLY DIVERSIFIED STOCK PORTFOLIOS REAP THE BEST RETURNS WITH THE LOWEST RISK

Wharton School Professor of Finance Jeremy Siegel is the author of the investing classic *Stocks for the Long Run* (McGraw-Hill), in which he explains how stocks have performed over the generations and why they offer solid potential for long-term returns. His explanations regarding the value of investing globally are outstanding and summarized for your benefit in this sidebar.

Siegal says that the financial markets are now clearly globalized. The United States is no longer the "unchallenged giant" but is one of many countries that offer wealth-building opportunities to investors. About 90 percent of the value of all stocks worldwide resided in the United States just after World War II. Today, that percentage is about 50 and the portion is continuing to shrink. "To invest only in the United States is to ignore the majority of the world's equity capital," says Siegel.

The developed world (Australia, Canada, Hong Kong, Japan, New Zealand, Singapore, South Korea, Taiwan, the United States, and Western Europe) are still overrepresented economically and in the world's stock markets. Although these countries contain just 15 percent of the world's population, they account for more than 50 percent of the world's economic activity and more than 90 percent of the world's equity capital.

According to Siegel, "The emerging nations' share of output and equity capital has been rising rapidly and will continue to do so . . . and market capitalism will push countries such as China and India to the forefront of the world economy."

Although world markets have tended to move more in tandem in recent years, especially over shorter time periods, investing opportunities outside Canada and the United States provide investors greater ability to diversify and spread risk. When investing outside of Canada, investors gain diversification exposure to currencies beyond the Canadian dollar but also are exposed to the risks of investing in stocks denominated in other currencies. As Siegel explains, ". . . for investors with long-term horizons, hedging currency risk in foreign stock markets is not important . . . it is not worth the cost. . . ."

Economic historians have shown that during the 17th and 18th centuries, China and India accounted for roughly one-third of world economic activity and were powerhouses. Siegel predicts that by 2050, these two countries will again account for about that amount of world gross domestic product (GDP) — he predicts 38 percent (it's currently 22 percent) — and will account for about 36 percent of world stock-market values. Siegel warns, however, ". . . the increase in a country's share of world

(continued)

(continued)

capital . . . does not necessarily represent capital appreciation of existing shares. Rather, most of the increases come from the flotation of new capital, as well as the acquisition of old capital . . . economic growth does not guarantee good returns. . . ."

His conclusion: "Only those investors who have a fully diversified world portfolio will be able to reap the best returns with the lowest risk."

Another way in which foreign stocks are categorized is between developed markets and emerging markets. Developed markets are characterized by more mature, stable, and secure economies with relatively high standards of living; examples include countries such as Australia, Canada, France, Germany, Japan, Switzerland, and the United Kingdom. Emerging markets tend to be more volatile and typically higher-growth economies that are in their early economic stages; examples include countries such as Brazil, China, Chile, India, Indonesia, Malaysia, Mexico, Russia, South Africa, and Thailand.

Discovering the relative advantages of mutual funds

TIP

Efficiently managed mutual funds offer investors low-cost access to high-quality money managers. Mutual funds span the spectrum of risk and potential returns, from nonfluctuating money-market funds (which are similar to savings accounts) to bond funds (which generally pay higher yields than money-market funds, but fluctuate with changes in interest rates) to stock funds (which offer the greatest potential for appreciation but also the greatest short-term volatility).

Selecting and investing in individual securities should be done only by those who really enjoy doing it and are aware of and willing to accept the risks in doing so. Mutual funds, if properly selected, are a low-cost, quality way to hire professional money managers. Over the long haul, you're highly unlikely to beat full-time professional managers who are investing in securities of the same type and at the same risk level. Chapter 10 is devoted to mutual funds.

Understanding exchange-traded funds, hedge funds, and managed accounts

Mutual funds aren't the only game in town when it comes to hiring a professional money manager. Three additional options you may hear about include

>> **ETFs:** These funds are the most similar to mutual funds except that they trade on a major stock exchange and, thus, can be bought and sold during the trading day. The best ETFs have low fees and, like an index fund (see Chapter 10), invest to track the performance of a stock-market index.

>> **Hedge funds:** These privately managed funds are for wealthier investors and are generally riskier than a typical mutual fund (some hedge funds even go bankrupt). The fees can be steep — typically 20 percent of the hedge fund's annual returns, as well as an annual management fee of 1 percent or so. They're also generally illiquid — there are usually lockup periods, and it can still be difficult to get your money back out later when needed. We generally don't recommend them.

>> **Managed accounts:** The major brokerage firms, which employ brokers on commission, offer access to private money managers. In reality, this option isn't really different from getting access to fund managers via mutual funds, but you'll generally pay a much higher fee, which reduces this option's attractiveness.

Investing in individual stocks

Our experience is that plenty of people choose to invest in individual securities because they think that they're smarter or luckier than the rest. We don't know you personally, but it's safe to say that in the long run, your investment choices are highly unlikely to outperform those of the best full-time investment professionals and index funds.

Speaking with many folks about how they approach investing, we've noticed a distinct difference between the sexes on this issue. Perhaps because of the differences in how people are raised, testosterone levels, or whatever, men tend to have more of a problem swallowing their egos and admitting that they're better off not selecting their own individual securities. Maybe the desire to be a stock picker is genetically linked to not wanting to ask for directions!

WARNING

Investing in individual stocks entails numerous drawbacks and pitfalls:

>> **You need to spend a significant amount of time doing research.** When you're considering the purchase of an individual security, you need to know a lot about the company in which you're thinking about investing. Relevant questions to ask about the company include the following:

- What products or services does it sell?

- What are its prospects for future growth and profitability?

- How much debt does the company have?

You need to do your homework not only before you make your initial investment but also on an ongoing basis for as long as you hold the investment. Research takes your valuable free time and sometimes costs money.

>> **Your emotions will probably get in your way.** Analyzing financial statements, corporate strategy, and competitive position requires great intellect and insight. However, those skills aren't nearly enough. Will you have the stomach to hold on after what you thought was a sure-win stock plunges 20 percent, 30 percent, 40 percent, or more? Will you have the courage to dump such a stock if your new research suggests that the plummet is the beginning of the end rather than just a big bump in the road? When your money is on the line, emotions often kick in and undermine your ability to make sound long-term decisions. Few people have the psychological constitution to invest in individual stocks and handle and outfox the financial markets.

>> **You're less likely to diversify.** Unless you have tens of thousands of dollars to invest in different stocks, you probably can't cost-effectively afford to research, develop, and monitor a diversified portfolio. For example, when you're investing in stocks, you should hold companies in different industries, different companies within an industry, and so on. By not diversifying, you unnecessarily add to your risk.

>> **You'll face accounting and bookkeeping hassles.** When you invest in individual securities outside registered retirement plans, every time you sell a specific security, you must report that transaction on your tax return. Even if you pay someone else to complete your tax return, you still have the hassle of keeping track of statements and receipts.

WARNING

Of course, you may find some people (with a vested interest) who try to convince you that picking your own stocks and managing your own portfolio of stocks is easy and more profitable than investing in, say, a mutual fund or ETF. In our experience, such stock–picking cheerleaders fall into at least one of the following categories:

>> **Newsletter writers:** Whether in print, on TV, or online, some pundits pitch the notion that professional money managers are just overpaid buffoons and that you can handily trounce the pros with little of your time by simply putting your money into the pundits' stock picks. Of course, what these self-anointed gurus are really selling is either an ongoing newsletter (which can run upwards of several hundred dollars per year) or your required daily visitation of their advertising-stuffed websites. How else will you be able to keep up with their announced buy-and-sell recommendations? These supposed experts want you to be dependent on continually following their advice. (We discuss investment newsletters in Chapter 8 and websites in Chapters 20 and 21.)

>> **Book authors:** You can easily find investing books claiming that they can teach you a stock-picking strategy for beating the system. Never mind the fact that the author has no independently audited track record demonstrating her success! The book publisher of at least one investment group (Beardstown Ladies) was successfully sued over hyping and misrepresenting the group's

actual investment success. Other disreputable book authors (for example, Wade Cook) have ended up with penalties and even jail time for such unsubstantiated claims in their investment advisory or related businesses.

>> **Stockbrokers and investment advisors:** Some brokers steer you toward individual stocks for several reasons that benefit the broker and not you:

- As we discuss in Chapter 8, the high-commission brokerage firms can make handsome profits for themselves by getting you to buy stocks.

- Brokers can use changes in the company's situation to encourage you to then sell and buy different stocks, generating even more commissions.

- As with newsletter writers, this whole process forces you to be dependent on the broker, leaving you broker!

TIP

Researching individual stocks can be more than a full-time job, and if you choose to take this path, remember that you'll be competing against the professionals who do so on a full-time basis. If you derive pleasure from picking and following your own stocks, or you want an independent opinion of some stocks you currently own, useful research reports are available from Value Line (800-825-8354; www.valueline.com). We also recommend that you limit your individual stock holdings to no more than 20 percent of your overall investments.

INDIVIDUAL STOCK-DIVIDEND REINVESTMENT PLANS

Many corporations allow existing shareholders to reinvest their *dividends* (their share in company profits) in more shares of stock without paying brokerage commissions. In some cases, companies allow you to make additional cash purchases of more shares of stock, also commission-free.

In order to qualify, you must first generally buy some shares of stock through a broker (although some companies allow the initial purchases to be made directly from them). Ideally, you should purchase these initial shares through a discount broker to keep your commission burden as low as possible.

Some investment associations — including ShareOwner (www.shareowner.com) — also have plans that allow you to buy one or just a few shares to get started. You typically need to complete some forms to invest in a number of different companies' stock.

Finally, even with those companies that do sell stock directly without charging an explicit commission like a brokerage firm, you pay plenty of other fees. Many plans charge an upfront enrollment fee, fees for reinvesting dividends, and a fee when you want to sell.

Generating wealth with real estate

Over the generations, real-estate owners and investors have enjoyed rates of return comparable to those produced by the stock market, thus making real estate another time-tested method for building wealth. However, like stocks, real estate goes through good- and bad-performance periods. Most people who make money investing in real estate do so because they invest over many years and do their homework when they buy to ensure that they purchase good property in solid locations at an attractive/fair price.

TIP

Buying your own home is the best place to start investing in real estate. Your home's *equity* (the difference between the market value of the home and the loan owed on it), which builds over the years, can become a significant part of your net worth. Among other things, you can tap this equity to help finance other important personal goals, such as retirement, university (going yourself or helping your kids), and starting or buying a business. Moreover, throughout your adult life, owning a home should be less expensive than renting a comparable home. See Chapter 15 for the best ways to buy and finance real estate.

Real estate: Not your ordinary investment

Real estate differs from most other investments in several respects. Here's what makes real estate unique as an investment:

>> **You can live in it.** You can't live in a stock, bond, or mutual fund (although we suppose you could glue together a substantial fortress with all the paper some of these companies fill your mailbox with each year). Real estate is the only investment you can use (by living in it or renting it out) to produce income.

>> **Land is in limited supply.** The percentage of the Earth occupied by land is relatively constant. And because humans like to reproduce, the demand for land and housing continues to grow. Consider the areas that have the most expensive real-estate prices in the world — Hong Kong, Tokyo, Hawaii, San Francisco, and Manhattan. In these densely populated areas, little if any new land is available for building new housing.

>> **Zoning shapes potential value.** Local government regulates the zoning of property, and zoning determines what a property can be used for. In most communities these days, local zoning boards are against big growth. This position bodes well for future real-estate values. Also, know that in some cases, a particular property may not have been developed to its full potential. If you can figure out how to develop the property, you can reap large profits.

>> **You don't need a lot of cash upfront.** Real estate is also different from other investments because you can borrow a lot of money to buy it — 80 percent to 90 percent or more of the value of the property. This borrowing is known as

exercising *leverage:* With only a small investment of 10 percent to 25 percent down, you're able to purchase and own a much larger investment. When the value of your real estate goes up, you make money on your investment and on all the money you borrowed. (In case you're curious, you can leverage non-retirement-plan stock and bond investments through margin borrowing. However, you have to make a much larger "down payment" — about double to triple the percentage you need to buy real estate.)

For example, suppose you plunk down $25,000 to purchase a property for $100,000. If the property appreciates to $125,000, you make a profit of $25,000 (on paper) on your investment of just $20,000. In other words, you make a 100 percent return on your investment. But leverage cuts both ways. If your $100,000 property decreases in value to $75,000, you actually lose (on paper) 100 percent of your original $25,000 investment, even though the property value drops only 25 percent.

>> **You can discover hidden value.** In an *efficient market,* the price of an investment accurately reflects its true worth. Some investment markets are more efficient than others because of the large number of transactions and easily accessible information. Real-estate markets can be inefficient at times. Information is not always easy to come by, and you may find an ultra-motivated or uninformed seller. If you're willing to do some homework, you may be able to purchase a property below its fair market value (perhaps by as much as 10 percent to 20 percent).

Just as with any other investment, real estate has its drawbacks. For starters, buying or selling a property generally takes time and significant cost. When you're renting property, you discover firsthand the occasional headaches of being a landlord. And especially in the early years of rental-property ownership, the property's expenses may exceed the rental income, producing a net cash drain.

The best real-estate-investment options

Although real estate is unique in some ways, it's also like other types of investments in that prices are driven by supply and demand. You can invest in homes or small apartment buildings and then rent them out. In the long run, buyers of investment property hope that their rental income and the value of their properties will increase faster than their expenses.

When selecting real estate for investment purposes, remember that local economic growth is the fuel for housing demand. In addition to a vibrant and diverse job base, you want to look for limited supplies of both existing housing and land on which to build. When you identify potential properties in which you may want to invest, run the numbers to understand the cash demands of owning the property and the likely profitability. See Chapter 15 for help determining the costs of real-estate ownership.

COMPARING REAL ESTATE AND STOCKS

Real estate and stocks have historically produced comparable returns. Deciding between the two depends less on the performance of the markets than on you and your situation. Consider the following major issues when deciding which investment may be better for you:

- **The first and most important question to ask yourself is whether you're cut out to handle the responsibilities that come with being a landlord.** Real estate is a time-intensive investment (property managers can help, but their cost takes a sizable chunk of your rental income). Investing in stocks can be time-intensive as well, but it doesn't have to be if you use professionally managed mutual funds and ETFs (see Chapter 10).

- **An often-overlooked drawback to investing in real estate is that you earn no tax benefits while you're accumulating your down payment.** Registered retirement plans (see Chapter 11) give you an immediate tax deduction as you contribute money to them. If you haven't exhausted your tax-deductible contributions to these accounts, consider doing so before chasing after investment real estate.

- **Ask yourself which investments you have a better understanding of.** Some folks feel uncomfortable with stocks and funds because they don't understand them. If you have a better handle on what makes real estate tick, you have a good reason to consider investing in it.

- **Figure out what will make you happy.** Some people enjoy the challenge that comes with managing and improving rental property; it can be a bit like running a small business. If you're good at it and you have some good fortune, you can make money and derive endless hours of enjoyment.

Although few will admit it, some real-estate investors get an ego rush from a tangible display of their wealth. Sufferers of this "edifice complex" can't obtain similar pleasure from a stock portfolio detailed on a piece of paper (although others have been known to boast of their stock-picking prowess). When you want to invest directly in real estate, residential housing — such as single-family homes or small multiunit buildings — may be an attractive investment. Buying properties close to home offers the advantage of allowing you to more easily monitor and manage what's going on. The downside is that your investments will be less diversified — more of them will be dependent on the local economy.

TIP

If you don't want to be a hands-on landlord (one of the biggest drawbacks of investment real estate), consider investing in real estate through *real-estate investment trusts* (REITs). REITs are real-estate investment companies that purchase and manage a diverse portfolio of rental real estate for investors. A typical

REIT invests in one or two particular types of property, such as shopping centres, apartments, and other rental buildings. You can invest in REITs either by purchasing them directly on the major stock exchanges or by investing in a real-estate mutual fund that invests in numerous different REITs (see Chapter 10).

The worst real-estate investments

WARNING

Not all real-estate investments are good; some aren't even real investments. The bad ones are characterized by burdensome costs and problematic economic fundamentals:

>> **Limited partnerships (LPs):** Avoid LPs sold through brokers and financial consultants. LPs are inferior investment vehicles. Limited partnerships are so burdened with high sales commissions and ongoing management fees (which deplete your investment) that you can do better elsewhere. The investment salesperson who sells you such an investment stands to earn a commission of up to 10 percent or more — so only 90 cents of each dollar gets invested. Each year, LPs typically siphon off another several percent for management and other expenses. Most partnerships have little or no incentive to control costs. In fact, they have a conflict of interest that forces them to charge more to enrich the managing partners.

Unlike a mutual fund, you can't vote with your dollars. If the partnership is poorly run and expensive, you're stuck. LPs are *illiquid* (not readily convertible into cash without a substantial loss). You can't access your money until the partnership is liquidated, typically seven to ten years after you buy in.

Many of the yields on LPs have turned out to be bogus. In some cases, partnerships prop up their yields by paying back investors' principal (without telling them, of course). As for returns, well, historically too many LPs have been turkeys. The only thing limited about a limited partnership is its ability to make you money.

>> **Time-shares:** Time-shares are another nearly certain money loser. With a time-share, you buy a week or two of ownership of, essentially, the right to use a particular unit (usually a condominium in a resort location) each year. If, for example, you pay $8,000 for a week (in addition to ongoing maintenance fees), you're paying the equivalent of more than $400,000 for the whole unit, when a comparable unit nearby may sell for only $150,000. The extra markup pays the salespeople's commissions, administrative expenses, and profits for the time-share development company.

People usually get enticed into buying a time-share when they're enjoying a vacation someplace. They're easy prey for salespeople who want to sell them a souvenir of the trip. The "cheese in the mousetrap" is an offer of something free (for example, a free night's stay in a unit) for attending the sales presentation. As someone Tony once profiled in his "Me and My Money" column for *The Globe and Mail* quipped, "I went in to a room for a free piña colada, and came out with a time-share!"

If you can't live without a time-share, consider buying a used one. Usually, you'll find that many previous buyers, who more than likely have lost a good chunk of their original investment, are trying to dump their units (which should tell you something). In this case, you may be able to buy a time-share at a fair price. But why commit yourself to taking a vacation in the same location and building at the same time each year? Many time-shares let you trade your weeks for other times and other places; however, doing so is a hassle — you're charged an extra fee, and your choices are usually limited to time slots that other people don't want (that's why they're trading them!).

>> **Second homes:** The weekend getaway is a sometimes-romantic notion, and a dream of many Canadians. And when your cottage or cabin is not in use, you may be able to rent it out and earn some income to help defray the expense of keeping it up. However, most second-home owners seldom rent out their property — typically 10 percent or less of the time. As a result, second homes are usually money drains, not investments.

If you aren't going to rent out a second home most of the time, ask yourself whether you can afford such a luxury. Can you accomplish your other financial goals — saving for retirement, paying for the home in which you live, and so on — with this added expense? Even if you're successful at renting it out, the season for doing so is typically very short. Suppose you buy a lakefront cottage that isn't winterized. At best, you'll only be able to rent it during July and August, along with a few weekends in the last spring and early fall. Keeping a second home is more of a consumption than an investment decision. Few people can afford more than one home.

Investing in small business (and your career)

TIP

Small business is the leading investment through which folks have built the greatest wealth. You can invest in small business by starting one yourself (and, thus, finding yourself the best boss you've probably ever had), buying an existing business, or investing in someone else's small business. Even if small business doesn't interest you, hopefully your own job does, so in this section we present some tips on making the most of your career.

Launching your own enterprise

When you have self-discipline and a product or service you can sell, starting your own business can be both profitable and fulfilling. Consider first what skills and expertise you possess that you can use in your business. You don't need a "eureka" type of idea or invention to start a small business. Millions of people operate successful businesses that are hardly unique, such as dry cleaners, restaurants, tax-preparation firms, and so on.

TIP

Begin exploring your idea by first developing a written business plan. Such a plan should detail your product or service, how you're going to market it, your potential customers and competitors, and the economics of the business, including the start-up costs.

Of all the small-business investment options, starting your own business involves the most work. Although you can do this work on a part-time basis in the beginning, most people end up running their businesses full-time — it's your new job, career, or whatever you want to call it.

We've both been running our own businesses for most of our working years, and we wouldn't trade that experience for the corporate life. That's not to say that running our own businesses doesn't have its drawbacks and down moments. But in our experience dealing with small-business owners, we've seen many people of varied backgrounds, interests, and skills succeed and be happy with running their own businesses.

In most people's eyes, starting a new business is the riskiest of all small-business investment options. But if you're going into a business that uses your skills and expertise, the risk isn't nearly as great as you may think. Many businesses can be started with little cash by leveraging your existing skills and expertise. You can build a valuable company and job if you have the time to devote. As long as you check out the competition and offer a valued service at a reasonable cost, the principal risk with your business comes from not doing a good job marketing what you have to offer. If you can market your skills and have a plan to get through the inevitable economic down cycles that affect every business, you're home free.

TIP

As long as you're thinking about the risks of starting a business, consider the risks of staying in a job you don't enjoy or that doesn't challenge or fulfill you. If you never take the plunge, you may regret that you didn't pursue your dreams.

Buying an existing business

If you don't have a specific product or service you want to sell, but you're skilled at managing and improving the operations of a company, buying a small business may be for you. Finding and buying a good small business takes much time and patience, so be willing to devote at least several months to the search. You may also need to enlist financial and legal advisors to help inspect the company, look over its financial statements, and hammer out a contract.

Although you don't have to go through the riskier start-up period if you buy a small business, you'll likely need more capital to buy an established enterprise. You'll also need to be able to deal with stickier personnel and management issues. The history of the organization and the way things work will predate your ownership of the business. If you don't like making hard decisions, firing people who don't fit with your plans, and coercing people into changing the way they do things, buying an existing business likely isn't for you.

WARNING

Some people perceive buying an existing business as being safer than starting a new one. Buying someone else's business may actually be riskier. You're likely to shell out far more money upfront, in the form of a down payment, to buy an existing business. If you don't have the ability to run the business and it does poorly, you have more to lose financially. In addition, the business may be for sale for a reason — it may not be very profitable, it may be in decline, or it may generally be a pain in the neck to operate.

Good businesses don't come cheap. If the business is a success, the current owner has already removed the start-up risk from the business, so the price of the business should be at a premium to reflect this lack of risk. When you have the capital to buy an established business and you have the skills to run it, consider going this route.

Investing in someone else's small business

Are you someone who likes the idea of profiting from successful small businesses but doesn't want the day-to-day headaches of being responsible for managing the enterprise? Then investing in someone else's small business may be for you. Although this route may seem easier, few people are actually cut out to be investors in other people's businesses. The reason: Finding and analyzing opportunities isn't easy.

Are you astute at evaluating corporate financial statements and business strategies? Investing in a small, privately held company has much in common with investing in a publicly traded firm (as is the case when you buy stock), but it also has a few differences. One difference is that private firms aren't required to produce comprehensive, audited financial statements that adhere to certain accounting principles. So, you have a greater risk of not having sufficient or accurate information when evaluating a small, private firm.

Another difference is that unearthing private, small-business investing opportunities is harder. The best private companies who are seeking investors generally don't advertise. Instead, they find prospective investors through networking with people such as business advisors. You can increase your chances of finding private companies to invest in by speaking with tax, legal, and financial advisors who work with small businesses. You can also find interesting opportunities through your own contacts or experience within a given industry.

Don't consider investing in someone else's business unless you can afford to lose all of what you're investing. Also, you should have sufficient assets so that what you're investing in small, privately held companies represents only a small portion (20 percent or less) of your total financial assets.

Investing in your career

In working with clients and from observing friends and colleagues over the years, we've witnessed plenty of people succeed working for employers. So, we don't want to leave you with the impression that financial success requires starting, buying, or investing in someone else's small business.

You can and should invest in your career. Some time-tested, proven ways to do that include

>> **Networking:** Some people wait to network until they've been laid off or they're really hungry to change jobs. Take an interest in what others do for a living, and you'll learn and grow from the experience, even if you choose to stay with your current employer or in your chosen field. In addition to personal networking, create an account on LinkedIn (`www.linkedin.com`).

>> **Continuing your education:** Whether it's through reading quality books or other publications or taking some night courses, find ways to build on your knowledge base.

>> **Weighing the risk in the status quo:** Many folks are resistant to change and get anxious thinking about what could go wrong when taking a new risk. We know when we were ready to walk away from our jobs with prestigious organizations and open our own businesses, a number of relatives and friends thought we'd lost our marbles. That's not to say that they didn't have some valid concerns; they just weren't really considering the risks inherent in our staying put and didn't see the upside of our small-business ventures.

Off the Beaten Path: Investment Odds and Ends

The investments that we discuss in this section sometimes belong on their own planet (because they're neither ownership nor lending vehicles). Here are the basics on these other common, but odd, investments.

Precious metals

Gold and silver have been used by many civilizations as currency or a medium of exchange. One advantage of precious metals as a currency is that they can't be debased by the government. With paper currency, such as the Canadian or U.S. dollars, the government can simply print more. This process can lead to the devaluation of a currency and inflation.

Holdings of gold and silver can provide a so-called *hedge* against inflation. In the late 1970s and early 1980s, inflation rose dramatically in North America. This largely unexpected rise in inflation depressed stocks and bonds. Gold and silver, however, rose tremendously in value — in fact, more than 500 percent (even after adjusting for inflation) from 1972 to 1980 (see Chapter 8). Such periods are unusual. Precious metals produced decent returns in the 2000s, but, after peaking in 2011, prices fell steeply.

Over many decades, precious metals tend to be lousy investments. Their rate of return tends to keep up with the rate of inflation but not surpass it.

TIP

When you want to invest in precious metals as a hedge against inflation, your best option is to do so through mutual funds or ETFs (see Chapter 10). Don't purchase precious-metals futures. They're not investments; they're short-term gambles on which way gold or silver prices may head over a short period of time. We also recommend staying away from firms and shops that sell coins and *bullion* (bars of gold or silver). Even if you can find a legitimate firm (not an easy task), the cost of storing and insuring gold and silver is quite costly. You won't get good value for your money — markups can be substantial.

Bitcoin and other cryptocurrencies

Perhaps you've heard of Bitcoin, the online "currency." We find that far more young adults know about it than older folks do. That makes sense because it's a digital currency used for Internet transactions.

Increasingly, Bitcoin has been in the news and making news more and more as its price climbs to ever dizzying higher heights. In December 2017, the price of a Bitcoin neared the $20,000 mark.

So, what exactly is Bitcoin? For starters, it's not actually a coin — calling it a coin is a way to make it sound like a real currency. Bitcoin and other similar cryptocurrencies only exist in the online world. Bitcoin's creators have limited the number of Bitcoins that can be "mined" and put into online circulation to about 21 million (more on mining later in this section).

As its promoters have talked up its usefulness and dizzying rise, many people who have Bitcoins continue to hold onto them in the hopes that the price will keep rising. Like shares of stock in the next Amazon or Apple, its owners and promoters are hoping and expecting for further steep price increases. People don't hoard real currencies with similar pie-in-the-sky hopes for large investment returns.

Online Bitcoin transactions can be done anonymously, and they can't be contested, disputed, or reversed. So, if you buy something using Bitcoin and have a problem with the item you bought, that's too bad — you have no recourse, unlike, for example, with a purchase made on your credit card. The clandestine nature of cryptocurrencies makes them attractive to folks trying to hide money or engage in illegal activities (for example, criminals, drug dealers, and so on).

In May 2018, about $375 billion was tied up in these cryptocurrencies according to CoinMarketCap (http://coinmarketcap.com), which now tracks about 1,600 cryptocurrencies. Over the previous years, Bitcoin's market share has dropped from nearly 90 percent to about 35 percent. CoinMarketCap tracks the 100 largest cryptocurrencies as measured by their market capitalizations — number 100 on the list recently had a market cap of about $160 million.

So, what is a given cryptocurrency like Bitcoin worth? Cryptocurrencies have no inherent value. Let's contrast that with gold. Not only has gold had a long history of being used as a medium of exchange (currency), but gold has commercial and industrial uses. Plus, gold costs real money to mine out of the ground, which provides a floor of support under the price of gold in the range of $800 to $900 per ounce, not far below the recent price of gold at about $1,280 per ounce. (Bitcoin has a made-up "mining process" whereby you need special computer equipment and end up using a bunch of electricity to solve complex math problems.)

The supply of Bitcoin is currently artificially limited. And Bitcoin is hardly unique — it's one of hundreds of cryptocurrencies. So, if another cryptocurrency or two or three is easier to use online and perceived as attractive (in part because it's far less expensive), Bitcoin will eventually tumble in value.

Ethereum is the second most popular cryptocurrency as people discover that it allows for incorporating *smart contracts,* which are computer-based and enforced contracts that delineate specific conditions that must be met in order for the transaction to be completed.

Even though Bitcoin has been the most popular cryptocurrency in recent years, few merchants actually accept it. And, to add insult to injury, Bitcoin users get whacked with unfavourable conversion rates, which adds greatly to the effective price of items bought with Bitcoin.

We can't tell you what will happen to Bitcoin's price next month, next year, or next decade. But we can tell that it has virtually no inherent value as a digital currency, so those paying thousands of dollars for a Bitcoin will eventually be very disappointed. With more than 1,500 of these cryptocurrencies, the field keeps growing as creators hope to get in on the ground floor of the next cryptocurrency, which they hope will soar in value.

According to a recent *Wall Street Journal* investigation, "Hundreds of technology firms raising money in the fevered market for cryptocurrencies are using deceptive or even fraudulent tactics to lure investors. . . . *The Wall Street Journal* has found 271 with red flags that include plagiarized investor documents, promises of guaranteed returns, and missing or fake executive teams."

Annuities

Annuities are a peculiar type of insurance and investment product. They're a sort of savings-type account with slightly higher yields, and they're backed by insurance companies. *Fixed annuities* pay a preset interest rate determined by the insurance company. This rate is typically set one year ahead at a time. *Variable annuities'* return varies over time depending on the returns provided by the investments chosen within the annuity offerings.

As with other types of registered retirement plans, money placed in an annuity compounds without taxation until it's withdrawn. Plus, similar to money contributed to a Registered Retirement Savings Plan (RRSP) or used to purchase a registered GIC, you can also get an upfront tax break by purchasing a registered deferred annuity. you don't receive upfront tax breaks on contributions you make to an annuity. Ongoing investment expenses also tend to be much higher than in RRSPs. So, consider an annuity generally only after you fully fund tax-deductible registered retirement plans.

There's one other possible personal use for annuities: Those nearing or in retirement with limited resources can insure against the risk of outliving their assets by buying an annuity and annuitizing it — again, at a cost, so proceed carefully. For more help on deciding whether to invest in an annuity, see Chapter 13.

Collectibles

The collectibles category is a catchall for antiques, art, autographs, baseball cards, clocks, coins, comic books, diamonds, dolls, gems, photographs, rare books, rugs, stamps, vintage wine, and writing utensils — in other words, any material object that, through some kind of human manipulation, has become more valuable to certain humans.

WARNING

Notwithstanding the few people who discover on *Antiques Roadshow* that they own an antique of significant value, collectibles are generally lousy investment vehicles. Dealer markups are enormous, maintenance and protection costs are draining, research is time-consuming, and people's tastes are quite fickle. All this for returns that, after you factor in the huge markups, rarely keep up with inflation.

TIP

Buy collectibles for your love of the object, not for financial gain. Treat collecting as a hobby rather than as an investment. When buying a collectible, try to avoid the big markups by cutting out the middlemen. Buy directly from the artist or producer if you can.

Chapter **10**

Investing in Funds

When you invest in a mutual fund or its close sibling, an exchange-traded fund (ETF) that trades on a stock exchange, an investment company pools your money with the money of many other like-minded individuals and invests it in stocks, bonds, and other securities. Think of it as a big investment club without the meetings! When you invest through a typical fund, several hundred million to billions of dollars are typically invested along with your money.

If you're thinking of joining the club, read on to discover the benefits of investing in mutual funds and ETFs and the types of funds available (see Chapter 9 for a discussion of alternatives to mutual funds and ETFs). In this chapter, we advise you on analyzing and choosing your *funds* (a term we use to generally describe both mutual funds and ETFs), explain how to track your investments, and help you decide when to sell.

Understanding the Benefits of Mutual Funds and Exchange-Traded Funds

Mutual funds and ETFs rank right up there with microwave ovens, sticky notes, and smartphones as some of the best modern inventions. Here are the benefits you receive when you invest in mutual funds and ETFs:

>> **Professional management:** Mutual funds and ETFs are managed by a portfolio manager and research team whose full-time jobs are to screen the universe of investments for those that best meet each fund's stated objectives. These professionals call and visit companies, analyze companies' financial statements, and speak with companies' suppliers and customers. In short, the team does more research and analysis than you can ever hope to do in your free time.

Fund managers are typically graduates of the top business and finance schools in the country, where they learn the principles of portfolio management and securities valuation and selection. The best fund managers typically have at least a decade of experience in analyzing and selecting investments; many measure their experience in decades rather than years.

>> **Low fees:** The most efficiently managed stock mutual funds charge you less than 2 percent per year in fees, and bond and money-market funds cost even less. ETFs are even cheaper, costing less than 1 percent. Because funds typically buy or sell tens of thousands of shares of a security at a time, the percentage of commissions these funds pay is far less than what you pay to buy or sell a few hundred shares on your own. In addition, when you buy a *no-load fund,* you avoid paying sales commissions (known as *loads*) on your transactions. We discuss these types of funds throughout this chapter. You can buy an ETF for a low transaction fee through the best online brokers (see Chapter 19).

>> **Diversification:** Fund investing enables you to achieve a level of diversification that's difficult to reach without having tens of thousands of dollars and a lot of time to invest. If you go it alone, you should invest money in at least 8 to 12 different securities in different industries to ensure that your portfolio can withstand a downturn in one or more of the investments. Proper diversification allows a fund to receive the highest possible return at the lowest possible risk given its objectives. The most unfortunate investors during major stock-market downswings have been individuals who had all their money riding on only a few stocks that plunged in price by 90 percent or more.

>> **Low cost of entry:** Most mutual funds have low minimum-investment requirements, especially if you're investing inside a Registered Retirement Savings Plan (RRSP). (ETFs essentially have no minimum, although you don't

want to do transactions involving small amounts because the brokerage fee takes up a larger percentage of your investment amount.) Even if you have a lot of money to invest, consider funds for the low-cost, high-quality money-management services they provide.

>> **Audited performance records and expenses:** In their prospectuses, all funds are required to disclose historical data on returns, operating expenses, and other fees. Each province's securities regulators are charged with checking these disclosures for accuracy. Also, several organizations (such as Globefund and Morningstar) report hundreds of fund statistics, allowing comparisons of performance, risk, and many other factors.

>> **Flexibility in risk level:** Among the different funds, you can choose a level of risk that you're comfortable with and that meets your personal and financial goals. If you want your money to grow over a long period of time, you may want to select funds that invest more heavily in stocks. If you need current income and don't want investments that fluctuate in value as widely as stocks, you may choose more-conservative bond funds. If you want to be sure that your invested principal doesn't drop in value (perhaps because you may need your money in the short term), you can select a money-market fund.

Exploring Various Fund Types

REMEMBER

When fund companies package and market funds, the names they give their funds aren't always completely accurate or comprehensive. For example, a stock fund may not be *totally* invested in stocks. Twenty percent of it may be invested in bonds. Don't assume that a fund invests exclusively in Canadian companies, either — it may invest in international firms, as well.

Note: If you haven't yet read Chapters 8 and 9, which provide an overview of investment concepts and vehicles, doing so can enhance your understanding of the rest of this chapter.

Money-market funds

Money-market funds are generally considered the safest type of mutual funds and ETFs (although not insured or guaranteed) for people concerned about losing their invested dollars. As with bank savings accounts, the value of your original investment does not fluctuate. (For more background on the advantages of money-market funds, see Chapter 10.)

General-purpose money-market funds invest in safe, short-term guaranteed investment certificates (GICs), Government of Canada Treasury bills, and *corporate commercial paper* (short-term debt), which is issued by the largest and most creditworthy companies.

Since their origination in the early 1970s, money-market funds have a track record of being extremely safe. The risk difference compared to a bank account is nil. Hundreds of billions of dollars have flowed into and out of money-market funds over the decades without any retail investors losing principal. Only twice have funds broken the buck (one by 6 percent, the other by 3 percent), and both these funds were American and used by institutional investors.

Money-market funds can only invest in the most creditworthy securities and must have an average maturity of less than 120 days. In the unlikely event that an investment in a money-market fund's portfolio goes sour, the mutual-fund company that stands behind the money-market fund will almost certainly cover the loss.

TIP

If the lack of insurance on money-market funds still spooks you, select a money-market fund that invests exclusively in Government of Canada. Government securities, which are virtually risk-free because they're backed by the full strength and credit of the federal government. These types of accounts typically pay less interest.

Bond funds

Bonds are IOUs. When you buy a newly issued bond, you typically lend your money to a corporation or government agency. A bond fund is nothing more than a large group of bonds.

Bond funds typically invest in bonds of similar *maturity* (the number of years that elapse before the borrower must pay back the money you lend). The names of most bond funds include a word or two that provides clues about the average length of maturity of their bonds. For example, a *short-term bond fund* typically concentrates its investments in bonds maturing in the next one to three years. An *intermediate-term bond fund* generally holds bonds that come due within three to ten years. The bonds in a *long-term bond fund* usually mature in more than ten years.

In contrast to an individual bond that you buy and hold until it matures, a bond fund is always replacing bonds in its portfolio to maintain its average maturity objective. Therefore, if you know that you absolutely, positively must have a certain principal amount back on a particular date, individual bonds may be more appropriate than a bond fund.

TIP

Bond funds are useful when you want to live off interest income or you don't want to put all your money in riskier investments such as stocks and real estate (perhaps because you plan to use the money soon). Also, making small incremental investments in a bond fund is easier, as opposed to the cost of buying a single individual bond, which can be many thousands of dollars. Bonds are among the most inefficient parts of the securities markets. Most individuals can't easily determine the bonds' true value and pay steep markups or markdowns, all of which a larger institutional trader (like a mutual fund) can more easily avoid.

Stock funds

Stock funds, as their name implies, invest in stocks. These funds are often referred to as *equity funds. Equity* — not to be confused with equity in real estate — is another word for stocks. Stock funds are often categorized by the type of stocks they primarily invest in.

Stock types are first defined by size of company (small, medium, or large). The total market value *(capitalization)* of a company's outstanding stock determines its size. Small and midsize Canadian company stocks, for example, are usually defined as companies with total market capitalization of less than $500 million. (Contrast that with the United States, where small-company stocks are generally seen as companies with total market capitalization of less than $1 billion.) Stocks are further categorized as growth or value stocks:

>> **Growth stocks** represent companies that are experiencing rapidly expanding revenues and profits and typically have high stock prices relative to their current earnings or asset (book) values. These companies tend to reinvest most of their earnings in their infrastructure to fuel future expansion. Thus, growth stocks typically pay low dividends. (See the later "Dividends" section for more information.)

>> **Value stocks** are at the other end of the spectrum. Value-stock investors look for good buys. They want to invest in stocks that are cheaply priced in relation to the profits per share and *book value* (assets less liabilities) of the company. Value stocks are usually less volatile than growth stocks.

These categories are combined in various ways to describe how a mutual fund invests its money. One fund may focus on large-company growth stocks, while another fund may limit itself to small-company value stocks. Funds are further classified by the geographical focus of their investments: Canadian, U.S., international, worldwide, and so on (see the section "Canadian, U.S., international, and global funds").

Balancing bonds and stocks: Hybrid funds

Hybrid funds invest in a mixture of different types of securities. Most commonly, they invest in bonds and stocks. These funds are usually less risky and volatile than funds that invest exclusively in stocks. In an economic downturn, bonds usually hold up in value better than stocks do. However, during good economic times when the stock market is booming, the bond portions of these funds tend to drag down their performance a bit.

Hybrid mutual funds are typically known as *balanced funds*, which generally try to maintain a fairly constant percentage of investments in stocks and bonds, or *asset-allocation funds*, which tend to adjust the mix of different investments according to the portfolio manager's expectations of the market. Of course, exceptions do exist — some balanced funds make major shifts in their allocations, whereas some asset-allocation funds maintain a relatively fixed mix.

REMEMBER

Most funds that shift money around instead of staying put in good investments rarely beat the market averages over a number of years.

There are also now increasing numbers of *target-maturity funds* (also known as *target-date funds* or *retirement-date funds*), which tend to decrease their risk (and stock allocation) over time. Such funds appeal to investors who are approaching a particular future goal, such as retirement or a child's university education, and want their fund to automatically adjust as that date approaches.

TIP

Hybrid funds are a way to make fund investing simple. They give you extensive diversification across a variety of investing options. They also make it easier for stock-skittish investors to invest in stocks while avoiding the high volatility of pure stock funds.

Canadian, U.S., international, and global funds

Unless they have words like *international, global, worldwide,* or *world* in their names, most Canadian funds focus their investments in Canada. But even funds without one of these terms attached may invest money internationally.

TIP

The only way to know for sure where a fund is currently invested (or where the fund may invest in the future) is to investigate. You can start by calling the toll-free number of the fund company you're interested in. A fund's annual report (which often can be found on the fund company's website) also details where the fund is investing (the prospectus will also detail where the fund can be invested).

FUNDS OF FUNDS

An increasing number of fund providers are responding to overwhelmed investors by offering a simplified way to construct a portfolio: a fund that diversifies across numerous other funds — or a *fund of funds*. When a fund of funds is done right, it helps focus fund investors on the important big-picture issue of asset allocation — how much of your investment money you put into bonds versus stocks. Although the best funds of funds appear to deliver a high-quality, diversified portfolio of funds in one fell swoop, funds of funds are not all created equal, and not all are worthy of your investment dollars.

The fund of funds idea isn't new. In fact, the concept has been around for many years. High fees gave the earlier funds of funds, run in the United States in the 1950s by the late Bernie Cornfeld, a bad name. Cornfeld established a fund of funds outside the United States and tacked on many layers of fees. Although the funds were profitable for his enterprise, duped investors suffered a continual drain of high fees. The Cornfeld episode is an important reason why regulators have generally been careful in approving new funds of funds.

When a fund has the term *international* or *foreign* in its name, it typically means that the fund invests anywhere in the world *except* Canada. The term *worldwide* or *global* generally implies that a fund invests everywhere in the world, *including* Canada.

Index funds

Index funds are funds that can be (and are, for the most part) managed by a computer. An index fund's assets are invested to replicate an existing market index such as the Toronto Stock Exchange's S&P/TSX Index, or the Standard & Poor's 500, an index of 500 large U.S. company stocks. (Some ETFs are index funds with the added twist that they trade on a major stock exchange.)

Over long periods (ten years or more), index funds outperform about three-quarters of their peers! How is that possible? How can a computer making mindless, predictable decisions beat an intelligent, creative, MBA-endowed portfolio manager with a crack team of research analysts scouring the market for the best securities? The answer is largely cost. The computer doesn't demand a high salary or need a big corner office. And index funds don't need a team of research analysts.

Most active fund managers can't overcome the handicap of high operating expenses that pull down their funds' rates of return. As we discuss later in this chapter, operating expenses include all the fees and profit that a mutual fund extracts from a fund's returns before the returns are paid to you. For example, the average Canadian stock fund has an operating expense ratio of 2.5 percent per year. So, a Canadian stock index fund (or its peer ETF, which is an index fund that trades on a stock exchange) with an expense ratio of just 1 percent per year has an advantage of 1.5 percent per year.

Another not-so-inconsequential advantage of index funds is that they can't underperform the market. Some funds do just that because of the burden of high fees and/or poor management. For money invested outside retirement plans, index funds have an added advantage: Lower taxable capital gains distributions are made to shareholders because less trading of securities is conducted and a more stable portfolio is maintained.

Yes, index funds may seem downright boring. When you invest in them, you give up the opportunity to brag to others about your shrewd investments that beat the market averages. On the other hand, with a low-cost index fund, you have no chance of doing much worse than the market (which more than a few mutual-fund managers do).

TIP

Index funds and ETFs make sense for a portion of your investments, because beating the market is difficult for portfolio managers. Here are the lowest-cost providers of these funds:

>> BlackRock, whose funds go by the iShares name (866-474-2737; www. blackrock.com/ca)

>> Horizons Exchange Traded Funds (866-641-5739; www.horizonsetfs.com)

>> TD e-Series Funds (800-640-2150; www.td.com/ca/products-services/ investing-at-td)

>> Vanguard (www.vanguardcanada.ca)

Specialty (sector) funds

Specialty funds don't fit neatly into the previous categories. These funds are often known as *sector funds*, because they tend to invest in securities in specific industries.

WARNING

In most cases, you should avoid investing in specialty funds. Investing in stocks of a single industry defeats one of the major purposes of investing in funds: diversification. Another good reason to avoid specialty funds is that they tend to carry much higher expenses than other funds.

IDENTIFYING SOCIALLY RESPONSIBLE FUNDS

Select funds label themselves *socially responsible.* This term means different things to different people. In most cases, though, it implies that the fund avoids investing in companies whose products or services harm people or the world at large — tobacco manufacturers, for example. Because cigarettes and other tobacco products kill hundreds of thousands of people and add billions of dollars to healthcare costs, most socially responsible funds shun tobacco companies. The term *socially responsible* can also include investing only in companies with fair labour practises, such as not using child workers, providing decent and safe working conditions, limiting the maximum hours per week, paying overtime, and so on.

Socially responsible investing presents some challenges. For example, your definition of *social responsibility* may not match the definition offered by the investment manager who's running a fund. Another problem is that, even if you can agree on what's socially irresponsible (such as selling tobacco products), funds aren't always as clean as you would think or hope. Even though a fund avoids tobacco manufacturers, it may well invest in retailers that sell tobacco products. Another drawback is that these funds tend to have higher-than-average costs, even when they take an indexing approach.

If you want to consider a socially responsible fund, review the fund's recent annual report, which lists the specific investments the fund owns. Also, consider giving directly to charities (and getting a tax deduction) instead.

TIP

Specialty funds that invest in real estate or precious metals may make sense for a small portion (10 percent or less) of your investment portfolio. These types of funds can help diversify your portfolio, because they can do better during times of higher inflation.

Selecting the Best Funds

When you go camping in the wilderness, you can do a number of things to maximize your chances for happiness and success. You can take maps and a GPS to keep you on course, food for nourishment, proper clothing to stay dry and warm, and some first-aid gear to treat minor injuries. But regardless of how much advance preparation you do, you may have a problematic experience. You may take the wrong trail, trip on a rock and break your ankle, or lose your food to a tenacious bear that comes romping through camp one night.

And so it is with funds. Although most fund investors are rewarded for their efforts, you get no guarantees. You can, however, follow some simple, common-sense guidelines to help keep you on the trail and increase your odds of investment success and happiness. The issues in the following sections are the main ones to consider.

Reading prospectuses and annual reports

Fund companies produce information that can help you make decisions about fund investments. Every fund is required to issue a *prospectus*. This legal document is reviewed and audited by securities regulators. The most valuable information — the fund's investment objectives, costs, performance history, and primary risks — is summarized in the first few pages of the prospectus. Make sure that you read this part. Skip the rest, which is composed mostly of tedious legal details. Funds also produce what's called a *simplified prospectus,* which is an abbreviated version of the full-length prospectus and hits the important highlights.

A better starting point are *Fund Facts,* three- to four-page summaries available directly from fund companies and on their websites. Not only do Fund Facts contain a great deal of useful information, but they're typically written in easy-to-understand language. As their name implies, these reports will help you quickly understand many key facts about a fund and assist you in assessing how well a particular fund may or may not meet your needs and circumstances.

In particular, a Fund Facts document details the following:

>> The costs to you of buying and owning the fund

>> The percentage of the fees you'll pay that would go to your advisor

>> The fund's relative level of risk

>> What the fund holds as investments

>> Up to ten years of the fund's annual returns

Funds also produce *annual reports,* which discuss how the fund has been doing and provide details on the specific investments a fund holds. If, for example, you want to know which countries an international fund invests in, you can find this information in the fund's annual report.

Keeping costs low

The charges you pay to buy or sell a fund, as well as the fund's ongoing operating expenses, can have a big impact on the rate of return you earn on your investments. Many novice investors pay too much attention to a fund's prior performance (in the case of stock funds) or to the fund's current yield (in the case of bond funds) and too little attention to fees. Doing so is dangerous because a fund can inflate its return or yield in many risky ways. Plus, what worked yesterday may flop tomorrow.

Fund costs are an important factor in the return you earn from a fund. Fees are deducted from your investment. All other things being equal, high fees and other charges depress your returns. What are a fund's fees, you ask? Good question — read on to find the answers.

Eliminating loads

Loads are upfront or ongoing annual commissions paid to brokers who sell mutual funds. Loads typically range from 2 percent to as high as 7 percent or 8 percent of your investment. Sales loads have two problems:

>> **They're an extra cost that drags down your investment returns.** Because commissions are paid to the salesperson and not to the fund manager, the manager of a load fund doesn't work any harder and isn't any more qualified than a manager of a no-load fund. Common sense suggests, and studies confirm, that load funds perform *worse,* on average, than no-load funds when factoring in the load, because the load charge is subtracted from your payment before your payment is invested.

>> **The power of self-interest can bias your broker's advice.** Although this issue is rarely discussed, it's even more problematic than the issue of sales loads. Brokers who work for a commission are interested in selling you commission-based investment products; therefore, *their* best interests often conflict with *your* best interests.

Although you may be mired in high-interest debt or underfunding your retirement plan, salespeople almost never advise you to pay off your credit cards or put more money into your employer's pension plan. To get you to buy, they tend to exaggerate the potential benefits and obscure the risks and drawbacks of what they sell. They don't take the time to educate investors. We've seen too many people purchase investment products through brokers without understanding what they're buying, how much risk they're taking, and how these investments will affect their overall financial lives.

WARNING

TIP

Invest in no-load funds. The only way to be sure that a fund is truly no-load is to look at the prospectus for the fund. Only there, in black and white and without marketing hype, must the truth be told about sales charges and other fund fees. When you want investing advice, hire a financial advisor on a fee-for-service basis (see Chapter 19), which should cost less and minimize potential conflicts of interest.

Minimizing operating expenses

All funds charge ongoing fees. The fees pay for the operational costs of running the fund — employees' salaries, marketing, website development and maintenance, staffing the toll-free phone lines, printing and mailing published materials, computers for tracking investments and account balances, accounting fees, and so on. Despite being labeled "expenses," the profit a fund company earns for running the fund is added to the tab as well.

The fund's operating expenses are quoted as an annual percentage of your investment and are essentially invisible to you, because they're deducted before you're paid any return. The expenses are charged on a daily basis, so you don't need to worry about trying to get out of a fund before these fees are deducted. You can find a fund's operating expenses in the fund's prospectus. Look in the "Expenses" section and find a line that says something like "Total Fund Operating Expenses." You can also call the fund's toll-free number and ask a representative.

TIP

Within a given sector of funds (for example, money market, short-term bond, or international stock), funds with low annual operating fees can more easily produce higher total returns for you. Although expenses matter on all funds, some types of funds are more sensitive to high expenses than others. Expenses are critical on money-market funds and very important on bond funds. Fund managers already have a hard time beating the averages in these markets; with higher expenses added on, beating the averages is nearly impossible.

With stock funds, expenses are a less important (but still significant) factor in a fund's performance. Don't forget that, over time, stocks average returns of about 10 percent per year. So, if one stock fund charges 1 percent more in operating expenses than another fund, you're already giving up an extra 10 percent of your expected returns.

Some people argue that investing in stock funds that charge high expenses may be justified if those funds generate higher rates of return. However, evidence doesn't show that these stock funds actually generate higher returns. In fact, funds with higher operating expenses tend to produce *lower* rates of return. This trend makes sense, because operating expenses are deducted from the returns a fund generates.

REMEMBER

Stick with funds that maintain low total operating expenses and don't charge loads. Both types of fees come out of your pocket and reduce your rate of return. You have no reason to pay a lot for the best funds. (In Chapters 12 and 13, we provide some specific fund recommendations as well as sample portfolios for investors in different situations.)

Evaluating historic performance

A fund's *performance* (historic rate of return) is another factor to weigh when selecting a fund. As all funds are supposed to tell you, past performance is no guarantee of future results. An analysis of historic fund performance proves that some of yesterday's stars turn into tomorrow's skid-row bums.

Many former high-return funds achieved their results by taking on high risk. Funds that assume higher risk should produce higher rates of return. But high-risk funds usually decline in price faster during major market declines. Thus, in order for a fund to be considered a *best* fund, it must consistently deliver a favourable rate of return given the degree of risk it takes.

TIP

When assessing an individual fund, compare its performance and volatility over an extended period of time (five or ten years will do) to a relevant market index. For example, compare funds that focus on investing in large Canadian companies to the S&P/TSX Index. For large U.S. companies, look at the S&P 500 Index. Compare funds that invest in U.S. stocks of all sizes to the Dow Jones U.S. Total Stock Market Index. Indexes also exist for bonds, foreign stock markets, and almost any other type of security you can imagine.

Assessing fund-manager and fund-family reputations

Much is made of who manages a specific mutual fund. As Peter Lynch, the retired and famous former manager of the Fidelity Magellan fund, said, "The financial press made us Wall Street types into celebrities, a notoriety that was largely undeserved. Stock stars were treated as rock stars. . . ."

Although the individual fund manager is important, no fund manager is an island. The resources and capabilities of the parent company are equally important. Different companies have different capabilities and levels of expertise in relation to the different types of funds.

TIP

When you're considering a particular fund, examine the performance history and fees not only of that fund but also of similar foreign-stock funds at the same company. If the company's other foreign-stock funds have done poorly, or it offers no other foreign-stock funds, those are strikes against the fund you're looking at.

Also, be aware that "star" fund managers tend to be associated with higher-expense funds to help pay their rock-star salaries. And star managers tend to leave or get hired away after several years of stellar performance, so you may not be getting the manager who created that good past performance in the first place. Index and asset class funds that use a team approach avoid this issue.

Rating tax-friendliness

Investors often overlook tax implications when selecting mutual funds to hold outside tax-sheltered accounts such as RRSPs, Registered Retirement Income Funds (RRIFs), Registered Education Savings Plan (RESPs), or Tax-Free Savings Accounts (TFSAs). Numerous funds effectively reduce their shareholders' returns because of their tendency to produce more taxable distributions — that is, capital gains and dividends. (See the "Dividends" and "Capital gains" sections later in this chapter.)

Fund capital-gains distributions have an impact on an investor's after-tax rate of return. All fund managers buy and sell stocks over the course of a year. Whenever a fund manager sells securities, any gain or loss from those securities must be distributed to fund shareholders. Securities sold at a loss can offset securities sold at a profit. When a fund manager has a tendency to cash in more winners than losers, investors in the fund receive taxable gains. So, even though some funds can lay claim to producing higher total returns, *after* you factor in taxes, they actually may not produce higher total returns.

Choosing funds that minimize capital-gains distributions helps you defer taxes on your profits. By allowing your capital to continue compounding as it would in a tax-sheltered registered retirement plan, you receive a higher total return. When you're a long-term investor, you benefit most from choosing funds that minimize capital-gains distributions. The more years that appreciation can compound without being taxed, the greater the value to you as the investor.

TIP

If you're purchasing shares in funds outside tax-sheltered retirement plans or accounts, consider the time of year when making your purchases. December is the most common month in which funds make capital-gains distributions. When making purchases late in the year, ask if the fund may make a significant capital-gains distribution. Consider delaying purchases in such funds until after the distribution date.

Determining your needs and goals

Selecting the best funds for you requires an understanding of your investment goals and risk tolerance. What may be a good fund for your next-door neighbour may not necessarily be a good fund for you. You have a unique financial profile.

REMEMBER

If you've already determined your needs and goals, terrific! If you haven't, refer to Chapter 4. Understanding yourself is a good part of the battle. But don't short-change yourself by not being educated about the investment you're considering. If you don't understand what you're investing in and how much risk you're taking, stay out of the game.

Deciphering Your Fund's Performance

REMEMBER

As a fund investor, you can't simply calculate your return by comparing the share price of the fund today to the share price you originally paid. Why not? Because funds make distributions of dividends and capital gains, which, when reinvested, give you more shares of the fund.

Even if you don't reinvest distributions, they create an accounting problem, because they reduce the share price of a fund. (Otherwise, you can make a profit from the distribution by buying into a fund just before a distribution is made.) Therefore, over time, following just the share price of your fund doesn't tell you how much money you've made or lost.

TIP

The only way to figure out exactly how much you've made or lost on your investment is to compare the total value of your holdings in the fund today with the total dollar amount you originally invested. If you invested chunks of money at various points in time and you want to factor in the timing of your various investments, this exercise becomes complicated. (Check out our investment website, app, and software recommendations in Chapter 20 if you want to harness technology to help you crunch the numbers.)

The *total return* of a fund is the percentage change of your investment over a specified period. For example, a fund may tell you that in 2017, its total return was 15 percent. Therefore, if you invested $10,000 in the fund on the last day of 2016, your investment would be worth $11,500 at the end of 2017. To find out a fund's total return, you can visit the company's website, call the fund company's toll-free number, or read the fund's annual report.

The following three components make up your total return on a fund:

» Dividends (including interest paid by money-market or bond funds)

» Capital-gains distributions

» Share-price changes

In short, you calculate a fund's total return as follows:

Dividends + Capital-Gains Distributions + Share-Price Changes = Total Return

The following sections discuss each of these components in more detail.

Interest and dividends

Interest and dividends are income paid by investments. Bond funds and stocks can pay out both dividends and interest. *Bond-fund dividends* (the interest paid by the individual bonds in a fund) tend to be higher (as a percentage of the amount you have invested in a fund). When a dividend distribution is made, you can receive it as cash (which is good if you need money to live on) or reinvest it into more shares in the fund. In either case, the share price of the fund drops to offset the payout. So, if you're hoping to strike it rich by buying into a bunch of funds just before their dividends are paid, don't bother. You'll just end up paying more in income taxes.

If you hold your mutual fund outside a tax-sheltered plan or account, the distributions are taxable. You have to pay tax on these gains whether you receive them in the form of cash or you reinvest them as additional shares in the fund.

Interest is taxed at your full marginal tax rate. Dividends, however, are taxed at a much lower rate, thanks to the dividend tax credit. As a result, dividend funds are a good bet if you're investing to earn income outside of a tax-sheltered plan, such as an RRSP. (See Chapter 7 for more on how different types of investments are taxed.)

Capital gains

When a fund manager sells a security in the fund, net gains realized from that sale (the difference from the purchase price) must be distributed to you as a *capital gain*. Typically, funds make one annual capital gains distribution in December, but distributions can be paid multiple times per year.

As with a dividend distribution, you can receive your capital gains distribution as cash or as more shares in the fund. In either case, the share price of the fund drops to offset the distribution.

For funds held outside tax-sheltered retirement plans, your capital gains distribution is taxable. As with dividends, capital gains are taxable whether or not you reinvest them in additional shares in the fund. Capital-gains distributions can be partly composed of short-term and long-term gains.

TIP

If you want to avoid making an investment in a fund that is about to make a capital-gains distribution, check with the fund to determine when capital gains are distributed. Capital-gains distributions increase your current-year tax liability for investments made outside of registered retirement plans. (We discuss this concept in more detail in Chapter 13.)

Share-price changes

You also make money with a fund when the share price increases. This occurrence is just like investing in a stock or piece of real estate. If the fund is worth more today than it was when you bought it, you've made a profit (on paper, at least). In order to realize or lock in this profit, you need to sell your shares in the fund.

Evaluating and Selling Your Funds

WARNING

How closely you follow your funds is up to you, depending on what makes you happy and comfortable. We don't recommend tracking the share prices of your funds (or other investments, for that matter) on a daily basis; it's time-consuming and nerve-racking, and it can make you lose sight of the (long-term) big picture. When you track your investments too closely, you're more likely to panic when times get tough. And with investments held outside of registered retirement plans, every time you sell an investment at a profit, you get hit with taxes.

TIP

A monthly or quarterly check-in is more than frequent enough for following your funds. Many publications carry total return numbers over varying periods so you can determine the exact rate of return you're earning.

Trying to time and trade the markets so you buy at lows and sell at highs rarely works. Yet an entire industry of investment newsletters, hotlines, online services, and the like purport to be able to tell you when to buy and sell. Don't waste your time and money on such predictive nonsense. (See Chapter 8 for more info about gurus and newsletters.)

Consider selling a fund only when it no longer meets the criteria mentioned in "Selecting the Best Funds" earlier in this chapter. If a fund underperforms its peers for at least a two-year period, or if a fund jacks up its management fees, it may be a good time to sell. But if you do your homework and buy good funds from good fund companies, you shouldn't have to do much trading.

REMEMBER

Finding and investing in good funds isn't rocket science. Chapters 12 and 13 recommend some specific funds using the criteria discussed earlier in this chapter.

Chapter **11**

Taking Advantage of Registered Retirement Savings Plans

A Registered Retirement Savings Plan (RRSP) is the single best, easiest, and most efficient way to save for retirement. RRSPs also offer one of the best ways to reduce the tax you pay. To make the most out of RRSPs, you need to know not only how to use them, but also how they work and what their benefits are.

Understanding How RRSPs Work

The phrase *Registered Retirement Savings Plan* is perhaps the best-known financial term in the country. Unfortunately, it's also one of the most often misunderstood. For example, many people think of an RRSP as an investment. The reality is that an RRSP is a special holding account where you can place most generally available Canadian and foreign investments.

When you open an RRSP, you enter into an agreement with the government. By "registering" your retirement savings plan, you agree to put away money for your retirement and not spend it. In return, the government gives you two valuable benefits:

>> **Money that you contribute to your RRSP is deductible from your taxable income.** This means that any income you contribute to your savings plan is not taxed.

>> **The government lets the savings in your RRSP grow tax-free.** Any profits your RRSP investments earn are not taxable until you collapse your plan and withdraw the funds.

The benefits of tax-deductible contributions and tax-deferred growth combine to supercharge your retirement savings. In this section, we look at the powerful impact they can have on your ability to save for the future.

The benefits of tax-deductible contributions

Money you contribute to an RRSP can be deducted from your income before your income tax is calculated for the year. Say you made $50,000 and contributed $5,000 to your RRSP. If you claimed that $5,000 as a deduction on your tax return, your income tax would be calculated as though you had made only $45,000 that year.

Suppose you're in a 42 percent tax bracket, which means the government takes 42 cents of the last dollar you earn. If you contribute $1,000 to your RRSP, you save yourself $420 in tax. So the *real* out-of-pocket cost of a $1,000 contribution is only $580. Contributing $1,000 to your RRSP only leaves you short $580 in after-tax money you can put your hands on.

The tax savings from contributing to an RRSP are substantial regardless of your tax bracket, as Table 11-1 shows.

TABLE 11-1 **Short-Term Benefits of Tax-Deductible RRSP Contributions**

Where	Investment Amount	Tax Rate	Tax Reduction	After-Tax Cost in Dollars
Outside RRSP	$5,000	All	$0	$5,000
Inside RRSP	$5,000	25%	$1,250	$3,750
Inside RRSP	$5,000	34%	$1,700	$3,300
Inside RRSP	$5,000	42%	$2,100	$2,900
Inside RRSP	$5,000	46%	$2,300	$2,700
Inside RRSP	$5,000	50%	$2,500	$2,500

The payoff from tax-deferred compound growth

When you put your money into an RRSP, any profits you earn with that money aren't taxed until you take the money out of your plan. That means you can reinvest 100 percent of those profits, and they, in turn, can earn their own profits, again, unrestrained by taxes.

When interest and earnings on investments aren't taxed, the full value is added to the original amount. This new, larger amount then earns further gains, which again are added to, or compounded with, your investments. This phenomenon is called *compound growth*, and over time it will lead to your retirement savings growing exponentially.

TIP

Just how well does compound growth work? A good guideline to remember is the "Rule of 72." Take 72, divide it by your rate of return, and the result is the approximate number of years it will take for your investment to double in value. For example, an investment earning 7 percent will double in about ten years.

The benefits of tax-deductible contributions increase over time. Suppose you're 35 and you invest $5,000 of your salary this year outside an RRSP. Assuming that given your province's tax rate you're in a combined federal and provincial tax bracket of 40 percent, the Canada Revenue Agency (CRA) would first take $2,000 in tax, leaving you with $3,000. You invest that $3,000 in a mutual fund that earns a 10 percent compound return. After 30 years, you would've amassed a tidy $52,000. (This doesn't take into account the taxes you would likely have to pay each year on the distribution of capital gains, dividends, and interest, which would further reduce your average compound return outside an RRSP.)

Now, how would the numbers look if you had contributed that money to your RRSP? Because the CRA doesn't take any tax off your contributions, you can invest the full $5,000. Right away, that puts you $2,000 ahead. (In the real world, of course, you would've had the tax already taken off your income as it was earned. But you would then receive a $2,000 tax rebate for your $5,000 contribution, so, at the end of the day, the real cost is only $3,000.)

If you invest that $5,000 in the same mutual fund inside an RRSP earning an average 10 percent compound return for 30 years, you're left with $87,000, or almost $35,000 more than you would have if you had put the money in a mutual fund. Table 11-2 shows just how valuable a tax-sheltered RRSP contribution can be to the long-term growth of your savings.

TABLE 11-2

Long-Term Payoff of Tax-Favoured RRSP Contributions

Where	Pretax Savings	Available for Investment (with 10-percent Growth)	Value in 30 Years
Inside RRSP	$5,000	$5,000	$87,000
Outside RRSP	$5,000	$3,000 (after-tax)	$52,000

As Table 11-2 demonstrates, the more money you invest to begin with, the more money you end up with for any given investment.

Maximizing Your RRSP's Growth

You can maximize the growth of your RRSP in two simple steps:

>> Begin contributing as early as you can in life.

>> Try to maximize your RRSP's returns.

The payoff from starting an RRSP early

Your RRSP needs a good, long runway to get off the ground, but when it takes flight, it will gain altitude quickly. The real value in starting as early in life as possible is not simply the total amount of the extra contributions you manage to put in. It's that the longer you have money in an RRSP, the more time your savings have to compound.

Take someone who starts an RRSP when she's 28, making annual $2,000 contributions each year until she's 65. If she puts her money into a family of mutual funds that earns an average return of 10 percent, the total accumulation would be about $660,000.

But she could've accumulated that same amount if she had begun putting $2,000 a year into an RRSP when she was 21 — and contributed for only seven years (see Table 11-3).

TABLE 11-3

The Money-Earning Potential of Starting an RRSP When You're Young

Annual Contribution	Age Beginning	Age Ended	Total Years	Final Value at Age 65
$2,000	21	27	7	$709,722
$2,000	28	65	37	$660,000

Note: This table assumes a 10 percent annual rate of return.

TIP

Even if you're just 25 and you have only $1,000 to spare, put it in an RRSP! If you earn an average of 10 percent a year, you'll have an extra $45,000 in your plan when you retire at 65.

TIP

Examples like the previous one are commonly used to sell the benefits of putting money into an RRSP from an early age. The problem is that if you aren't young, these examples can be unsettling. If you didn't find out about the benefits of RRSPs when you were young or you didn't have money to contribute, you likely find it dispiriting to realize the tax savings and compound growth you missed out on. Whatever you do, don't let that stop you from taking action today. To rework that old cliché, today is the first day of the rest of your financial life!

Increasing your returns

Despite the benefits of tax-free contributions and compounding, you still need to choose appropriate investments to maximize the growth of your RRSP. And the more years you have before you have to collapse your plan, the larger the impact of boosting your returns by even just 1 percent or 2 percent.

Say you contribute $5,000 a year to your plan for 30 years, and you earn an average return of 8 percent. The final value of your plan would be just over $566,000.

But consider the results if you had taken a little more time in choosing your RRSP investments and you had managed to earn 9 percent a year — just 1 percent more. In 30 years' time, your plan would be worth over $681,000.

By improving your fund's performance by only 1 percent, you would end up with an extra $115,000 (see Table 11-4).

TABLE 11-4   **The Payoff from Profitable Investing: How a $5,000 Annual Contribution Will Grow**

Value at Growth Rate of . . . Years	8%	9%
5	$29,333	$29,924
10	$72,433	$75,965
30	$566,416	$681,538

TIP

HOW TO GET MOTIVATED TO MAKE RRSP CONTRIBUTIONS

To help stem your appetite for a large expense that you may desperately want but not necessarily need, it can help to get a firm grip on the substantial payoff from contributing to an RRSP.

For example, suppose you were able to put $6,000 every year into your RRSP and earned an average return of 9 percent. After 30 years, you would've accumulated an impressive $817,845.

But what if you put in only $4,500 annually, using the extra $1,500 to give yourself a week in the sun? Your total would still be a respectable $613,384. But look at it another way. Indulging yourself a little today will cost you more than $200,000 in your retirement. Are your beach vacations really worth having $200,000 less when you retire?

Do you find it tough to come up with anywhere near your maximum allowable contribution when the RRSP deadline comes around? Try an automatic deduction plan. You can tell your financial institution or RRSP holder to take a certain amount out of your bank account every few weeks — for example, when your paycheque comes in. You likely won't miss the money, and you'll be surprised at how much more you can put away.

Examining the Contribution Rules

As long as you're 71 years old or younger and you've received income from a job, running a business, or even net rental income — that is, as long as you've received *earned income* — you generally can contribute to an RRSP. No minimum age requirement applies — even a child can have an RRSP, as long as the child has earned income.

Checking out the contribution limits

Three factors determine the maximum you can contribute to your RRSP in any year.

>> **The absolute maximum amount that anyone can contribute in any one year:** The maximum for 2017 was $26,010; for 2018, $26,230. After 2018, this ceiling will be indexed, meaning it will be increased at the same rate as the cost of living.

>> **Your income:** Regardless of the absolute ceiling on contributions, the amount you earn the right to contribute to your RRSP in any year is also limited to 18 percent of your earned income from the previous year (see the sidebar "What's earned income?" for more information about what qualifies as earned income). For example, the most you can contribute in the 2019 tax year would be 18 percent of your 2018 earned income to the year's maximum.

>> **Membership in a company pension plan or a deferred profit-sharing plan (DPSP):** The employer makes an estimate of the value of the pension you earned in the previous year. This amount, called your *pension adjustment* (PA), is subtracted from whichever is lower, the dollar maximum contribution allowable or 18 percent of your earned income, to arrive at the most you can put into your RRSP.

In the spring or summer of each year, the CRA sends all taxpayers a Notice of Assessment for the previous year. Your contribution limit for the current year is included on the statement. For example, if you've filed your 2018 tax return, you'll find your allowable contribution for 2019 on your assessment statement, which you should receive in the first half of 2019.

Review your allowable maximum contribution to ensure the government has come up with the right figure. If the CRA's number is too high and you over-contribute, you may risk having to pay a penalty. If the figure is too low, your plan will suffer because you won't have maximized your contribution.

MAKING THE MOST OF YOUR UNUSED CONTRIBUTIONS

If you don't contribute the full amount you're allowed to in a given year — or don't make a contribution at all — the unused portion can be carried forward and used in later years.

For example, if you were allowed to contribute $7,000 this year and contributed only $5,000, you would have $2,000 of what's called *unused contribution room* to use in the future. Say the next year your income meant that you could contribute an additional $10,000. The total amount you could contribute to your RRSP in that year would be $12,000 — the $2,000 of allowable contributions brought forward from the previous year, and the $10,000 allowable contribution for the current year. In the jargon of RRSPs, this amount is not called your *allowable contribution,* but your *contribution room.* If you've saved enough money for a contribution that uses contribution room that you haven't been able to take advantage of in the past, congratulations are in order.

You don't have to deduct contributions to an RRSP from your taxable income in the same year they're made. In fact, it often makes sense not to claim some or even all of your contribution on this year's tax return. Why would you not want to deduct your contributions as soon as possible? When you deduct an RRSP contribution, the tax you save is determined by your marginal tax bracket. If your income fluctuates or is unusually low (perhaps you've taken time off to care for a baby, start a new business, or just smell the roses), you may save more in taxes by putting off claiming the deduction for some or even all of a contribution until your income is higher. By doing so, you'll be in a higher marginal bracket, which means your deduction will save you that much more in taxes.

Also, a large deduction can decrease your taxable income so that you actually drop a tax bracket. For example, suppose you earn $49,000, which means your marginal tax rate is approximately 34 percent. But only the last $3,000 of your income is taxed at this rate. Income below about $46,000 down to $12,000 is taxed at only about 25 percent. You can maximize your tax savings from a large RRSP contribution by claiming only about $3,000 — just enough to reduce your taxable income so that none of it is taxed at 34 percent. You can then use the same strategy for the remainder of the contribution in future years.

How much can you contribute?

To begin with, realize that the government puts absolute maximums on how much people, regardless of situation, can contribute each year — the *allowable contribution.*

WHAT'S EARNED INCOME?

Now, you probably quite naturally believe that when it comes to your income, you've earned all of it — but the government has other ideas. When determining what qualifies as your *earned income,* certain types of earnings are excluded.

Earned income includes only income sources such as these:

- Salary
- Net self-employment income
- Bonuses and commissions
- Net business income
- Taxable alimony, maintenance, and child-support payments you receive
- Net rental income
- Royalties
- Disability pension received under the Canada Pension Plan (CPP) or Quebec Pension Plan (QPP)
- Income from an employee profit-sharing plan
- Unemployment benefits
- Some types of taxable employment incomes, including disability and sick benefits

The following reduce your earned income:

- Deductible alimony, maintenance, and child-support payments you make
- Most deductible employment-related expenses, including travel expenses and union dues
- Rental losses
- Union or professional dues

Finally, many types of income are simply excluded from your earned income. In addition to most income from investments, including interest, dividends, and capital gains, you may not include pension benefits, retiring allowances or severance pay, death benefits, or money received from an RRSP, Registered Retirement Income Fund (RRIF), or DPSP.

The most you can contribute in any given year, then, is the *lower* of the following:

>> The annual maximum amount for that year (see the previous section)

>> Eighteen percent of your earned income in the previous year

Note: If no one in your family has a company pension plan, you can skip this next section. Those with company pension plans, stay with the program.

If you belong to a pension plan or DPSP, the government further scales back the amount it lets you contribute. The thinking is that because you have alternative sources of retirement income, you shouldn't get the full tax break allotted to people without pensions.

The government reduces your otherwise maximum allowable contribution by the value attributed for the contributions that both you and your employer make to your pension or DPSP. This figure is called your *pension adjustment* (PA) *factor*. How that figure is arrived at depends on the type of plan you belong to.

Your pension adjustment is then subtracted from the lower of 18 percent of your earned income or the year's maximum to arrive at your RRSP limit. Your pension adjustment is listed on your T4 slip, which you should receive from your employer before the end of every February. In general, the higher your pension, the larger your pension adjustment, and the lower your maximum allowable contribution.

If you belong to a defined-benefit pension plan

With a defined-benefit pension plan, the amount you receive when you retire is based upon your years of service and your income level. When you belong to this kind of plan, your pension adjustment (PA factor) is based on a calculation of the future value attributed to your pension of your previous year of employment. Your maximum contribution for 2018, for example, would be 18 percent of your 2017 earned income, up to a maximum of $26,230, less your 2017 PA factor.

If you belong to a money-purchase pension plan

Your pension adjustment under this kind of pension plan is the total combined amount put into your pension by both you and your employer for the previous year. Your maximum contribution for 2018, for example, would be 18 percent of your 2017 earned income to a maximum of $26,230, less all the 2017 pension contributions (PA factor).

THE CONTRIBUTION DEADLINE

For any given tax year, you can make a contribution any time up to and including the 60th day in the next year. The last day you're allowed to contribute for the 2018 tax year, for instance, is March 1, 2019. You could contribute as early as January 1, 2018, of course. The exception is that, in the year in which you turn 71, you must contribute to your plan before December 31.

Note that the deadline is the 60th day in the new year, and not fixed as March 1. Why do we point this out? Leap year. Every fourth year, if you waited until March 1 to make your contribution, you'd be too late. In a leap year, because February has one extra day, the deadline is not March 1, but February 29. The only positive thing that can be said about leaving your contribution to the last minute is that it's probably good for an adrenaline rush. But consider this: If you plan ahead and make your contributions well in advance, you'll likely earn enough in extra interest over the years to pay for hours of heart-stopping bungee jumping and skydiving when you retire.

Every February, many people dash around trying to get their RRSP contributions in before the deadline. Rushed contributions, however, are usually made without considering investment options.

If you can't avoid making your contribution at the last minute, don't rush into making any major investment decisions. Consider putting your money into a money-market fund or other cashlike investment, and then moving your money into better-performing investments when you have the time and energy to consider your options. By carefully assessing your RRSP investments, you can greatly boost the value of your plan, which translates directly into thousands of dollars more income to live on during retirement.

If you belong to a deferred profit-sharing plan

If your employer contributes money to a DPSP on your behalf, your pension adjustment equals the total of the contributions made (up to the maximum allowable DPSP contribution) for the previous year. For example, your 2018 maximum would be 18 percent of your 2017 earned income to a maximum of $26,230, minus your 2017 PA factor.

Types of Registered Retirement Savings Plans

You'll often hear about three different types — *guaranteed, mutual-fund,* and *self-directed* or *brokerage-house RRSPs*. The names are often partly dictated by the financial institution that is offering them. Here's how to interpret what the different names mean:

>> **Guaranteed RRSPs:** Guaranteed RRSPs are really just RRSPs in which you put your money into investments where your principal is protected, such as guaranteed investment certificates (GICs). When you do so, you lend your money to a bank or other financial institution in return for regular interest payments. Guaranteed plans pay fixed returns, and your money, if invested in GICs, is usually protected by the Canada Deposit Insurance Corporation (CDIC).

>> **Mutual-fund RRSPs:** Mutual-fund RRSPs are investments in —drumroll, please — mutual funds. Mutual fund RRSPs offer two benefits:

- By using mutual funds, you can invest your money in stocks and bonds, which over the long haul, will handily beat the returns from guaranteed investments.

- If you set up an RRSP with a mutual-fund company, you can diversify your savings by putting them into several different types of funds with the same company.

Note: Some mutual-fund companies charge an annual trustee fee ranging from $25 to $50 a year for RRSP accounts.

>> **Self-directed and brokerage-house RRSPs:** This type of RRSP allows you to invest in a wide range of securities. In addition to GICs and mutual funds, you can invest in individual stocks and bonds and a wide range of other securities.

You can set up a self-directed plan with most investment dealers and discount brokerages. Some of these companies charge an annual fee, which typically runs around $100. Some institutions are willing to reduce or eliminate their fees for self-directed plans. The discount brokerages run by the big banks and trust companies often waive the first-year fee for new plans. If you do have to pay a fee, make sure you pay it out of your regular savings, not out of the funds in your plan.

You can get an RRSP just about anywhere — your local bank, trust company, brokerage house, insurance company, credit union, or mutual-fund company. And you aren't limited to a specific number of RRSPs. You can, for example, open a handful of RRSPs, each in different types of investments with different companies.

Drawbacks do exist to having several plans, however. The paperwork can be burdensome, and it can become a real chore to follow your investments. Also, if you invest with a number of different mutual-fund companies, the trustee fees can start to add up.

REDUCING YOUR FAMILY'S TAX BILL WITH A SPOUSAL RRSP

A spousal RRSP can help reduce your household's future tax bill if you're married or living common-law and anticipate a big gap between your income and your spouse's income when you both retire.

A spousal RRSP is simply a special kind of RRSP to which one spouse makes the contributions and is able to claim the tax deduction. However, the money then belongs to the other spouse. (Although this change in official ownership worries some potential contributing partners, it shouldn't. In most cases the money in RRSPs is simply counted as part of your combined assets and divided equally between you and your spouse if you separate or divorce.) A spousal RRSP allows you to move some future income out of the hands of the person in the higher tax bracket and into the hands of the spouse with the lower retirement income and, therefore, the lower tax bracket.

You need to know some specific rules. The total contributions made by a spouse to both his or her own plan and a spousal RRSP can't exceed that individual's allowable maximum individual contribution. In addition, restrictions exist that prevent the higher-earning spouse from contributing to a spousal plan, claiming the deduction against income that is taxed at a high marginal rate, and then having the lower-earning spouse remove the money from the plan and being taxed at the lower marginal rate. If you contribute to a spousal plan, the money immediately belongs to your spouse. However, if he or she withdraws any of the contribution in that year or during the next two calendar years, the withdrawal is treated as though you had earned it, and it's taxed at your marginal rate. (This rule does not apply if you and your spouse are separated or divorced.)

You have to close down your RRSP by the end of the year in which you turn 71. But if you have earned income in any year, you still earn RRSP contribution room. And it doesn't have to go to waste. If you're married or living with a common-law partner, and your partner is 71 or younger, you can contribute to a spousal RRSP and claim a deduction. You can continue to do so until the year after your partner turns 71.

Taking Money Out of Your Plan before Retirement

It's called a *retirement* savings plan, but you don't have to wait until you've left the working world to take money out of an RRSP. In fact, you're allowed to withdraw money out of your RRSP whenever you like. When you do, though, the government will want to collect the taxes it had earlier forgone on your contributions (with two exceptions, which we discuss in the section "Special circumstances").

Regular withdrawals before retirement

When you withdraw money from your RRSP, the plan holder is required to withhold taxes on your withdrawals. As of 2018, the rates in all provinces (except Quebec) were 10 percent on amounts up to $5,000, 20 percent on the next $10,000, and 30 percent on withdrawals of more than $15,000. In Quebec, for any single withdrawal, the amount withheld is one-half of the federal withholding rates, plus another 16 percent.

WARNING

When you prepare your next income-tax return, you have to declare your withdrawals as income in the year you took the money out of your plan. For most people, that will mean an additional tax bill because the withholding rates in most cases are lower than the marginal tax rate.

TIP

The withholding tax rates are calculated on each individual withdrawal. If you do need to get at your RRSP funds, take out separate withdrawals of no more than $5,000 each time to minimize the amount of withholding tax.

Special circumstances

In two cases, you can withdraw funds from your RRSP without paying taxes: to help purchase a house or to pay for an education.

The Home Buyers' Plan

You can tap the money you've saved inside an RRSP to help you buy or build a home by using the Home Buyers' Plan (HBP). You can borrow up to $25,000 from your RRSP under the HBP, and the money does not have to be added to your income (like a regular withdrawal would), so it's not taxed. You do, however, have to repay the money you've withdrawn over 15 years, beginning in the second year after you've taken the money out. For the full details of the plan, see Chapter 15.

The Lifelong Learning Plan

You can also tap your RRSP savings to help pay for an education. Under the Lifelong Learning Plan, you can take a loan out from your RRSP to help pay for post-secondary education or full-time training. You or your spouse can withdraw up to a maximum of $10,000 a year over a four-year period. The total withdrawn can't be more than $20,000. Like money taken out under the HBP, money "borrowed" from your RRSP must be repaid, but the rules are different.

PENSIONS AND YOUR CONTRIBUTION LIMITS

Sometimes, pension benefits under a defined-benefit pension plan are improved retroactively. If this happens, your RRSP contribution limit may be further reduced by a past-service pension adjustment (PSPA).

On the other hand, you may find your contribution limits increased. For example, you may work for a company that has a pension plan. As a result, your RRSP contribution limits will be reduced by your pension adjustment. However, you may leave the company before you fully earn the rights to those benefits — before they vest. To give you back some of the RRSP contribution room that had been taken away because of the supposed pension benefits you were due to receive, you will get a pension adjustment reversal (PAR). A PAR increases your allowable RRSP contribution in the year you leave that particular job.

The Lifelong Learning Plan repayments must start in the fifth year after the first withdrawal was made, and the full amount must be put back into your RRSP within ten years. For more details on the Lifelong Learning Plan, see Chapter 14.

Closing Down Your RRSP

You must close down, or *mature,* your RRSP by the end of the year during which you turn 71. You can make a final contribution to your plan in that year; however, instead of having 60 days into the next year to get your money in, the deadline for your final contribution is December 31.

WARNING

Deciding just when to fold your plan and what to do with your funds are two of the most important financial decisions you'll ever make. Time your moves correctly and make some astute choices, and you'll find you have a much larger financial comfort zone than you expected. However, if you make your decisions at the last minute without doing your homework, you may find that your lack of attention costs you in terms of a lower standard of living.

You have three basic options to choose from when your RRSP matures:

>> **Cash out.** Take all the money right out of your RRSP and do what you want with it. The CRA will treat the sum total of your plan as taxable income in that year. The resulting tax bill will lop off anywhere from one-third to half of your

retirement savings, right then and there. Ugh! Because we don't think this is a sensible decision, this is all we'll say about this option.

>> **Convert your RRSP into an RRIF.** RRIFs allow you to continue to enjoy tax-deferred compounding. However, RRIFs require that you take out a certain minimum amount every year.

>> **Use the funds to buy an annuity.** Hand over your money to a financial institution (usually an insurance company), which then pays out regular sums to you for a period of time that you choose. This can be as short as ten years or as long as the rest of your life.

You aren't limited to just one of these three options. You can choose to split your RRSP funds and use two or even all three of these different strategies.

TIP

To make the right decision for your individual circumstances, you have to consider a lot more than simply how much cash flow each option will bring in. Each strategy has its own specific tax burden and a different schedule on when those tax bills will come due to consider. Plus, you need to decide how much control you want to have over how your funds are invested and whether you want to have access to your funds. Finally, each option offers different levels of estate or survivorship protections.

REMEMBER

Although you can close out your RRSP earlier than the year in which you celebrate your 71st birthday, the best strategy for most people is to leave your RRSP intact for as long as you're allowed. This is almost always the case if you decide to turn it into an RRIF. If you choose to go the annuity route, collapsing your plan a year or two early can make sense. If interest rates are relatively high, closing your plan out early may make sense if it allows you to lock in a higher-than-average return.

Registered Retirement Income Funds

An RRIF is similar in many ways to an RRSP. An RRIF allows your money to continue to grow tax-deferred. You can invest your funds in most of the eligible RRSP investments, from money-market funds to individual stocks. And, just as with RRSPs, you can have one, two, or a handful of different RRIFs.

The only difference between an RRIF and an RRSP is that you aren't allowed to put any money into your RRIF. Instead, you're required to take out a certain minimum amount each year.

These minimum payments are required to start the year after you set up your RRIF. You can choose monthly, quarterly, semi-annual, or annual payments. What's more, you don't have to take your payments in cash. You can move any investment out of your RRIF without selling it. However, you must pay tax on the fair market value at the time of the withdrawal, just as if it had been taken out as income.

The minimum amount you're required to withdraw is based on your age, and increases each year. The withdrawals are fully taxable. If you have a younger spouse, you can use your spouse's age, not yours, to determine your minimum withdrawal each year. If you don't need the additional cash, this can be a profitable strategy. The lower the age, the smaller the minimum required withdrawal, and, thus, the less tax you'll pay.

The amount is determined by taking a percentage of the value of your RRIF at the beginning of the year. The percentage starts low — just 3.33 percent at age 60 — and increases slightly for every year beyond that, eventually leveling out at a flat 20 percent the year you turn 95.

TIP

The main benefit of an RRIF is that you continue to have control over how and where your money is invested. This control gives you the best chance of earning healthier returns on your money. In particular, it allows you to invest in equities and bonds.

RRIFs also let you have a say about how much income you have. As long as you withdraw the required minimums, you can take out as little or as much as you wish in any given year. If you suddenly come into some money, you can leave your RRIF essentially untouched and keep ringing up tax-free growth. If you have a medical emergency, you can quickly get your hands on as much as you need at the time.

TIP

RRIFs are usually a good choice if you enjoy managing your money, have an indexed company pension plan that guarantees you a basic level of income, and don't immediately need to start drawing on your funds. Another advantage of RRIFs is that you can convert them to an annuity at any time, whereas an annuity is for life: After you sign up for an annuity, you can't change your mind. Plus, with an RRIF you have a lot more control over what happens to your money at your death.

Your minimum withdrawals are a percentage of the market value of your RRIF at the end of the previous year. The requirement for each year is determined by your age on January 1 of that year (see Table 11-5).

TABLE 11-5

Minimum RRIF Withdrawals

Age (Beginning of Year)	RRIF Minimum
60	3.33%
61	3.45%
62	3.57%
63	3.7%
64	3.85%
65	4%
66	4.17%
67	4.35%
68	4.55%
69	4.76%
70	5%
71	5.28%
72	5.4%
73	5.53%
74	5.67%
75	5.82%
76	5.98%
77	6.17%
78	6.36%
79	6.58%
80	6.82%
81	7.08%
82	7.38%
83	7.71%
84	8.08%
85	8.51%
86	8.99%
87	9.55%

Age (Beginning of Year)	RRIF Minimum
88	10.21%
89	10.99%
90	11.92%
91	13.06%
92	14.49%
93	16.34%
94 and up	18.79%
95 and older	20%

Annuities

When you use your RRSP funds to buy an annuity, you transfer your funds over to a financial institution (usually an insurance company), which then pays them back to you a little bit at a time. You don't pay tax on any RRSP funds at the time you turn them into an annuity. The regular payments from the annuity, though, are taxable and treated by the CRA as "pension" income. If you have no other pension income, up to $2,000 of the annuity payments will qualify for the Pension Income Tax Credit.

TIP

The biggest decision when buying an annuity is the length of time you want your payments to run for. One option is to pick a specific number of years, such as 5, 10, or 20. At the end of the specific time, your payments end and your annuity is fully depleted. Another choice is a *life annuity,* which provides you with payments for the rest of your life; a *joint-life annuity* continues payments as long as you or your spouse is still alive.

If you select a life annuity, the size of your payments depends on your age and sex. Men tend to die at an earlier age than women do, so life-annuity payments for males are generally higher because the funds have to last for fewer years. And, obviously, the younger you are, the smaller your payments will be, because (we hope) your payments will have to stretch far into the future.

You can also add a couple of wrinkles to your annuity. If you choose a life annuity, even if you die the very next week, the insurance company gets to keep all the money. But if you choose a *guaranteed annuity,* you ensure that if you die before a certain number of years have passed, the payments will continue and will go to your beneficiaries. You can also choose to have your payments increase gradually from year to year; these *indexed annuities* help your income keep up with inflation.

REMEMBER

Just how much your funds will pay you, how long you want them to continue, and the options you want are all put through complex calculations by the technical climbers of the accounting world, actuaries. After you decide on your options, your payments can be calculated by using the statistics of how long you're likely to live and the likelihood of your dying at various ages. (Don't ask to see these numbers, because you probably don't want to know.) After you select your options, they can never be changed; they'll remain in place until the annuity contract ends with your death or, if you choose the spousal survivor option, your spouse's death.

This means that options such as indexing and guarantees all come at a price. Because these features mean that the insurance company will in all likelihood have to pay out more money, your regular payments will be lower than if you chose to go with a basic, stripped-down *defined-term annuity*.

TIP

Annuities are usually best when you

>> Have small retirement savings that absolutely need to last a number of years, especially if you're young and your family has a history of living a long time

>> Must have the peace of mind that comes with knowing just how much you have to live on

>> Don't want to have to make ongoing decisions about how to invest your money

WARNING

On the flip side of these advantages are several drawbacks, including these:

>> You lose all control of your savings.

>> Your rate of return is fixed when you buy your plan and will likely be lower than what you can earn investing in good mutual funds. If the investment world suddenly becomes littered with far more profitable options, you'll just have to lump it.

>> If you don't accept lower payments in return for an indexed annuity, you may be faced with having less buying power over the years if inflation takes off.

>> If you don't take out a guarantee, or you die after the guarantee period expires, your family or other beneficiaries won't get anything on your death.

The largest drawback to annuities is that you lose all input in how your money is invested and in how much it earns for you. You also have to accept lower initial payments if you want your annuity to increase with the cost of living.

UNLOCKING LOCKED-IN RRSPs AND RETIREMENT ACCOUNTS

If you leave a company in which you were a member of a pension plan, you may have earned the right to your pension benefits. However, you may not be allowed to gain access to those benefits due to the pension regulations (locking-in legislation). In this case, your pension benefits may be transferred to a special type of RRSP called a Locked-in RRSP or Locked-in Retirement Account (LIRA), depending on the province you live in.

When you're ready to start drawing on this money, you generally have two options. You can take the money and purchase an annuity. The other option is to convert such locked-in plans and accounts into an LIF. These accounts are similar to RRIFs, but with a few extra wrinkles. Like an RRIF, you typically have to withdraw a set minimum as a percentage of the funds in your LRIF or LIF every year. However, unlike an RRIF, on which no maximums exist, there's generally also a ceiling on how much you can withdraw each year.

WARNING

The world of retirement plans and funds — including Life Income Funds (LIFs) and Locked-in Retirement Income Funds (LRIFs) — has no shortage of complexities and acronyms. In addition, to being regulated differently across the country, the rules have been in flux for many years. Be sure to check with your province or territory's regulators or tax department or territory to get the most up-to-date information before making any key decisions about moving money or opening or closing one of these plans, accounts, or funds.

Chapter **12**

Investing in Retirement Plans

This chapter helps you decide how to invest money you currently hold inside — or plan to contribute to — a Registered Retirement Savings Plan (RRSP) or another retirement plan, such as an employer's Registered Pension Plan (RPP).

When compared to the often-overwhelming world of investing outside retirement plans, investing inside tax-sheltered retirement plans — RRSPs, Registered Retirement Income Funds (RRIFs), and company plans — is less complicated for two reasons:

» **The range of possible registered retirement plan investments is more limited.** Direct investments, such as real estate and investments in small, privately owned companies, aren't generally available or accessible in most RRSPs or other registered retirement plans.

» **When you invest in a tax-sheltered retirement plan, your returns aren't taxed as you earn them.** Money inside registered retirement plans compounds and grows without taxation. You generally pay taxes on these funds only when you withdraw money from the account. (Direct transfers to registered retirement plans at another investment firm are not withdrawals, so they're not taxed.) So, when you choose an investment for your registered retirement plan, don't rack your brain over dividends and capital gains; save all that worry for the money you invest in nonregistered retirement accounts.

Allocating Your Money in Retirement Plans

With good reason, people are concerned about placing their retirement plan money in investments that can decline in value. You may feel that you're gambling with dollars intended for the security of your golden years.

Most working folks need to make their money work hard in order for it to grow fast enough to provide this security. This need involves taking some risk; you have no way around it. Luckily, if you have 15 to 20 years or more before you need to draw on the bulk of your retirement plan assets, time is on your side. As long as the value of your investments has time to recover, what's the big deal if some of your investments drop a bit over a year or two? The more years you have before you're going to retire, the greater your ability to take risk.

TIP

Think of your retirement plans as part of your overall plan to generate retirement income. Then allocate different types of investments between your tax-deferred retirement plans and other taxable investment accounts to get the maximum benefit of tax deferral. This section helps you determine how to distribute your money in retirement plans. Chapters 9 and 13 can help you decide how to divide your money among different nonretirement investment options based on your time frame and risk tolerance.

Understanding the difference between a retirement plan and the investments inside a retirement plan

Many people get confused when discussing the investments they make in retirement plans, especially those held inside RRSPs. Often, they don't realize that you can have an RRSP at a variety of financial institutions (for example, a mutual-fund company or brokerage firm). At each financial institution, you can choose among the firm's investment options for putting your RRSP money to work.

INAPPROPRIATE RETIREMENT-PLAN INVESTMENTS

Some investments, such as those that are treated favourably by the taxman, often don't make a lot of sense inside tax-sheltered registered retirement plans.

Although annuities are retirement vehicles, they have no place inside retirement plans. Annuities allow your investment dollars to compound without taxation. In comparison to other investments that don't allow such tax deferral, annuities carry much higher annual operating expenses, which depress your returns. Purchasing an annuity inside an RRSP is like wearing a belt and suspenders together. Either you have a peculiar sense of style, or you're spending too much time worrying about your pants falling down. In our experience, many people who mistakenly invest in annuities inside retirement plans have been misled by investment salespeople.

Limited partnerships are treacherous, high-commission, high-cost (and hence low-return) investments sold through investment salespeople. Part of their supposed allure, however, is the tax benefits they generate. But when you buy and hold a limited partnership in an RRSP or other retirement plan, you lose the ability to take advantage of many of the tax deductions. The illiquidity of limited partnerships may also mean that you can't make required retirement-plan withdrawals when needed. These are just some of the many reasons to avoid investing in limited partnerships. (For more reasons, see Chapter 9.)

No-load (commission-free) mutual fund and discount brokerage firms are your best bet for establishing an RRSP. For more specifics, see our recommendations in Chapter 10.

Prioritizing retirement contributions

When you have access to various retirement plans, prioritize which account you're going to use first by determining how much each gives you in return. Your first contributions should be to employer-based plans that match your contributions. After that, contribute to any other employer plans that allow tax-deductible contributions or to a self-directed RRSP. After you contribute as much as possible to these tax-deductible plans, consider an annuity (see "Annuities: An Odd Investment," in this chapter). For information on how to set up an RRSP, refer to Chapter 11.

Allocating money when your employer selects the investment options

In some company-sponsored plans, such as RPPs, you're typically limited to the predetermined investment options your employer offers. In the following sections, we discuss common investment options for employer-sponsored plans in order of increasing risk and, hence, likely return. Then we follow with examples for how to allocate your money across the different types of common employer retirement-plan options.

Money-market funds or savings accounts

For regular contributions that come out of your paycheque, a money-market fund or savings account doesn't make much sense. Some people who are skittish about the stock and bond markets are attracted to money-market funds and savings accounts because they can't drop in value. However, the returns are low — so low that you have a great risk that your investment won't stay ahead of, or even keep up with, inflation and taxes (which are due upon withdrawal of your money from the retirement plan).

REMEMBER

Don't be tempted to use a money-market fund as a parking place until you think stocks and bonds are cheap. In the long run, you won't be doing yourself any favours. As we discuss in Chapter 8, timing your investments to try to catch the lows and avoid the peaks isn't possible.

TIP

You may need to keep money in a money-market fund if you use the borrowing feature that some retirement plans allow. Check with your employee benefits department for more details. After you retire, you may also want to use a money-market fund to hold money you expect to withdraw and spend within a year or so.

Bond mutual funds

Bond mutual funds (see Chapter 10) invest in a mixture of typically high-quality bonds. Bonds pay a higher rate of interest or dividends than money-market funds. Depending on whether your plan's option is a short-term, intermediate-term, or long-term fund (maybe you have more than one type), the bond fund's current yield is probably a percent or two higher than the money-market fund's yield. (*Note:* During certain time periods, the yield difference may be more, whereas during other time periods, it may be less.)

Bond funds carry higher yields than money-market funds, but they also carry greater risk, because their value can fall if interest rates increase. However, bonds tend to be more stable in value over the shorter term (such as a few years) than stocks.

TIP

Aggressive, younger investors should keep a minimum amount of money in bond funds. Older folks who want to invest conservatively can place more money in bonds (see the asset-allocation discussion in Chapter 8).

Guaranteed-investment certificates

Guaranteed investment certificates (GICs) are backed by a bank, trust company, or insurance company, and they typically quote you a rate of return projected one year or a few years forward. So, you don't have the uncertainty that you normally face with bond or stock investments (unless, of course, the insurance company fails).

The attraction of these investments is that your account value doesn't fluctuate (at least, not that you can see). Financial institutions normally invest your money mostly in bonds and maybe a bit in stocks. The difference between what these investments generate for the financial institution and what they pay in interest to GIC investors is profit to the seller. A GIC's yield is usually slightly less than that of a bond fund.

TIP

For people who hit the eject button the moment a bond fund slides a bit in value, GICs are soothing to the nerves. And they're certainly higher yielding than a money-market fund or savings account.

Like bonds, however, GICs don't give you the opportunity for much long-term growth above the rate of inflation. Over the long haul, you can expect to earn a better return in a mixture of bond and stock investments. In GICs, you pay for the peace of mind of a guaranteed return with lower long-term returns.

Balanced and target-date mutual funds

Balanced mutual funds invest primarily in a mixture of stocks and bonds. This one-stop-shopping concept makes investing easier and smoothes out fluctuations in the value of your investments — funds investing exclusively in stocks or bonds make for a rougher ride. These funds are solid options and, in fact, can be used for a significant portion of your retirement plan contributions. See Chapter 10 to find out more about balanced funds.

Some fund companies offer funds of funds known as a *target-date fund.* These funds include a mixture of stocks and bonds; the mix gets gradually more conservative (less risky) over the years as a person nears retirement.

Stock mutual funds

Stock mutual funds invest in stocks, which often provide greater long-term growth potential but also wider fluctuations in value from year to year. Some companies offer a number of different stock funds, including funds that invest overseas. Unless you plan to borrow against your funds to purchase a home (if your plan allows), you should have a healthy helping of stock funds. See Chapter 10 for an explanation of the different types of stock funds as well as for details on how to evaluate a stock fund.

Stock in the company you work for

WARNING

Some companies offer employees the option of investing in the company's stock. We generally advocate avoiding this option for the simple reason that your future income and other employee benefits are already riding on the success of the company. If the company hits the skids, you may lose your job and your benefits. You certainly don't want the value of your retirement plan to depend on the same factors.

In the early 2000s, you may have heard all the hubbub about companies such as Enron going under and employees losing piles of money in their retirement plans. Enron's bankruptcy in and of itself shouldn't have caused direct problems in Enron's retirement plan. The problem was that Enron required employees to hold substantial amounts of Enron company stock. So, when the company tanked, employees lost their jobs *and* their retirement savings balances invested in the company's stock.

If you think that your company has its act together and the stock is a good buy, investing a portion of your retirement account is fine — but no more than 20 percent to 25 percent. Now, if your company is on the verge of hitting it big and the stock is soon to soar, you'll of course be kicking yourself for not putting more of your money into the company's stock. But when you place a big bet on your company's stock, be prepared to suffer the consequences if the stock tanks. Consider all those Nortel and Blackberry employees who piled their savings into their employer's stock, only to watch it plummet in value (and, in Nortel's case, become worthless.) Don't forget that lots of smart investors track companies' prospects, so odds are that the current value of your company's stock is reasonably fair.

TIP

Some employers offer employees an additional option to buy company stock at a discount, sometimes as much as 15 percent, when compared to its current market value. If your company offers a discount on its stock, take advantage of it. When you sell the stock, you'll usually be able to lock in a decent profit over your purchase price.

Some asset-allocation examples

Using the methodology that we outline in Chapter 8 for allocating money, Table 12-1 shows a couple examples of how people in different employer plans may choose to allocate their retirement investments among the plan's investment options.

TABLE 12-1   ## Allocating Company RPP Investments

	25-Year-Old, Aggressive-Risk Investor	45-Year-Old, Moderate-Risk Investor	60-Year-Old, Moderate-Risk Investor
Bond fund	0%	35%	50%
Balanced fund (50% stock, 50% bond)	10%	0%	0%
Blue-chip or larger-company stock fund(s)	30%–40%	20%–25%	25%
Smaller-company stock fund(s)	20%–25%	15%–20%	10%
International stock fund(s)	25%–35%	20%–25%	15%

REMEMBER

Making allocation decisions is not a science. Use the formulas in Chapter 8 as a guideline.

Allocating money in retirement plans you design

With RRSPs, you may select the investment options, as well as the allocation of money among them. In the sections that follow, we give some specific recipes that you may find useful for investing at some of the premier investment companies.

To establish an RRSP at one of these firms, simply pick up your telephone, dial the company's toll-free number, and ask the representative to mail you an account application. You can also have the company mail you background information on specific mutual funds. (If you're less patient, and you're a fan of the Internet, many investment firms provide downloadable account applications. However, downloading an application can be a tedious process, especially if you also need other information such as investment prospectuses and annual reports.)

Note: In the examples, we make recommendations for a conservative portfolio and an aggressive portfolio for each firm. We use the terms *conservative* and *aggressive* in a relative sense. Because some of the funds we recommend don't maintain fixed percentages of their different types of investments, the actual percentage of stocks and bonds that you end up with may vary slightly from the targeted percentages. Don't sweat it.

TIP

Where you have more than one fund choice, you can pick one or split the suggested percentage among them. If you don't have enough money today to divvy up your portfolio as we suggest, you can achieve the desired split over time as you add more money to your RRSP.

TIP

SHOULD I USE MORE THAN ONE INVESTMENT FIRM?

The firms we recommend in this chapter offer a large-enough variety of investment options, managed by different fund managers, that you can feel comfortable concentrating your money at one firm. Your investments themselves aren't at risk based on the financial health of the fund company itself. Discovering the nuances and choices of just one firm rather than several and having fewer administrative hassles are the advantages of a focused approach.

If you like the idea of spreading your money around, you may want to invest through a number of different firms using a discount brokerage account (see Chapter 8). You can diversify across different mutual-fund companies through one brokerage firm. However, you may pay small transaction fees on some of your purchases and sales of funds.

TD Asset Management

TD Asset Management (800-465-5463; www.tdassetmanagement.com) is a large provider of funds and operates a discount brokerage division. The real stars of TD's long list of funds are its *e-funds*, funds that can only be purchased electronically (in other words, online). You can buy them through an EasyWeb Mutual Fund account or a TD Direct Investment account.

The *management expense ratios* (MERs) of TD's e-funds are some of the very lowest in the industry, ranging from 0.33 percent to 0.55 percent. The expense ratios on good index exchange-traded funds [ETFs] are lower still — generally 0.05 percent to 0.3 percent. But, unlike ETFs, you don't have to pay any fees or costs to buy or sell TD e-funds. See the nearby sidebar, "Management fees and management expense ratio" for more information.

TIP

If you want to maintain a conservative portfolio, try this:

>> **TD Canadian Bond Index Fund - e:** 50 percent

>> **TD Canadian Index Fund - e (stocks):** 25 percent

>> **TD International Index Fund - e (stocks):** 15 percent

>> **TD US Index Fund - e (stocks):** 10 percent

MANAGEMENT FEES AND MANAGEMENT EXPENSE RATIOS

Mutual funds are a business. And, like most businesses, they like to make a profit. Here's how they do it, and how you pay for it.

Every mutual fund charges all investors in the fund a fee for the services of the manager. This is called the *management fee.* The management fee is calculated as a percentage of the total dollar value of the assets in the fund. This fee also includes money that is paid out each year to the advisor, dealer, or broker who sold you the fund. This fee is called a *trailing commission* or *trailer.* Charging you a trailing commission is usually defended as being a justifiable payment to the advisor for the services and advice he supposedly offers you on an ongoing basis. We say "supposedly" because the reality is that, often, when you buy a fund, you receive little, if any, true service for this fee, a fee that many funds make mandatory. The reality is that the function of trailing commissions is to, shall we say, "encourage" you to keep your money invested in that particular fund and not to move it to another fund.

In addition to the management fee, fund companies also pass along their operating costs, including, but not limited to, day-to-day operating expenses, including record keeping, fund-valuation costs, audit and legal fees, as well as the costs of sending out prospectuses and annual reports. Finally, they tack on taxes.

Added together, these three different fees — the management fee, the operating costs, and taxes — are known as the management expenses. However, you'll typically only hear people refer to the *management expense ratio* (MER). The reason is that, similar to the basic management fee, the amount of the management expenses charged by a fund are a percentage of the total value of the fund's assets.

MERs are tremendously important to you as an investor. The higher they are, the less your investment earns you. By way of illustration, a 2 percent MER may sound quite reasonable, if not a downright bargain! But the money is paid out of the profits the fund earns in the year. So, if a fund made a gross return of 8 percent on its investments over the year, and charged a 2 percent MER, you would only earn 6 percent. Put another way, the mutual-fund company is pocketing a full 25 percent of the fund's gains!

Contrast that with a fund with a low MER of just 0.5 percent, such as an index fund or ETF, which rang up the same gross return of 8 percent. Deducting its 0.5 percent MER, the low-cost fund would leave you with a return of 7.5 percent. At the risk of this becoming a math class, the lower-MER fund, by giving you a return of 7.5 percent, compared to the high-cost fund's return of 6 percent, gives you an extra profit of 1.5 percent. In other words, the low-cost fund provides you with a 25 percent higher return than the high-cost fund.

TIP

If you want to maintain an aggressive portfolio, try this:

- » **TD Canadian Index Fund - e (stocks):** 25 percent
- » **TD International Index Fund - e (stocks):** 25 percent
- » **TD Canadian Bond Index Fund - e:** 20 percent
- » **TD DJ Average Index Fund - e (stocks):** 15 percent
- » **TD S&P 500 Index ETF (stocks):** 15 percent

Mawer

Mawer Investment Management (800-889-6248; www.mawer.com) is a small Calgary-based firm that was an early leader in no-load funds that featured both strong returns and low MERs, and none of the far-too-common hidden fees the industry has an affection for. As Mawer puts it, ". . . no sales or trailing commissions, no setup fees, and no purchase, transfer, or redemption fees." For those with a higher net worth, Mawer offers its funds directly — along with investment advice. You can also purchase Mawer's funds through discount brokers.

TIP

If you want to maintain a conservative portfolio, try this:

- » **Mawer Balanced:** 50 percent
- » **Mawer Canadian Bond:** 25 percent
- » **Mawer Canadian Equity:** 25 percent

TIP

If you want to maintain an aggressive portfolio, try this:

- » **Mawer Balanced:** 35 percent
- » **Mawer Canadian Equity:** 20 percent
- » **Mawer Global Equity Fund:** 20 percent
- » **Mawer Global Small Cap Fund (stocks):** 20 percent
- » **Mawer Canadian Bond:** 5 percent

PH&N Investment Services

PH&N Investment Services (800-661-6141; www.phn.com) was originally known as Phillips, Hager & North. Founded in 1964, the Vancouver-based company built a well-deserved reputation for a focused portfolio of funds with low MERs and strong performances. Its run as one of the longest-standing customer-focused independent Canadian fund companies came to an end in 2008, when it was bought by RBC. The list of offerings has greatly expanded over the years, but the combination of low expense ratios, no commissions to buy or sell, and solid returns has remained a constant.

TIP

If you don't want to risk too much, try this:

>> **PH&N Balanced:** 40 percent

>> **PH&N Bond:** 30 percent

>> **PH&N Canadian Equity Value:** 20 percent

>> **PH&N Global Equity:** 10 percent

TIP

If you want to be aggressive, try this:

>> **PH&N Global Equity:** 25 percent

>> **PH&N Bond:** 20 percent

>> **PH&N Canadian Equity:** 20 percent

>> **PH&N U.S. Equity:** 20 percent

>> **PH&N Canadian Growth:** 15 percent

Vanguard

Vanguard (www.vanguardcanada.ca) is a mutual fund and ETF powerhouse in the United States, where it also operates a discount brokerage division. It's the largest no-load fund company, and it consistently has the lowest operating expenses in the business. Historically, Vanguard's funds have shown excellent performance when compared to those of the company's peers, especially among conservatively managed bond and stock funds. In Canada, Vanguard offers some four dozen different ETFs, as well as a small number of low-cost index funds.

Note: You can only reach Vanguard online and not by phone, because it isn't yet registered in Canada to deal directly with investors.

TIP

If you're looking for the ultimate in simplicity, but you don't want to give up performance and the safety that comes with proper diversification — or the very low cost of index ETFs — consider looking into Vanguard's four new asset-allocation ETFs. Launched in 2018, each allocation ETF is a "fund of funds," composed of a basket of seven different Vanguard ETFs. All are balanced funds, offering a professionally selected mix of both stocks and bonds. But you don't pay the management fees on each of those seven individual funds — you only pay an MER a single time, and it's on the asset-allocation ETF itself. And the costs are no higher than on Vanguard's regular ETFs, even though you're getting the benefit of someone managing the asset allocation for you. Three of Vanguard's ETF Portfolio offerings — the Balanced, Conservative, and Growth ETFs — charge just 0.22 percent. The fourth — the Global Balanced Fund — charges 0.28 percent.

>> **Vanguard Balanced ETF Portfolio:** Focuses on long-term capital growth, along with moderate income levels. The fund is approximately 60 percent stocks and 40 percent fixed income.

>> **Vanguard Conservative ETF Portfolio:** Aims to provide a combination of income and moderate long-term capital growth. The asset allocation is 40 percent stocks and 60 percent fixed income.

>> **Vanguard Global Balanced Fund:** Offers a combination of long-term capital growth with some current income. The target is to have two-thirds of the portfolio in stocks and one-third in fixed income.

>> **Vanguard Growth ETF Portfolio:** Designed to provide long-term capital growth. As the word *growth* in the name implies, the majority of this fund is in equities. The goal is around 80 percent in stocks and 20 percent in fixed income.

Discount brokers

You don't have to set up your RRSP with one particular mutual-fund company. As we discuss in Chapter 8, a discount brokerage account can allow you centralized, one-stop shopping and the ability to hold funds from a variety of leading fund companies.

Some funds are available without transaction fees, although most of the better funds require you to pay a small transaction fee when you buy funds through a discount broker. The reason: The discounter is a middleman between you and the fund companies. You have to weigh the convenience of being able to buy and hold funds from multiple fund companies in a single account versus the lower cost of buying funds directly from their providers. A $25 to $30 transaction fee can gobble a sizable chunk of what you have to invest, especially if you're investing smaller amounts.

Discount brokers allow you to set up *self-directed RRSPs*, in which you can choose from a huge range of investments — including mutual funds. When you buy through discount brokerages, you can buy hundreds of different mutual funds without paying transaction fees. However, there may be a charge for switching funds or selling within a certain period.

ASSESSING ROBO ADVISORS

So-called *robo advisors* walk you through a self-assessment, come up with a recommended asset allocation, and invest your money in a corresponding mix of low-cost ETFs and index funds. The *robo* part is that almost everything is automated, from account registration to *rebalancing* (adjusting how much money is invested in each fund to maintain the preferred asset allocation). The result is an alternative for investors to managing their portfolios on their own, but at a lower cost than that charged by brokers and investment counsellors. Robo advisors also have minimal initial investment requirements, unlike the $250,000, $500,000 or even $1 million necessary to open an account with many firms whose service is built around personalized asset allocation and rebalancing.

Robo advisors do offer low fees (typically 0.25 percent to 0.5 percent), but there are other costs you need to consider. In particular, you also have to pay the expenses charged by each individual ETF or index fund the robo advisor invests you in. The cost of the bulk of ETFs used by robo advisors runs between about 0.05 percent and 0.28 percent, with an average of around 0.2 percent. Taken together with the robo advisor's fee, that means the overall cost is more in the range of 0.45 percent to 0.7 percent.

Besides being excellent investments, the four Vanguard portfolio allocation fund of funds we discuss in this chapter are clearly meant to compete against robo advisors. In fact, many of the individual funds they hold — along with BlackRock iShares ETFs — are often used by robo advisors. But you save the extra 0.25 percent to 0.5 percent charged by the robo advisor.

Here is a suggested conservative portfolio and an aggressive portfolio using a basket of funds from different fund companies.

If you want to maintain a conservative portfolio, try this:

>> **BMO Aggregate Bond Index ETF:** 50 percent

>> **iShares Core MSCI All Country World ex Canada Index ETF:** 25 percent

>> **Vanguard FTSE Canada All Cap Index ETF:** 25 percent

If you want to maintain an aggressive portfolio, try this:

>> **iShares Core MSCI All Country World ex Canada Index ETF:** 30 percent

>> **BMO S&P TSX Capped Composite IDX ETF and/or Vanguard FTSE Canada All Cap Index ETF:** 25 percent

- » **iShares Core S&P US Total Market Index ETF and/or Vanguard S&P 500 Index ETF:** 20 percent
- » **BMO Aggregate Bond Index ETF:** 15 percent
- » **Vanguard Canadian Short-Term Bond Index ETF:** 5 percent
- » **Vanguard FTSE Emerging Markets All Cap Index ETF:** 5 percent

Understanding annuities: An odd investment

Annuities are contracts that are backed by an insurance company. If you, the annuity holder (investor), die during the so-called *accumulation phase* (that is, prior to receiving payments from the annuity), your designated beneficiary is guaranteed to receive the amount of your contribution. In this sense, annuities look a bit like life insurance.

Annuities, like RRSPs, allow your capital to grow and compound without taxation. You defer taxes until withdrawal. Unlike RRSPs, which have an annual contribution limit, you can deposit as much as you want into an annuity in any year — even a million dollars or more if you have it! However, you get no upfront tax deduction for your contributions.

TIP

Contributing to an annuity may make sense if

- » **You've exhausted contributions to RRSPs and employer-sponsored and self-employed plans.** Your contributions to these retirement plans are tax-deductible, while annuity contributions are not.

- » **You expect to leave the money compounding in the annuity for at least 15 years.** It typically takes this long for the benefits of tax-deferred compounding to outweigh the higher annuity fees and treatment of all withdrawn annuity earnings at the higher ordinary income-tax rates. If you're close to or are actually in retirement, tax-friendly investments made outside of registered retirement plans are preferable.

For details about other investment options and the best places to purchase annuities, see Chapter 13, where we discuss investing money outside of registered retirement plans.

Transferring Retirement Plans

Except for plans maintained by your current employer that limit your investment options, you can move your money held in an RRSP or other type of retirement plan, to almost any major investment firm. Moving the money is pretty simple: If you can fill out some forms and send them back in a postage-paid envelope (or complete them online), you can transfer a plan. The investment firm to which you're transferring your plan does the rest.

Transferring retirement plans you control

Here's a step-by-step list of what you need to do to transfer a retirement plan to another investment firm. Even if you're working with a financial advisor, you should be aware of this process (called a *direct trustee-to-trustee transfer*) to ensure that no hanky-panky takes place on the advisor's part and to ensure that the transfer is not taxable.

1. **Decide where you want to move the plan.**

We recommend several investment companies in this chapter, along with some sample portfolios within those firms. You may also want to consult the latest edition of our other book, *Investing For Canadians For Dummies* (Wiley) and visit Tony's website at www.moneygrower.ca.

2. **Obtain an application and asset transfer form.**

Call the toll-free number of the firm you're transferring the money to and ask for an application and asset transfer form for the type of plan you're transferring. You can also visit the firm's website, but for this type of request, most people find it easier to speak directly to someone.

TIP

Ask for the form for the same type of plan you currently have at the company from which you're transferring the money. You can determine the plan type by looking at a recent plan statement — the plan type should appear near the top of the statement or in the section with your name and address. If you can't figure out the type on a cryptic statement, call the firm where the plan is currently held and ask a representative to tell you what kind of plan you have.

WARNING

Never, ever sign over assets such as cheques and security certificates to a financial advisor, no matter how trustworthy and honest she may seem. Transfers should not be completed this way. The advisor can bolt with them quicker than you can say "Bonnie and Clyde." Besides, you'll find it easier to handle the transfer by following the information in this section.

3. **Figure out which securities you want to transfer and which need to be liquidated.**

Transferring existing investments in your plan or account to a new investment firm can sometimes be a little sticky. Transferring such assets as cash (money-market funds) or securities that trade on any of the major stock exchanges is not a problem.

TIP

If you own publicly traded securities, transferring them as is (also known as transferring them *in kind*) to your new investment firm is better, especially if the firm offers discount brokerage services. You can then sell your securities through that firm more cheaply.

If you own mutual funds unique to the institution you're leaving, check with your new firm to see whether it can accept them. If not, you need to contact the firm that currently holds them to sell them.

WARNING

GICs are tricky to transfer. Ideally, you should send in the transfer forms several weeks or so before the GICs mature — few people do this. If the GIC matures soon, call the bank and say that when the GIC matures, you would like the funds to be invested in a high-interest savings account, regular savings account, or money-market fund that you can access without penalty when your transfer request lands in the bank's mailbox.

4. **Complete and mail the application and asset transfer form.**

Completing this paperwork for your new investment firm opens your new plan and authorizes the transfer.

WARNING

Don't take possession of the money in your retirement plan when moving it over to the new firm. The tax authorities impose huge penalties if you perform a transfer incorrectly. For example, if you make the mistake of withdrawing your investments from an RRSP during the transfer process, the full amount gets included in your taxable income for that year, and you'll have to pay tax on it at your marginal tax rate. Let the company to which you're transferring the money do the transfer for you. If you have questions or problems, the firm to which you're transferring your plan has armies of capable employees waiting to help you. *Remember:* These firms know that you're transferring your money to them, so they should roll out the red carpet.

5. **Let the firm from which you're transferring the money know that you're doing so. (This step is optional.)**

If the place you're transferring the money from doesn't assign a specific person to your plan, you can definitely skip this step. When you're moving your investments from a brokerage firm where you dealt with a particular broker, deciding whether to follow this step can be more difficult.

Most people feel obligated to let their representative know that they're moving their money. In our experience, calling the person with the "bad news" is usually a mistake. Brokers or others who have a direct financial stake in your decision to move your money will try to sell you on staying. Some may try to make you feel guilty for leaving, and some may even try to bully you.

TIP

Writing a letter may seem like the coward's way out, but writing usually makes leaving your broker easier for both of you. You can polish what you have to say, and you don't put the broker on the defensive. Although we don't want to encourage lying, not telling the *whole* truth may be an even better idea. Excuses, such as that you have a family member in the investment business who will manage your money for free, may help you avoid an uncomfortable confrontation.

Then again, telling an investment firm that its charges are too high or that it misrepresented and sold you a bunch of lousy investments may help the firm improve in the future. Don't fret too much — do what's best for you and what you're comfortable with. Brokers are not your friends. Even though your broker may know your kids' names, your favorite hobbies, and your birthday, you have a *business* relationship with him.

Transferring your existing assets typically takes two to four weeks to complete. If the transfer is not completed within one month, get in touch with your new investment firm to determine the problem. If your old company isn't cooperating, call a manager there to help get the ball rolling.

The unfortunate reality is that an investment firm will cheerfully set up a new plan to *accept* your money on a moment's notice, but it will drag its feet, sometimes for months, when the time comes to relinquish your money. To light a fire under the folks at the investment firm, tell a manager at the old firm that you're going to send a letter to the provincial securities regulator if it doesn't complete your transfer within the next week.

Moving money from an employer's plan

WARNING

When you leave a job, particularly if you're retiring or being laid off after many years of service, money-hungry brokers and financial planners probably will be on you like a pack of bears on a tree leaking sweet syrup. If you seek financial help, tread carefully — Chapter 19 helps you avoid the pitfalls of hiring such assistance.

When you leave a job, you're confronted with a slightly different transfer challenge: If you've earned the right to some or all of your pension benefits (called *vesting*), you have the option of moving them into a special account called a

Locked-in Retirement Account (LIRA). In some provinces, these are called Locked-in RRSPs. (As long as your employer allows it, you may be able to leave your money in your old employer's plan. Evaluate the quality of the investment choices using the information we provide in this part of the book.)

REMEMBER

Never take personal possession of money from your employer's retirement plan. If you want to transfer your pension funds, establish an appropriate account at the investment firm you intend to use. Then tell your employer's benefits department where you'd like your retirement money transferred. You can send your employer the Canada Revenue Agency (CRA) forms and lock-in agreement (if required) that have been signed by the investment firm's retirement-plan trustee. These forms will contain the investment firm's mailing address and your account number.

Chapter **13**

Investing Outside Tax-Sheltered Retirement Plans

I n this chapter, we discuss investment options for money held outside registered retirement plans, and we include some sample portfolio recommendations. (Chapter 12 reviews investments for money *inside* registered retirement plans and accounts.) This distinction may seem somewhat odd — it's not one that's made in most financial books and articles. However, thinking of these two types of investment accounts differently can be useful because

» **Investments held outside registered retirement plans are subject to taxation.** You have a whole range of different investment options to consider when taxes come into play.

» **Money held outside registered retirement plans is more likely to be used sooner than funds held inside registered retirement plans.**

Why? Because you'll generally have to pay far more in income taxes to access money inside rather than outside registered retirement plans. (And you may be subject to penalties if you need to make early withdrawals from registered retirement plans.)

>> **Funds inside registered retirement plans have their own nuances.** For example, when you invest through your employer's Registered Pension Plan (RPP), your investment options are usually limited to a handful of choices. And special rules govern transfer of your retirement-plan balances.

Getting Started

Suppose that you have some money sitting in a bank savings account or money-market mutual fund, earning a pitiful amount of interest, and you want to invest it more profitably. You need to remember two things about investing this type of money:

>> **Earning a little is better than losing 20 percent to 50 percent or more.** Just talk to anyone who didn't do his homework and ended up buying a lousy investment. Be patient. Educate yourself *before* you invest.

>> **To earn a higher rate of return, you must be willing to take more risk.** In order to earn a better rate of return, you need to consider investments that fluctuate in value — of course, the value can drop as well as rise.

You approach the vast sea of investment options and start stringing up your rod to go fishing. You hear stories of people catching big ones — cashing in big on stocks or real estate that they bought years ago. Even if you don't have delusions of grandeur, you'd at least like your money to grow faster than the cost of living.

But before you cast your investment line, consider the following often overlooked ways to put your money to work and earn higher returns without much risk. These options may not be as exciting as hunting the big fish out there, but they can easily improve your financial health.

Paying off high-interest debt

TIP

Many folks have credit-card debt or other consumer debt that costs more than 10 percent — or even 20 percent, or higher — per year in interest. Paying off this debt with savings is like putting your money in an investment with a guaranteed return that's equal to the interest rate you're paying on the debt.

For example, if you have credit-card debt outstanding at 25 percent interest, paying off that loan is the same as putting your money to work in an investment with a sure 25 percent annual return. Remember that the interest on consumer debt is not tax-deductible, so you actually need to earn *more* than 25 percent investing your money elsewhere in order to net 25 percent after paying taxes. (See Chapter 5 for more details if you're still not convinced.)

If you can't pay off your credit cards, then the next best thing is to transfer your outstanding balances from cards with high interest rates to a card with a low interest rate. Be careful, however, that you don't sign up for a card with an attractively low *initial* interest rate, only to find that it gets bumped way up after six months or a year, if you're going to take at least that long to pay off the balance. You can find a current listing of our recommended low-rate credit cards on Tony's website, www.moneygrower.ca.

Paying off some or all your mortgage may make sense, too. This financial move isn't as clear as erasing consumer debt, because the mortgage interest rate is lower than it is on consumer debt.

Taking advantage of tax breaks

TIP

Make sure that you take advantage of the tax benefits offered on Registered Retirement Savings Plans (RRSPs) and other plans. If you work for a company that offers to match your contributions to a retirement savings plan, try to fund it at the highest level you can manage. If you earn self-employment income, consider an RRSP. (Refer to Chapters 11 and 12 for more about RRSPs.)

If you need to save money outside retirement plans for shorter-term goals (for example, to buy a car or a home, or to start or buy a small business), then by all means, save money outside registered retirement plans. This chapter shows you how to save and invest money in two valuable tax-friendly accounts: Tax-Free Savings Accounts (TFSAs) and Registered Disability Savings Plans (RDSPs). You also learn the best ways to invest in taxable accounts (nonregistered retirement plans that are exposed to taxation).

Taking Advantage of Tax-Free Savings Accounts

If you're 18 or older, and you have more than enough in a savings or chequing account to handle your regular ongoing cash needs and bill payments — say, a few thousand dollars — take advantage of a TFSA.

Think of a TFSA as being the reverse of an RRSP. Unlike an RRSP, you don't get to deduct money you put into a TFSA from your taxable income. However, any funds withdrawn aren't taxed.

Any interest, dividends, and capital gains you earn on the money and investments inside your TFSA are tax-free. That means your money can enjoy compound growth without the headwind of taxes slowing it down. TFSAs are easy to understand and a breeze to set up, and they'll help you save on taxes and help your money grow faster. What's not to like?

You can take out your money — and your profits — at any time, tax-free. So, a TFSA can help you reach both your short-term and long-term goals.

REMEMBER

Understanding how much you can contribute

Starting in 2009, you automatically earn the right to contribute to a TFSA each year. (For 2009 to 2002, the maximum was $5,000 per year. For 2013 and 2014, that amount was increased to $5,500. In 2015, the limit was nearly doubled to $10,000, after which it reverted to $5,500 for 2016 and subsequent years.) If you don't contribute the maximum allowed in any given year, the unused portion gets added to a running total of what you can contribute in any year in the future. In the jargon of the tax world, this is known as "carrying forward your unused contribution room." Unlike RRSPs, the allowable contribution is not affected in any way by your level of income or whether you're a member of a pension plan.

You can hold more than one TFSA, but the contribution ceiling applies to the total amount contributed, not the contributions made to each individual account.

REMEMBER

If you're married or living in common law, TFSAs offer an additional way to save on your taxes. If one spouse earns more than the other, the higher-earning spouse can give money to his or her partner, which the partner can use to make contributions to his or her own TFSA. (The maximum amounts are governed by the available contribution room of the person making the contribution.)

TIP

Normally, when you give money to your spouse and he or she then invests it, the Canada Revenue Agency (CRA) treats any gains as though you had earned them. In other words, the CRA attributes the gains to the giver, under the logically named *attribution income rules*. However, the attribution rules do not apply to funds put into a TFSA. This means that if a couple can come up with $10,000 total, they can contribute that full amount regardless of who put up what (each investing $5,000 into a TFSA) and enjoy tax-free growth on the full amount.

Understanding your investment choices

Most of the common types of investments that are allowed inside an RRSP are also eligible for use in a TFSA. This includes cash, term deposits, and guaranteed investment certificates (GICs). Exchange-traded funds (ETFs), mutual funds, bonds, and stocks are also allowed, as are shares of small-business corporations in certain cases. Regardless of the type of investment, your gains are not taxable. (Note that if you sell an investment inside a TFSA at a loss, that loss can't be used to reduce taxes on the gains on other investments outside your account.)

TIP

If you don't have actual cash on hand, you can start building up your TFSA if you own investments that aren't inside a registered plan. Most investments — including GICs, stocks, and units of mutual funds — can be contributed to a TFSA in the place of cash.

WARNING

If you do contribute an investment that has appreciated in value since you bought it, moving that investment into your TFSA will trigger a tax bill. When you do this — called making a *contribution in kind* — the tax department assesses your gains and taxes them, by using the value you originally paid for the investment and the value of the investment at the time you transfer it into your TFSA.

Making withdrawals

You can make withdrawals of any size from your TFSA at any time, and your withdrawals won't be taxed. One valuable wrinkle in the TFSA rules to be aware of is that the dollar amount of any withdrawal is added on to your available contribution room for the following year. This means you can take money out of your TFSA when needed and, beginning with the start of the next year, "re-contribute" that same amount of money at any point in the future. This rule not only applies to your original contributions, but also works with any profits you've earned inside your account and subsequently withdrawn.

The ability to re-contribute withdrawn funds opens up some potentially valuable strategies. In essence, you can enjoy tax-free gains, get access to those profits if you need them, and still leave yourself with the option of replacing the full amount you've withdrawn in future years. For example, say you invested $5,000 in a mutual fund inside your TFSA. The fund has a lucky streak, and in a few years' time, it's worth $8,500. You can sell the units, withdraw the $8,500, and at any point in the future have the right to put the full $8,500 back into your account. This is in addition to the annual maximum allowed, along with any other contribution room you've built up.

WARNING

Although you can replace any money you've taken out of a TFSA, you have to wait until the next calendar year. If you re-contribute money in the same year you've withdrawn it, that contribution will be added to any other contributions you've made that year. If the total is more than your allowable contribution, you'll be hit with a penalty of 1 percent per month on the overcontribution amount.

Understanding Registered Disability Savings Plans

If you or someone in your family has a disability, an RDSP is a valuable tool to help you provide for the longer-term financial needs you or your family member will face.

RDSPs work in a similar fashion to Registered Education Savings Plans (RESPs), which we explore in Chapter 14. Similar to RESPs and TFSAs (which we cover earlier), your contributions aren't tax-deductible. In other words, contributions have to be made with after-tax dollars. Inside the plan, your contributions can be invested in most common investments and any interest or gains you then earn aren't taxed.

Determining whether you're eligible for an RDSP

In order to open up an RDSP for yourself, you must be eligible for the disability tax credit, which in turn requires that the disability must be a severe and prolonged impairment that restricts your daily life and has lasted, or is expected to last, for at least 12 months. Parents or guardians can also open up an RDSP for a minor child with a disability that meets this definition.

The only restriction on contributions is a lifetime maximum limit of $200,000. Until that limit is reached, you can contribute as much as you like at any time, and no annual maximums exist. However, contributions can't be made beyond the end of the year the beneficiary turns 59.

TIP

Unlike all other special tax-friendly savings accounts and plans, no restrictions exist on who can put money into an RDSP. Beyond the beneficiary and his or her family, this means even distant relatives and friends can make contributions after an RDSP is set up.

Earning disability grants

Contributions to an RDSP earn the plan a government grant called the Canada Disability Savings Grant (CDSG). This grant is similar to the grant that accompanies RESP contributions (see Chapter 14). The grant isn't provided automatically — you have to apply for it through the financial institution where you have your RDSP.

Depending on our family's net income, and how much is contributed, the CDSG matches contributions at 100 percent, 200 percent, or 300 percent. A beneficiary of an RDSP can receive up to $3,500 in grants per year, and the maximum lifetime total grant is $70,000. One important point is that, for some reason, the grant is available only to those under the age of 49.

Lower-income families may qualify for a grant of Canada Disability Savings Bonds up to a value of $1,000 every year. The lifetime maximum is $20,000.

Withdrawing funds

Two different types of withdrawals, or *payments from an RDSP*, exist. Regardless of the method chosen, an annual maximum is placed on how much can be taken out.

It's important to watch the timing of these payments in order to protect the money received from government contributions to the plan. When payments from an RDSP are made, any grants or bonds that have been received in the previous ten years have to be returned to the government.

For a long time, there was a rule that required you to wait a minimum of ten years after you received your latest grant or bond before you withdrew money from the plan. If you withdrew money from the plan before the ten years were up, you generally were required to repay any grants or bonds (excluding interest) you'd received in the last ten years. This rule was revamped in 2014. Starting in January 2014, if you withdraw money before the ten-year period had gone by, for every dollar you take out of your RDSP, you only have to repay $3 of grants or bonds that went into your plan.

Lifetime disability assistance payments

One way to withdraw funds from an RDSP is through recurring annual payments. These are referred to as *lifetime disability assistance payments* (LDAPs). They can be started at any age, but at the latest they must begin the year the beneficiary turns 60. After they're started, they have to be continued until the death of the beneficiary.

The maximum that can be paid out each year is capped by an amusingly complex — and a tad too real — calculation. The formula is:

Current Value of Plan ÷ (3 + Life Expectancy – Current Age)

For example, take a plan where the beneficiary is 65, has a life expectancy of 80, and the plan is worth $100,000. You divide the value of the plan ($100,000) by 18 (3 + 80 − 65), making the maximum allowable annual payments $5,555.

Disability assistance payments

The second way that money can be paid out from an RDSP is through individual lump-sum payments called *disability assistance payments* (DAPs). A maximum exists for any single DAP, which is determined using the same formula as for LDAPs (see the preceding section).

Understanding Taxes on Your Investments

When you invest money outside of a registered retirement plan, investment gains — such as interest, dividends, and capital gains — are subject to tax. Too many folks (and too many of their financial advisors) ignore the tax impact of their investment strategies. You need to pay attention to the tax implications of your investment decisions *before* you invest your money.

Consider a person in a combined 34 percent tax bracket (federal plus provincial taxes) who keeps extra cash in a bond paying 3 percent interest. If he pays 34 percent of his interest earnings in taxes, he ends up keeping just 2 percent. If he weren't using that money as an emergency fund, he might consider putting it into a dividend-producing investment, such as a dividend mutual fund. The effective tax rates on dividend income are much lower than the tax rates for interest income. For someone in a 34 percent tax bracket, the effective tax rate on dividends is just a few percent. Table 13-1 shows the approximate effective tax rates on capital gains for 2018.

In the sections that follow, we give specific advice about investing your money while keeping an eye on taxes.

TABLE 13-1

Approximate Effective Tax Rates on Capital Gains for 2018

Taxable Income	Tax Rate (Bracket)
$0–$12,000	0%
$12,000–$46,000	0%
$46,000–$92,000	7.5%–12.5%
$92,000–$142,000	25%
$142,000–$203,000	31%
More than $203,000	39%

Fortifying Your Emergency Reserves

In Chapter 4, we explain the importance of keeping sufficient money in an emergency reserve account. From such an account, you need two things:

>> **Accessibility:** When you need to access your money for an emergency, you want to be able to do so quickly and without penalty.

>> **Highest possible return:** You want to get the highest rate of return possible without risking your principal. This factor doesn't mean that you should simply pick the money-market or savings option with the highest yield, because other issues, such as taxes, are a consideration. What good is earning a slightly higher yield if you pay a lot more in taxes?

The following sections give you information on investments that are suitable for emergency reserves.

Bank and credit-union accounts

When you have a few thousand dollars or less, your best and easiest path may be to keep this excess savings in a local bank or credit union. Look first to the institution where you keep your chequing account.

TIP

Keeping this stash of money in your chequing account, rather than in a separate savings account, makes financial sense if the extra money helps you avoid monthly service charges when your balance occasionally dips below the minimum. Compare the service charges on your chequing account with the interest earnings from a savings account.

For example, suppose you're keeping $4,000 in a savings account to earn 1 percent interest versus earning no interest on your chequing-account money. Over the course of a year, you earn $40 in interest on that savings account. If you incur a service charge of $9 per month on your chequing account, you pay $108 per year. So, keeping your extra $4,000 in a chequing account may be better financially if it keeps you above a minimum balance and erases that monthly service charge. (However, if you're more likely to spend the extra money in your chequing account, keeping it in a separate savings account where you won't be tempted to spend it may be better.)

High-interest savings accounts

A good choice for your short-term savings or emergency funds is a high-interest savings account. High-interest savings accounts fill the gap between a bank account (where you park a little money to cover your regular bill payments and cash needs) and mutual funds and other investments (in which you invest your savings for the longer term).

High-interest savings accounts usually don't offer all the usual features of regular bank accounts such as ATM access, bill payments, cheque writing, and so on, but in return you're rewarded with a much better interest rate.

TIP

You can arrange to have your paycheque deposited directly to a high-interest savings account, and have the account set up in conjunction with a chequing account.

TIP

Some of the best deals in high-interest savings accounts are with companies that don't have any actual branches in your neighbourhood or town. Although this may be somewhat unnerving, your money is generally just as safe as if it were in a traditional savings account. Just be sure to check that, like companies we mention in the following sections, the institution is a member of the Canada Deposit Insurance Corporation (CDIC), an insurance program that protects your savings up to $100,000. We recommend a few high-interest savings accounts here. Where we haven't mentioned the specific name of the account, it's because the institution offers more than one, with slightly different features.

But high-interest accounts are far from perfect. Don't expect the convenience of your everyday chequing account and 24/7 access to your money. Most don't come with debit cards — meaning no ATM withdrawals or retail purchases — or cheques. You'll likely be able to make bill payments, but you're generally limited to just a few e-transfers per month.

TIP

Here are some of the high-interest accounts we recommend. Just keep in mind that banks and credit unions regularly add new products or change the names of existing products, so these account names may change:

>> **Alterna Bank High Interest eSavings:** 866-560-0120; www.alternabahk.ca

>> **BMO Savings Builder:** 877-225-5266; www.bmo.com

>> **Canadian Tire High Interest Savings:** 866-681-2837; www.myctfs.com

>> **CIBC eAdvantage Savings:** 866-525-8622; www.cibc.com

>> **DUCA Credit Union Earn More Savings (Ontario only):** 866-900-3822; www.duca.com

>> **EQ Bank Savings Plus:** 844-437-2265; www.eqbank.ca

>> **Implicity Financial High Interest Savings:** 855-594-0990; www.implicity.ca

>> **Outlook Financial High-Interest Savings:** 877-958-7333; www.outlookfinancial.com

>> **RBC High-Interest eSavings:** 800-769-2511; www.rbcroyalbank.com

>> **Scotiabank Savings Accelerator:** 800-472-6842; www.scotiabank.com

>> **Simplii Financial High Interest Savings:** 888-723-8881; www.simplii.com

>> **Tangerine Saving:** 888-826-4374; www.tangerine.ca

>> **TD ePremium Savings:** 866-222-3456; www.td.com

TIP

For up-to-date listings of the best high-interest savings accounts, as well as the latest special offers, check out Tony's website, www.moneygrower.ca.

Money-market funds

Money-market funds, a type of mutual fund (see Chapter 10), are just like bank savings accounts — but better, in most cases. Although the best money-market funds pay higher yields than bank savings accounts, they generally don't come close to that of high-interest savings account. (For more, see the following sidebar, "High-interest savings accounts versus money-market funds.")

REMEMBER

The cost of a money-market fund is an important consideration. The operating expenses deducted before payment of dividends is the single biggest determinant of yield. All other things being equal (which they usually are with different money-market funds), lower operating expenses translate into higher yields for you. With interest rates as low as they have been in recent years, seeking out the money-market fund with the lowest operating expenses is more vital than ever.

Doing most or all your fund shopping (money market and otherwise) at one good fund company can reduce the clutter in your investing life. Chasing after a slightly higher yield offered by another company sometimes isn't worth the extra paperwork and administrative hassle. On the other hand, there's no reason why you can't invest in funds at multiple firms (as long as you don't mind the extra paperwork), using each for its relative strengths.

Most mutual-fund companies don't have many local branch offices, so you may have to open and maintain your money-market mutual fund over the phone, online, or through the mail. Distance has its advantages. Because you can conduct business remotely, you don't need to go schlepping into a local branch office to make deposits and withdrawals.

REMEMBER

Despite the distance between you and your mutual-fund company, you can usually have money transferred to your local bank on any business day, as well as having the fund company simply mail you a cheque. Don't fret about a deposit being lost in the mail; it rarely happens, and no one can legally cash a cheque made payable to you, anyway. Just be sure to endorse the cheque with the notation "for deposit only" under your signature.

TIP

Some of our favourite money market mutual funds include

>> **Beutel Goodman Money Market Fund:** 800-461-4551; www.beutelgoodman.com

>> **BMO Money Market Fund:** 844-837-9228; www.bmo.com

>> **Fidelity Canadian Money Market Fund:** 800-263-4077; www.fidelity.ca

>> **Leith Wheeler Money Market Fund:** 888-292-1122; www.leithwheeler.com

>> **Mawer Canadian Money Market Fund:** 800-889-6248; www.mawer.com

>> **PH&N Canadian Money Market Fund:** 800-661-6141; www.phn.com

>> **Sentry Money Market Fund:** 866-221-7692; www.sentry.ca

>> **Steadyhand Savings Fund:** 888-888-3147; www.steadyhand.com

>> **Sun Life Money Market Fund:** 877-344-1434; www.sunlifeglobal investments.com

>> **TD Canadian Money Market Fund:** 866-222-3456; www.tdcanadatrust.com

Canadian Treasury bill (T-bill) money-market funds are appropriate if you prefer a fund that invests solely in government-issued debt, which has the safety of government backing. Note that some of these funds are permitted to invest in other money-market securities. If the additional security is important to you, call the specific fund to ensure that it's 100 percent in T-bills before you invest.

HIGH-INTEREST SAVINGS ACCOUNTS VERSUS MONEY-MARKET FUNDS

High-interest savings are generally a better choice than money-market funds, which for years were the most popular place to park cash. Unlike money-market funds, high-interest savings accounts don't required a minimum deposit, nor do you have to worry about getting dinged with commissions, charges, or fees for withdrawing your money within a certain time frame. Another big plus is that, unlike a money-market fund, you can access your money quickly (although this may require first transferring it into a regular account) as long as your money has been in the account the required number of days. Most of these accounts allow you to access your cash simply by using a bank card at an ATM.

The purpose of money-market funds is to invest in short-term, highly liquid, and safe securities. In addition to government-backed T-bills, this includes GICs and *corporate commercial paper* (short-term debt) issued by the largest and most creditworthy companies. The value of these investments doesn't change. The returns from money-market funds come from the interest that they generate.

But when overall interest rates are low, so too are the returns on this class of investments. The challenge that simply can't be overcome by money-market funds is cost.

Here, in addition to the first wave of actual, self-title high-interest savings accounts, we're including the growing number of savings accounts available only online that offer rates far beyond what traditional bank savings accounts pay.

But what really tips the balance in favour of high-interest savings accounts? The returns. With the low interest rates we've seen in recent years, it has been a somewhat futile effort to search for good places to park your cash that allow you easy and fast access to your money, but that earn you any sort of reasonable interest in the meantime.

Money-market accounts still make sense if you're parking cash in an account with a brokerage firm or mutual fund company. Many also offer some version of a high-interest account, but moving your money in and out of them is sometimes not as simple as it is with a money-market fund. Additionally, some of these high-interest accounts charge a fee when you move money in or out of them. Others hit you with a hefty penalty fee if you take money out of the high-interest account within a few months of transferring it in.

>> **BMO T-Bill Fund:** 844-837-9228; www.bmo.com

>> **CIBC Canadian T-Bill Fund:** 800-465-2422; www.cibc.com

>> **Franklin Templeton Treasury Bill Fund:** 800-387-0830; www.frank lintempleton.ca

» **RBC Canadian T-Bill Fund:** 800-463-3863; www.rbcgam.com

» **Renaissance Canadian T-Bill Fund:** 888-888-3863; www.renaissance investments.ca

» **Scotia T-Bill Fund:** 800-268-9269; www.scotiabank.com

Investing for the Longer Term (Several Years or Decades)

REMEMBER

This section (together with its recommended investments) assumes that you have a sufficient emergency reserve stashed away and are taking advantage of tax-deductible retirement account contributions. (See Chapter 4 for more on these goals.)

Asset allocation refers to the process of figuring out what portion of your wealth to invest in different types of investments. You often (and most appropriately) practise asset allocation with retirement plans, because this money is earmarked for the long term. Ideally, more of your saving and investing should be conducted through tax-sheltered retirement accounts. These accounts generally offer the best way to lower your long-term tax burden (see Chapters 11 and 12 for details).

If you plan to invest outside retirement plans, asset allocation for these accounts depends on how comfortable you are with risk. But your choice of investments should also be suited to how much *time* you have until you plan to use the money. That's not because you won't be able to sell these investments on short notice if necessary (in most cases, you can). Investing money in a more volatile investment is simply riskier if you need to liquidate it in the short term.

For example, suppose that you're saving money for a down payment on a house and you're about one to two years away from having enough to make your foray into the real-estate market. If you had put this "home" money into the stock market near the beginning of one of the stock market's 20 percent to 50 percent declines (such as what happened in the early 2000s and then again in the late 2000s), you would've been mighty unhappy. A substantial portion of your money would've *vanished* in short order and your home-ownership dreams would've been put on hold.

Defining your time horizons

The different investment options in the remainder of this chapter are organized by time frame. All the recommended investment funds that follow assume that you have *at least* a several-year time frame, and they're all *no-load* (commission-free) mutual funds and ETFs. Funds can be sold on any business day, usually with a simple phone call or the click of a mouse. Funds come with all different levels of risk, so you can choose funds that match your time frame and desire to take risk. (Chapter 10 discusses all the basics of mutual funds.)

The recommended investments are also organized by your tax situation. (If you don't know your current tax bracket, review Chapter 7.) Here are summaries of the different time frames associated with each type of fund:

>> **Short-term investments:** These investments are suitable for a period of a few years — perhaps you're saving money for a home or some other major purchase in the near future. When investing for the short term, look for liquidity and stability — features that rule out real estate and stocks. Recommended investments include shorter-term bond funds, which are higher-yielding alternatives to money-market funds. If interest rates increase, these funds drop slightly in value — a couple of percent or so (unless rates rise tremendously). We also discuss Treasury bonds and GICs later in this chapter.

>> **Intermediate-term investments:** These investments are appropriate for more than a few years but less than ten years. Investments that fill the bill are intermediate-term bonds and well-diversified hybrid funds (which include some stocks as well as bonds).

>> **Long-term investments:** If you have a decade or more for investing your money, you can consider potentially higher-return (and therefore riskier) investments. Stocks, real estate, and other growth-oriented investments can earn the most money if you're comfortable with the risk involved. (See Chapter 8 for information on investing the portion that you intend to hold for the long term.)

Bonds and bond funds

Bond funds pay taxable distributions (mostly interest) that generally are taxed at your full marginal tax rate. Just like interest earned from a savings account, you have to pay tax on any interest generated by bond funds each year, whether the interest is distributed to you or reinvested in your fund. As a result, you're far better off holding bond funds inside your RRSP or RPP, where the interest isn't taxed and the full amount of your earnings can be reinvested.

INFLATION-INDEXED TREASURY BONDS

Like a handful of other nations, the Government of Canada now offers inflation-indexed government bonds. Because a portion of these Treasury bonds' return is pegged to the rate of inflation, the bonds offer investors a safer type of bond-investment option.

To understand the relative advantages of an inflation-indexed bond, take a brief look at the relationship between inflation and a normal bond. When an investor purchases a normal bond, she's committing herself to a fixed payment over a set period of time — for example, a bond that matures in ten years and pays 5 percent interest. However, changes in the cost of living (inflation) aren't fixed, so they're difficult to predict.

Suppose that an investor put $10,000 into a regular bond in the 1970s. During the life of her bond, she would've unhappily watched inflation escalate. During the time she held the bond, and by the time her bond matured, she would've witnessed the erosion of the purchasing power of her $500 of annual interest and $10,000 of returned principal.

Enter the inflation-indexed Treasury bond. Suppose you have $10,000 to invest and you buy a ten-year, inflation-indexed bond that pays you a "real" rate of return (the return above and beyond the rate of inflation) of, say, 2 percent (or $200). This portion of your return is paid out in interest. The other portion of your return is from the inflation adjustment to the principal you invested. The inflation portion of the return gets put back into the principal. So, if inflation were running at about 2 percent, as it has in recent years, your $10,000 of principal would be indexed upward after one year to $10,200. In the second year of holding this bond, the 2 percent real return of interest ($204), would be paid on the increased principal base ($10,200).

If inflation skyrocketed and was running at, say, 8 percent (as happened back in the 1970s and early 1980s) rather than 2 percent per year, your principal balance would grow 8 percent per year, and you'd still get your 2 percent real rate of return on top of that. Thus, an inflation-indexed Treasury bond investor doesn't see the purchasing power of his invested principal or annual interest earnings eroded by unexpected inflation.

The inflation-indexed Treasuries can be a good investment for conservative bond investors who are worried about inflation, as well as taxpayers who want to hold the government accountable for increases in inflation. The downside: Inflation-indexed bonds may yield slightly lower returns, because they're less risky compared to regular Treasury bonds.

Guaranteed investment certificates

For generations, GICs have been a popular investment for folks with some extra cash that they don't need in the near future. With a GIC, you get a higher rate of return than you get on a bank savings account. And unlike with bond funds, your principal doesn't fluctuate in value.

Compared to bonds, however, GICs have a couple of drawbacks:

>> **Inaccessibility:** In a GIC, your money isn't accessible unless you cough up a fairly big penalty — typically six months' interest. With a no-load (commission-free) bond fund, you can access your money without penalty — whether you need some or all your money next week, next month, or next year.

>> **Taxability:** A good deal of your earnings on GICs usually ends up in the CRA's hands. Unless you hold them in your RRSP, the interest earned on a GIC is taxed at your full marginal tax rate, the same rate as your salary.

TIP

In the long run, you can expect to earn more — perhaps 1 percent to 2 percent more per year — and have better access to your money in bond funds than in GICs.

One final piece of advice: Don't buy GICs simply for the CDIC insurance. Much is made, particularly by banks, of the CDIC insurance that comes with bank certificates of deposit (CDs). The lack of this insurance on high-quality bonds shouldn't be a big concern for you. High-quality bonds rarely default; even if a fund were to hold a bond that defaulted, that bond would probably represent only a tiny fraction (less than 1 percent) of the value of the fund, having little overall impact.

Besides, the CDIC itself is no Rock of Gibraltar. Banks have failed and will continue to fail. Yes, you're insured if you have less than $100,000 in a bank. However, if the bank fails, you may have to wait a long time and settle for less interest than you thought you were getting. You're not immune from harm, CDIC or no CDIC.

TIP

If the government backing you receive through CDIC insurance provides you with peace of mind, you can invest in T-bills (see "Bonds and bond funds," earlier in this chapter), which are government-backed bonds.

Stocks and stock funds

Stocks have stood the test of time for building wealth. (In Chapter 9, we discuss picking individual stocks versus investing through stock funds.) Remember that when you invest in stocks in taxable accounts (nonregistered retirement plans), all the distributions on those stocks, such as dividends and capital gains, are taxable. Stock dividends and capital gains do benefit from lower tax rates.

Additionally, increasing numbers of fund companies offer tax-friendly stock funds, which are appropriate if you don't want current income or you're in a high tax bracket and you want to minimize receiving taxable distributions on your funds. In general, the less a fund *turns over* (sells some holdings to buy different stocks), the lower the capital gains distributed to you each year, and the lower the amount of tax you'll have to pay on the fund's gains. As a result, index funds tend to have the best returns after taxes are accounted for.

Annuities

As we discuss in Chapter 12, *annuities* are accounts that are partly insurance but mostly investment. Consider contributing to an annuity only after you exhaust contributions to all your available retirement plans. Because annuities carry higher annual operating expenses than comparable mutual funds, you should consider them only if you plan to leave your money invested, preferably for 15 years or more. Even if you leave your money invested for that long, the tax-friendly funds discussed in the previous sections of this chapter can allow your money to grow without excessive annual taxation.

Real estate

Real estate can be a financially and psychologically rewarding investment. It can also be a money pit and a real headache if you buy the wrong property or get a "tenant from hell." (We discuss the investment particulars of real estate in Chapter 9 and the nuts and bolts of buying real estate in Chapter 15.)

Small-business investments

Investing in your own business or someone else's established small business can be a high-risk but potentially high-return option. The best investments are those you understand well. (See Chapter 9 for more on small-business investments.)

IN THIS CHAPTER

» **Understanding the financial-aid system**

» **Examining the right and wrong ways to save for university or college**

» **Figuring out how much you need to save**

» **Finding ways to pay for university or college when the time comes**

» **Exploring educational investment options**

Chapter **14**

Investing for Educational Expenses

I f you're like most parents (or potential future parents), just turning to this chapter makes you anxious. Such trepidation is understandable. According to much of what you read about educational expenses (particularly university expenses), if costs keep rising at the current rate, you'll have to spend upward of tens of thousands of dollars to give your youngster a quality postsecondary education.

Whether you're about to begin a regular education investment plan or you've already started saving, your emotions may lead you astray. The hype about educational costs may scare you into taking a financially detrimental path. However, quality education for your child doesn't have to — and probably won't — cost you as much as those gargantuan projections suggest. In this chapter, we explain the inner workings of the financial-aid system, help you gauge how much money you'll need, and discuss educational investment options so that you can keep a cool head (and some money in your pocket) when all is said and done.

Strategizing to Pay for Educational Expenses

TIP

We don't have just one solution to paying for your kids' education, because how you help pay for your child's university costs depends on your own unique situation. However, in most cases, you may have to borrow *some* money, even if you have some available cash that can be directed to pay the university bills as you receive them.

By concentrating on contributing to your Registered Retirement Savings Plan (RRSP) or company pension plan and paying down your mortgage today, you'll have a number of options when your kids graduate from high school. If you've paid down some — or all — of your mortgage, you can borrow against the paid-up value of your home (your *home equity*), usually at or near the lowest interest rate available (the *prime rate*).

You'll already have some strong momentum and compounding going on if you've been building up your retirement savings. You've also established a savings habit. When your kids get close to university age, you can divert your RRSP or other retirement-plan contributions to help pay their education costs. When they graduate, you can easily résumé your RRSP contributions.

You can even take advantage of the allowable RRSP contributions you missed out on because you're allowed to carry forward unused contributions indefinitely. (The Canada Revenue Agency [CRA] tracks this for you. You'll find a summary on the income-tax return assessment notice you receive every year.) This will leave you in much better financial shape than if you had forgone contributions to your RRSP or company retirement savings plan when you were younger in order to start an educational savings program.

Plus, when your kids are ready to go to university, you'll likely be in your peak earning years, so some extra funds will probably be available.

Estimating university or college costs

University or college can cost a lot. The total costs — including tuition, fees, books, supplies, room, board, and transportation — vary substantially from school to school. The total average annual cost for tuition in the 2017–2018 school year was $6,571 for undergraduate programs, while the average cost for graduate programs was just over $6,900, according to Statistics Canada. If the student wants to study away from home, you can ballpark doubling that figure to include room and board.

TIP

These numbers hide a great variance in the price of postsecondary education across the country. According to Statistics Canada, for example, the average annual cost of undergraduate tuition for social and behavioural sciences was $5,721 for 2017–2018. But that cost ranged from just $2,550 in Newfoundland to $6,860 in Nova Scotia. Meanwhile, Quebec had the lowest tuition for undergraduate studies in business, management, and public administration, at $2,731. Pursue those same studies in Ontario, and you'll be looking at an average tuition of over $10,000. Ouch!

Is all this expense worth it? Although many critics of higher education claim that the cost shouldn't be rising faster than inflation and that costs can, and should, be contained, denying the value of going to university is hard. Whether you're considering a local community college, your friendly nearby university, or a select high-end business school, investing in education is usually worth the effort and the cost.

REMEMBER

An *investment* is an outlay of money for an expected profit. Unlike a car, which depreciates in value, an investment in education yields monetary, social, and intellectual profits. A car is more tangible in the short term, but an investment in education (even if it means borrowing money) gives you more bang for your buck in the long term.

Universities and colleges are now subject to the same types of competition that companies confront. As a result, many schools are clamping down on rising costs. As with any other product or service purchase, it pays to shop around. You can find good values — schools that offer competitive pricing *and* provide a quality education. Although you don't want your kids to choose a university simply because it costs the least, you also shouldn't allow them to choose a university without any consideration or recognition of cost.

Setting realistic savings goals

If you have money left over *after* taking advantage of retirement plans, by all means try to save for your children's university costs.

Be realistic about what you can afford for university expenses given your other financial goals, especially saving for retirement (see Chapter 4). Being able to personally pay 100 percent of the cost of a university education is a luxury of the very affluent. If you're not a high-income earner, consider trying to save enough to pay a third or, at most, half of the cost. You can make up the balance through loans, your child's employment before and during university, and the like.

Use Table 14-1 to help get a handle on how much you should be saving for university.

TABLE 14-1   # How Much to Save for University or College*

Figure Out This	Write It Here
1. Cost of the school you think your child will attend**	$ _____
2. Percentage of costs you'd like to pay (for example, 20% or 40%)	× _____ %
3. Line 1 times line 2 (the amount you'll pay in today's dollars)	= $ _____
4. Number of months until your child reaches university or college age	÷ _____ months
5. Line 3 divided by line 4 (amount to save per month in today's dollars)***	= $ _____

Don't worry about correcting the overall analysis for inflation. This worksheet takes care of that through the assumptions made on the returns of your investments, as well as the amount that you save over time. This way of doing the calculations works because you assume that the money you're saving will grow at the rate of inflation of education costs. (In the happy event that your investment return exceeds the rate of university or college inflation, you end up with a little more than you expected.)

** The average cost of a four-year university education today is about $50,000.*

*** The amount you need to save (calculated in line 5) needs to be increased once per year to reflect the increase in university or college inflation — 5 percent or 6 percent should do.*

Strategies for Saving for Education Expenses

If you have enough money to take care of your other needs, such as contributing to an RRSP, terrific! You can also start putting away money for your children's postsecondary education. Just as important as the specific investments you choose is the way in which you organize your savings efforts.

There are two basic ways to set up an effective savings plan for postsecondary education expenses:

>> **Registered Education Savings Plans (RESPs):** For many people, an RESP is a great way to save, thanks in part to a generous government grant program.

>> **In-trust accounts:** Under an in-trust account arrangement, you put money into a special account and invest it on your child's behalf. If your children might not attend university or college, this could be a better choice.

Registered Education Savings Plans

If you're familiar with RRSPs (see Chapter 11), RESPs will be fairly easy to grasp. However, a few major differences between these two savings plans exist.

One of the big attractions of an RESP is that, as with an RRSP, money inside the plan can grow without being taxed. As a result, all your profits — whether interest, dividends, or capital gains from the appreciation in the value of stocks and mutual funds — can be put right back to work for you to deliver further gains.

Unlike contributions to an RRSP, however, your contributions to an RESP are not exempt from taxation. You don't get to deduct the money you put into an RESP when arriving at your taxable income.

But one other — and very valuable — difference between RRSPs and RESPs exists. Money put into an RESP earns you a contribution to your plan in the form of a grant from the federal government. The official name of the grant is the Canada Education Savings Grant (CESG). The CESG can make a sizable dent in the cost of postsecondary education, particularly if you start contributing to an RESP when your children are young.

To qualify for the grant, the RESP beneficiary must be a resident of Canada and be 17 or younger. The beneficiary must also have a Social Insurance Number; these can take several weeks to obtain. Contact Human Resources and Skills Development Canada for an application. (For more information, see "Maximizing RESP grants," later in this section.)

The total lifetime contribution limit per child is $50,000. There is no limit on the amount you can contribute to an RESP in any given year. (Prior to 2007, there was a yearly maximum of $4,000 per year for each child.) Over contributions are taxed at 1 percent for each month they remain in the plan.

You're allowed to contribute money for up to 31 years. (If the beneficiary has a disability, contributions can be made for 35 years.) The plan can be kept open — and the money inside earning tax-sheltered gains — for another four years. However, the maximum life span of an RESP is 35 years, after which the plan must be wound up. (For beneficiaries with a disability, the RESP can remain in operation for 40 years.)

You'll find two basic types of RESPs:

TIP

>> **"Scholarship" plans:** Because these plans are limited to mostly guaranteed investments, the rate of return on your plan is mediocre.

>> **Self-directed or mutual-fund RESPs:** You can open one with most brokerage and mutual-fund firms, often at no charge. A self-directed or mutual fund RESP allows you to choose from a wide range of investments. If you start an RESP when your children are still in diapers, these plans are a much better choice because they allow you to benefit from the larger earning potential of equities and equity mutual funds.

Making withdrawals

Money that you contribute to an RESP isn't tax-deductible, but any gains inside the plan are not taxed. When your child is ready to go to school, money from the plan can be taken out and used for a variety of education-related expenses. The original money that you contributed isn't taxed, but any gains on the money inside the plan, as well as the CESG, is subject to tax. However, it's taxed as income or gains to the student. Given that students typically have a very low income, as well as many education-related deductions and credits, your child will probably pay little, if any, tax on the withdrawals.

Investigating what happens if your child doesn't go to university

In the past, a major drawback to RESPs was that if your child didn't go to a post-secondary institution, you forfeited the earnings — either to another child, to an educational institution, or, in the case of pooled or "scholarship" RESPs, to other children in the program.

The rules have been greatly relaxed, however. You can now transfer up to $50,000 of the earnings from an RESP to your RRSP or your spouse's RRSP, as long as you have the contribution room available. The tax deduction you get on the money going into your RRSP offsets the tax on the funds you withdraw from the RESP. In order to transfer out profits from an RESP in this way, the plan must have been running for a minimum of ten years, with none of the beneficiaries being postsecondary students by age 21. And although any grants received under the CESG program must be repaid, any money earned inside the plan on the grants can be kept.

For an individual RESP, another option is to name a sibling as a replacement for the original beneficiary. (For a family plan, another child can be added.) If this is done, the grant doesn't have to be repaid and can be used by the new beneficiary for postsecondary education.

WARNING

Any earnings that can't be transferred in this way can still be moved out of the RESP, but they're taxed at your marginal tax rate plus an additional 20 percent penalty. (You can take out your original contributions — your principal — without any penalties or restrictions.)

Also, you can open a family plan, into which you can make contributions for several children. If one of the children in the plan chooses not to pursue a post-secondary education, both the money you've contributed to the plan for that child, as well as any gains it has rung up, can be used by the other children in the plan.

Maximizing RESP grants

Under the CESG program, the government will make a contribution to the RESP of 20 percent of the first $2,500 of contributions you make in a year. The maximum grant (as of 2018) was $500 per year per child for each year the beneficiary is under 18.

Grant rates for lower- and middle-income families are enhanced. For 2018, families with incomes of $46,605 or less earned a 40 percent CESG on their first $500 of RESP contributions. Families with incomes between $46,605 and $93,208 earned a 30 percent CESG on the first $500 they contributed. The maximum CESG payable each year is also increased to accommodate the enhanced grants.

NEGLECTING RRSPs: A BIG MISTAKE

You want what's best for your children. As a parent, that's a given. Not only do you want to be able to provide good learning opportunities for them when they're young, but you also want to give them choices. When little Dweezil and Moon Unit fill out their university applications, you don't want to have to say that you can't afford to send them to their dream school.

We know you're going to think that our advice sounds selfish. But consider this reality: You have to provide for your own financial security before saving for your child.

If you're a frequent flyer, think back to your most recent trip by airplane. Remember what the flight attendants instructed you to do in an emergency? In the event of a loss of air pressure that necessitates the use of oxygen masks, put your own oxygen mask on *first.* Only then should you help your children with their oxygen masks.

Consider for a moment why airlines recommend this approach. Although your instinct may be to ensure that your children are safe before taking care of yourself, by taking care of yourself first, you're stronger and better able to help your children.

Similarly, in regard to your personal finances, you need to take care of yourself first. You should save and invest through an RRSP or other retirement savings plan that gives you significant tax benefits.

Take care of your long-term financial needs first (for example, by saving through an RRSP). By doing so, you strengthen your financial health, which better enables you in the long run to help your kids with their educational expenses. (See Chapters 7 and 11 to find out how to reduce your taxes and save for retirement.)

If you don't contribute enough in any year to get the full $500 grant, you can earn the unused portion in later years. (For the years 1998 to 2006, the annual CESG contribution room was $2,000.) However, regardless of how much unused CESG you have, the maximum per beneficiary in any one year is capped at whichever is lower, $1,000 or 20 percent of any unused RESP room. The total lifetime maximum you can receive under this program is $7,200. The grants aren't included in assessing your yearly and lifetime contribution limits.

WARNING

The government has removed the ceiling on how much you can contribute to an RESP in any given year, as long as you don't exceed the overall lifetime limit of $50,000. However, before contributing more than the amount needed to earn the maximum CESG for the year, weigh the extra profits a large lump-sum contribution can earn over time against the loss of potential grants. The problem is that if you contribute in excess of what's needed to earn you the maximum grant in one year, that "overcontribution" can't be used to earn a grant in future years.

In-trust accounts

In-trust accounts — also known as *informal trusts* — allow you to save money for your child's future and have a portion of your earnings compound tax-free.

TECHNICAL
STUFF

You'll likely see these accounts referred to as *ITF account.* The acronym *ITF* stands for "in trust for." The account is "in trust" because minors can't enter into financial contracts.

No restrictions exist on contributions to an in-trust account. You can put in as much or as little you wish at any time.

When money is inside an informal trust, it belongs to the child. All profits on investments inside the trust are taxed. The person who contributes the money pays taxes on the dividends and income, but the child is responsible for paying taxes on any capital gains. Because most children don't have enough income to actually have to pay any tax, that portion of the account can compound tax-free. Because of this, the best investments for an in-trust account, especially when many years are left before the child will need the money, are equity mutual funds, where most of the profits are in the form of capital gains.

REMEMBER

If you set up an in-trust account and contribute only Child Tax Benefit payments, these tax rules don't apply. All the gains — whether in the form of capital gains, interest, or dividends — are taxed to the child.

USING YOUR RRSP SAVINGS TO PAY UNIVERSITY OR COLLEGE EXPENSES

You can use the money inside an RRSP to help finance a postsecondary education or full-time training for either yourself or your spouse. Under the federal government's Lifelong Learning Plan, you can withdraw up to $10,000 per year from your RRSP for four years. The maximum amount you can withdraw over that time is $20,000.

Much like the RRSP Home Buyers' Plan (see Chapter 15), using your RRSP to fund an education has several drawbacks. Although the withdrawals are not taxed, you have to repay the money to your RRSP in equal instalments over ten years. The first payment has to be made within 60 days after the end of the fifth year after your first withdrawal.

Any repayments not made are included in the taxable income of the person who made the withdrawal. In addition, you'll likely find it difficult to repay what you've taken out for education expenses, as well as continue your regular contributions. In that case, you'll have to be able to get by on less if you've been factoring your tax rebate from a regular RRSP contribution into your cash flow, because your repayments don't earn you a deduction. Plus, borrowing money from your plan, as well as delaying new contributions while you repay those funds, will significantly reduce the long-term growth of your retirement savings.

WARNING

The big drawback to informal trusts is that when the child turns 18, the money and all the profits legally become hers to spend as she wishes. No rules specify what the money must be spent on, so your child can use it for purposes other than an education, such as starting her own small business. Although you can hope that little Moon Unit will spend the money wisely, you can't do anything if, on the day of her 18th birthday, she empties her account and buys a convertible.

Certain steps are involved in setting up an in-trust account. When you open the account, you must clearly delineate the role of everybody involved. The person who puts money into the account is known as the *settlor* or *contributor.* The law requires that a different person (the *trustee*) have the responsibility of overseeing how the money is invested on behalf of the child (the *beneficiary*). When you set up an account, ensure that you use the proper phrasing: your name (if you are the trustee) followed by "in trust for" and then your child's name.

Obtaining Loans, Grants, and Scholarships

A host of financial aid programs, including a number of loans programs, enable you to borrow at fair interest rates. Additionally, a wide range of grants and scholarships are available from schools, service clubs, local companies, and other sources.

TIP

Your child can work and save money during high school and university. In fact, if your child qualifies for financial aid, he may be expected to contribute a certain amount to education costs from savings and from employment during the school year or summer breaks. Besides giving your child a stake in his own future, this training encourages sound personal financial management down the road.

Government student-loans programs

The Canada Student Loans Program (CSLP) is the largest source of college and university student loans in the country. The program is run by the federal government in conjunction with the provinces. The provinces administer the loans through their own separate student-aid offices.

Each province also has its own loan scheme that's rolled in with the CSLP. (Want to find out more about your province's student-loans program? Go to `www.canada.ca/en/services/jobs/education/student-financial-aid`, click the Student Loans link, and then click the Provincial and Territorial Information for Canada Student Loans and Grants link.)

To qualify, students must be citizens or permanent residents of Canada, attend an institution recognized by the program, and meet the criteria for being either part-time or full-time students. Students must also live in a province that participates in the CSLP; if your province doesn't, it will run its own distinct loans program to which the federal government contributes.

You generally need to submit only one application to receive loans from both programs, although interest and conditions on the federal loan and the provincial loan differ slightly. Regardless of where they're going to go to school, your kids must apply to the province in which they live. Applications can be obtained from any university or college or by calling your provincial student-loans program. Find the number online. The school needs to be a *designated educational institution*. See the sidebar "Are you eligible for loans or grants at your preferred postsecondary institution or school?" for the details.

TIP

Part of the assessment process involves examining your entire family's income. The assessment is based solely on cash flow — assets don't come into the picture at all. As a result, it doesn't pay to neglect contributing to your RRSP or company retirement savings plan or paying down your mortgage.

WARNING

The loans programs demand that parents assist in paying the education costs of any dependent children. Even if parents absolutely refuse to assist their children, their ability to pay will still be taken into account when the application is assessed. In order not to be classified as a dependant, a child must have graduated from high school at least four years earlier or have been in the workforce for at least 24 months.

ARE YOU ELIGIBLE FOR LOANS OR GRANTS AT YOUR PREFERRED POSTSECONDARY INSTITUTION OR SCHOOL?

The list of universities, colleges, and schools to which you can apply for government loans and grants is long and extensive. To check whether the institution your child wants to attend qualifies, go to www.canada.ca/en/services/jobs/education and click the List of Designated Educational Institutions link. (It's usually located under the "Most Requested" heading. If it's no longer there, search for "List of Designated Educational Institutions" using the search box at the top of the page.) The Master List gives you the four-digit Educational Institution Code for each school, along with its name and address.

If you can't find the name of the school you're thinking of attending, don't assume studying there means you won't qualify for loans or grants. The Master List isn't quite as "masterful" as its name suggests. Strangely, if a borrower has not recently attended a particular educational institution, it may disappear from this list! Contact your provincial or territorial student financial-aid authority to get a definitive answer.

If the loan is approved, your children should go to the financial-aid office when they enroll at their university or college. They'll be given some loan documents, which they can then take to the bank of their choice. (The loans are administered through the big banks, but the provincial and federal governments guarantee them.) A number of credit unions and *caisses populaires* are also approved student-loan providers. The maximum amount available varies depending on which province the student lives in.

TECHNICAL STUFF

The interest rate on the two components is calculated differently. The rate on the federal part of the loan is fixed once a year at a percentage or so above the best rates offered by financial institutions (the *prime rate*). The provinces tend to use a floating rate. For example, a province may charge prime plus 1 percent on its loans, with the rate rising and falling along with the going prime rate.

The federal and provincial governments pay the interest on the debt until the student either graduates or withdraws. At that point, the federal government stops paying its share of the interest, and the student is responsible for the debt. Some provinces, however, will continue to pay the debt costs on their part of the loan for an additional six months.

Even though the federal government stops paying the interest on its portion of the combined loan at graduation, students aren't required to start repaying the federal or provincial component of their loan until six months after graduation. Generally, this due date falls on November 1. At that time, students must negotiate a schedule with their bank. Although students are largely free to choose whatever repayment time frame they like, both the federal and provincial loans must be completely paid off within 114 months (ten years minus six months, or basically nine and a half years). After the student signs agreements for the two separate loans, most institutions will consolidate the debts and work out a single payment schedule.

WARNING

Both Ottawa and the provinces have become aggressive in tracking down delinquents and getting their money back. The federal government can even take what it's owed out of the tax refunds of those who are behind on their payments. Worse yet, many past-due student loans are now routinely handed over to collection agencies, and the students end up with a nick on their credit rating.

WARNING

In addition to the negative impact it will have on the student's credit rating, declaring bankruptcy if student loans become overwhelming comes with strict conditions. Changes to the bankruptcy rules in the late 2000s mean that a student who declares bankruptcy after July 7, 2008, cannot have his loans discharged until seven years after he has finished attending school.

If a student mistakenly files for bankruptcy before that period is deemed to have officially passed, the student loans will not be forgiven. As a result, it's best to be cautious. Count the seven years from the day of the student's last exam, or from the day he actually stopped attending school, whichever is the later. Then add 30 or 60 days to that, just to be safe. (The seven-year waiting period may be reduced to five years in the case of extreme financial hardships.)

Canada Student Grants

Canada Student Grants is the umbrella name for a number of grants available to students in a variety of circumstances enrolled at a designated postsecondary institution. (The money used to be distributed through the Canada Access Grants program. That program has ended, but the grants for each specific situation are now available under a matching name.)

In general, an application for any relevant grant is made automatically when you apply and qualify for student financial assistance through your province or territory for studying at a designated postsecondary institution. For the details on which schools qualify as designated postsecondary institutions, see the sidebar earlier in this chapter, "Are you eligible for loans or grants at your preferred postsecondary institution or school?"

To get an estimate of how much you can get in grants, check out the Government of Canada's Student Financial Assistance Estimator. You can find it at www.canada.ca/en/services/benefits/education/grants. In this section, we include the latest maximum amounts available for the different grants, which are for the 2017–2018 school year. With any luck, they'll increase for future years.

Canada Student Grant for Full-Time Students

The Canada Student Grant for Full-Time Students is available to students from low- and middle-income families who are enrolled in a full-time undergraduate program. The grant can be for up to $3,000 per eight-month school year, or $375 per month.

You're eligible if *all* of the following apply to you:

>> You've applied and qualified for student financial assistance. (You must have at least $1 of assessed financial need.)

>> You're from a low- or middle-income family as defined by the CSLP.

>> You're enrolled full-time in an undergraduate degree, diploma, or certificate program that's at least two years (60 weeks) in duration at a designated postsecondary institution.

Canada Student Grant for Full-Time Students with Dependants

You may be able to get the Canada Student Grant for Full-Time Students with Dependants if you have a young dependant, are from a low-income family (as defined by the CSLP), and are in a full-time program.

The grant can be worth up to $200 a month for every dependent child you have. The grant is available every year that you're studying full-time, including both undergraduate- and graduate-level studies. Any grant you receive under this program is in addition to any money that you receive from the Canada Student Grant for Students from Low-Income Families.

For example, suppose you qualify for a government grant, and your assessed need is $2,500. In that case, you would get a $1,600 Grant for Students with Dependants for each qualifying child, as well as a Grant for Students from Low-Income Families of $2,500, assuming eight months of study.

You're eligible if *all* of the following apply to you:

>> You've applied and qualified for student financial assistance. (You have at least a $1 of assessed financial need.)

>> You come from a family deemed low-income by the CSLP.

>> You're enrolled in a full-time degree, diploma, or certificate program. The program must run at least 12 weeks in a 15-week period at a designated postsecondary institution.

>> You have at least one dependant who will be less than 12 years of age when you begin your studies. (You also qualify if you have a dependant 12 years of age or older who has a permanent disability.)

Canada Student Grant for Students with Permanent Disabilities

If you have a permanent disability, this grant is available — for each year of your studies — as long as you continue to qualify. This includes both undergraduate- and graduate-level studies. The grant is $2,000 for each school year, which runs from August 1 to July 31. (There is also a separate grant available to assist you in paying for education-related costs, called the Canada Student Grant for Services and Equipment for Students with Permanent Disabilities.)

To be eligible, *all* the following must apply to you:

>> You've applied and qualified for full-time or part-time student financial assistance. (You have at least a $1 of assessed financial need.)

>> You're enrolled in a full-time or part-time program at a designated postsecondary institution.

>> You qualify as a student with a *permanent disability,* which is defined as "a functional limitation caused by a physical or mental impairment that restricts the ability of a person to perform the daily activities necessary to participate in studies at a postsecondary school level or the labour force; and is expected to remain with the person for the person's expected life."

>> You include proof of your disability with your loan application. This can be in the form of one of the following:

- A medical certificate

- A psycho-educational assessment

- Documents that prove you've received federal or provincial permanent disability assistance

Canada Student Grant for Part-Time Studies

The Canada Student Grant for Part-Time Studies is available for students studying part-time and who meet the definition of *low income*. The grant is $1,800 for each school year.

To qualify, *all* of the following must apply to you:

>> You've applied and qualified for part-time student financial assistance.

>> You have a low family income as defined by the CSLP. Your spouse or common-law partner, if you have one, is included in this calculation.

>> You're enrolled in a part-time degree, diploma, or certificate program. The program has to be at least 12 weeks in length and fall within a period of 15 weeks in a row at a designated postsecondary institution.

>> You've successfully completed all courses for which you previously received a grant.

Canada Student Grant for Part-Time Students with Dependants

If you have a low income, you're studying part-time, and you have dependants, you may be eligible for the Canada Student Grant for Part-Time Students with Dependants. If you have one or two dependants, you can get up to $40 for each week you're at school. If you have more than two dependants, the weekly maximum is $60. There is also a limit of $1,920 per school year.

To be eligible, *all* of the following must apply to you:

>> You've applied and qualified for part-time student financial assistance.

>> You have a low family income as defined by the CSLP. (If you're married or living in common law, this is assessed using both your income and that of your spouse or common-law partner.)

>> You're enrolled in a part-time degree, diploma, or certificate program that runs at least 12 weeks within a 15-week period at a designated postsecondary institution.

>> You have a dependant who will be under 12 years of age at the start of the study period, or a dependant with a permanent disability who is 12 or older.

>> The province or territory where you lived most recently for at least 12 months in a row assesses that your financial need meets its requirements.

Additional grants worth investigating

In addition to these specific grants, there are several other worth looking into:

>> **Apprenticeship Completion Grant:** This grant is given to registered apprentices who have completed their apprenticeship training and get their journeyperson certification.

>> **Apprenticeship Incentive Grant:** This grant is for apprentices who've completed either their first or second year or level of an apprenticeship program in a designated Red Seal trade.

>> **Athlete Assistance Program:** The program provides funding for athletes who are training for world-class performances while working or in school.

>> **Legal Studies for Aboriginal People Program:** Métis or Non-Status Indians who want to go to law school may be eligible for this bursary.

>> **Post-Secondary Student Support Program:** This program offers financial assistance to First Nations and eligible Inuit students who are enrolled in eligible postsecondary programs.

>> **University and College Entrance Preparation Program for Aboriginal People:** This program provides financial assistance for First Nations and Inuit students for courses they need to take in order to meet the admission requirements for postsecondary studies.

Tips for getting loans, grants, and scholarships

A number of grant programs are available through schools and the government, as well as through independent sources. Employers, banks, credit unions, and community groups also offer grants and scholarships. In addition to the aid offices at universities and colleges, look into directories and databases at your local library, and speak with your child's school counselling department. Also try local organizations, churches, employers, and so on. You have a better chance of getting scholarship money through these avenues.

WARNING

Postsecondary scholarship search services are generally a waste of money — and in some cases, they're scams. Some of these services charge up to $100 or more just to tell you about scholarships that either you're already being considered for or that you aren't even eligible for.

Investing Educational Funds

Financial companies pour millions of dollars into advertising for investment and insurance products that they claim are best for making your money grow for your children. Don't get sucked in by these ads.

What makes for good and bad investments in general applies to investments for educational expenses, too. Stick with basic, proven, lower-cost investments. (Chapter 9 explains what you generally need to look for and beware of.) The following sections focus on considerations specific to investing to pay for university or college.

Good investments: No-load mutual funds and exchange-traded funds

As we discuss in Chapter 10, the professional management and efficiency of the best no-load mutual funds makes them a tough investment to beat. Chapters 12 and 13 provide recommendations for investing money in funds both inside and outside tax-sheltered retirement plans.

Gearing the investments to the time frame involved until your children will need to use the money is the most important issue with no-load mutual funds and exchange-traded funds (ETFs). The closer your child gets to attending university or college and using the money, the more conservatively the money should be invested.

Bad investments

Life-insurance policies that have cash values are some of the most oversold investments for funding university costs. Here's the usual pitch: "Because you need life insurance to protect your family, why not buy a policy that you can borrow against to pay for university?"

The reason you shouldn't invest in this type of policy to fund university costs is that you're better off contributing to an RRSP that gives you an immediate tax deduction — which saving through life insurance doesn't offer. Because life insurance that comes with a cash value is more expensive, parents are also more likely to make another mistake — not buying enough coverage. If you need and want life insurance, you're better off buying lower-cost term life insurance (see Chapter 17).

Another poor investment for university expenses is one that fails to keep you ahead of inflation, such as savings or money-market accounts. You need your money to grow so that you can afford educational costs down the road.

Prepaid tuition plans — offered by a few U.S. schools — should generally be avoided. The allure of these plans is that, by paying today, you eliminate the worry of not being able to afford rising costs in the future. This logic doesn't work for several reasons:

>> Odds are quite high that you don't have the money today to pay in advance.

>> Putting money into such plans reduces your eligibility for financial aid dollar for dollar.

>> You don't know which school your child will want to attend and how long it may take him to finish. Coercing your child into the school you've already paid for is a sure ticket to long-term problems in your relationship.

If you have that kind of extra dough around, you're better off using it for other purposes — and you're not likely to worry about rising costs anyway. You can invest your own money — that's what the school's going to do with it anyway.

Overlooked investments

Too often, we see parents knocking themselves out to make more money so that they can afford to buy a bigger home, drive more expensive cars, take better vacations, and send their kids to more expensive (and, therefore, supposedly better) private schools. Families stretch themselves with outrageous mortgages or complicated living arrangements so that they can get into neighbourhoods with top-rated public schools or send their kids to expensive private elementary schools.

The best school in the world for your child is you and your home. The reason many people we know were able to attend some of the top educational institutions in this country is that their concerned parents worked hard — not just at their jobs, but at spending time with the kids when they were growing up. Instead of working to make more money (with the best of intentions of buying educational games or trips, or sending your kids to better schools), try focusing more attention on your kids. In our humble opinion, you can do more for your kids by spending more time with them.

We see parents scratching their heads about their children's lack of academic interest and achievement — they blame the school, TV, video games, or society at large. These factors may contribute to the problem, but education begins in the home. Schools can't do it alone.

REMEMBER

Living within your means not only allows you to save more of your income but also frees up more of your time for raising and educating your children. Don't underestimate the value of spending more time with your kids and giving them your attention.

Chapter **15**

Investing in Real Estate: Your Home and Beyond

Buying a home or investing in real estate can be financially and psychologically rewarding. On the other hand, owning real estate can be a real pain in the posterior, because purchasing and maintaining property can be quite costly, time-consuming, and emotionally draining. Perhaps you're looking to escape your rented apartment and buy your first home. Or maybe you're interested in becoming a local real-estate investing tycoon. In either case, you can learn many lessons from real-estate buyers who've travelled before you.

Note: Although this chapter focuses primarily on real estate in which you're going to live — otherwise known by those in the trade as *owner-occupied property* — much of what this chapter covers is relevant to real-estate investors as well. For additional information on buying *investment real estate* — property that you rent out to others — see Chapter 9.

Deciding Whether to Buy or Rent

You may be tired of moving from rental to rental. Perhaps your landlord doesn't adequately keep up the place, or you have to ask permission to hang a picture on the wall. You may want the financial security and rewards that seem to come with home ownership. Or maybe you just want a place to call your own.

Any one of these reasons is good enough to *want* to buy a home. But before you head down that path to homeownership, you should take stock of your life and your financial health so you can decide whether you still want to buy a home and how much you can really afford to spend. You need to ask yourself some bigger questions.

Assessing your timeline

TIP

From a financial standpoint, you really shouldn't buy a place unless you can anticipate being there for at least three years (preferably five or more). Buying and selling a property entails a lot of expenses, which can include getting an inspection, moving costs, land transfer tax, harmonized sales tax (HST) for new homes, lawyers' fees, real-estate agents' commissions, and title insurance. To cover these transaction costs plus the additional costs of ownership, a property needs to appreciate about 15 percent.

If you need or want to move in a couple of years, counting on 15 percent appreciation is risky. If you're fortunate and you happen to buy before a sharp upturn in housing prices, you may get it. If you're unlucky, you'll probably lose money on the deal.

Some people are willing to invest in real estate even when they don't expect to live in it for long and are open to turning their home into a rental. Doing so can work well financially in the long haul, but don't underestimate the responsibilities that come with being a landlord. Also, most people need to sell their current home in order to tap all the cash that they have in it so they can buy the next one.

Determining what you can afford

Although buying and owning your own home can be a wise financial move in the long run, it's a major purchase that can send shockwaves through the rest of your personal finances. You'll probably have to take out a 25-year mortgage to finance your purchase. The home you buy will need maintenance over the years. Owning a home is a bit like running a marathon: Just as you should be in good physical shape to successfully run a marathon, you should be in solid financial health when you buy a home.

We've seen too many people fall in love with a home and make a rushed decision (with pressure from salespeople) without taking a hard look at the financial ramifications. Take stock of your overall financial health and goals (especially where you stand in terms of retirement planning and saving toward your other goals) *before* you buy property and agree to a particular mortgage. Don't let the financial burdens of a home control your financial future.

Don't rely upon a lender who tells you what you can "afford" according to some formulas the bank uses to figure out what kind of a credit risk you are. To determine how much a potential home buyer can borrow, lenders look primarily at their annual income; they pay no attention to some major aspects of a borrower's overall financial situation. Even if you don't have money tucked away into retirement savings, or you have several children to clothe, feed, and help put through university or college, you still qualify for the same loan amount as other people with the same income (assuming equal outstanding debts). Take the time and make the effort to understand how much you can afford, because only you know and really care about what your other financial goals are and how important they are to you.

Here are some important financial questions that no lender will ask or care about, but that you should ask yourself before buying a home:

>> Are you saving enough money monthly to reach your retirement goals?

>> How much do you spend (and want to continue spending) on fun things such as travel and entertainment?

>> How willing are you to budget your expenses in order to meet your monthly mortgage payments and other housing expenses?

>> How much of your children's expected university or college educational expenses do you want to be able to pay for?

The other chapters in this book can help you answer these important questions. Chapter 4, in particular, helps you think through saving for important financial goals.

Many homeowners run into financial trouble because they don't know their spending needs and priorities or how to budget for them. For this reason, a surprisingly large percentage — some studies say about half — of people who borrow additional money against their home equity use the funds to pay consumer debts.

Calculating how much you can borrow

Mortgage lenders want to know your ability to repay the money you borrow. So, you have to pass a few tests that calculate the maximum amount the lender is willing to lend you. For a home in which you'll reside, lenders total up your housing expenses. They define your housing costs as

Mortgage Payment + Property Taxes + Heat + 50% of Condominium Fees = Housing Costs

This amount is then used in the gross debt service formula by comparing it to your gross income. The result is your gross debt service ratio:

(Mortgage Payment + Property Taxes + Heat + 50% of Condominium Fees) ÷ Gross Annual Income = Gross Debt Service Ratio

Lenders typically limit the amount they'll loan so your total housing costs are no more than 30 percent to 35 percent of your gross (before taxes) income for the housing expense. Lenders will often want to see your financial statements and income tax returns from the last several years, and many decide on a case-by-case basis.

Lenders also consider your other debts when deciding how much to lend you. These other debts diminish the funds available to pay your housing expenses. Lenders add the amount you need to pay down your other consumer debts (for example, auto loans and credit cards) to your housing expense. This is known as your *total debt service ratio*. The total costs of these debt payments plus your housing costs compared to your gross annual income typically cannot exceed 40 percent to 42 percent.

(Mortgage Payment + Property Taxes + Heat + 50% of Condominium Fees + Other Debt Obligations) ÷ Gross Annual Income = Total Debt Service Ratio

One general rule says that you can borrow up to three times (or two and a half times) your annual income when buying a home. But this rule is a really rough estimate. The maximum that a mortgage lender will loan you depends on interest rates. If rates fall, the monthly payment on a mortgage of a given size also drops. Thus, lower interest rates make real estate more affordable.

Table 15-1 gives you an estimate of the maximum amount you may be eligible to borrow. Multiply your gross annual income by the number in the second column to determine the approximate maximum you may be able to borrow. For example, if you're getting a mortgage with a rate around 7 percent and your annual income is $50,000, multiply 3.5 by $50,000 to get $175,000 — the approximate maximum mortgage allowed.

TABLE 15-1

The Approximate Maximum You Can Borrow

When Mortgage Rates Are	Multiply Your Gross Annual Income* by This Figure
3%	5
4%	4.6
5%	4.2
6%	3.8
7%	3.5
8%	3.2
9%	2.9
10%	2.7
11%	2.5

If you're self-employed, your gross annual income is your net business income (before taxes).

Comparing owning versus renting costs

The cost of owning a home is an important financial consideration for many renters. Some people assume that owning costs more. In fact, owning a home doesn't have to cost much more or more at all; at times, it may even cost *less* than renting.

On the surface, buying a place seems a lot more expensive than renting. You're probably comparing your monthly rent (measured in hundreds of dollars to more than $2,000 or $3,000, depending on where you live) to the purchase price of a property, which is usually a much larger number — perhaps $250,000 to $750,000 or more. When you consider a home purchase, you may be thinking about your housing expenses in one huge chunk rather than in small monthly installments (like a rent cheque).

Tallying up the costs of owning a place can be a useful and not-too-complicated exercise. To make a fair comparison between ownership and rental costs, you need to figure what it will cost on a *monthly basis* to buy a place you desire versus what it will cost to rent a *comparable* place. The worksheet in Table 15-2 enables you to do such a comparison. *Note:* In the interest of reducing the number of variables, all this "figuring" assumes a fixed-rate mortgage, *not* an adjustable-rate mortgage. (For more info on mortgages, see "Financing Your Home" later in this chapter.)

TABLE 15-2

Monthly Expenses: Renting versus Owning

Figure Out This	Write It Here
1. Monthly mortgage payment (see "Mortgage")	$ _____
2. Plus monthly property taxes (see "Property taxes")	+ $ _____
3. Equals total monthly mortgage plus property taxes	= $ _____
4. Plus insurance ($50 to $175 per month, depending on property value)	+ $ _____
5. Plus maintenance (1% of property cost divided by 12 months)	+ $ _____
6. Equals total cost of owning (add lines 3, 4, and 5)	= $ _____

TECHNICAL STUFF

Also, we ignore what economists call the *opportunity cost of owning.* In other words, when you buy, the money you put into your home can't be invested elsewhere, and the foregone investment return on that money, say some economists, should be considered a cost of owning a home. We choose to ignore this concept because we don't agree with this line of thinking. When you buy a home, you're investing your money in real estate, which historically has offered solid returns over the decades (see Chapter 8). And second, we have you ignore opportunity cost because it greatly complicates the analysis and wouldn't lead to a dramatic change in the numbers.

Now compare line 9 in Table 15-2 with the monthly rent on a comparable place to see which costs more — owning or renting.

Mortgage

To determine the monthly payment on your mortgage, simply multiply the relevant number (or multiplier) from the 15-year or 25-year Amortization column in Table 15-3 by the size of your mortgage, expressed in thousands of dollars (divided by 1,000). For example, if you're taking out a $100,000, 25-year mortgage at 3 percent, you multiply 100 by 4.73, for a $473 monthly payment. If you were taking out a $400,000 mortgage amortized over 15 years at 4 percent, multiply 400 by a multiplier of 7.38, giving you monthly payments of $2,952.

Property taxes

You can ask a real-estate person, a mortgage lender, or your local assessor's office what your annual property tax bill would be for a house of similar value to the one you're considering buying. Divide this amount by 12 to arrive at your monthly property tax bill.

TABLE 15-3

Your Monthly Mortgage Payment Multiplier

Interest Rate	15-Year Amortization	25-Year Amortization
2%	6.43	4.23
2.5%	6.66	4.48
3%	6.9	4.73
3.5%	7.14	4.99
4%	7.38	5.26
4.5%	7.63	5.53
5%	7.88	5.82
5.5%	8.14	6.1
6%	8.4	6.4
6.5%	8.66	6.7
7%	8.93	7
7.5%	9.21	7.32
8%	9.49	7.63
8.5%	9.77	7.96
9%	10.05	8.27
9.5%	10.34	8.61
10%	10.62	8.94
10.5%	10.92	9.29
11%	11.21	9.62
11.5%	11.51	9.97
12%	11.81	10.32

Tax savings in home ownership

Owning a home in Canada offers one of the biggest and most straightforward tax breaks for Canadians. Unlike other types of investments, when you sell your home, any profits you make are tax-free. This exemption covers most types of homes, including houses, condominiums, and shares in co-op housing corporations.

To qualify, the property must be your "principal residence." This means you, your spouse, or your child must have generally inhabited it. (You can't claim the exemption for property that you rent out or for vacant land.) But this doesn't mean it only covered your, well, actual "principal" residence. Although a family can have only one "principal residence," there is a fair bit of leeway in the definition. Suppose you're lucky enough to have a cottage, as well as a home in the city. If you sell the cottage, you can claim it as your principal residence that year, making any profits exempt from tax. A few years out, if you sell your house, you can then deem it your principal residence, again keeping all the proceeds without having to pay any tax on them.

TIP

Even if you've rented out your home, either before *or* after it was your principal residence, you may still be able to claim the exemption. If you move out of your home, you're allowed to rent it out for up to four years while still deeming it your principal residence. During that time you cannot claim another property as your principal residence. (To qualify, when you submit your tax return for the year you began renting your home, you need to file a special election.) Further, if you began renting your home because either your or your spouse's job has required you to move, you can rent it out and generally have the home remain designated as your residence indefinitely, as long as you move back into it when that employment ends.

New housing rebate

You may also be eligible for a rebate of some of the goods and services tax (GST) or the federal portion of the HST you've paid if you've purchased a new or substantially renovated home, mobile home, or floating home. However, you must have bought the home from the builder. You can generally also claim the rebate if you or someone you've hired has built a home on land you own or done a major overhaul of a home you already own. (To meet the qualification as a substantial renovation, at least 90 percent of the house's interior has to be removed or replaced.) Similarly, the rebate is available on the cost of a major addition, meaning you have at least double the living area. Adding a sunroom or turning the attic into a lovely new master bedroom unfortunately, doesn't meet the requirements.

The Home Buyers' Plan (HBP) offers another tax benefit. Under the plan, you can take up to $25,000 out of your Registered Retirement Savings Plan (RRSP) to use toward a down payment or toward building a qualifying home. The money can be used either for a home for yourself or for a related person with a disability. However, you have to replace the money you've taken out of your RRSP. You have 15 years to do this, starting in the second year after the year in which you withdraw the money. (See Chapter 11 for more on the HBP and RRSPs.)

Considering the long-term costs of renting

When you crunch the numbers to find out what owning rather than renting a comparable place may cost you on a monthly basis, you may discover that owning isn't as expensive as you thought. Or you may find that owning costs more than renting. This discovery may tempt you to think that, financially speaking, renting is cheaper than owning.

WARNING

Be careful not to jump to conclusions. Remember that you're looking at the cost of owning versus renting *today*. What about 5, 10, 20, or 25 years from now? As an owner, your biggest monthly expense, the mortgage payment, doesn't rise steadily — it fluctuates, and only if interest rates are at a different level when your mortgage term expires and you renew. If interest rates are higher or lower at that time, your payments will rise — or fall — accordingly. Your property taxes, homeowner's insurance, and maintenance expenses — which are generally far less than your mortgage payment — will increase over time with the cost of living.

When you rent, however, your entire monthly rent is subject to the vagaries of inflation. Living in a rent-controlled unit, where the annual increase allowed in your rent is capped, is the exception to this rule. Rent control does not eliminate price hikes; it just limits them.

Suppose you're comparing the costs of owning a home that costs $500,000 to renting that same home for $2,200 a month. Table 15-4 compares the cost of owning the home to your rental costs over 25 years. The comparison assumes that you take out a mortgage loan equal to 75 percent of the cost of the property at a fixed interest rate of 5 percent, meaning your mortgage payments would be $1,097 (rounded up to $1,100) and that the rate of inflation of your homeowner's insurance, property taxes, maintenance (which for the ownership example starts off at $450 per month), and rent is 4 percent per year. (This is higher than inflation has been running the last few years, but inflation can and does rise quickly.)

TABLE 15-4

Cost of Owning versus Renting over 30 Years

Year	Ownership Cost per Month	Rental Cost per Month
1	$1,470	$1,300
5	$1,570	$1,521
10	$1,730	$1,850
20	$2,180	$2,739
30	$2,880	$4,054

TIP

Depending on where you live, these costs may seem high or, if you live in a place such as Toronto or Vancouver, unrealistically low. But there are still a couple of points you can take away from the chart. The first is the relative cost of buying versus renting, and how that changes the more years you take into account.

Second, you can easily adapt the chart if you're in a high-rent, high-home-cost city. If you're in Vancouver or Toronto, for instance, to get a better sense of the comparative cost of buying versus renting a home now and down the road, you can roughly double the numbers shown in the chart.

As you can see in Table 15-4, in the first few years, owning a home costs a little more than renting it. In the long run, however, owning is less expensive, because more of your rental expenses increase with inflation. And don't forget that as a homeowner you're building equity in your property; that equity will be quite substantial by the time you have your mortgage paid off.

Recognizing advantages to renting

Although owning a home and investing in real estate generally pay off handsomely over the long term, to be fair and balanced, we must say that renting has its advantages. Some of the financially successful renters we've seen include people who pay low rent, either because they've made housing sacrifices or they live in a rent-controlled building. If you're consistently able to save 10 percent or more of your earnings, you're probably well on your way to achieving your future financial goals.

As a renter, you can avoid worrying about or being responsible for fixing up the property — that's your landlord's responsibility. You also have more financial and psychological flexibility as a renter. If you want to move, you can generally do so a lot more easily as a renter than you can as a homeowner.

Having a lot of your money tied up in your home is another challenge that you don't face when renting over the long haul. Some people enter their retirement years with a substantial portion of their wealth in their homes. As a renter, you can have all your money in financial assets that you can tap into more easily. Homeowners who have a major chunk of equity in their home at retirement can downsize to a less-expensive property to free up cash and/or take out a reverse mortgage (which we discuss later in this chapter) on their home equity.

Financing Your Home

After you look at your financial health, figure out your timeline, and compare renting costs to owning costs, you need to confront the tough task of taking on debt to buy a home (unless you're independently wealthy). If you're new to the world of home buying, the term *mortgage* may sound confusing and complicated. It's not. In fact, it's one of the simplest concepts you need to learn about in personal finance.

When you buy a home, you likely won't have anywhere near enough money saved to buy it outright. So, you need to borrow the difference between what you can pay — your down payment — and the purchase price. You'll typically borrow the needed extra money from a bank, trust company, credit union, or other major lender. But because it's such a lot of money, the lender will want to minimize its risk and protect itself against a big loss if you suddenly stop making your regular repayments and walk away from the loan. To protect itself against this happening, the lender will include a condition in your loan agreement that if you don't make good on your repayments, the lender will get legal ownership of the property. A mortgage, then, is simply a loan you take out to buy a property that is backed — or guaranteed — by the property itself.

Understanding mortgage essentials

Several different types and configurations of mortgages are available. The differences can be important or trivial, expensive or not. The best way to understand them is to consider that all mortgages have three main features:

>> **The total amount of time you want to take to pay your loan back:** This is called the *amortization*. By far the most common amortization is 25 years.

>> **The term that your mortgage agreement runs for:** This typically will range from six months to five years or more. When the term expires, you essentially take out a new mortgage and can negotiate different conditions, and even move your business to a different lender.

>> **Whether you can pay off the balance of your mortgage at any time (called an *open mortgage*) or have to continue making your payments until the end of the term (called a *closed mortgage*).**

You can put yourself in the driver's seat when it comes to negotiating a mortgage with potential lenders by deciding on the type of mortgage that's best for you before you go out to purchase a piece of real estate or refinance a loan. In the real world, however, most people ignore this advice. The excitement of purchasing a home tends to cloud a person's judgment. Our experience has been that it is, in fact, quite common for people to make major real-estate decisions without first assessing their overall larger financial circumstances. This means you risk ending up with a mortgage that can someday seriously overshadow your delight in your little English herb garden out back.

We help you understand your choices on these three fronts in the following sections.

Amortization

If you decide to take out a loan to buy a car, you'll have to decide how long you want to take to pay back the money. The shorter the period, the higher your regular payments will be. Suppose you choose a repayment period of four years. Over that time, you'll have to pay back the full amount you originally borrowed, plus interest. When the four years are up, you'll have paid your lender all the money you borrowed and all the interest on the borrowed funds. But that may not be immediately evident, because your lender will crunch the numbers and come up with a total, set amount you'll need to send in each payment period.

Mortgages are similar, in that instead of a car, you're borrowing to buy a home. But, in the same way, your payments will be a blended total of interest charges and repayment of the original loan. That said, there is one significant difference that can, at first, be confusing.

Similar to a car loan, when you take out a mortgage, you can choose the number of years you want to take to repay the money. This is called the *amortization*.

Most mortgages in Canada are amortized over 25 years. You can, however, choose a shorter or sometimes longer period. This can range from 5 to as many as 35 years. When the amortization is decided on, your interest costs for that entire period are calculated and used to arrive at the amount of your regular mortgage payments.

Your mortgage term

The length of the amortization you choose is distinct and separate from the *term*. The term of your mortgage is the length of time you want your loan agreement with a particular lender to run. In contrast to an amortization of, say, 25 years, mortgage terms typically run anywhere from just 6 months to 5 years.

When the term ends, your loan expires. You can choose to sign up for another loan for whatever term you like, either with the same lender or a different financial institution. You can pay off some of or your entire mortgage at that point if you have the money available. You can even alter the amortization at that point.

To help explain this, consider an example. Suppose you can take out a mortgage with the total cost spread out — or *amortized* — over 25 years. You can also select a term of just two years, meaning the actual mortgage agreement lasts for only two years. When those two years are up, you renew your mortgage and can select different features, including a different amortization and term. For instance, you can decide to choose a shorter amortization of just 15 years, but sign up for a five-year term.

CONSIDERING SHORT-TERM AND LONG-TERM MORTGAGES

You can typically choose a term of anywhere from six months or a year to five years. (Some lenders also offer seven- and even ten-year terms.)

The longer your term, the longer you have a specific rate locked in. If rates rise in the meantime, your lender earns less than if you had to renew earlier, and sign up for a higher interest rate. To protect themselves, lenders will charge you a higher interest rate — the longer the term you choose, the higher the rate. In contrast, a short term means that you have to renew much more frequently, putting you at the mercy of current interest rates. If rates have moved up by the time your term ends and you have to renew, your monthly payments will also be higher. If rates stay level, though, your payments will be less than what they would be with a longer-term mortgage, which generally comes with a higher interest rate. Of course, if rates have fallen when you come to renew, you'll be even farther ahead.

DECIDING BETWEEN A SHORT-TERM AND LONG-TERM MORTGAGE

When choosing your term, you're making a trade-off. If you choose a short term, your monthly payments will be lower, but you risk having rates rise between now and your next renewal date. If you select a longer term that comes with higher payments, you may end up paying more than you needed to if rates haven't risen in the meantime. If they have, however, you'll have saved yourself some money.

It's easy to get tangled up trying to get some sort of confirmation of where interest rates are likely to be one to five years down the road. Our advice? Don't waste much time on this. No experts have ever been able to consistently and accurately predict the future level of interest rates.

Instead, focus on what term and size of payments makes sense given your finances and your temperament. Selecting a longer term (four to five years, or more) locks in your payments for that entire period. This may be a valuable feature for those on a tightly controlled budget. A longer term is often a good choice if you're in the early years of home ownership. When you're locked in, you know exactly how much your mortgage will cost for years to come. You don't have to make any new decisions about your home loan for a long time. If an unexpected jump in rates would push your payments beyond what you can comfortably handle, then lock in at a rate you know you can afford for several years.

But this peace of mind comes at a price. Rates for a five-year term, for example, typically range anywhere from 1 percent to more than 3 percent higher than the rates for a six-month term. You pay a kind of insurance premium to protect yourself against the possibility of higher rates in the future. Ask yourself if the cost is worth it. Often, you'll find that both the financial and security risks of going short are not as great as you think.

When is it a good idea to consider a shorter term? When rates are at historical all-time highs. *Remember:* The reason for going long is to lock in a rate that protects you from renewing at an even higher rate. Otherwise, everyone would select a short term. Sure, it's hard to know if rates have peaked. But by staying short, you can quickly capture the gains when rates fall back down again.

TIP

If you choose a short term, you'll have to take your chances at the mortgage-rate roulette wheel more often. If you can handle the uncertainty — both psychologically and financially — you'll be rewarded by rates that are consistently lower than long-term rates. Making decisions more often also allows you to fine-tune your strategy and gives you more opportunity to reduce your principal.

Whatever you do, don't base your decisions on short-term movements. Interest rates fluctuate. If they jump quickly, they can just as easily fall back to where they started or even lower. Just make sure you have enough of a financial cushion to afford the higher payments that you'll have to make if rates have risen by the time your renewal date rolls around.

TIP

Your decision depends on your ability to live with risk. Staying short means more uncertainty, but you're almost certain to have lower mortgage costs unless rates keep marching up without coming back down. Choose long and you may sleep better, but you pay a premium for those worry-free nights.

If you're still unsure about which route to follow, don't worry. It's something that everybody goes through. Next time you're at a party, just start asking people about the choices they've made with their mortgages. You're bound to hear all sorts of tales about thousands of dollars lost or saved.

Open and closed mortgages

A *closed mortgage* means you're stuck with the terms of the deal until your loan agreement ends, or *matures.* You can refinance only if your lender lets you, and often that can involve paying stiff penalties. The upside of a closed mortgage is that, because the lender knows it can depend on your regular payments, your rates are lower.

Growing competition, however, has forced lenders to build in ways for you to pay off significant portions of your loan even within a closed mortgage. For example, the right to pay off 10 percent of your initial principal amount on each anniversary of your agreement is common.

An *open mortgage,* on the other hand, allows you to pay off part or all of the loan at any time without penalty. That can be a valuable option if you expect to come into a substantial sum of money or if you know you'll sell your home shortly. By completely paying off an open mortgage, you effectively terminate your contract with the lender. An open loan gives you flexibility to adapt your loan to changes in your financial picture or the economic situation. You have to pay more for this feature, usually a percent or so.

TIP

If falling rates are too tough to resist, but you want something less risky than a variable rate (which we describe in the next section), consider a fixed open mortgage. Your rate is guaranteed, but if rates fall to an even more attractive level, you can lock in at that point without any penalty. If you want to play the interest game, this allows you to keep your options open while still protecting you should rates go up instead of down. It's usually not worth paying the premium that lenders charge for open mortgages, though, and you have other options.

Today's numerous prepayment options allow you to pay down significant sums during the life of your mortgage. In addition, more and more homeowners opt for shorter and shorter terms. Simply rolling over six-month terms, for example, can be a sensible strategy. At the end of each term, you're free to pick whatever term you like, from whatever lender you want, if you meet the lender's basic requirements. You also have the option of paying off any amount of your principal that you choose.

Otherwise, however, if you're trying to take advantage of low or falling rates, a much better alternative is now available, called a six-month convertible. We talk more about convertible mortgages later in this chapter.

Examining the difference between fixed- and variable-rate mortgages

With a *fixed-rate mortgage,* your payments won't change during your mortgage term. You lock in an interest rate that's fixed for the entire length of your term — nothing complicated to track, and no uncertainty. If you like getting your daily newspaper delivered at the same time every day, you're gonna like fixed-rate mortgages.

A *variable-rate mortgage* (sometimes referred to as an *adjustable mortgage*) carries an interest rate that (no surprise here!) varies. Usually tied to the lender's prime rate, it moves, jumps, rises, falls, and otherwise can't sit still, just like a fidgeting child.

The return for putting up with this volatility is that the rate is usually the lowest available at any point in time. Variable rates generally are set at, or slightly above, the lender's prime rate, and they rise and fall accordingly.

Some lenders offer protection from soaring rates by putting an absolute ceiling on how high your rate can go. You pay a slightly higher rate for a capped variable, usually around 1 percent above that of a regular variable.

If rates are on their way up, you're better off locking in to a fixed-rate mortgage before the rates go any higher. And if rates are going down, you should select a variable rate and go along for the ride.

TIP

So, some people ask, "Shouldn't the likelihood of interest rates going up or down determine whether I take a fixed-rate or variable-rate mortgage?" Good question. The problem is that there really is no accurate way to predict which way rates are going. If you feel strongly that rates are likely to fall and you prefer the variable option, you should understand the risks involved. A rise in interest rates can mean that at some point your monthly payment won't even cover the interest cost of your loan. If this happens, the outstanding interest is added to your balance. When that figure hits about 105 percent to 110 percent of the original loan amount, you can expect to hear from your lender. You'll either have to make a lump-sum payment against your principal or lock in to a fixed term.

If you decide that a variable-rate mortgage is the way to go, you also have to pass some extra tests. Due to their volatility, variable-rate mortgages often have lower lending limits. Many lenders won't let you borrow more than 70 percent of your property's appraised value. In some cases, you must also select an amortization period of 20 years or less. And in 2010, the federal government brought in a new rule requiring that borrowers qualify for a five-year, fixed-rate mortgage in order to take out a mortgage, even if the actual mortgage selected has a lower interest rate or a shorter term and, thus, lower payments.

Variables are variable in another way: No other type of mortgage differs so much from lender to lender. Every aspect, from the terms available to whether you can pay the loan off early, varies widely depending on the institution. It's important to ask specific questions about any variable mortgage — and make sure that the answers are there on paper — before signing on the dotted line.

TIP

A relatively unpromoted player on the mortgage scene can save you from having to decide whether the potential savings from lower rates is worth all this worry. It's called a *convertible mortgage,* and it's one of the best-kept secrets in the mortgage game. A convertible loan offers many of the benefits of a variable-rate mortgage, with very little downside. For more information, see the "Convertible mortgages" sidebar.

Checking out the Home Buyers' Plan

You can borrow up to $25,000 from your RRSP to buy a house without paying any extra taxes or penalties under the federal government's HBP (up to January 28, 2009, the maximum was $20,000). For hopeful home buyers, the plan can be useful, but it's by no means perfect. The plan has a number of strict conditions and some potentially big costs, too.

CONVERTIBLE MORTGAGES

Although the bells and whistles of convertible mortgages vary from lender to lender, the basic principle remains the same: You get a mortgage with a term of six months — or sometimes a year — typically with the same interest rate available for fixed mortgages for the same term. This is generally the best mortgage rate available. At any point during the term of your convertible mortgage, you can "convert" your mortgage to a different term; you can also choose between an open or closed loan.

The benefit of a convertible mortgage is that it allows you to avoid paying a premium for longer-term fixed rates. You're also protected against rapidly rising rates because you can lock in at any time, instead of having to wait until your term expires or paying a hefty penalty. If rates suddenly move up, you can simply lock in a longer-term rate. Meanwhile, you also save yourself the extra premium for an open mortgage.

If rates are falling, you can lock in the lower rates at any point. It often pays to simply ride out the term and, if rates are still falling at that point, just sign up for another six-month convertible.

The important point with a convertible mortgage is to check the fine print for specific conditions. One institution, for example, allows you to convert only to a five-year term. Even if you let the six months elapse, you're automatically signed up. In essence, this is really a five-and-a-half-year mortgage, with the possibility of lower rates for a maximum of the first six months.

Most lenders allow you to convert at any time to any term you wish. The only across-the-board restriction is that you can't convert during the term to another six-month convertible. The other drawback to convertibles is that if you want to renew partway through the six months, you can't change lenders. That means losing some bargaining power, which can cost you a quarter or half of a percentage point.

REMEMBER

Understand all the specifics, despite their positively desertlike aridity. Knowing what you're getting into now can save you a lot of financial worries down the road.

One important restriction is that the funds that you're withdrawing from your RRSP for the HBP must have been in your RRSP for at least 90 days. The government doesn't want you to put money into your plan, get the tax break, and then draw on the same funds to use as part of a down payment. If you've been making regular contributions to your RRSP, and you've been building the tax refund into your budget, you need to prepare for this loss in cash flow.

BEWARE OF PREPAYMENT PENALTIES

Avoid loans with prepayment penalties. You pay this charge, usually 2 percent to 3 percent of the loan amount, when you pay off your loan before you're supposed to.

Prepayment penalties can also apply when you pay off a loan because you sell the property. (These penalties may be waived if you're selling to buy another property on which you take out a new mortgage with your current lender.) But if you refinance such a loan in order to take advantage of lower interest rates, you almost always get hit by prepayment penalties if the loan calls for such penalties.

The only way to know whether a loan has a prepayment penalty is to ask. If the answer is yes, find yourself another mortgage.

Repayment rules

Strict rules govern how quickly you have to repay the money you've borrowed from your RRSP. You must repay the money into your RRSP within 16 years. The minimum you have to repay each year starting with the second year after you make your withdrawal is the equivalent of $1/15$ of the amount borrowed.

Keep in mind those payments aren't considered RRSP contributions, and you don't get any tax write-offs for them. And if you miss a payment or part of a payment, the government treats that money as if you had withdrawn it directly from your RRSP. The sum is included as part of your income for that year, and you have to pay tax on it. Ouch!

WARNING

If you're currently finding it tough to put money into your RRSP, it will be twice as hard if you use your retirement funds for a down payment. Before you can even think of making a fresh contribution, you have to replace the required portion of the borrowed funds for that year. If that leaves you unable to make a direct RRSP contribution for that year, you miss out on a big tax break and a large tax refund. You also forgo the tax-free compound growth you could've earned from that new contribution.

Loss of potential growth in your RRSP

WARNING

By taking money out, you lose all the potential growth from those funds as long as that money isn't in your plan. The younger you are, the higher the cost is to you. Unfortunately, the only way to understand the dangers this option poses for your RRSP is to do battle with a few numbers.

Suppose you're 30 and you borrow $18,000 from your plan to buy a home. You have to repay $1,200 a year, or $100 a month, for the next 15 years. The alternative would have been to borrow the money, say, as a second mortgage. If you borrowed the money at 10 percent and spread the loan over 15 years, the monthly payments would be $193.50. So, the extra cost of borrowing the money from a bank or trust company instead of your RRSP is $93.50 a month.

But you have to balance that against the gains possible by leaving that $18,000 in your RRSP. Earning an average of 10 percent a year, in 40 years that money would grow to more than $800,000. By comparison, if it were left in for 35 years, it would be worth just over $500,000.

This is an extreme example, but it amply demonstrates the true cost of borrowing "free" from your RRSP. The actual cost depends on how old you are and how quickly you're able to repay the borrowings. In general, if you're over 40, the price may not be too steep. In addition, if you use the plan to buy a home and it appreciates steadily, the growth on the value of your house will offset some of the forgone growth in your RRSP. You may be able to get the best of both worlds by borrowing from your RRSP and repaying the loan quickly, say in the first three or four years after you've settled into your new home.

TIP

In general, you're probably better off borrowing the money, even if that means taking out a second mortgage or a high-ratio mortgage. Just make sure you can afford the higher interest-rate charges or the mortgage insurance premium.

Avoiding the down-payment blues

You can generally qualify for the most favorable mortgage terms by making a down payment of at least 20 percent of the purchase price of the property.

Why? Because you can generally qualify for the most favourable terms on a mortgage with such a down payment, and you can avoid the added cost of mortgage insurance. Mortgage insurance protects lenders against losing money in the event you default on your loan and can cost several hundred dollars per year on a typical mortgage.

TIP

Many people don't have the equivalent of 20 percent or more of the purchase price of a home to avoid paying private mortgage insurance. Here are a number of solutions for coming up with that 20 percent more quickly or buying with less money down:

>> **Go on a spending diet.** Take a tour through Chapter 6 to find strategies for cutting back on your spending.

>> **Consider lower-priced properties.** Smaller properties and ones that need some work can help reduce the purchase price and, therefore, the required down payment.

>> **Find financial partners.** You can often get more home for your money when you buy a building in partnership with one, two, or a few people. Prepare a legal contract to specify what's going to happen if a partner wants out, divorces, or passes away.

>> **Seek reduced down-payment financing.** Some lenders will offer you a mortgage even though you may be able to put down only as little as 5 percent to 10 percent of the purchase price. You can't be as picky about properties because not as many are available under these terms — many need work or haven't yet sold for other reasons. You must have solid credit to qualify for such loans, and you generally have to obtain and pay for the extra expense of mortgage insurance, which protects the lender if you default on the loan.

>> **Get assistance from family.** If your parents, grandparents, or other relatives have money dozing away in a savings account or a guaranteed investment certificate (GIC), they may be willing to lend (or even give) you the down payment. You can pay them an interest rate higher than the rate they're currently earning but lower than what you'd pay to borrow from a bank — a win/win situation. Lenders generally ask whether any portion of the down payment is borrowed and will reduce the maximum amount they're willing to loan you accordingly.

OBTAINING A HIGH-RATIO MORTGAGE

If you have a down payment of at least 5 percent of the purchase price, you can obtain a high-ratio mortgage from most lenders. However, you're required to buy special mortgage insurance. If your application is approved, your lender will generally organize this for you. The insurance is available from the Canada Mortgage and Housing Corporation (CMHC), which is run by the federal government, or Genworth (formerly GE Capital), and Canada Guarantee Mortgage Insurance Company. The insurance is there to protect your lender — not you — in case you fail to meet your payments.

Your down payment determines your insurance rate, which can run from 0.5 percent to 3.25 percent. You pay the premium only once — when you take out your mortgage. You're required to insure the entire loan, not just the difference between your down payment and the 20 percent required for a conventional loan. On a $100,000 mortgage, an insurance rate of 2.5 would mean paying $2,500 in insurance. If you don't have the money, you can ask your lender to add the insurance premium to your loan. Of course, that means you'll likely end up paying twice or three times that amount back over the life of the mortgage when all the interest costs have been added in.

Finding the best lender

As with other financial purchases, you can save a lot of money by shopping around. It doesn't matter whether you shop around on your own or hire someone to help you. Just do it!

On a 25-year, $150,000 mortgage, for example, getting a mortgage that costs 0.5 percent less per year saves you around $15,000 to $20,000 in interest over the life of the loan (given current interest rates). That's enough to buy a decent car! On second thought, save it!

Shopping for a lender on your own

In most areas, you can find many mortgage lenders. Although having a large number of lenders to choose from is good for competition, it also makes shopping a chore.

Large banks whose names you recognize from their advertising usually don't offer the best rates. Make sure that you check out some of the smaller lending institutions in your area, as well as credit unions and alternative lenders such as PC Financial and Tangerine Bank.

Real estate agents can also refer you to lenders with whom they've previously done business. These lenders may not necessarily offer the most competitive rates — the agent simply may have done business with them in the past.

TIP

Head to Tony's website at www.moneygrower.ca for up-to-date rates from all major lenders and many less-known ones as well.

Hiring a mortgage broker

Insurance agents peddle insurance, real-estate agents sell real estate, and mortgage brokers deal in mortgages. They buy mortgages at wholesale from lenders and then mark them up to retail before selling them to you. The mortgage brokers get their income from the difference, or *spread,* in the form of a commission. The terms of the loan obtained through a broker are generally the same as the terms you obtain from the lender directly.

TIP

Mortgage brokers get paid a percentage of the loan amount — typically 0.5 percent to 1 percent or 2 percent. This commission is negotiable, especially on larger loans that are more lucrative. Ask a mortgage broker what his cut is. Many people don't ask for this information, so some brokers may act taken aback when you inquire. *Remember:* It's your money!

The chief advantage of using a mortgage broker is that the broker can shop among lenders to get you a good deal. If you're too busy or disinterested to shop around for a good deal on a mortgage, a competent mortgage broker can probably save you money. A broker can also help you through the tedious process of filling out all those horrible documents lenders demand before giving you a loan. And if you have credit problems or an unusual property you're financing, a broker may be able to match you up with a hard-to-find lender who's willing to offer you a mortgage.

WARNING

When evaluating a mortgage broker, be on guard for those who are lazy and don't continually shop the market looking for the best mortgage lenders. Some brokers place their business with the same lenders all the time, and those lenders don't necessarily offer the best rates. Also, watch out for salespeople who earn big commissions pushing certain loan programs that aren't in your best interests. These brokers aren't interested in taking the time to understand your needs and discuss your options. Thoroughly check a broker's references before doing business.

TIP

When a loan broker quotes you a really good deal, ask who the lender is. (Most brokers refuse to reveal this information until you pay the few hundred dollars to cover the appraisal and credit report.) You can check with the actual lender to verify the interest rate and points the broker quotes you and make sure that you're eligible for the loan.

Understanding other lender fees

In addition to charging you the ongoing interest rate, lenders nickel-and-dime you with a number of fees when processing your loan. You need to know the total of all lender fees so you can compare different mortgages and determine how much completing your home purchase is going to cost you.

Actually, you pay more than nickels and dimes — $300 here and $50 there add up in a hurry! Here are the main culprits:

>> **Application and processing fees:** Most lenders charge several hundred dollars to complete your paperwork and process it through their *underwriting* (loan evaluation) department. The justification for this fee is that if your loan is rejected or you decide not to take it, the lender needs to cover the costs. Some lenders return this fee to you upon closing if you go with their loan (after you're approved).

>> **Appraisal:** The property for which you're borrowing money needs to be valued. If you default on your mortgage, your lender doesn't want to get stuck with a property worth less than you owe. For most residential properties, the appraisal cost is typically several hundred dollars.

Get a written itemization of charges from all lenders you're seriously considering so you can more readily compare different lenders' mortgages and so you have no surprises when you close on your loan. And to minimize your chances of throwing away money on a loan for which you may not qualify, ask the lender whether you may not be approved for some reason. Be sure to disclose any problems you're aware of that are on your credit report or with the property.

Increasing your approval chances

A lender can take several weeks to complete your property appraisal and an evaluation of your loan package. When you're under contract to buy a property, having your loan denied after waiting several weeks can mean that you lose the property, as well as the money you spent applying for the loan and having the property inspected. Some property sellers may be willing to give you an extension, but others won't.

Here's how to increase your chances of having your mortgage approved:

>> **Get your finances in shape before you shop.** You won't have a good handle on what you can afford to spend on a home until you whip your personal finances into shape. Do so before you begin to make offers on properties. This book can help you. If you have consumer debt, eliminate it — the more credit card, auto loan, and other consumer debt you rack up, the less mortgage you qualify for. In addition to the high interest rate and the fact that it encourages you to live beyond your means, you now have a third reason to get rid of consumer debt. Hang onto the dream of owning a home, and plug away at paying off consumer debts.

>> **Clear up credit-report problems.** If you think you may have errors on your credit report, get a copy before you apply for a mortgage. Chapter 2 explains how to obtain a free copy of your credit report, as well as correct any mistakes or clear up blemishes.

>> **Get preapproved or prequalified.** When you get prequalified, a lender speaks with you about your financial situation and then calculates the maximum amount she's willing to lend you based on what you tell her. Preapproval is much more in-depth and includes a lender's review of your financial statements. Just be sure not to waste your time and money getting preapproved if you're not really ready to get serious about buying.

>> **Be upfront about problems.** Late payments, missed payments, or debts that you never bothered to pay can come back to haunt you. The best defence against loan rejection is to avoid it in the first place. You can sometimes head off potential rejection by disclosing to your lender anything that may cause a problem before you apply for the loan. That way, you have more time to

correct problems and find alternate solutions. Mortgage brokers (see the preceding section) can also help you shop for lenders who are willing to offer you a loan despite credit problems.

>> **Work around low/unstable income.** When you've been changing jobs or you're self-employed, your recent economic history may be as unstable as a country undergoing a regime change. Making a larger down payment is one way around this problem. You may try getting a cosigner, such as a relative or good friend. As long as he isn't borrowed up to his eyeballs, he can help you qualify for a larger loan than you can get on your own. Be sure that all parties understand the terms of the agreement, including who's responsible for monthly payments!

>> **Consider a backup loan.** You certainly should shop among different lenders, and you may want to apply to more than one for a mortgage. Although applying for a second loan means additional fees and work, it can increase your chances of getting a mortgage if you're trying to buy a difficult-to-finance property or if your financial situation makes some lenders leery. Be sure to disclose to each lender what you're doing — the second lender to pull your credit report will see that another lender has already done so.

Finding the Right Property

Shopping for a home can be fun. You get to peek inside other people's closets. But for most people, finding the right house at the right price can take a lot of time. When you're buying with partners or a spouse (or children, if you choose to share the decision-making with them), finding the right place can also entail a lot of compromise. A good agent (or several who specialize in different areas) can help with the legwork. The following sections cover the main things you need to consider when shopping for a home to call your own.

Condo, town house, co-op, or detached home?

Some people's image of a home is a single-family dwelling — a stand-alone house with a lawn and white picket fence. In some areas, however — particularly in higher-cost neighborhoods — you find *condominiums* (you own the unit and a share of everything else); *town houses* (attached or row houses); and *cooperatives*, also known as *co-ops* (you own a share of the entire building). The allure of such higher-density housing is that it's generally less expensive. Often, you don't have to worry about some of the general maintenance, because the owner's association (which you pay for, directly or indirectly) takes care of it.

If you don't have the time, energy, or desire to keep up a property, shared housing may make sense for you. You generally get more living space for your dollars, and it may also provide you with more security than a stand-alone home.

As investments, however, single-family homes generally do better in the long run. Shared housing is easier to build and, thus, overbuild; on the other hand, single-family houses are harder to put up because more land is required. And most people, when they can afford it, still prefer a stand-alone home.

That said, you should remember that a rising tide raises all boats. In a good real-estate market, all types of housing generally appreciate, although single-family homes tend to do better. Shared-housing values tend to fare better in densely populated urban areas with little available land for new building.

From an investment return perspective, if you can afford a smaller single-family home instead of a larger shared-housing unit, buy the single-family home. Be especially wary of buying shared housing in suburban areas with lots of developable land.

Casting a broad net

You may have an idea about the type of property and location you're interested in or think you can afford before you start your search. You may think, for example, that you can only afford a condominium in the neighborhood you're interested in. But if you take the time to check out other communities, you may be surprised to find one that meets most of your needs and also has single-family homes you can afford. You'd never know about this community if you were to narrow your search too quickly.

Even if you've lived in an area for a while and you believe you know it well, look at different types of properties in a number of communities before you narrow your search. Be open-minded and figure out which of your many criteria for a home you *really* care about.

Finding out actual sale prices

Don't look at just a few of the homes listed at a particular price and then get depressed because they're all lousy or you can't afford what you really want. Before you decide to renew your apartment lease, remember that properties often sell for less than the price at which they're listed.

TIP

Find out what the places you look at eventually sell for. Doing so gives you a better sense of what places are really worth and what properties you may be able to afford. Until recently, that has been all but impossible. The problem is that real-estate boards worked to keep this information — compiled by the Multiple Listing Service (MLS) — secret, saying only their agents had the right to share that information with clients. But in late 2017, the courts upheld a ruling against the Toronto Real Estate Board (the country's largest real-estate board) practise by the Competition Bureau. The competition watchdog said the group's practise of keeping information about home sale prices and real-estate agent commissions secret is anticompetitive and bad for consumers, and had ordered the board to open the information up to the public.

The board appealed the decision, but in August 2018, the Supreme Court of Canada refused to hear the appeal. Meanwhile, a number of house-sale-price websites sprang up, including HouseSigma (www.housesigma.com) and Sold.Watch (www.sold.watch). This is all good news for consumers in the Toronto area, and with luck, real-estate boards across the country will have to fall in line and make the information public. In the meantime, try asking the agent or owner who sold the property what the sale price was, or contact the town's assessor's office for information on how to obtain property sale-price information.

Researching the area

TIP

Even (and especially) if you fall in love with a house at first sight, go back to the neighborhood at various times of the day and on different days of the week. Travel to and from your prospective new home during commute hours to see how long your commute will really take. Knock on some doors and meet your potential neighbors. You may discover, for example, that a flock of chickens lives in the backyard next door or that the street and basements frequently flood.

Go visit the schools. Don't rely on statistics about test scores. Talk to parents and teachers. What's really going on at the school? Even if you don't have kids, the quality of the local school has direct bearing on the value of your property. Is crime a problem? Call the local police department. Will future development be allowed? If so, what type? Talk to the planning department. What are your property taxes going to be? Is the property located in an area susceptible to major risks, such as floods, mudslides, fires, or earthquakes? Consider these issues even if they're not important to you, because they can affect the resale value of your property. Make sure you know what you're getting yourself into *before* you buy.

Working with Real-Estate Agents

When you buy (or sell) a home, you'll probably work with a real-estate agent. Real-estate agents earn their living on commission. As such, their incentives can be at odds with what's best for you. Real-estate agents usually don't hide the fact that they get a cut of the deal. Property buyers and sellers generally understand the real-estate commission system. We credit the real-estate profession for calling its practitioners "agents" instead of coming up with some silly obfuscating title such as "housing consultants."

A top-notch real-estate agent can be a significant help when you purchase or sell a property. On the other hand, a mediocre, incompetent, or greedy agent can be a real liability. The following sections help you sort the best from the rest.

Recognizing conflicts of interest

WARNING

Real-estate agents, because they work on commission, face numerous conflicts of interest. Some agents may not even recognize the conflicts in what they're doing. The following list presents the most common conflicts of interest that you need to watch out for:

>> Because agents work on commission, it costs them when they spend time with you and you don't buy or sell. They want you to complete a deal, and they want that deal as soon as possible — otherwise, they don't get paid. Don't expect an agent to give you objective advice about what you should do given your overall financial situation. Examine your overall financial situation *before* you decide to begin working with an agent.

>> Because real-estate agents get a percentage of the sale price of a property, they have a built-in incentive to encourage you to spend more.

>> Agents often receive a higher commission when they sell listings that belong to other agents in their office. Beware! Sometimes the same agent represents both the property seller and the property buyer in the transaction — a real problem. Agents who hold open houses for sale may try to sell to an unrepresented buyer they meet at the open house. There's no way one person can represent the best interests of both sides.

>> Because agents work on commission and get paid a percentage of the sale price of the property, many aren't interested in working with you if you can't or simply don't want to spend a lot. Some agents may reluctantly take you on as a customer and then give you little attention and time. Before you hire an agent, check references to make sure that he works well with buyers like you.

>> Real-estate agents typically work a specific territory. As a result, they usually can't objectively tell you the pros and cons of the surrounding regions. Most won't admit that you may be better able to meet your needs by looking in another area where they don't normally work. Before you settle on an agent (or an area), spend time figuring out the pros and cons of different territories on your own. If you want to seriously look in more than one area, find more than one agent — one agent who specializes in each area.

>> Some agents may refer you to a more expensive lender who has the virtue of high approval rates. If you don't get approved for a mortgage loan, your entire real-estate deal may unravel. Be sure to shop around — you can probably get a loan more cheaply. Be especially wary of agents who refer you to mortgage lenders and mortgage brokers who pay agents referral fees. Such payments clearly bias a real-estate agent's "advice."

>> Agents may encourage you to use a particular inspector with a reputation for being "easy" — meaning he may not "find" all the house's defects. Home inspectors are supposed to be objective third parties who are hired by prospective buyers to evaluate the condition of a property. ***Remember:*** It's in the agent's best interest to seal the deal, and the discovery of problems may sidetrack those efforts.

>> Under pressure to get a house listed for sale, some agents agree to be accomplices and avoid disclosing known defects or problems with the property. In most cover-up cases, it seems, the seller doesn't explicitly ask an agent to help cover up a problem; the agent just looks the other way or avoids telling the whole truth. Never buy a home without having a home inspector look it over from top to bottom.

Looking for the right qualities in real-estate agents

When you hire a real-estate agent, you want to find someone who's competent and with whom you can get along. Working with an agent costs a lot of money (which is built into the price of houses sold and generally deducted from the seller's proceeds) — so make sure you get your money's worth.

TIP

Interview several agents. Check references. Ask agents for the names and phone numbers of at least three clients they've worked with in the past six months (in the geographical area in which you're looking). Look for the following traits in any agent you work with:

>> **Full-time employment:** Some agents work in real estate as a second or even third job. Information in this field changes constantly. The best agents work at it full-time so they can stay on top of the market.

- >> **Experience:** Hiring someone with experience doesn't necessarily mean looking for an agent who's been kicking around for decades. Many of the best agents come into the field from other occupations, such as business or teaching. Some sales, marketing, negotiation, and communication skills can certainly be picked up in other fields, but experience in buying and selling real estate does count.

- >> **Honesty and integrity:** If your agent doesn't level with you about what a neighborhood or particular property is really like, you suffer the consequences.

- >> **Interpersonal skills:** An agent must be able to get along not only with you but also with a whole host of other people who are typically involved in a real-estate deal: other agents, property sellers, inspectors, mortgage lenders, and so on.

- >> **Negotiation skills:** Is your agent going to exhaust all avenues to negotiate the best deal possible for you? Be sure to ask the agent's references how well the agent negotiated for them.

- >> **High-quality standards:** Sloppy work can lead to big legal or logistical problems down the road. If an agent neglects to recommend thorough and complete inspections, for example, you may be stuck with undiscovered problems after the deal is done.

TIP

Agents sometimes market themselves as *top producers*, which means that they sell a relatively large volume of real estate. This title doesn't count for much for you, the buyer. It may be a red flag for an agent who focuses on completing as many deals as possible. When you're buying a home, you need an agent who has the following additional traits:

- >> **Patience:** You need an agent who's patient and willing to allow you the necessary time it takes to get educated and make the best decision for yourself.

- >> **Local market and community knowledge:** When you're looking to buy a home in an area in which you're not currently living, an informed agent can have a big impact on your decision.

- >> **Financing knowledge:** As a buyer, you should look for an agent who knows which lenders can best handle your type of situation. This advice is especially true if you're a first-time buyer or you have credit problems.

TIP

Buying real estate requires somewhat different skills than selling real estate. Few agents can do both equally well. No law or rule says that you must use the same agent when you sell a property as you do when you buy a property.

Putting Your Deal Together

After you do your homework on your personal finances, discover how to choose a mortgage, and research neighborhoods and home prices, you'll hopefully be ready to close in on your goal. Eventually you'll find a home you want to buy. Before you make that first offer, though, you need to understand the importance of negotiations, inspections, and the other elements of a real-estate deal.

Negotiating 101

TIP

When you work with an agent, the agent usually handles the negotiation process. But you need to have a plan and strategy in mind; otherwise, you may end up overpaying for your home. Here are some recommendations for getting a good deal:

>> **Never fall in love with a property.** If you have money to burn and can't imagine life without the home you just discovered, pay what you will. Otherwise, remind yourself that other good properties are out there. Having a backup property in mind can help.

>> **Find out about the property and owner before you make your offer.** How long has the property been on the market? What are its flaws? Why is the owner selling? The more you understand about the property and the seller's motivations, the better able you'll be to draft an offer that meets both parties' needs.

>> **Get comparable sales data to support your price.** Too often, home buyers and their agents pick a number out of thin air when making an offer. But if the offer has no substance behind it, the seller will hardly be persuaded to lower her asking price. Pointing to recent and comparable home sales to justify your offer price strengthens your case.

>> **Remember that price is only one of several negotiable items.** Sometimes sellers get fixated on selling their homes for a certain amount. Perhaps they want to get at least what they paid for it years ago. You may be able to get a seller to pay for certain repairs or improvements, to pay some of your closing costs, or to offer you an attractive loan without the extra loan fees that a bank would charge. Likewise, the real-estate agent's commission is negotiable.

Inspecting before you buy

When you buy a home, you may be making one of the biggest (if not *the* biggest) purchases of your life. Unless you build homes and do contracting work, you probably have no idea what you're getting yourself into when it comes to furnaces, fungus, and termites.

TIP

Spend the time and money to locate and hire good inspectors and other experts to evaluate the major systems and potential problem areas of the home. Areas that you want to check include

>> Overall condition of the property

>> Electrical, heating, cooling, and plumbing systems

>> Foundation

>> Roof

>> Pest control, dry rot, fungus, and mold

>> Seismic, mudslide, and flood risk

Inspection fees often pay for themselves. When problems that you weren't aware of are uncovered, the inspection reports give you the information you need to go back and ask the seller to fix the problems or reduce the purchase price of the property to compensate you for correcting the deficiencies yourself.

As with other professionals whose services you retain, interview several inspection companies. Ask which systems they inspect and how detailed a report they're going to prepare for you (ask for a sample copy). Request names and phone numbers of three people who have used their service within the past six months.

WARNING

Never accept a seller's inspection report as your only source of information. When a seller hires an inspector, he may hire someone who won't be as diligent and critical of the property. What if the inspector is a buddy of the seller or his agent? By all means, review the seller's inspection reports if available, but get your own as well.

And here's one more inspection for you to do: The day before you close on the purchase, do a brief walk-through of the property. Make sure that everything is still in good order and that all the fixtures, appliances, curtains, and other items that were to be left per the contract are still there. Sometimes sellers (and their movers) "forget" what they're supposed to leave or try to test your powers of observation.

Remembering title insurance

Everything from clerical errors and misrepresentations to outright fraud can turn owning a home into a legal nightmare. The role of title insurance is to provide you with some legal protection against these kinds of problems.

The major purpose of title insurance is to protect you against someone else claiming legal title to your property. This claim can happen, for example, when a husband and wife split up and the one who remains in the home decides to sell and take off with the money. If both spouses are listed as owners on the title, the spouse who sells the property (possibly by forging the other's signature) has no legal right to do so.

Both you and the lender can get stuck holding the bag if you buy the home that one spouse of this divided couple is selling. But title insurance acts as the salvation for you and your lender. Title insurance protects you against the risk that the spouse whose name was forged will come back and reclaim rights to the home after it's sold.

In addition to problems of who actually owns title to the property, title insurance can help you if problems crop up with your survey. This coverage can also protect you against smaller annoyances, such as vendors not having paid utility bills they claim to have settled, or not receiving a parking spot the seller asserted you were entitled to as part of your purchase.

TIP

When you call around for title-insurance quotes, make sure you understand all the fees. Many companies tack on all sorts of charges for things such as courier fees and express mail. If you find a company with lower prices and want to use it, ask for an itemization in writing so that you don't have any surprises.

Real-estate agents and mortgage lenders can be a good starting point for referrals because they usually have a broader perspective on the cost and service quality of different companies. Call other companies as well. Agents and lenders may be biased toward a company simply because they're in the habit of using it or they've referred clients to it before.

After You Buy

After you buy a home, you'll make a number of important decisions over the months and years ahead. This section discusses the key issues you need to deal with as a homeowner and tells what you need to know to make the best decision for each of them.

Refinancing your mortgage

Three reasons motivate people to *refinance,* or obtain a new mortgage to replace an old one:

>> To save money because interest rates have dropped

>> To raise capital for some other purpose

>> To get out of one type of loan and into another

The following sections can help you decide on the best option in each case.

Options for open and closed mortgages

If you have an open mortgage, of course, you can renew whenever current rates are more attractive. Find a new term you're comfortable with and sit back and count your savings. Better yet, keep your payments at the previous level and use the drop-in rates to take years off your mortgage.

REMEMBER

When you refinance, you terminate your deal with your current lender. You're free to shop around your mortgage to other lenders. Or you can get a few offers to use as leverage to get your current lender to chop a quarter or even half a percent off its published rates.

Most mortgages, however, are closed. And although your lender may be willing to allow you to refinance early, it will want to be compensated for some — or all — of its losses. After all, if you want to refinance to reduce your rate from 11 percent to 8 percent, the banks aren't exactly going to leap at the chance to make 3 percent less on your loan, are they?

TIP

The first step is to get your mortgage agreement out and read the fine print. Growing competition means that some lenders have made it easier for you to get out of your current loan. But this is a marketing edge they don't particularly want to tout unless they have to. After all, if you don't read your agreement and you simply assume that you're stuck paying higher rates than you may need to, you don't really expect banks and trust companies to bring that to your attention, do you?

The three months' interest penalty

Your mortgage agreement may allow you to refinance your loan by paying the equivalent of three months' interest on your outstanding balance. By law, any mortgage with a term longer than five years also becomes open on the fifth anniversary, with the same three-month penalty applying.

TIP

Although they don't widely promote the fact, several of the big banks now allow you to refinance under the same terms at any point after the third anniversary of your present agreement. But remember, it's unlikely that your lenders will alert you to the money you could be saving.

Whether the three-month penalty is worth paying is different in every case. It depends on the difference between your existing rate and what current rates are, as well as on how much remains in your principal. Your best bet is to ask your lender to work the numbers out for you. The lender may not be that happy about doing so, but you should get the answers you need.

The interest-rate-differential penalty

The most common penalty is something called the *interest-rate differential* (IRD). The IRD is the value today of the income the lender gives up by allowing you to refinance.

WARNING

Say you're paying 10 percent and you have two years left in your term. Your lender calculates how much it can make by taking the balance of your loan and lending it out elsewhere. Then it will ask you to make up the difference so that it can break even on the deal. The problem is that paying the IRD leaves you breaking even as well. The money you save with lower rates will be wiped out by the compensation you'll have to pay.

WARNING

Another potential problem is that nobody can say with certainty where interest rates are headed. You lose out if rates fall and are lower at the end of your present term. If that happens, you've gone through an awful lot of tedious paperwork only to be locked in at a higher term than you would be paying if you had simply sat tight.

Considering mortgage life insurance

Shortly after you buy a home or close on a mortgage, you start getting mail from all kinds of organizations that keep track of publicly available information about mortgages. Most of these organizations want to sell you something, and they don't tend to beat around the bush. "What will your dependants do if you meet with an untimely demise and they're left with a gargantuan mortgage?," these organizations ask. In fact, this is a good financial-planning question. If your family is dependent on your income, can it survive financially if you pass away?

TIP

Don't waste your money on mortgage life insurance. You may need life insurance to provide for your family and help meet large obligations such as mortgage payments or educational expenses for your children, but mortgage life insurance is typically grossly overpriced. (Check out the life insurance section in Chapter 17 for advice about term life insurance.) Consider mortgage life insurance only if you have a health problem and the mortgage life insurer doesn't require a physical examination. Be sure to compare it with term life options.

HOME-EQUITY LINES OF CREDIT AND HOME-EQUITY LOANS

A home-equity line of credit or a home-equity loan can be a useful source of financing to help buy or improve a home.

A home-equity line of credit is somewhat like a credit card, in that it gives you the ability to withdraw money against it, up to a set maximum, with the paid-off value of your home as security. You're required to make at least the set minimum monthly payments on it, depending on how much you've taken out. After it's set up, a home-equity line of credit allow you to tap it as you need or want to so you can use the money for many purposes, including a home remodel, university expenses for your kids, or as an emergency source of funds.

A home-equity loan (sometimes referred to as a second mortgage) is similar, except you borrow a fixed amount in one lump sum. You then repay the money over an agreed-upon period.

Home-equity lines of credit have their downsides. The biggest negative in our experience is that they encourage homeowners to view their homes as piggybanks from which they can keep borrowing. The interest rate can increase instantaneously. Also, beware that lenders can generally cancel your home-equity line of credit at their discretion (for example, if the value of your home falls too much or your credit score deteriorates).

Weighing the pros and cons of a reverse mortgage

An increasing number of homeowners are finding, particularly in their later years of retirement, that they lack cash. The home in which they live is usually their largest asset. Unlike other investments, such as bank accounts, bonds, or stocks, a home does not provide any income to the owner unless he decides to rent out a room or two.

A *reverse mortgage* allows a homeowner who is low on cash to tap home equity. For an elderly homeowner, using home equity can be a difficult thing to do psychologically. Most people work hard to pay a mortgage month after month, year after year, until it's finally all paid off. What a feat and what a relief after all those years!

Taking out a reverse mortgage reverses this process. Each month, the reverse mortgage lender sends you a check that you can spend on food, clothing, travel, or whatever you want. The money you receive each month is really a loan from the bank against the value of your home, which makes the monthly check free from taxation. A reverse mortgage also allows you to stay in your home and use its equity to supplement your monthly income.

The main drawback of a reverse mortgage is that it can diminish the estate that you may want to pass on to your heirs or use for some other purpose. Also, some loans require repayment within a certain number of years. The fees and the effective interest rate you're charged to borrow the money can be quite high.

Because some loans require the lender to make monthly payments to you as long as you live in the home, lenders assume that you'll live many years in your home so they won't lose money when making these loans. If you end up keeping the loan for only a few years because you move, for example, the cost of the loan is extremely high.

TIP

You may be able to create a reverse mortgage with your relatives. This technique can work if you have family members who are financially able to provide you with monthly income in exchange for ownership of the home when you pass away.

You have other alternatives to tapping the equity in your home. Simply selling your home and buying a less expensive property (or renting) is one option. Generally, any profit you make on the sale of the home you live in is not taxable.

Selling your house

The day may come when you want to sell your house. If you're going to sell, make sure you can afford to buy the next home you desire. Be especially careful if you're a trade-up buyer — that is, if you're going to buy an even more expensive home. All the affordability issues we discuss earlier in this chapter apply. You also need to consider the following issues.

Selling through an agent

When you're selling a property, you want an agent who can get the job done efficiently and sell your house for as much as possible. As a seller, you need to seek an agent who has marketing and sales expertise and is willing to put in the time and money necessary to sell your house. Don't necessarily be impressed by an agent who works for a large company. What matters more is what the agent will do to market your property.

When you list your house for sale, the contract you sign with the listing agent includes specification of the commission to be paid if the agent is successful in selling your house. In most areas of the country, agents usually ask for a 6 percent commission. In an area that has lower-cost housing, they may ask for 7 percent.

SHOULD YOU KEEP YOUR HOME UNTIL PRICES GO UP?

Many homeowners are tempted to hold on to their properties (when they need to move) if the property is worth less than when they bought it or if the real-estate market is soft. Renting out your property probably isn't worth the hassle, and holding on to it probably isn't worth the financial gamble. If you need to move, you're better off, in most cases, selling your house.

You may reason that, in a few years (during which you'd rent the property), the real-estate storm clouds will clear, and you'll be able to sell your property at a much higher price. Here are three risks associated with this line of thinking:

- **You can't know whether property prices in the next few years are going to rebound, stay the same, or drop even further.** A property generally needs to appreciate at least a few percent per year just to make up for all the costs of holding and maintaining it.

- **You may be unprepared for legal issues and dealings with your tenants.** If you've never been a landlord, don't underestimate the hassle and headaches associated with this job.

- **If you convert your home into a rental property in the meantime and it appreciates in value, you're going to pay capital-gains tax on your profit when you sell it (and the taxable profit will be higher if you've taken tax deductions for depreciation during the rental period).** This capital-gains tax wipes out much of the advantage of having held on to the property until prices recovered.

However, if you would realize little cash from selling *and* you lack other money for the down payment to purchase your next property, you have good reason for holding on to a home that has dropped in value.

Commissions are *always* negotiable. Because the commission is a percentage, you have a much greater possibility of getting a lower commission on a higher-priced house. If an agent makes 6 percent selling both a $200,000 house and a $100,000 house, the agent makes twice as much on the $200,000 house. Yet selling the higher-priced house does not take twice as much work. (Selling a $400,000 house certainly doesn't take four times the effort of selling a $100,000 house.)

If you're selling a higher-priced home (above $450,000), you have no reason to pay more than a 5 percent commission. For expensive properties ($900,000 and up), a 4 percent commission may be reasonable. You may find, however, that your ability to negotiate a lower commission is greatest when an offer is on the table. Because you don't want to give other agents (working with buyers) a reason not to sell your house, have your listing agent cut his take rather than reduce the commission that you advertise you're willing to pay to an agent who brings you a buyer.

In terms of the length of the listing sales agreement you make with an agent, three months is reasonable. When you give an agent a listing that's too long (6 to 12 months) in duration, the agent may simply toss your listing into the multiple listing book and not put much effort into selling your property. Practically speaking, if your home hasn't sold, you can fire your agent whenever you want, regardless of the length of the listing agreement. However, a shorter listing may be more motivating for your agent.

Selling without a real-estate agent

You may be tempted to sell without an agent so you can save the commission that's deducted from your house's sale price. If you have the time, energy, and marketing experience and you can take the time to properly value your home, you can sell your house without an agent and possibly save some money.

The major problem with trying to sell your house on your own is that agents who are working with buyers don't generally look for or show their clients properties that are for sale by owner (FSBO). Besides saving you time, a good agent can help ensure that you're not sued for failing to disclose the known defects of your property. If you decide to sell your house on your own, make sure you have access to a legal advisor who can review the contracts.

KEEPING YOUR HOME AS AN INVESTMENT PROPERTY AFTER YOU MOVE

TIP

Converting your home into rental property is worth considering if you need or want to move. Don't consider doing so unless it really is a long-term proposition (ten years or more). Selling rental property has tax consequences.

If you want to convert your home into an investment property, you have an advantage over someone who's looking to buy an investment property, because you already own your home. Locating and buying investment property takes time and money. You also know what you have with your current home. If you go out and purchase a property to rent, you're starting from scratch.

If your property is in good condition, consider what damage renters may do to it; few renters will take care of your home the way that you would. Also, consider whether you're cut out to be a landlord. For more information, see the section on real estate as an investment in Chapter 9.

4

Insurance: Protecting What You Have

Understand the fundamentals of insurance and determine when you need it and when you don't.

Find out how to secure insurance on yourself to protect your income earning ability for yourself and loved ones and shield against major medical expenses.

Know what's available to protect your assets such as your home, cars, and wealth.

Chapter **16**

Insurance: Getting What You Need at the Best Price

Unless you work in the industry, you may find insurance to be a dreadfully boring topic. Most people associate insurance with disease, death, and disaster and would rather do just about anything other than review their policies or spend money on insurance. But because you won't want to deal with money hassles when you're coping with catastrophes — illness, disability, death, fires, floods, earthquakes, and so on — you should secure insurance well *before* you need it.

Insurance is probably the most misunderstood and least monitored area of personal finance. Studies by the U.S. nonprofit National Insurance Consumer Organization show that about 90 percent of people purchase and carry the wrong types and amounts of insurance coverage. Most people are overwhelmed by all the jargon in sales and policy statements. Thus, they pay more than necessary for their policies and get coverage they don't really need while failing to obtain coverage that they really should have.

In this chapter, we tell you how to determine what kinds of insurance you need, explain what you can do if you're denied coverage, and give you advice on getting your claims paid. Later chapters discuss types of insurance in detail, including insurance on people (Chapter 17) and possessions (Chapter 18).

Discovering the Three Laws of Buying Insurance

We know your patience and interest in finding out about insurance is surely limited, so in this section we boil down the subject to three fairly simple but powerful concepts that can easily save you big bucks:

>> Insure for the big stuff; don't sweat the small stuff.

>> Buy broad coverage.

>> Shop around and buy direct.

And while you're saving money, you can still get the quality coverage you need in order to avoid a financial catastrophe.

Insure for the big stuff; don't sweat the small stuff

What if you could buy insurance that would pay for the cost of a restaurant meal if you got food poisoning? Even if you were splurging at a fancy restaurant, you wouldn't have a lot of money at stake, so you'd probably decline that coverage.

REMEMBER

The point of insurance is to protect against losses that would be financially catastrophic to you, not to smooth out the bumps of everyday life. The preceding example about restaurant insurance is silly, but some people buy equally foolish policies without knowing it. In the following sections, we tell you how to get the most appropriate insurance coverage for your money. We start off with the "biggies" that are worth your money, and then we work down to some insurance options that are less worthy of your dollars.

Buying insurance to cover financial catastrophes

TIP

You want to insure against what could be a huge financial loss for you or your dependents. The price of insurance isn't cheap, but it's relatively small in comparison to the potential total loss from a financial catastrophe.

The beauty of insurance is that it spreads risks over millions of other people. If your home were to burn to the ground, paying the rebuilding cost out of your own pocket probably would be a financial catastrophe. If you have insurance, the premiums paid by you and all the other homeowners collectively can easily pay the bills.

Think for a moment about what your most valuable assets are. Also consider potential large expenses. Perhaps they include the following:

>> **Future income:** During your working years, your most valuable asset is probably your future earnings. If you were disabled and unable to work, what would you live on? Long-term disability insurance exists to help you handle this type of situation. If you have a family that's financially dependent on your earnings, how would your family manage if you died? Life insurance can fill the monetary void left by your death.

>> **Business:** If you're a business owner, what would happen if you were sued for hundreds of thousands of dollars or a million dollars or more for negligence in some work that you messed up? Liability insurance can protect you.

>> **Health:** In this age of soaring medical costs, you can easily rack up significant bills in short order. Depending on your situation, it may pay to buy extended medical health insurance coverage that covers you for expenses your provincial plan doesn't, such as prescription drugs, dental care, physical therapists, and counselling. (See Chapter 17 for more on health insurance.)

Psychologically, buying insurance coverage for the little things that are more likely to occur is tempting. You don't want to feel like you're wasting your insurance dollars. You want to get some of your money back, darn it! You're more *likely* to get into a fender bender with your car or have a package lost in the mail than you are to lose your home to fire or suffer a long-term disability. But if the fender bender costs $500 (which you end up paying out of your pocket because you took our advice to take a high deductible; see the next section) or the post office loses your package worth $50 or $100, you won't be facing a financial disaster.

On the other hand, if you lose your ability to earn an income because of a disability, or if you're sued for $1 million and you're not insured against such catastrophes, not only will you be extremely unhappy, but you may also face financial ruin. We hear people rationalize, "Yes, but what are the odds that I'll suffer a long-term disability or that I'll be sued for $1 million?" We agree that the odds are quite low, but the risk is there. The problem is that you just don't know what, or when, bad luck may befall you.

And don't make the mistake of thinking that you can figure the odds better than the insurance companies can. The insurance companies predict the probability of your making a claim, large or small, with a great deal of accuracy. They employ armies of number-crunching actuaries to calculate the odds that bad things will happen and the frequency of current policyholders' making particular types of claims. The companies then price their policies accordingly.

So, buying (or not buying) insurance based on your perception of the likelihood of needing the coverage is foolish. Insurance companies aren't stupid; in fact, they're ruthlessly smart! When insurance companies price policies, they look at a number of factors to determine the likelihood of your filing a claim. Take the example of auto insurance. Who do you think will pay more for auto insurance: A single 20-year-old male who lives the fast life in a city known for car thefts, drives a turbo sports car, and has received two speeding tickets in the past year? Or a couple in their 40s, living in an area where car thefts are rare, driving a four-door sedan, with clean driving records?

Taking the highest deductible you can afford

Most insurance policies have *deductibles* — the maximum amount you must pay in the event of a loss before your insurance coverage kicks in and begins paying out. On many policies, such as auto and homeowner's or renter's coverage, many folks opt for a $100 to $250 deductible.

Here are some benefits of taking a higher deductible:

>> **You save premium dollars.** Year in and year out, you can enjoy the lower cost of an insurance policy with a high deductible. You may be able to shave 15 percent to 20 percent off the cost of your policy. Suppose, for example, that you can reduce the cost of your policy by $150 per year by raising your deductible from $250 to $1,000. That $750 worth of coverage is costing you $150 per year. Thus, you'd need to have a claim of $1,000 or more every five years — highly unlikely — to come out ahead. If you're that accident-prone, guess what? The insurance company will raise your premiums.

>> **You don't have the hassles of filing small claims.** If you have a $300 loss on a policy with a $100 deductible, you need to file a claim to get your $200 (the amount you're covered for after your deductible). Filing an insurance claim can be an aggravating experience that takes hours. In some cases, you may even have your claim denied after jumping through all the necessary hoops. Getting your due may require prolonged haggling.

When you have low deductibles, you may file more claims (although this doesn't necessarily mean that you'll get more money). After filing more claims, you may be "rewarded" with higher premiums — in addition to the headache you get from preparing all those blasted forms! Filing more claims may even cause cancellation of your coverage!

Avoiding small-potato policies

A good insurance policy can seem expensive. A policy that doesn't cost much, on the other hand, can fool you into thinking that you're getting something for next to nothing. Policies that cost little also cover little — they're priced low because they don't cover large potential losses.

Following are examples of common "small-potato" insurance policies that are generally a waste of your hard-earned dollars. As you read through this list, you may find examples of policies that you bought and that you feel paid for themselves. We can hear you saying, "But I collected on that policy you're telling me not to buy!" Sure, getting "reimbursed" for the hassle of having something go wrong is comforting. But consider all such policies that you bought or may buy over the course of your life. You're not going to come out ahead in the aggregate — if you did, insurance companies would lose money! These policies aren't worth the cost relative to the small potential benefit. On average, insurance companies pay out just 60 cents in benefits on every dollar collected. Many of the following policies pay back even less — around 20 cents in benefits (claims) for every insurance-premium dollar spent:

>> **Extended-warranty and repair plans:** Isn't it ironic that right after a sales-person persuades you to buy a particular television, computer, car, or smartphone — in part by saying how reliable the product is — he tries to convince you to spend more money to insure against the failure of the item? If the product is so good, why do you need such insurance?

Extended-warranty and repair plans are expensive and unnecessary short-term insurance policies. Product manufacturers' warranties typically cover any problems that occur in the first year or even several years. After that, paying for a repair out of your own pocket isn't a financial catastrophe. (Some credit-card issuers automatically double the manufacturer's warranty without additional charge on items purchased with their cards. However, the cards that do this typically are higher-cost premium cards, so this is no free lunch — you're paying for this protection in terms of higher fees.)

>> **Home-warranty plans:** A third-party new-home warranty is mandatory for most buyers in Ontario and Quebec, as well as Albert, British Columbia, and, likely starting in 2020, Manitoba. In other provinces (at least as of 2018), they're still optional. If you're buying a home in another province, and your real-estate agent or the seller of a home wants to pay the cost of a home-warranty plan for you, turning down the offer would be ungracious. (As Grandma would say, you shouldn't look a gift horse in the mouth.) But don't buy this type of plan for yourself unless you're required to by provincial regulations. In addition to requiring some sort of fee (around $50 to $100), home-warranty plans limit how much they'll pay for problems.

Your money is best spent hiring a competent inspector to uncover problems and fix them *before* you purchase the home. If you buy a house, you should expect to spend money on repairs and maintenance; don't waste money purchasing insurance for such expenses.

- **Dental insurance:** If your employer pays for dental insurance, you can take advantage of it. But don't pay for this coverage on your own. Dental insurance generally covers a couple of teeth cleanings each year and limits payments for more expensive work.

- **Credit life and credit disability policies:** *Credit life policies* pay a small benefit if you die with an outstanding loan. *Credit disability policies* pay a small monthly income in the event of a disability. Banks and their credit-card divisions usually sell these policies. Some companies sell insurance to pay off your credit-card bill in the event of your death or disability, or to cover minimum monthly payments for a temporary period during specified life transition events (such as loss of a job, divorce, and so on).

   The cost of such insurance seems low, but that's because the potential benefits are relatively small. In fact, given what little insurance you're buying, these policies are expensive. If you need life or disability insurance, buy it. But get enough coverage, and buy it in a separate, cost-effective policy (see Chapter 17 for more details).

TIP

   If you're in poor health and you can buy these insurance policies without a medical evaluation, you may be an exception to the "don't buy it" rule. In this case, these policies may be the only ones to which you have access — another reason these policies are expensive. The people in good health are paying for the people with poor health who can enroll without a medical examination and who undoubtedly file more claims.

- **Insuring packages in the mail:** You buy a $40 gift for a friend, and when you go to the post office to ship it, the friendly postal clerk asks whether you want to insure it. For a few bucks, you think, "Why not?" Canada Post rarely loses or damages things. Go spend your money on something else — or better yet, invest it.

- **Cellphone insurance:** We understand that if you just shelled out $700 or more for the latest smartphone (especially if you bought one for a teenager in your household), you'd like to protect against the loss or damage of said device. If you can't afford to replace such a costly cellphone, then, we would argue don't spend that much on one in the first place. But if you insist on a costly smartphone purchase, the insurance isn't worth it. Our reviews of recent plans show that the coverage will cost you $150 to $300 just for the first two years and, if you do have a loss, you'll also get whacked with a $100 to $200 deductible!

- **Contact-lens insurance:** The things that people come up with to waste money on just astound us. Contact-lens insurance really does exist! The money goes to replace your contacts if you lose or tear them. Lenses are relatively inexpensive. Don't waste your money on this kind of insurance.

>> **Little-stuff riders:** Many policies that are worth buying, such as auto and disability insurance, can have all sorts of riders added on. These *riders* are extra bells and whistles that insurance agents and companies like to sell because of the high profit margin they provide (for *them*). On auto insurance policies, for example, you can buy a rider for a few bucks per year that pays you $25 each time your car needs to be towed. Having your vehicle towed isn't going to bankrupt you, so it isn't worth insuring against.

Likewise, small insurance policies that are sold as add-ons to bigger insurance policies are usually unnecessary and overpriced. For example, you can buy some disability-insurance policies with a small amount of life insurance added on. If you need life insurance, purchasing a sufficient amount in a separate policy is less costly.

Buy broad coverage

Purchasing coverage that's too narrow is another major mistake people make when buying insurance. Such policies often seem like cheap ways to put your fears to rest. For example, instead of buying life insurance, some folks buy flight insurance at an airport self-service kiosk. They seem to worry more about their mortality when getting on an airplane than they do when getting into a car. If they die on the flight, their beneficiaries collect. But if they die the next day in a car accident or get some dreaded disease — which is statistically far, *far* more likely than going down in a jet — the beneficiaries get nothing from flight insurance. Buy life insurance (broad coverage to protect your loved ones financially in the event of your untimely demise no matter the cause), not flight insurance (narrow coverage).

WARNING

The medical equivalent of flight insurance is cancer insurance. Older people, who are fearful of having their life savings depleted by a long battle with this dreaded disease, are easy prey for this narrow insurance. If you get cancer, cancer insurance pays the bills. But what if you get heart disease, diabetes, or some other disease? Cancer insurance won't pay these costs. Purchase major-medical coverage, not cancer insurance.

Recognizing fears

Fears, such as getting cancer, are natural and inescapable. Although you may not have control over the emotions that your fears invoke, you must often ignore those emotions in order to make rational insurance decisions. In other words, getting shaky in the knees and sweaty in the palms when boarding an airplane is okay, but letting your fear of flying cause you to make poor insurance decisions is not okay, especially when those decisions affect the financial security of your loved ones.

TIP

EXAMINING MISPERCEPTIONS OF RISKS

How high do you think your risks are for expiring prematurely if you're exposed to toxic wastes or pesticides, or if you live in a dangerous area that has a high murder rate? Well, actually, these risks are quite small when compared to the risks you subject yourself to when you get behind the wheel of a car or light up yet another cigarette.

Now-retired reporter John Stossel (formerly with ABC News and Fox News) was kind enough to share the results of a study done for him by physicist Bernard Cohen. In the study, Cohen compared different risks. Cohen's study showed that people's riskiest behaviours are smoking and driving. Smoking whacks an average of seven years off a person's life, whereas driving a car results in a bit more than half a year of life lost, on average. Toxic waste shaves an average of one week off an American's life span.

Unfortunately, you can't buy a formal insurance policy to protect yourself against all of life's great dangers and risks. But that doesn't mean that you have to face these dangers as a helpless victim; simple changes in behaviour can help you improve your security.

Personal health habits are a good example of the types of behaviour you can change. If you're overweight and you eat unhealthy foods, drink alcohol excessively, and don't exercise, you're asking for trouble, especially after middle age. Engage in these habits, and you dramatically increase your risk of heart disease and cancer.

You can buy all the types of traditional insurance that we recommend in this book and still not be well protected for the simple reason that you're overlooking uninsurable risks. However, not being able to buy formal insurance to protect against some dangers doesn't mean that you can't drastically reduce your exposure to such risks by modifying your behaviour. For example, you can't buy an auto-insurance policy that protects your personal safety against drivers who are under the influence of alcohol and/or drugs, who are responsible for some half of motor-vehicle crashes in Canada. However, you can choose to drive a safe car, practise safe driving habits, and minimize driving on the roads during the late-evening hours and on major holidays when drinking is prevalent (such as New Year's Eve, Canada Day, and so on).

Preparing for natural disasters — insurance and otherwise

In the chapters following this one, in which we discuss specific types of insurance such as disability insurance and homeowner's insurance, we highlight the fact that you'll find it nearly impossible to get coverage that includes every possibility of catastrophe. For example, when purchasing homeowner's coverage, you may find that losses from floods and earthquakes are excluded. You may be able to secure such coverage in separate policies, which you should do if you live in an area subject to such risks (see more on this in Chapter 18). Many people don't understand these risks, and insurers don't always educate customers about such gaping holes in their policies.

TIP

In addition to filling those voids, also think about and plan for the nonfinancial issues that inevitably arise in a catastrophe. For example, make sure you have

>> A meeting place for you and your loved ones if you're separated during a disaster (and a friend or family member who lives outside your area to serve as a common point of contact)

>> An escape plan in the event that your area is hit with flooding or some other natural disaster (tornado, hurricane, earthquake, fire, or mudslide)

>> The security of having taken steps to make your home safer in the event of an earthquake or fire (for instance, securing shelving and heavy objects from falling and tipping, and installing smoke detectors and fire extinguishers)

>> A plan for what you'll do for food, clothing, and shelter if your home becomes uninhabitable

You get the idea. Although you can't possibly predict what's going to happen and when, you can find out about the risks for your area. In addition to buying the broadest possible coverage, you should also make contingency plans for disasters.

Shop around and buy direct

Whether you're looking at auto, home, life, disability, or other types of coverage, some companies may charge double or triple the rates that other companies charge for the same coverage. Insurers that charge the higher rates may not be better about paying claims, however. You may even end up with the worst of both possible worlds — high prices *and* lousy service.

Most insurance is sold through agents and brokers who earn commissions based on what they sell. The commissions, of course, can bias what they recommend.

Not surprisingly, policies that pay agents the biggest commissions also tend to be more costly. In fact, insurance companies compete for the attention of agents by offering bigger commissions. When we browse publications targeted to insurance agents, we often see ads in which the largest text is the commission percentage offered to agents who sell the advertiser's products.

Besides the attraction of policies that pay higher commissions, agents also get hooked, financially speaking, on companies whose policies they sell frequently. After an agent sells a certain amount of a company's insurance policies, she's rewarded with bigger commission percentages (and other perks) on any future sales. Just as airlines bribe frequent flyers with mileage bonuses, insurers bribe agents with heftier commissions and awards such as trips and costly goods.

Shopping around is a challenge not only because most insurance is sold by agents working on commission, but also because insurers set their rates in mysterious ways. Every company has a different way of analyzing how much of a risk you are; one company may offer low rates to your friend but not to you, and vice versa.

Despite the obstacles, several strategies exist for obtaining low-cost, high-quality policies. The following sections offer smart ways to shop for insurance. (Chapters 17 and 18 recommend how and where to get the best deals on specific types of policies.)

Looking at employer and other group plans

When you buy insurance as part of a larger group, you generally get a lower price because of the purchasing power of the group. Most of the health and disability policies that you can access through your employer are less costly than equivalent coverage you can buy on your own.

TIP

Likewise, many occupations have professional associations through which you may be able to obtain lower-cost policies. Not all associations offer better deals on insurance — compare their policy features and costs with other options.

Life insurance is an exception to the rule that states that group policies offer better value than individual policies. Group life-insurance plans usually aren't cheaper than the best life-insurance policies that you can buy individually. However, group policies may have the attraction of convenience (ease of enrollment and avoidance of lengthy sales pitches from life-insurance salespeople). Group life-insurance policies that allow you to enroll without a medical evaluation are usually more expensive, because such plans attract more people with health problems who can't get coverage on their own. If you're in good health, you should definitely shop around for life insurance (see Chapter 17 to find out how).

WARNING

Insurance agents who want to sell you an individual policy can come up with 101 reasons why buying from them is preferable to buying through your employer or some other group. In most cases, agents' arguments for buying an individual policy from them include self-serving hype.

One valid issue that agents raise is that if you leave your job, you'll lose your group coverage. Sometimes that may be true. For example, if you know that you're going to be leaving your job to become self-employed, securing an individual disability policy before you leave your job makes sense. However, your employer's health insurer may allow you to buy an individual policy when you leave.

In Chapter 17, we explain what you need in the policies you're looking for so you can determine whether a group plan meets your needs. In most cases, group plans, especially through an employer, offer good benefits. So as long as the group policy is cheaper than a comparable individual policy, you'll save money overall buying through the group plan.

Buying insurance without paying sales commissions

Buying policies from the increasing number of companies that are selling their policies directly to the public without the insurance agent and the agent's commission is your best bet for getting a good insurance value. Just as you can purchase no-load mutual funds directly from an investment company without paying any sales commission (see Chapter 10), you also can buy no-load insurance. Be sure to read Chapters 17 and 18 for more specifics on how to buy insurance directly from insurance companies.

Annuities, investment/insurance products traditionally sold through insurance agents, are also now available directly to the customer, without commission.

THE STRAIGHT SCOOP ON COMMISSIONS

The commission paid to an insurance agent is never disclosed through any of the documents or materials that you receive when buying insurance. The only way you can know what the commission is and how it compares with other policies is to ask the agent. Nothing is wrong or impolite about asking. After all, your money pays the commission. You need to know whether a particular policy is being pitched harder because of its higher commission.

Commissions are typically paid as a percentage of the first year's premium on the insurance policy. (Many policies pay smaller commissions on subsequent years' premiums.) With life- and disability-insurance policies, for example, a 50 percent commission on the first year's premium is not unusual. With life-insurance policies that have a cash value, commissions of 80 percent to 100 percent of your first year's premium are possible. Commissions on health insurance are lower but generally not as low as commissions on auto and homeowner's insurance.

Dealing with Insurance Problems

When you seek out insurance or have insurance policies, sooner or later you're bound to hit a roadblock. Although insurance problems can be among the more frustrating in life, in the following sections, we explain how to successfully deal with the more common obstacles.

Knowing what to do if you're denied coverage

Just as you can be turned down when you apply for a loan, you can also be turned down when applying for insurance. With life or disability insurance, a company may reject you if you have an existing medical problem (a pre-existing condition) and are, therefore, more likely to file a claim. When it comes to insuring assets such as a home, you may have difficulty getting coverage if the property is deemed to be in a high-risk area.

TIP

Here are some strategies to employ if you're denied coverage:

>> **Ask the insurer why you were denied.** Perhaps the company made a mistake or misinterpreted some information that you provided in your application. If you're denied coverage because of a medical condition, find out what information the company has on you and determine whether it's accurate.

>> **Shop other companies.** Just because one company denies you coverage (for example, with disability or life insurance) doesn't mean all insurance companies will do the same. Some insurers better understand certain medical conditions and are more comfortable accepting applicants with those conditions. Most insurers charge higher rates to people with blemished medical histories than they do to people with perfect health records, but some companies penalize them less than others. An agent who sells policies from multiple insurers, called an *independent agent,* can be helpful, because she can shop among a number of different companies.

>> **Find out about provincial high-risk pools.** A number of provinces act as the insurer of last resort and provide insurance for those who can't get it from insurance companies. Provincial high-risk-pool coverage is usually bare-bones, but it beats going without any coverage. If you're turned down for health or property insurance, check with your provincial department of insurance (see the "Government" section of your local phone directory).

>> **Check for coverage availability before you buy.** If you're considering buying a home, for example, and you can't get coverage, the insurance companies are trying to tell you something. What they're effectively saying is, "We think that property is so high-risk, we're not willing to insure it even if you pay a high premium."

Getting your due on claims

In the event that you suffer a loss and file an insurance claim, you naturally hope that your insurance company will cheerfully and expeditiously pay your claims. Given all the money that you shelled out for coverage and all the hoops you jumped through to get approved for coverage in the first place, that's a reasonable expectation.

Insurance companies may refuse to pay you what you think they owe you for many reasons, however. In some cases, your claim may not be covered under the terms of the policy. At a minimum, the insurer wants documentation and proof of your loss. Other people who have come before you have been known to cheat, so insurers won't simply take your word for it, no matter how honest and ethical you are.

Some insurers view paying claims as an adversarial situation and take a "negotiate tough" stance. Thinking that all insurance companies are going to pay you a fair and reasonable amount even if you don't make your voice heard is a mistake.

The tips we discuss in this section can help you ensure that you get paid what your policy entitles you to.

Documenting your assets and case

TIP

When you're insuring assets, such as your home and its contents, having a record of what you own can be helpful if you need to file a claim. The best defence is a good offence. If you keep records of valuables and can document their cost, you should be in good shape. A video is the most efficient record for documenting your assets, but a handwritten list detailing your possessions works, too. Just remember to keep this record someplace away from your home — if your home burns to the ground, you'll lose your documentation, too!

If you're robbed or you're the victim of an accident, get the names, addresses, and phone numbers of witnesses. Take pictures of property damage and solicit estimates for the cost of repairing or replacing whatever has been lost or damaged. File police reports when appropriate, if for no other reason than to bolster your documentation for the insurance claim.

Preparing your case

Filing a claim should be viewed the same way as preparing for a court trial or a tax audit. Any information you provide verbally or in writing can and will be used against you to deny your claim. First, you should understand whether your policy covers your claim (this is why getting the broadest possible coverage helps). Unfortunately, the only way to find out whether the policy covers your claim is to read it. Policies are hard to read because they use legal language in non-user-friendly ways.

TIP

A possible alternative to reading your policy is to call the claims department and, *without* providing your name (and using caller ID blocking on your phone if you're calling from home or your personal cellphone), ask a representative whether a particular loss (such as the one that you just suffered) is covered under its policy. You have no need to lie to the company, but you don't have to tell the representative who you are and that you're about to file a claim either. Your call is so you can understand what your policy covers. However, some companies aren't willing to provide detailed information unless a specific case is cited.

After you initiate the claims process, keep records of all conversations and copies of all the documents you give to the insurer's claims department. If you have problems down the road, this "evidence" may bail you out.

For property damage, get at least a couple of reputable contractors' estimates. Demonstrate to the insurance company that you're trying to shop for a low price, but don't agree to use a low-cost contractor without knowing that she can do quality work.

Approaching your claim as a negotiation

To get what you're owed on an insurance claim, you must approach most claims' filings for what they are — a negotiation with a party that's often uncooperative. And the bigger the claim, the more your insurer will play the part of adversary.

A number of years ago, when Eric filed a homeowner's insurance claim after a major rain and wind storm significantly damaged his backyard fence, he was greeted on a weekday by a perky, smiley adjuster. When the adjuster entered his yard and started to peruse the damage, her demeanor changed dramatically. She had a combative, hard-bargainer type of attitude that Eric last witnessed when he worked on some labour-management negotiations during his days as a consultant.

The adjuster stood on Eric's back porch, a good distance away from the fences that had been blown over by wind and crushed by two large trees, and said that the insurer preferred to repair damaged fences rather than replace them. "With your deductible of $1,000, I doubt this will be worth filing a claim for," she said.

The fence that had blown over, she reasoned, could have new posts set in concrete. Because Eric had already begun to clean up some of the damage for safety reasons, he presented to her some pictures of what the yard looked like right after the storm; she refused to take them. She took some measurements and said that she'd have her settlement cheque to him in a couple of days. The settlement she faxed was for $1,119 — nowhere near what it cost Eric to fix the damage that was done.

Practicing persistency

When you take an insurance company's first offer and don't fight for what you're due, you may be leaving a lot of money on the table. To make Eric's long fence-repair story (see the preceding section) somewhat shorter, after *five* rounds of haggling with the adjusters, supervisors, and finally managers, he was awarded payment to replace the fences and clean up most of the damage. Even though all the contractors he contacted recommended that the work be done this way, the insurance adjuster discredited their recommendations by saying, "Contractors try to jack up the price and recommended work once they know an insurer is involved."

His final total settlement came to $4,888, more than $3,700 higher than the insurer's first offer. Interestingly, Eric's insurer backed off its preference for repairing the fence when the contractor's estimates for doing that work exceeded the cost of a new fence.

Eric understandably was disappointed with the behaviour of that insurance company. He knows from conversations with others that his homeowner's insurance company (at that time) was not unusual in its adversarial strategy, especially with larger claims. And to think that this insurer had, at that time, one of the better track records for paying claims!

Enlisting support

If you're doing your homework and you're not making progress with the insurer's adjuster, ask to speak with supervisors and managers. This is the strategy Eric used to get the additional $3,700 needed to get things back to where they were before the storm (see the previous sections).

The agent who sold you your policy may be helpful in preparing and filing the claim. A good agent can help increase your chances of getting paid — and getting paid sooner. If you're having difficulty with a claim for a policy obtained through your employer or other group, speak with the benefits department or a person responsible for interacting with the insurer. These folks have a lot of clout, because the agent and/or insurer doesn't want to lose the entire account.

WHEN INSURERS (AND GOVERNMENT) MOVE SLOWLY

When Hurricane Katrina caused unprecedented damage and loss along the Gulf Coast, Eric received many complaints from folks in that region. Typical is the following note he received from a New Orleans family more than three months after Hurricane Katrina:

> We had substantial damage to our home in New Orleans due to Hurricane Katrina. We had roof damage on August 29 and three feet of water August 31. Our flood insurance is through an insurance company acting as an agent for FEMA's program. [*Note:* FEMA is the Federal Emergency Management Agency, an agency of the U.S. government.] Our adjuster has still not turned in the necessary paperwork for our claim. Our home insurer made no allowance for proper removal and disposal of asbestos shingles, and we have gotten just $2,000 for living expenses out of the $21,000 we're now owed. We have just gotten a first partial payment ($40,000 out of $160,000) on the flood insurance, but it was made out to the wrong mortgage company, so we had to send the check back.

> It is shocking that it has gone on this long. It has been all over the papers about the delay of some flood-insurance payments being due to FEMA not having adequate money in the till. There's no doubt the insurers are overwhelmed, but why is this taking so long? I called the Louisiana Department of Insurance and was told that insurers normally have 30 days for claims according to the insurance department (which has said they can have 45 days in this case). It's been over 60 days since the adjuster came out to our home.

Stories like this make us disappointed and mad. There's simply no excuse for large insurance companies who are in the business of insuring for such events not to bring the proper resources to bear to make timely payments. The fact that they did not do so for Gulf Coast victims is even more reprehensible given the widespread problems in that area. In addition to home losses, many people also had job losses to deal with and could ill afford to be without money. Large insurers that wrote flood policies for which FEMA temporarily lacked money should've paid their policyholders. Although the federal government and FEMA officials should've been taken to task for allowing FEMA's accounts to run dry, customer-service-oriented insurers should've stepped up and advanced money that they knew would eventually come from FEMA.

In situations like this, if you do your homework and you're not making progress with the insurer's adjuster, ask to speak with supervisors and managers. If you're having problems getting a fair and timely settlement from the insurer, try contacting your province's insurance regulator. The person who wrote Eric was from Louisiana, where the state department of insurance had more than 1,600 hurricane-related complaints in the first three months after Hurricane Katrina. To our surprise, the department's Director of Public Information told Eric that no insurance companies had been fined and penalized for delaying payments. It's no wonder these companies weren't getting on the stick!

TIP

If you're having problems getting a fair settlement from the insurer of a policy you bought on your own, try contacting the provincial department that oversees insurance companies or the provincial regulator. You can find the phone number online or possibly in your insurance policy.

Hiring a public adjuster who, for a percentage of the payment (typically 5 percent to 10 percent), can negotiate with insurers on your behalf is another option.

When all else fails and you have a major claim at stake, try contacting a lawyer who specializes in insurance matters. You can find these specialists in the yellow pages under "Lawyers — Insurance Law" or enter those terms and your city into a search engine. Expect to pay at least $150 per hour. Look for a lawyer who's willing to negotiate on your behalf, help draft letters, and perform other necessary tasks on an hourly basis without filing a lawsuit. Your provincial insurance regulator, the local bar association, or other legal, accounting, or financial practitioners also may be able to refer you to someone.

Chapter **17**

Insurance on You: Life, Disability, Long Term Care, and Medical

During your working years, multiplying your typical annual income by the number of years you plan to continue working produces a pretty big number. That dollar amount equals what is probably your most valuable asset — your ability to earn an income. You need to protect this asset by purchasing some insurance on *you*.

This chapter explains the ins and outs of buying insurance to protect your income: life insurance in case of death, and disability insurance in case of an accident or severe medical condition that prevents you from working. We tell you what coverage you should have, where to look for it, and what to avoid.

We also fill you in on long-term-care insurance — what it is and whether you need it. We close the chapter with a discussion of travel medical insurance, which covers you in the event that you get sick or injured while out of the country.

Providing for Your Loved Ones: Life Insurance

You generally need life insurance only when other people depend on your income. The following folks don't need life insurance to protect their incomes:

>> Single people with no children

>> Working couples who could maintain a lifestyle acceptable to them on one of their incomes

>> Independently wealthy people who don't need to work

>> Retired people who are living off their retirement nest egg

>> Minor children (because you're not financially dependent upon them)

If others are either fully or partly dependent on your paycheque (usually a spouse and/or child), you need life insurance, especially if you have major financial commitments such as a mortgage or years of child-rearing ahead. You may also want to consider life insurance if an extended family member is currently or likely to be dependent on your future income.

Determining how much life insurance to buy

Determining how much life insurance to buy is as much a subjective decision as it is a quantitative decision. We've seen some worksheets that are incredibly long and tedious (some rivalling your tax returns). There's no need to get fancy. If you're like us, your eyes start to glaze over if you have to complete 20-plus lines of calculations. Figuring out how much life insurance you need doesn't have to be that complicated.

The main purpose of life insurance is to provide a lump-sum payment to replace the deceased person's income. Ask yourself how many years of income you want to replace. Table 17-1 provides a simple way to figure how much life insurance to consider purchasing. To replace a certain number of years' worth of income, simply multiply the appropriate number in the table by your annual after-tax income.

TIP

You can access a Canadian Retirement Income Calculator on the Canada Pension Plan (CPP) website at www.canada.ca/en/services/benefits/publicpensions/cpp/retirement-income-calculator.html. The calculator takes about 30 minutes to complete, but the tool will provide you with information on your government retirement income, including CPP and Old Age Security (OAS) retirement benefits.

When you've determined how much your survivors would receive per month in the event of your death, factor this benefit into the amount of life insurance that you calculate in Table 17-1. For example, suppose your annual after-tax income is $45,000 and your spouse will receive survivor's benefits for himself and your children worth $5,000 after tax per year. For the purposes of Table 17-1, you should determine the amount of life insurance needed to replace $40,000 annually ($45,000 − $5,000), not $45,000.

TABLE 17-1

Life-Insurance Calculation

Years of Income to Replace	Multiply Annual After-Tax Income* By
5	4.5
10	8.5
20	15
30	20

You can roughly determine your annual after-tax income by getting out last year's tax return and subtracting the federal, provincial, and other payroll deductions you paid from your gross employment income.

Another way to determine the amount of life insurance to buy is to think about how much would be needed to pay for major debts or expenditures, such as your mortgage, other loans, and university or college for your children. For example, suppose you want your spouse to have enough of a life-insurance death benefit to pay off your mortgage and half of your children's postsecondary education. Simply add your mortgage amount to half of your children's estimated university or college costs (see Chapter 14 for approximate numbers), and then buy that amount of life insurance.

Looking at the Canada Pension Plan and Quebec Pension Plan's survivor benefits

If you're covered, the CPP or Quebec Pension Plan (QPP) can provide *survivor benefits* to your spouse (this includes both those who are married and those who are living in common law) and children. (Note that the deceased must have ten calendar years, or one-third of the number of years included wholly or partly in his contributory period, but not for less than three years.)

Figuring out just how much the surviving spouse may get can be somewhat complicated. The amount — and the maximum available — is affected by the person's age, whether he or she is still working, what CPP benefits he or she may have been receiving and for how long, and how much his or her spouse paid into CPP.

To begin with, your surviving spouse is going to get little if any survivor benefits if he or she is working and earning even a modest amount of money.

If you're already receiving your own CPP or QPP retirement pension or disability benefits and you then become eligible to also receive survivor benefits due to the death of your spouse, it will be combined with what you're already receiving in one monthly payment. However, there are a number of limitations. This new combined total amount can't exceed the maximum retirement pension. If you're receiving a disability benefit, the total, after your survivor benefits are added in, can't exceed the maximum disability benefit.

TIP

Some couples choose to split one of their CPP or QPP payments as a way to balance their income and reduce their household's overall tax bill. This has no impact on the surviving spouse's benefits. If one spouse dies, the survivor benefits are calculated as if the splitting (officially called *assigning*) of benefits never took place.

For more on the exact formulas used, visit www.canada.ca/en/services/ benefits/publicpensions.html and click the Survivor's Pension link.

The impact on Old Age Security benefits

The Guaranteed Income Supplement (GIS) and OAS Allowance benefits are calculated using a couple's combined income. If you're receiving these benefits and your spouse or common-law partner dies, the monthly payments will be recalculated using your own income. If you start receiving a CPP or QPP survivor benefit, that benefit is included in your income for the purposes of calculating your eligibility for GIS or OAS Allowance benefits in the following year.

Benefits for surviving children

Children under the age of 18 of a contributor to the CPP may also be eligible for payments called the CPP Children's Benefit. Children between the ages of 18 and 25 who are attending school full-time may also be eligible, as well as part-time students in certain cases. The monthly benefit is a flat amount; in 2018, it was $244.64.

TIP

You may want to factor your government survivor's benefits into how much life insurance to buy, but be sure to consider the taxes you may owe on them. To find out how much your survivors will receive per month in the event of your death, contact Service Canada, which is part of Employment and Social Development Canada. You can find this information online by going to www.canada.ca/en/ employment-social-development.html and clicking the Public Pensions link. You can also request information by mail. You'll find the address for the Service Canada web office nearest you at the same website. You can also reach them by phone at 800-277-9914 (English) or 800-277-9915 (French).

EXAMINING "OTHER" LIFE INSURANCE

Contemplating the possibility of your untimely demise is surely depressing. You'll likely feel some peace of mind when purchasing a life-insurance policy to provide for your dependants. However, we suggest you take things a step further. Suppose you pass away. Do you think that simply buying a life-insurance policy will be sufficient "help" for the loved ones you leave behind? Surely your contribution to your household involves far more than being a breadwinner.

Do you have a will? See Chapter 18 for more details on wills and other estate-planning documents. Make sure all your important financial documents — investment-account statements, insurance policies, employee-benefits materials, small-business accounting records, and so on — are kept in one place (such as a file drawer) that your loved ones know about. You may also want to consider providing a list of key contacts — such as who you recommend your family or designated advocate call (or what you recommend they read) in the event of legal, financial, or tax quandaries.

So, in addition to trying to provide financially for your dependants, you should also take some time to reflect on what else you can do to help point them in the right direction on matters you normally handle. With most couples, it's natural for one spouse to take more responsibility for money management. That's fine; just make sure to talk about what's being done so that in the event that the responsible spouse dies, the surviving person knows how to jump into the driver's seat.

If you have kids (and even if you don't), you may want to give some thought to sentimental leave-behinds for your loved ones. These leave-behinds can be something like a short note telling them how much they meant to you and what you'd like them to remember about you.

Comparing term life insurance to cash-value life insurance

We're going to tell you how you can save hours of time and thousands of dollars. Ready? Buy term life insurance. If you've already figured out how much life insurance to purchase and this is all the advice you need, you can jump to the "Buying term insurance" section that follows.

If you want the details behind our recommendation for term insurance, the following information is for you. Or maybe you've heard (and you've already fallen prey to) the sales pitches from life-insurance agents, most of whom love selling cash-value life insurance because of its huge commissions.

Despite the variety of names that life insurance marketing departments have cooked up for policies, life insurance comes in two basic flavors:

>> **Term insurance:** This insurance is pure life insurance. You pay an annual premium for which you receive a particular amount of life-insurance coverage. If you, the insured person, pass away, your beneficiaries collect; otherwise, the premium is gone, but you're grateful to be alive!

>> **Cash-value insurance:** All other life-insurance policies (whole, universal, variable, and so on) combine life insurance with a supposed savings feature. Not only do your premiums pay for life insurance, but some of your dollars are also credited to an account that grows in value over time, assuming you keep paying your premiums. On the surface, this type of insurance sounds potentially attractive. People don't like to feel that their premium dollars are getting tossed away.

WARNING

But cash-value insurance has a big catch. For the same amount of coverage (for example, for $100,000 of life-insurance benefits), cash-value policies cost you about eight times (800 percent!) more than comparable term policies.

Insurance salespeople know the buttons to push to interest you in buying the wrong kind of life insurance. Here are some of the typical arguments they make for purchasing cash-value polices, and our perspective on each one:

>> **"Cash-value policies are all paid up after X years. You don't want to be paying life insurance premiums for the rest of your life, do you?"** Agents who pitch cash-value life insurance present projections that imply that after the first ten or so years of paying your premiums, you don't need to pay more premiums to keep the life insurance in force. The only reason you may be able to stop paying premiums is because you poured a lot of extra money into the policy in the early years. Remember that cash-value life insurance costs about eight times as much as term insurance.

Imagine that you're currently paying $500 a year for auto insurance and that an insurance company comes along and offers you a policy for $4,000 per year. The representative tells you that after ten years, you can stop paying and still keep your same coverage. We're sure you wouldn't fall for this sales tactic, but many people do when they buy cash-value life insurance.

You also need to be wary of the projections, because they may include unrealistic and lofty assumptions about the investment return that your cash balance can earn. When you stop paying into a cash-value policy, the cost of each year's life insurance is deducted from the remaining cash value. If the rate of return on the cash balance is not sufficient to pay the insurance cost, the cash balance declines, and eventually you receive notices saying that your policy needs more funding to keep the life insurance in force.

>> **"You won't be able to afford term insurance when you're older."** As you get older, the cost of term insurance increases because the risk of dying rises. But life insurance is not something you need all your life! It's typically bought in a person's younger years when financial commitments and obligations outweigh financial assets. Twenty or 30 years later, the reverse should be true — if you use the principles in this book!

When you retire, you don't need life insurance to protect your employment income, because there isn't any to protect! You may need life insurance when you're raising a family and/or you have a substantial mortgage to pay off, but by the time you retire, the kids should be out on their own (you hope!), and the mortgage should be paid down.

In the meantime, term insurance saves you a tremendous amount of money. For most people, it takes 20 to 30 years for the premium they're paying on a term life insurance policy to finally catch up to (equal) the premium they've been paying all along on a comparable amount of cash-value life insurance.

>> **"You can borrow against the cash value at a low interest rate."** Such a deal! It's your money in the policy, remember? If you deposited money in a savings or money-market account, how would you like to pay for the privilege of borrowing your own money back? Borrowing on your cash-value policy is potentially dangerous: You increase the chances that the policy will lapse — leaving you with nothing to show for your premiums.

>> **"Your cash value grows tax-deferred."** Ah, a glimmer of truth at last. The cash-value portion of your policy grows without taxation until you withdraw it, but if you want tax deferral of your investment balances, you should first take advantage of funding your Registered Retirement Savings Plan (RRSP). An RRSP gives you an immediate tax deduction for your current contributions in addition to growth without taxation until withdrawal.

The money you pay into a cash-value life policy gives you no upfront tax deductions. (See Chapter 11 for details on RRSPs.)

Life insurance tends to be a mediocre investment at best. The insurance company generally quotes you an interest rate for the first year; after that, the company changes the rate annually. If you don't like the future interest rates, you can be penalized for quitting the policy. Would you ever invest your money in a bank account that quoted an interest rate for the first year and then penalized you for moving your money within the next seven to ten years?

>> **"Cash-value policies are forced savings."** Many agents argue that a cash-value plan is better than nothing — at least it's forcing you to save. This line of thinking is silly because so many people drop cash-value life-insurance policies after just a few years of paying into them. You can accomplish "forced savings" without using life insurance. An RRSP, as discussed in Chapter 11, can be set up for automatic monthly transfers. Employers offering such a plan can

deduct contributions from your paycheque — and they don't take a commission! You can also set up monthly electronic transfers from your bank chequing account to contribute to mutual funds (see Chapter 10).

Making your decision

Insurance salespeople aggressively push cash-value policies because of the high commissions that insurance companies pay them. Commissions on cash-value life insurance range from 50 percent to 100 percent of your first year's premium. An insurance salesperson, therefore, can make *eight to ten times more money* (yes, you read that right) selling you a cash-value policy than he can selling you term insurance. And as you can imagine, that's a powerful motivator many insurance salespeople just can't ignore. Cash-value life insurance is the most oversold insurance and financial product in the financial services industry.

Ultimately, when you purchase cash-value life insurance, you pay the high commissions that are built into these policies. As you can see in the policy's cash-value table, you don't get back any of the money that you dump into the policy if you quit the policy in the first few years. The insurance company can't afford to give you any of your money back in those early years because so much of it has been paid to the selling agent as commission. That's why these policies explicitly penalize you for withdrawing your cash balance within the first seven to ten years.

WARNING

Perhaps the biggest strike again cash-value life insurance is that, despite — or, rather because of — the huge cost, you likely won't end up with the point of parting with so much money: ensuring your family has a financial safety net should you die. Because cash-value policies are so expensive, relative to the cost of a term policy for the same amount of coverage, you're more likely to buy less life insurance coverage than you need. This is the sad part of the insurance industry's pushing of this stuff. The vast majority of life-insurance buyers need more protection than they can afford to buy with cash-value coverage.

Cash-value life insurance isn't completely without its uses. A cash-value policy can make sense for a small number of people in somewhat-unique circumstances with particular needs. For example, a cash-value policy may be a useful purchase for a small-business owner who owns a business worth at least several million dollars and don't want her heirs to be forced to sell their business to pay taxes in the event of her death. (See "Considering the purchase of cash-value life insurance" later in this chapter.)

TIP

In short? Purchase low-cost term insurance and do your investing separately. Life insurance is rarely a permanent need; over time, you can reduce the amount of term insurance you carry as your financial obligations lessen and you accumulate more assets.

Buying term insurance

Term insurance policies have several features from which to choose. We cover the important elements of term insurance in this section so you can make an informed decision about purchasing it.

Selecting how often your premium adjusts

Term insurance can be purchased so your premium adjusts (increases) annually or after 5, 10, 15, or 20 years. The less frequently your premium adjusts, the higher the initial premium and its incremental increases will be. (**Remember:** As you get older, the risk of dying increases, so the cost of your insurance goes up.)

The advantage of a premium that locks in for, say, 15 years is that you have the security of knowing how much you'll be paying annually for the next 15 years. You also don't need to go through medical evaluations as frequently to qualify for the lowest rate possible. The disadvantage of a policy with a long-term rate lock is that you pay more in the early years than you do on a policy that adjusts more frequently. In addition, you may want to change the amount of insurance you carry as your circumstances change. Thus, you may throw money away when you dump a policy with a long-term premium guarantee before its rate is set to change.

TIP

Policies that adjust the premium every five to ten years offer a happy medium between price and predictability.

Ensuring guaranteed renewability

Guaranteed renewability, which is standard practise on the better policies, assures that the policy can't be cancelled because of poor health. Don't buy a life-insurance policy without this feature unless you expect that your life insurance needs will disappear when the policy is up for renewal.

TIP

When assessing the price tag of a policy, what really matters is the total amount you'll pay for your coverage for all the years that you'll require life insurance. Be sure that the premiums you'll pay each time you renew are guaranteed and laid out term by term in your policy.

To evaluate different policies, have the agent do a *net-present-value* (NPV) *comparison* of the total amount you'll pay in premiums over the period you estimate you'll require life insurance. This figure represents what a policy would cost if you had to pay for all your years of coverage in a single payment today. Suppose you're trying to compare the costs of two policies. The premium adjusts every ten years on both of them, but policy A has somewhat higher premiums for the first ten years. However, for years 11 through 20, policy A's premiums fall significantly below those you would pay with policy B. Then, in the third decade, policy A's premiums once again are higher than policy B's premiums, but only by a small percentage. If you just use the raw numbers, you can stand on your head all day trying to get a sense of which of the two policies is cheaper, and be no closer to an answer.

The only way to tell which of the two policies is cheaper is to make an apples-to-apples comparison. And the only way to do that is to do an NPV comparison.

Deciding where to buy term insurance

A number of sound ways to obtain high-quality, low-cost term insurance are available. You may choose to buy through a local agent because you know him or prefer to buy from someone close to home. However, you should invest a few minutes of your time getting quotes from one or two of the following sources to get a sense of what's available in the insurance market. Gaining familiarity with the market can prevent an agent from selling you an overpriced, high-commission policy.

Here are some sources for high-quality, low-cost term insurance:

- » **Blue Cross Canada:** You can find a phone number for Blue Cross in your province at www.bluecross.ca.

- » **Canadian Automobile Association:** Call 877-942-4222 or go to www.caa.ca.

- » **Insurance-agency quotation services:** These services provide proposals from the highest-rated, lowest-cost companies available. Like other agencies, the services receive a commission if you buy a policy from them, which you're under no obligation to do. They ask questions such as your date of birth, whether you smoke, some basic health questions, and how much coverage you want. Tony has links to several insurance quote services, along with their contact information, on his website, www.moneygrower.ca.

See Chapter 20 for information on how to use your computer when making life-insurance decisions.

Considering the purchase of cash-value life insurance

WARNING

Don't expect to get objective information from the typical salesperson who sells cash-value life insurance. Beware of insurance salespeople masquerading under the guise of self-anointed titles, such as estate-planning specialists or financial planners.

As we discuss earlier in the chapter, purchasing cash-value life insurance may make sense if you expect to have an estate-tax "problem." However, cash-value life insurance is just one of many ways to reduce your estate taxes (see the section on estate planning in Chapter 18).

TIP

If you want to obtain some cash-value life insurance, tread carefully with local insurance agents. Most agents aren't as interested in educating as they are in selling. Besides, the best cash-value policies can be obtained commission-free when you buy them from the sources in the preceding list. The money saved on commissions (which can easily be thousands of dollars) is reflected in a much higher cash value for you.

Getting rid of cash-value life insurance

If you were snookered into buying a cash-value life-insurance policy and you want to part ways with it, go ahead and do so. But don't cancel the coverage until you first secure new term coverage. When you need life insurance, you don't want to have a period when you're not covered (Murphy's Law says that's when disaster will strike).

Ending a cash-value life insurance policy has tax consequences. For most of these policies, you must pay tax on the amount you receive in excess of the premiums you paid over the life of the policy. If you want to withdraw the cash balance in your life-insurance policy, consider checking with the insurer or a tax advisor to clarify what the tax consequences may be.

Preparing for the Unpredictable: Disability Insurance

As with life insurance, the purpose of disability insurance is to protect your employment income. The only difference is that with disability insurance, you're protecting the income for yourself (and perhaps also your dependents). If you're completely disabled, you still have living expenses, but you probably can't earn employment income.

We're referring here to *long-term* disabilities. If you strain your back while reliving your athletic glory days and you wind up in bed for a couple weeks, it likely won't be a financial disaster. But what if you were disabled in such a way that you can't work for several years? This section helps you figure out whether you need disability insurance, how much to get, and where to find it.

Deciding whether you need coverage

Most large employers offer disability insurance to their employees. But whether your employer pays for some or all the premiums, or you have to pay the cost yourself, the amount of income your company policy provides may not be sufficient. And many small-company employees — and all self-employed people — are left to fend for themselves without disability coverage. Being without disability insurance is a risky proposition, especially if, like most working people, you need your employment income to live on.

If you're married and your spouse earns a large enough income that you can make do without yours, consider skipping disability coverage. The same is true if you've already accumulated enough money for your future years (in other words, you're financially independent). Keep in mind, though, that your expenses may go up if you become disabled and require specialized care.

For most people, dismissing the need for disability coverage is easy. The odds of suffering a long-term disability seem so remote — and they are. But if you suffer bad luck, disability coverage can relieve you (and possibly your family) of a major financial burden.

Most disabilities are caused by medical problems, such as arthritis, heart conditions, hypertension, and back/spine or hip/leg impairments. Some of these ailments occur with advancing age, but more than one-third of all disabilities are suffered by people under the age of 45. The vast majority of these medical problems can't be predicted in advance, particularly those caused by random accidents. Other disabilities are caused by accidents, which no one can predict.

WARNING

If you've always just assumed that there's a government program that will take care of you if you become disabled, you're not alone. It's an easy enough mistake to make, in part because of Canada's universal healthcare. But if think you have good disability coverage through government programs, you'd better think again:

>> **Government benefits:** In order to receive CPP or QPP disability benefits, you generally must have paid into the CPP or QPP for at least four of the six years leading up to the point at which you became disabled. Your disability must be severe, which means it prevents you from doing not only your former job but also *any* job on a regular basis, in order to qualify. The disability must also be prolonged, meaning it's expected to last at least a year or be likely to result in death. CPP/QPP disability payments are quite low because they're intended to provide only for basic, subsistence-level living expenses. The average in 2009 was $971.23, and the maximum was $1,335.83. The amount you'll receive is a combination of the basic fixed monthly amount ($485.20 for 2018), plus an amount based on how much you contributed to the CPP or QPP during your entire working career.

   If you receive CPP or QPP disability benefits, your dependent children may also be eligible for a separate children's benefit. The benefit, a fixed amount, was $244.64 in 2018.

>> **Workers' compensation:** Workers' compensation (if you have such coverage through your employer) pays you benefits when you're injured on the job, but it doesn't pay any benefits if you become disabled away from your job. You need coverage that pays regardless of where and how you're disabled.

Determining how much disability insurance you need

You need enough disability coverage to provide you with sufficient income to live on until other financial resources become available. If you don't have much saved in the way of financial assets and you want to continue with the lifestyle supported by your current income if you suffer a disability, get disability coverage to replace your entire monthly take-home (after-tax) pay.

The benefits you purchase on a disability policy are quoted as the dollars per month you receive if disabled. So, if your job provides you with a $3,000-per-month income after taxes, seek a policy that provides a $3,000-per-month benefit.

If you pay for your disability insurance, the benefits are tax-free (but hopefully you won't ever have to collect them). If your employer picks up the tab, your benefits are taxable, so you need a larger benefit amount.

In addition to the monthly coverage amount, you also need to select the duration for which you want a policy to pay you benefits. You need a policy that pays benefits until you reach an age at which you become financially self-sufficient. For most people, that's around age 65, when their CPP/QPP and other government benefits kick in. If you anticipate needing your employment income past your mid-60s, you may want to obtain disability coverage that pays you until a later age.

If you crunch some numbers (see Chapter 3) and find that you're within five to ten years of being financially independent or able to retire, five-year and ten-year disability policies are available. You may also consider such short-term policies when you're sure that someone (for example, a family member) can support you financially over the long term.

Identifying other features you need in disability insurance

Disability-insurance policies have many confusing features. Here's what to look for — and look out for — when purchasing disability insurance:

>> **Definition of disability:** An *own-occupation* disability policy provides benefit payments if you can't perform the work you normally do. Some policies pay you only if you're unable to perform a job for which you are *reasonably trained*. Other policies revert to this definition after a few years of being own-occupation. Own-occupation policies are the most expensive because there's a greater chance that the insurer will have to pay you. The extra cost may not be worth it unless you're in a high-income or specialized occupation and you'd have to take a significant pay cut to do something else (and you wouldn't be happy about a reduced income and the required lifestyle changes).

>> **Noncancelable and guaranteed renewable:** These features ensure that your policy can't be cancelled because you've fallen into poor health. With policies that require periodic physical exams, you can lose your coverage just when you're most likely to need it.

>> **Waiting period:** This is the "deductible" on disability insurance — the time between the onset of your disability and the time you begin collecting benefits. As with other types of insurance, you should take the highest deductible (longest waiting period) that your financial circumstances allow. The waiting period significantly reduces the cost of the insurance and eliminates the hassle of filing a claim for a short-term disability. The minimum waiting period on most policies is 30 days. The maximum waiting period can be up to one to two years. Try a waiting period of three to six months if you have enough emergency reserves.

>> **Residual benefits:** This option pays you a partial benefit if you have a disability that prevents you from working full-time.

>> **Cost-of-living adjustments (COLAs):** This feature automatically increases your benefit payment by a set percentage annually or in accordance with changes in inflation. The advantage of a COLA is that it retains the purchasing power of your benefits. A modest COLA, such as 3 percent to 4 percent, is worth considering.

>> **Future insurability:** A clause that many agents encourage you to buy, future insurability allows you to buy additional coverage regardless of health. For most people, paying for the privilege of buying more coverage later is not worth it if the income you earn today fairly reflects your likely long-term earnings and spending desires. You may benefit from the future insurability option if your income is artificially low now and you're confident that it will rise significantly in the future. (For example, you just got out of medical school and you're earning a low salary while being a resident.)

>> **Insurer's financial stability:** As we discuss in Chapter 16, you should choose insurers that'll be here tomorrow to pay your claim. But don't get too hung up on the stability of the company; benefits are paid even if the insurer fails, because the government or another insurer will almost always bail out the unstable insurer.

Deciding where to buy disability insurance

The place to buy disability insurance with the best value is through your employer or professional association. Unless these groups have done a lousy job shopping for coverage, group plans generally offer a better value than disability insurance you can purchase on your own. Just make sure that the group plan meets the specifications discussed in the preceding section, especially any limitations of benefit amounts or stricter qualification terms, which are found on some group plans.

WARNING

Don't trust an insurance agent to be enthusiastic about the quality of a disability policy your employer or other group is offering. Agents have a conflict of interest when they criticize these options, because they won't make a commission if you buy through a group.

If you don't have access to a group policy, check with your agent or a company you already do business with. But tread carefully when purchasing disability insurance through an agent. Some agents try to load down your policy with all sorts of extra bells and whistles to pump up the premium along with their commission.

For a list of low-cost disability insurance providers, visit Tony's website at www. moneygrower.ca. The site also has a handy calculator that lets you figure out how much income protection you need.

Planning for Nursing-Home Care: Long-Term-Care Insurance

Insurance agents who are eager to earn a hefty commission will often tell you that long-term care (LTC) insurance is the solution to your concerns about an extended stay in a nursing home. Don't get your hopes up. Policies are complicated and filled with all sorts of exclusions and limitations. On top of all that, they're expensive.

The decision to purchase LTC insurance is a trade-off. Do you want to pay thousands of dollars annually to guard against the possibility of needing daily living support or a long-term stay in a nursing home (or possibly to pay for in-home assistance if you qualify)? If you live into or past your mid-80s, you can end up paying $100,000 or more on an LTC policy (not to mention the lost investment earnings on these insurance premiums).

People who end up in a nursing home for years on end may come out ahead financially when buying LTC insurance. The majority of people who stay in a nursing home are there for less than a year, though, because they either die or move out. (Provincial health plans will cover a portion of LTC costs, generally requiring you to pay a fixed amount that can range from around $12,000 to $25,000 or more per year.)

If you have relatives or a spouse who will likely care for you in the event of a major illness, you definitely should *not* waste your money on LTC insurance. You can also bypass this coverage if you have and don't mind using retirement assets to help pay nursing-home costs.

Even if you do deplete your assets, remember that you have a backup: government-assistance programs. However, this will usually cover only basic accommodation. To find out what may be available to you, contact your province's ministry of health.

TIP

Consider buying LTC insurance if you want to retain and protect your assets and it gives you peace of mind to know that a long-term nursing-home stay is covered. But do some comparison-shopping, and make sure that you buy a policy that pays benefits for the long term. A year's worth (or even a few years' worth) of benefits won't protect your assets if your stay lasts longer. Also be sure to get a policy that adjusts the daily benefit amount for increases in the cost of living. Get a policy that covers care in your home or other settings if you don't need to be in a high-cost nursing home, and make sure that it doesn't require prior hospitalization for benefits to kick in. To keep premiums down, also consider a longer exclusion or waiting period — three to six months or a year before coverage starts.

You may also want to consider retirement communities if you're willing to live as a younger retiree in such a setting. After paying an entrance fee, you pay a monthly fee, which usually covers your rent, care, and meals. Make sure that any such facility you're considering guarantees care for life and preferably has a continuum of care levels available.

Getting Care for the Road: Travel Medical Insurance

If you head out of Canada on vacation, for business, or even just for a day-shopping trip across the border, you need to make sure you're properly insured against unexpected medical expenses. An emergency ward or doctor's waiting room likely isn't on your list of must-sees when you head out of the country. But you simply can't predict whether a visit to a medical facility will end up being part of your itinerary when you leave our home and native land.

WARNING

Without sufficient travel medical coverage, an accident or illness that strikes while you're out of Canada can severely damage your financial health.

Determining what coverage you already have

As long as you belong to your province's healthcare plan, you already have some coverage outside of Canada. However, each provincial plan covers you only up to certain levels, with maximums established for various procedures and other medical costs. The amounts that provincial plans will pay have been shrinking, though, and what your provincial health plan pays may be only a fraction of the final bill.

WARNING

Don't assume that because you have a premium credit card that trumpets medical coverage you're adequately covered. The eligibility requirements can be highly confusing, and the rules are regularly changed. Some premium cards, for instance, cover you for only a certain number of days for each trip you make. You may be covered for trips up to 21 days in length, for instance, so if you're injured on the 22nd day, your credit-card company won't pay any of the medical expenses.

TIP

Always check with your benefits department before you leave on a business trip. Most corporations provide medical insurance for employees who are travelling on business, but the policies can be complicated and can leave you exposed. For instance, you may be covered during the week while you're on company business, but not if you choose to stay over for the weekend to enjoy a little skiing at a nearby resort. If you break your leg on the slopes, you may find yourself responsible for any bills because company policy doesn't cover injuries sustained on personal time.

Buying travel medical insurance

Be sure to take a look at your family's overall need. Many providers now offer plans that will cover your family. If you travel a lot, check into annual plans, which cover you up to a maximum number of days outside the country over 12 months.

TIP

For a complete list of low-cost travel medical insurance providers, visit Tony's website at www.moneygrower.ca. Some of the companies include

>> **Canadian Automobile Association:** www.caa.ca

>> **Ingle International:** 800-360-3234; www.ingleinternational.com

>> **travelcuts:** 866-246-9762; www.travelcuts.com

Chapter **18**

Covering Your Assets

I n Chapter 17, we discuss the importance of protecting your future income from disability, death, or large, unexpected medical expenses. But you also have to insure major assets that you've acquired: your home, your car, and your personal property. You need to protect these assets for two reasons:

» **Your assets are valuable.** If you were to suffer a loss, replacing the assets with money out of your own pocket can be a financial catastrophe.

» **A lawsuit can drain your finances.** If someone is injured or killed in your home or because of your car, a lawsuit can be financially devastating.

In this chapter, we explain why, how, and for how much to insure your home, personal property, and vehicle. We also discuss excess liability insurance and how to determine where your money will go in the event of your death.

Insuring Your Home

When you buy a home with a mortgage, most lenders require you to purchase homeowner's insurance. But even if they don't, you're wise to do so, because your home and the personal property within it are worth a lot and would cost a lot to replace.

As a renter, damage to the building in which you live is not your immediate financial concern, but you still have personal property you may want to insure. You also have the possibility (albeit remote) that you'll be sued by someone who's injured while in your rental.

When shopping for a homeowner's or renter's policy, consider the important features that we cover in the following sections.

Dwelling coverage: The cost to rebuild

How much would you have to spend to rebuild your home if it were completely destroyed, for example, in a fire? The cost to rebuild should be based on the size (square footage) of your home. Neither the purchase price nor the size of your mortgage should determine how much *dwelling coverage* you need.

If you're a renter, rejoice that you don't need dwelling coverage. If you're a condominium owner, find out whether the insurance the condo association bought for the entire building is sufficient.

Be sure that your homeowner's policy includes a *guaranteed replacement cost* provision. This useful feature ensures that the insurance company will rebuild the home even if the cost of construction is more than the policy coverage. If the insurance company underestimates your dwelling coverage, it has to make up the difference.

Unfortunately, insurers define *guaranteed replacement cost* differently. Some companies pay for the full replacement cost of the home, no matter how much it ends up costing, but most insurers set limits. For example, some insurers may pay up to only 25 percent more than the dwelling coverage on your policy. Ask your insurer how it defines guaranteed replacement cost.

TIP

If you have an older property that doesn't meet current building standards, consider buying a *rider* (supplemental coverage to your main insurance policy) that pays for code upgrades. This rider covers the cost of rebuilding your home, in the event of a loss, to comply with current building codes that may be more stringent than the ones in place when your home was built. Ask your insurance company what your basic policy does and doesn't cover. Some companies include a certain amount (for example, 10 percent of your dwelling coverage) for code upgrades in the base policy.

Personal property coverage: For your things

On your homeowner's policy, the amount of personal property coverage is typically derived from the amount of dwelling coverage you carry. Generally, you get personal property coverage that's equal to 50 percent to 75 percent of the dwelling coverage. This amount is usually more than enough.

Regarding riders to cover jewellery, computers, collectibles, and other somewhat costly items that may not be fully covered by typical homeowner's policies, ask yourself whether the out-of-pocket expense from the loss of such items would constitute a financial catastrophe. Unless you have more than several thousand dollars' worth of jewellery or computer equipment, skip such riders.

Some policies come with *replacement-cost guarantees* that pay you the cost to replace an item. This payment can be considerably more than what the used item was worth before it was damaged or stolen. When this feature is not part of the standard policy sold by your insurer, you may want to purchase it as a rider, if available.

As a renter or condominium owner, you need to choose a dollar amount for the personal property you want covered. Tally it up instead of guessing — the total cost of replacing all your personal property may surprise you.

TIP

Make a list of your belongings — or even better, take pictures or make a video (you can use your smartphone to do this) — with an estimate of what they're worth. Be sure to back up those files so that they're stored outside of your home. One option is to use an online storage service, or "cloud," many of which offer you a reasonable amount of storage space for free. You can also simply back them up onto a USB key and leave it for safekeeping with a neighbour or relative. Keep this list updated; you'll need it if you have to file a claim. Retaining receipts for major purchases may also help your case.

REMEMBER

No matter how you document your belongings, don't forget to keep the documentation somewhere besides your home — otherwise, it can be destroyed along with the rest of your house in a fire or other disaster.

Receipts can be a real hassle. One easy solution is to hang onto them, either in a wallet or purse, or throw them into a drawer or small container. Then, every so often, grab your smartphone and record them as photos.

Liability insurance: Coverage for when others are harmed

Liability insurance protects you financially against lawsuits that may arise if someone gets injured on your property, including wounds inflicted by the family's pernicious pup or terrible tabby. (Of course, you should keep Bruno restrained when guests visit — even your cranky in-laws.) At a minimum, get enough liability insurance to cover your financial assets — covering two times your assets is better. Buying extra coverage is inexpensive and well worth the cost.

The probability of being sued is low, but if you are sued and lose, you can end up owing big bucks. If you have substantial assets to protect, you may want to consider an *umbrella* (excess liability) policy (see "Protecting against Mega-Liability: Umbrella Insurance" later in this chapter).

Liability protection is one of the side benefits of purchasing a renter's policy — you protect your personal property as well as insure against lawsuits. (But don't be reckless with your banana peels even if you get liability insurance!)

Flood and earthquake insurance: Protection from Mother Nature

You should purchase the broadest possible coverage when buying any type of insurance (see Chapter 16). The problem with homeowner's insurance is that it's not comprehensive enough — it doesn't typically cover losses due to earthquakes and floods. You have to buy such disaster coverage separately.

TIP

Don't wait until you're hit by disaster to realize you should call your insurance agent to get flood or earthquake coverage. If you do, there's a good chance you'll run into the same kind of Catch-22 Tony once did. In the first home he rented, one rainy evening, he went down to the basement to get something out of storage. To his horror, he found that his small collection of boxes that had been neatly stacked in the corner were bobbing about in half a meter of backed-up sewage; many of the homes in the neighborhood had been similarly afflicted. Particularly after finishing the nasty cleanup job, he decided that was the first and last time. So, the next day, he rang up his insurance agent to see about making a claim. To his surprise — and edification — he was told that flood coverage was not included in his policy. Why not? Because it was a separate rider that needed to be purchased, and Tony hadn't requested it. (Which of course begged the question: Why had his agent not brought this to his attention?) That was obviously water under the bridge, in addition to under his main floor. So, he asked his agent the cost of the rider — which, especially compared to job items he lost not to mention the cleanup job, was minimal — and to have it added to his policy. The reply? It can't be done. Why not? Well, because it was now clear his property was susceptible to flooding!

If an earthquake or flood were to strike your area and destroy your home, you'd be out tens (if not hundreds) of thousands of dollars without proper coverage. Yet many people don't carry these important coverages, often as a result of some common misconceptions:

>> **"Not in my neighbourhood."** Many people mistakenly believe that earthquakes occur only in California and Japan. Those of us who live in the True North wish this were true, but it's not. Vancouver is built on a major fault line, and known (though not very active) fault lines lie in eastern Canada, including

the Ottawa–Hull region. The cost of earthquake coverage is based on insurance companies' assessment of the risk of your area and property type, so you shouldn't decide whether to buy insurance based on how small you think the risk is. The risk is already built into the price.

Many communities across the country face potential damage from floods. And as those living in southern Alberta when the Red Deer River overflowed its banks in 2005 found out, floods are a very real and often financially devastating catastrophe. Communities in Manitoba, Ontario, and Quebec have also recently suffered extensive and costly damage from floods. But, like earthquakes, floods are not a covered risk in standard homeowner's policies, so you need to purchase a flood-insurance rider. Check with your current insurer or with the insurers we recommend in this chapter.

>> **"The government will bail me out."** The vast majority of government financial assistance is obtained through low-interest loans. Loans, unfortunately, need to be repaid, and that money comes out of your pocket.

>> **"In a major disaster, insurers would go bankrupt anyway."** This is highly unlikely given the reserves insurers are required to keep and the fact that the insurance companies *reinsure* — that is, they buy insurance to back up the policies they write. Also, state regulatory agencies facilitate the merging of faltering insurers into strong entities.

People who have little equity in their property and are willing to walk away from their property and mortgage in the event of a major earthquake or flood may consider not buying earthquake or flood coverage. Keep in mind that walking away damages your credit report, because you're essentially defaulting on your loan.

TIP

You may be able to pay for much of the cost of earthquake or flood insurance by raising the deductibles (discussed in the next section) on the main part of your homeowner's or renter's insurance and other insurance policies (such as auto insurance). You can more easily afford the smaller claims, not the big ones. If you think flood or earthquake insurance is expensive, compare those costs with the expenses you would incur to completely replace your home and personal property. Buy this insurance if you live in an area that has a chance of being affected by these catastrophes.

To help keep the cost of earthquake insurance down, consider taking a 10 percent deductible. Most insurers offer deductibles of 5 percent, 10 percent, or 20 percent of the cost to rebuild your home. Ten percent of the rebuilding cost is a good chunk of money. But losing the other 90 percent is what you want to insure against. (For most people, a 20 percent deductible is too high.)

Deductibles: Your cost with a claim

As we discuss in Chapter 16, the point of insurance is to protect against catastrophic losses, not the little losses. By taking the highest deductibles you're comfortable with, you save on insurance premiums year after year, and you don't have to go through the hassle of filing small claims.

Special discounts

TIP

You may qualify for special discounts on your policy. Companies and agents that sell homeowner's and renter's insurance don't always check to see whether you're eligible for discounts. After all, the more you spend on policy premiums, the more money they make! If your property has a security system, you're older, or you have other policies with the same insurer, you may qualify for a lower rate. Remember to ask.

Also, be aware that insurers use your credit score as a factor in setting some of your insurance rates. They do this because their studies have shown that folks who have higher credit scores tend to have fewer accidents and insurance claims. (See Chapter 2 for how to assess and improve your credit reports and scores.)

Buying homeowner's or renter's insurance

Each insurance company prices its homeowner's and renter's policies based on its own criteria. So the lowest-cost company for your friend's property may not be the lowest-cost company for yours. You have to shop around at several companies to find the best rates. The following list features companies that historically offer lower-cost policies for most people and have decent track records regarding customer satisfaction and the payment of claims:

>> **belairdirect:** 888-280-8549; www.belairdirect.com

>> **COSECO Insurance Company:** 800-810-4990; www.coseco.ca

>> **Desjardins Insurance:** 877-699-9923; www.desjardinsgeneralinsurance.com

>> **President's Insurance:** 877-251-8652; www.pcinsurance.ca

TIP

You can find a full list of suggested companies and their up-to-date contact information on Tony's website, www.moneygrower.ca.

Don't worry that some of these companies require you to call a toll-free number for a price quote. This process saves you money, because these insurers don't have to pay commissions to local agents hawking their policies. These companies have local claims representatives to help you if and when you have a claim.

A number of the companies mentioned in the preceding list sell other types of insurance (for example, life insurance) that aren't as competitively priced. Be sure to check out the relevant sections in this part of the book for the best places to buy these other types of coverage if you need them.

Some provincial insurance departments conduct surveys of insurers' prices and tabulate complaints received. Look up your province or territory's department of insurance phone number in the government section of your local phone directory or visit the website of the Financial Services Commission of Ontario (www.fsco.gov.on.ca) for a list of provincial and federal regulators that oversee each province's insurance companies.

Auto Insurance 101

Over the course of your life, you may spend tens of thousands of dollars on auto insurance. Much of the money people spend on auto insurance is not spent where it's needed most. In other cases, the money is simply wasted. Look for the following important features when searching for an auto-insurance policy.

Bodily-injury and property-damage liability insurance

As with homeowner's liability insurance, auto liability insurance provides insurance against lawsuits. Accidents happen, especially with a car. To protect yourself, you need *third-party liability coverage*, which has two components:

>> **Bodily-injury liability insurance:** Coverage to pay for harm done to others.

>> **Property-damage liability insurance:** Coverage to pay for damage caused by your vehicle to someone else's property.

Third-party liability coverage is a provincial requirement, but the amounts are quite low — $50,000 to $200,000, depending on your province. (Typically, your premiums for the two coverage components are broken out, but with one single combined figure for your total liability coverage.)

If you're just beginning to accumulate assets, don't mistakenly assume that you don't need any more than the required minimum amount of coverage. Your future earnings, which are an asset, can be garnished in a lawsuit. Make sure that you have at least enough to cover your assets. Preferably, your coverage should be two to five times your assets.

Uninsured or underinsured motorist liability

When you're in an accident with another motorist and she doesn't carry her own liability protection (or doesn't carry enough), *uninsured- or underinsured-motorist liability coverage* allows you to collect for lost wages, medical expenses, and pain and suffering incurred in the accident.

If you already have comprehensive health and long-term disability insurance, uninsured- or underinsured-motorist liability coverage is largely redundant. However, it is still generally required.

REMEMBER

To provide a death benefit to those financially dependent on you in the event of a fatal auto accident, buy term life insurance (see Chapter 17).

Deductibles

To minimize your auto-insurance premiums and eliminate the need to file small claims, take the highest deductibles you're comfortable with. (Most people should consider a $500 to $1,000 deductible.) On an auto policy, two deductibles exist:

>> **Collision:** Collision applies to claims arising from collisions. (Note that if you have collision coverage on your own policy, you can generally bypass collision coverage when you rent a car. However, be sure to first check with your insurer as to whether this applies to your particular policy.)

>> **Comprehensive:** Comprehensive applies to other claims for damages not caused by collision (for example, a window broken by vandals).

As your car ages and loses its value, you can eventually eliminate your comprehensive and collision coverages altogether. The point at which you do this is up to you. Insurers won't pay more than the book value of your car, regardless of what it costs to repair or replace it. Remember that the purpose of insurance is to compensate you for losses that are financially catastrophic to you. For some people, this amount may be as high as $5,000 or more — others may choose $1,000 as their threshold point.

Special discounts: Auto edition

You may be eligible for special discounts on auto insurance. Don't forget to tell your agent or insurer if your car has a security alarm, air bags, or antilock brakes. If you're older or you have other policies or cars insured with the same insurer, you may also qualify for discounts. And make sure that you're given appropriate "good driver" discounts if you've been accident- and ticket-free in recent years.

TIP

Before you buy your next car, call insurers and ask for insurance quotes for the different models you're considering. The cost of insuring a car should factor into your decision of which car you buy, because the insurance costs represent a major portion of your car's ongoing operating expenses.

Little-stuff coverage to skip

Auto insurers have dreamed up all sorts of riders, such as towing and rental-car reimbursement. On the surface, these riders appear to be inexpensive. But they're expensive given the little amount you'd collect from a claim and the hassle of filing.

Riders that waive the deductible under certain circumstances make no sense, either. The point of the deductible is to reduce your policy cost and eliminate the hassle of filing small claims.

Accident benefits coverage replaces some of your income that is lost due to an accident, and pays for some other medical expenses. If you and your passengers are covered by a provincial health plan and you have disability insurance, this rider coverage isn't usually necessary. This is especially true when you're also covered by an extended health-benefit plan. However, almost all provinces require you to carry a minimum level of this type of coverage.

Roadside assistance, towing, and rental-car reimbursement coverage pay only small dollar amounts, and they aren't worth buying. In fact, you may already have some of these coverages through membership in an automobile club or as a feature of your credit card.

Buying auto insurance

You can use the homeowner's insurers list we present in the earlier section "Buying homeowner's or renter's insurance" to obtain quotes for auto insurance. University alumni associations and organizations such as the Canadian Automobile Association (CAA) also often offer competitive rates for both automobile and property insurance. In addition, you can visit Tony's website at `www. moneygrower.ca`.

DRIVING SAFELY: OVERLOOKED AUTO INSURANCE

Tragic events (murders, fires, hurricanes, plane crashes, and so on) are well covered by the media, but the number of deaths that make the front pages of our newspapers pales in comparison to the almost 2,000 people who die on Canada's roads every year. We're not suggesting that the national media should start reporting every automobile fatality. Even 24 hours of daily CNN coverage probably couldn't keep up with all the accidents on our roads. But the real story with auto fatalities lies not in the *who, what,* and *where* of specific accidents but in the *why.* Asking the *why* question reveals how many of them are preventable.

No matter what kind of car you drive, you can and should drive safely. Stay within the speed limits and don't drive while intoxicated or tired or in adverse weather conditions. Wear your seat belt — one U.S. Department of Transportation study found that 60 percent of auto passengers killed were not wearing their seat belts. And don't try to talk or text on your cellphone and write notes on a pad of paper attached to your dashboard while balancing your coffee cup between your legs! It's both extraordinarily unsafe *and* illegal.

You can also greatly reduce your risk of dying in an accident by driving a safe car. You don't need to spend buckets of money to get a car with desirable safety features. For a list of the safest cars along with links for more information, visit Eric's website at `www.erictyson.com`.

DIVERSIFICATION: INVESTMENT INSURANCE

Insurance companies don't sell policies that protect the value of your investments, but you can shield your portfolio from many of the dangers of a fickle market through diversification.

If all your money is invested in bank accounts or bonds, you're exposed to the risks of inflation, which can erode your money's purchasing power. Conversely, if the bulk of your money is invested in one high-risk stock, your financial future can go up in smoke if that stock explodes.

Chapter 9 discusses the benefits of diversification and tells you how to assemble a portfolio of investments that do well under different conditions.

Protecting against Mega-Liability: Umbrella Insurance

Umbrella insurance (which is also referred to as *excess-liability insurance*) is liability insurance that's added on top of the liability protection on your home and cars. If, for example, you have $700,000 in assets, you can buy a $1 million umbrella liability policy to add to the $300,000 liability insurance that you have on your home and car. Expect to pay a couple hundred dollars — a small cost for big protection. Each year, thousands of people suffer lawsuits of more than $1 million related to their cars and homes.

Umbrella insurance is generally sold in increments of $1 million. So, how do you decide how much you need if you have a lot of assets? You should have at least enough liability insurance to protect your assets and preferably enough to cover twice the value of those assets. To purchase umbrella insurance, start by contacting your existing homeowner's or auto insurance company.

Planning Your Estate

Estate planning is the process of determining what will happen to your assets after you die. Considering your mortality in the context of insurance may seem a bit odd. But the time and cost of various estate-planning manoeuvres is really nothing more than buying insurance: You're ensuring that, after you die, everything will be taken care of as you wish, and taxes will be minimized. Thinking about estate planning in this way can help you better evaluate whether certain options make sense at particular points in your life.

Depending upon your circumstances, you may eventually want to contact a lawyer who specializes in estate-planning matters. However, educating yourself first about the different options is worth your time. More than a few lawyers have their own agendas about what you should do, so be careful. And most of the estate-planning strategies that you're likely to benefit from don't require hiring a lawyer.

Wills, living wills, and medical powers of attorney

When you have children who are minors (dependents), a will is a necessity. The will names the guardian to whom you entrust your children if both you and your spouse die. Should you and your spouse both die without a will (called *intestate*), the province or territory (courts and social-service agencies) decides who will raise your children. Therefore, even if you can't decide at this time who you want to raise your children, you should *at least* appoint a trusted guardian who can decide for you.

Having a will makes good sense even if you don't have kids, because it gives instructions on how to handle and distribute all your worldly possessions. If you die without a will, your province or territory decides how to distribute your money and other property, according to provincial law. Therefore, your friends, distant relatives, and favorite charities will probably receive nothing. Without a will, your heirs are legally powerless, and the province may appoint a public executor to supervise the distribution of your assets at a fee of around 5 percent of your estate. A living will and a medical power of attorney are useful additions to a standard will. A *living will* (also known as an *advance healthcare directive*) tells your doctor what, if any, life-support measures you prefer. A *medical* (or *healthcare*) *power of attorney* grants authority to someone you trust to make decisions regarding your medical-care options.

The simplest and least costly way to prepare a will, a living will, and a medical power of attorney is to use the high-quality, user-friendly software packages that we recommend in Chapter 20, and then, if you prefer to be cautious, have them looked over by a lawyer. Be sure to give copies of these documents to the guardians and executors named in the documents. You don't need a lawyer to make a legal will. Most lawyers, in fact, prepare wills and living trusts using software packages! What makes a will valid is that two people witness your signing it.

TIP

If preparing the will all by yourself seems overwhelming, you can (instead of hiring a lawyer) use a paralegal typing service to help you prepare the documents. These services generally charge 50 percent or less of what a lawyer charges.

Avoiding probate through living trusts

Because of our quirky legal system, even if you have a will, some or all your assets must go through a court process known as probate. *Probate* is the legal process for administering and implementing the directions in a will.

Property and assets that are owned in joint tenancy generally pass to heirs without having to go through probate. If you have designated a beneficiary, proceeds from a Registered Retirement Savings Plan (RRSP), Registered Retirement Income Fund (RRIF), Tax-Free Savings Account (TFSA), or insurance policy also do not require probate. Your family home, joint bank account, and other assets should also not be subject to probate if you register their ownership as "joint and survivor," sometimes also referred to as "joint with rights of survivorship." Most other assets pass through probate.

A *living trust* effectively transfers assets into a trust. As the trustee, you control those assets, and you can revoke the trust whenever you desire. The advantage of a living trust is that upon your death, assets can pass directly to your beneficiaries without going through probate. Probate can be a lengthy, expensive hassle for your heirs — with legal fees tallying as high as 1.5 percent of the value of the estate, depending on your province. In addition, your assets become a matter of public record as a result of probate.

Living trusts are likely to be of greatest value to people who meet one or more of the following criteria (the more that apply, the more value trusts have):

>> Age 60 or older

>> Single

>> Assets worth more than $1 million that must pass through probate (including real estate, nonregistered retirement plans and accounts, and small businesses)

As with a will, you do *not* need a lawyer to establish a legal and valid living trust (see our software recommendations in Chapter 20 and consider the paralegal services that we mention in the preceding section on wills). Legal fees for establishing a living trust can range from hundreds to thousands of dollars. Hiring a lawyer is of greatest value to people with large estates (see the next section) who do not have the time, desire, or expertise to maximize the value derived from estate planning.

Note: Living trusts keep assets out of probate but have nothing to do with minimizing capital-gains taxes triggered by your death.

Planning your estate to minimize taxes triggered by your death

Even though Canada doesn't have estate-tax laws like those faced by Americans, your death will likely result in one final tax bill — a potentially large one! When you die, the government taxes your stocks, funds, real estate, and other assets as if you had sold them all at their fair market value at the time of your death. If those assets are worth more than their purchase price, the result will generally be a taxable capital gain.

TIP

The critical exception to this rule occurs when you leave your assets to your spouse, including a common-law spouse. If you do, the assets simply transfer tax-free to your spouse. When he or she dies, the difference between the original purchase price and the market value at that time will be used to calculate any taxable gains. The rule also doesn't apply when you leave your assets to a spousal trust.

In addition, the assets in your registered retirement plans, such as an RRSP or RRIF, are treated as regular income in the year that you die, and also taxed. However, you can avoid this tax bill by naming your spouse as the beneficiary of any RRSPs or RRIFs. Your spouse can then transfer the assets tax-free to his or her own RRSP or RRIF.

Whether you need to do some planning to reduce the tax bill that will arise when you die depends on several issues. How much of your assets you're going to use up during your life is the first and most important issue you need to consider. This amount depends on how much your assets grow over time, as well as how rapidly you spend money. During retirement, you'll (hopefully) be utilizing at least some of your money.

We've seen too many affluent individuals worry throughout their retirement about how taxes will impact their estates. If your intention is to leave your money to your children, grandchildren, or a charity, why not start giving while you're still alive so that you can enjoy the act? No limitations apply on the amount of money you can give away to adult family members other than your spouse.

WARNING

If you give assets to your spouse while you're living, you'll be subject to the *attribution rules.* Whether you give cash, stocks, or bonds, you'll generally be taxed on any income or loss or any capital gains (or losses) on that money or investments. If you give your children others assets beyond cold, hard cash, there may also be a tax bill to pay. If you give away assets, the Canada Revenue Agency (CRA) deems that you have sold those assets at their market value. Any difference between what you paid and the value at the time you gave them away will be deemed a taxable capital gain.

In addition to gifting, establishing in your will that a trust will be set up when you die — called a *testamentary trust* — can also help reduce taxes. With a testamentary trust, you can choose to have some or all your assets transferred to the trust when you die, with your intended heirs named as the beneficiaries.

Cash-value life insurance is another estate-planning tool. Unfortunately, it's a tool that's overused — or, we should say, oversold. People who sell cash-value insurance — that is, insurance salespeople and others masquerading as financial planners — too often advocate life insurance as the one and only way to minimize taxes due upon your death. Other methods for reducing these taxes are usually superior, because they don't require wasting money on life insurance.

TIP

Small-business owners whose businesses are worth several million dollars or more may want to consider cash-value life insurance under specialized circumstances. If you lack the necessary additional assets to pay expected taxes and don't want your beneficiaries to be forced to sell the business, you can buy cash-value life insurance to pay expected estate taxes.

5
Where to Go for More Help

Chapter **19**

Working with Financial Planners

H iring a competent and ethical financial planner to help you make and implement financial decisions can be money well spent. But if you pick a poor planner or someone who really isn't a financial planner but rather a salesperson in disguise, your financial situation can get worse instead of better. So, before we talk about the different types of help for hire, we discuss the options you have for directing the management of your personal finances.

Surveying Your Financial Management Options

Everyone has three basic choices for managing money: You can do nothing, you can do it yourself, or you can hire someone to help you. This section lays out these three options in more detail.

Doing nothing

The do-nothing (or do-little) approach has a large following. (And you thought you were alone!) People who fall into this category may be leading exciting, interesting lives and are, therefore, too busy to attend to something as mundane as dealing with their personal finances. Or they may be leading mundane existences but are too busy fantasizing about more appealing ways to spend their time.

WARNING

The dangers of doing nothing are many. Putting off saving for retirement or ignoring your accumulation of debt eventually comes back to haunt you. If you don't have adequate insurance, accidents can be devastating. Fires, earthquakes, floods, and hurricanes show how precarious living in paradise actually is.

If you've been following the do-nothing approach all your life, you're now officially promoted out of it! You bought this book to find out more about personal finance and make changes in your money matters, right? So, take control and keep reading!

Doing it yourself

The do-it-yourselfers learn enough about financial topics to make informed decisions on their own. Doing anything yourself, of course, requires you to invest some time in learning the basic concepts and keeping up with changes. The idea that you're going to spend endless hours on your finances if you direct them yourself is a myth.

What's the hardest part of managing money for most people? Simply catching up on things that they should have done before. The good news, which hopefully will serve as terrific motivation? After you get things in order, which you can easily do with this book as your companion, you shouldn't have to spend more than an hour or two every few months working on your personal finances (unless a major issue, like a real-estate purchase, comes up).

WARNING

Some people in the financial-planning business like to make what they do seem so complicated that they compare it to brain surgery! Their argument goes, "You wouldn't perform brain surgery on yourself, so why would you manage your money yourself?" Well, to this we say, "Personal financial management ain't brain surgery — not even close." You can manage on your own. In fact, you can do a better job than most planners. Why? Because you're not subject to their conflicts of interest, and you care the most about your money.

Hiring financial help

Realizing that you need to hire someone to help you make and implement financial decisions can be a valuable insight. Spending a few hours and several hundred dollars to hire a competent professional can be money well spent, even if you have a modest income or assets. But you need to know what your money is buying. Financial planners make money in three ways:

>> They earn commissions based on the sales of financial products.

>> They charge a percentage of the assets they invest and oversee or manage on your behalf.

>> They charge by the hour (this can also be done through fixed-fee arrangements).

The following sections help you differentiate among the three main types of financial planners.

Commission-based planners

WARNING

Commission-based planners aren't really planners, advisors, or counsellors at all — they're salespeople. What prior generations called "stockbrokers" and "insurance brokers" are now called *financial consultants* or *financial-service representatives* in order to glamourize the profession and obscure how they're compensated. Ditto for insurance salespeople calling themselves *estate-planning specialists*.

A stockbroker referring to himself as a financial consultant is like a Honda dealer calling himself a transportation consultant. A Honda dealer is a salesperson who makes a living selling Hondas — period. He's definitely not going to tell you nice things about Ford, Chrysler, or Toyota cars — unless, of course, he happens to sell those, too. He also has no interest in educating you about potentially moneysaving public-transit possibilities!

Salespeople and brokers masquerading as planners can have an enormous self-interest when they push certain products, particularly products that pay generous commissions. Getting paid on commission tends to skew their recommendations toward certain strategies (such as buying investment or life-insurance products) and to cause them to ignore or downplay other aspects of your finances. For example, they'll gladly sell you an investment rather than persuade you to pay off your high-interest debts or save and invest through your employer's retirement plan, thereby reducing your taxes.

Table 19-1 gives you an idea of the commissions that a financial planner/salesperson can earn by selling particular financial products.

TABLE 19-1

Financial Product Commissions

Product	Commission
Life Insurance ($250,000, Age 45)	
Term life	$150 to $600
Universal/whole life	$1,000 to $2,500
Disability Insurance	
$3,000 per month benefit, age 35	$300 to $1,500
Investments ($20,000)	
Mutual funds (loaded)	$200 to $1,200
Limited partnerships	$1,400 to $2,000
Annuities	$1,000 to $2,000

Percentage-of-assets-under-management planners

A financial planner who charges a percentage of the assets that are being managed or invested is generally a better choice than a commission-based planner. This compensation system removes the incentive to sell you products with high commissions and initiate lots of transactions (to generate more of those commissions).

REMEMBER

The fee-based system is an improvement over product pushers working on commission, but it has flaws, too. Suppose that you're trying to decide whether to invest in stocks, bonds, or real estate. A planner who earns his living managing your money likely won't recommend real estate because that will deplete your investment capital. The planner also won't recommend paying down your mortgage for the same reason — he'll claim that you can earn more investing your money (with his help, of course) than it'll cost you to borrow.

Fee-based planners are also only interested in managing the money of those who have already accumulated a fair amount of it — which rules out most people. Many have minimums of $100,000, $250,000, $500,000, or more.

Hourly planners

Your best bet for professional help with your personal finances may be a financial planner who charges for his time. Because he doesn't sell any financial products, he maintains his objectivity. He doesn't perform money management, so he can help you make comprehensive financial decisions with loans, retirement planning, and the selection of good investments, including real estate, mutual funds, and small business.

WARNING

Hiring someone incompetent is the primary risk you face when selecting an hourly planner. Be sure to check references and find out enough about finances on your own to discern between good and bad financial advice. Another risk comes from not clearly defining the work to be done and the approximate total cost of the planner's service before you begin, so consider getting these items in writing. You should also review some of the other key questions that we outline in "Interviewing Financial Planners: Asking the Right Questions" later in this chapter.

An entirely different kind of drawback occurs when you don't follow through on your planner's recommendations. You pay for his work but don't act on it, so you don't capture its potential value. If part of the reason you hired the planner in the first place was that you're too busy or not interested enough to make changes to your financial situation, look for this type of support in the services you buy from the planner.

Some planners charge a fixed fee to whip up a financial plan for you. Remember to ask how much of their time is involved in working with you so you can assess the amount you're paying per hour.

TIP

If you just need someone to act as a sounding board for ideas or to recommend a specific strategy or product, you can hire an hourly planner for one or two sessions of advice. You save money doing the legwork and implementation on your own. Just make sure the planner is willing to give you specific advice so you can properly implement the strategy.

Deciding Whether to Hire a Financial Planner

If you're like most people, you don't need to hire a financial planner, but you may benefit from hiring some help at certain times in your life. Good reasons for hiring a financial planner can be similar to the reasons you may have for hiring someone to clean your home or do your taxes. If you're too busy, you don't enjoy doing it, or you're terribly uncomfortable making decisions on your own, using a planner for a second opinion makes good sense. And if you shy away from numbers and bristle at the thought of long division, a good planner can help you.

How a good financial planner can help

The following list gives you a rundown of some of the important ways a competent financial planner can assist you:

>> **Identifying problems and goals:** Many otherwise-intelligent people have a hard time being objective about their financial problems. They may ignore their debts or have unrealistic goals and expectations given their financial situations and behaviours. And many are so busy with other aspects of their lives that they never take the time to think about what their financial goals are. A good financial planner can give you the objective perspective you need. Surprisingly, some people are in a better financial position than they think they are in relation to their goals. Good financial planners really enjoy this aspect of their jobs — good news is easier and much more fun to deliver.

>> **Identifying strategies for reaching your financial goals:** Your mind may be a jumble of various plans, ideas, and concerns, along with a cobweb or two. A good planner can help you sort out your thoughts and propose alternative strategies for you to consider as you work to accomplish your financial goals.

>> **Setting priorities:** You may be considering doing dozens of things to improve your financial situation, but making just a few key changes is likely to have the greatest value. Identifying the changes that fit your overall situation and that won't keep you awake at night is equally important. Good planners help you prioritize.

>> **Saving research time and hassle:** Even if you know which major financial decisions are most important to you, doing the research needed to make them can be time-consuming and frustrating if you don't know where to turn for good information and advice. A good planner will have done research to match the needs of people like you to the best available strategies and products. A good planner also can prevent you from making a bad decision based on poor or insufficient information.

>> **Purchasing commission-free financial products:** When you hire a planner who charges for his time, you can easily save hundreds or thousands of dollars by avoiding the cost of commissions in the financial products you buy. Purchasing commission-free is especially valuable when you buy investments and insurance.

>> **Providing an objective voice for major decisions:** When you're trying to figure out when to retire, how much to spend on a home purchase, and where to invest your money, you're faced with some big decisions. Getting swept up in the emotions that accompany these issues can cloud your perspective. A competent and sensitive planner can help you cut through the confusion and provide you with sound counsel.

>> **Helping you to just do it:** Deciding what you need to do is not enough — you have to actually do it. And although you can use a planner for advice, and then make all the changes on your own, a good planner can help you follow through

with your plan. After all, part of the reason you hired the planner in the first place may be that you're too busy or uninterested to manage your finances.

>> **Mediating:** If you have a spouse or partner, financial decisions can produce real fireworks, and not the fun, enjoyable Canada Day kind. Although a financial planner isn't a therapist, a good one can be sensitive to the different needs and concerns of each party and can try to find middle ground on the financial issues you're grappling with.

>> **Making you money and allowing you peace of mind:** The whole point of professional financial planning is to help you make the most of your money and plan for and attain your financial and personal goals. In the process, the financial planner should show you how to enhance your investment returns; reduce your spending, taxes, and insurance costs; increase your savings; improve your catastrophic-insurance coverage; and achieve your goals for financial independence.

Understanding why planners aren't for everyone

Finding a good financial planner isn't easy, so make sure you want to hire a planner before you venture out in search of a competent one. You should also consider your personality type before you decide to hire help. Our experience has been that some people (believe it or not) enjoy the research and number crunching. If this sounds like you, or if you're not really comfortable taking advice, you may be better off doing your own homework and creating your own plan.

TIP

If you have a specific tax or legal matter, you may be better off hiring a good professional who specializes in that specific field, rather than hiring a financial planner.

Recognizing conflicts of interest

WARNING

All professions have conflicts of interest. Some fields have more than others, and the financial planning field is one of those fields. Knowing where some of the land mines are located can certainly help. Here, then, are the most common reasons that planners may not have 20/20 vision when giving financial directions.

Selling and pushing products that pay commissions

If a financial planner isn't charging you a fee for his time, you can rest assured that he's earning commissions on the products he tries to sell you. A person who sells financial products and then earns commissions from those products is a salesperson, *not* a financial planner. Financial planning done well involves taking an objective, holistic look at your financial situation — something brokers are neither trained nor financially motivated to do.

To make discerning a planner's agenda even harder, you can't assume that planners who charge fees for their time don't also earn commissions selling products. This compensation double-dipping is common.

Selling products that provide a commission tends to skew a planner's recommendations. Products that carry commissions result in fewer of your dollars going to the investments and insurance you buy. Because a commission is earned only when a product is sold, such a product or service is inevitably more attractive in the planner's eyes than other options. For example, consider the case of a planner who sells disability insurance that you can obtain at a lower cost through your employer or a group trade association (see Chapter 17). He may overlook or criticize your most attractive option (buying through your employer) and focus on *his* most attractive option — selling you a higher-cost disability policy on which he derives a commission.

WARNING

Another danger of trusting the recommendation of a commission-based planner is that he may steer you toward the products that have the biggest payback for him. These products are among the *worst* for you, because they siphon off even more of your money upfront to pay the commission. They also tend to be among the costliest and riskiest financial products available.

Planners who are commission-greedy may also try to *churn* your investments. They encourage you to frequently buy and sell, attributing the need to trade frequently to changes in the economy or the companies you invested in. More trading generally means more commissions for the broker.

WARNING

FINANCIAL PLANNING IN BANKS

Many banks have "financial representatives" and "investment specialists" sitting in their branches, waiting to pounce on bank customers with big balances. In many banks, these "financial planners" are simply brokers who are out to sell investments that pay them (and the bank) hefty sales commissions.

Customers often have no idea that these bank reps are earning commissions and that those commissions are being siphoned out of customers' investment dollars. Many customers are mistaken (partly due to the banks' and salespeople's poor disclosure) in believing that these investments, like bank savings accounts, are insured by the Canada Deposit Insurance Corporation (CDIC) and can't lose value. Frequently, bank reps go to the media with stories of being pushed to sell products, often investments that aren't appropriate to the client.

Taking a narrow view

WARNING

Because of the way they earn their money, many planners are biased in favour of certain strategies and products. As a result, they typically don't keep your overall financial needs in mind. For example, if you have a problem with accumulated consumer debts, some planners may never know (or care), because they're focused on selling you an investment product. Likewise, a planner who sells a lot of life insurance tends to develop recommendations that require you to purchase it.

Not recommending saving through your employer's retirement plan

Taking advantage of saving through your employer's retirement savings plan is one of your best financial options. Although this method of saving may not be as exciting as risking your money in cattle futures or real estate in Dubai, it's not as dull as watching paint dry — and most important, it's typically tax-deductible. Some employers make it an even better choice by also making contributions to your plan when you do on some sort of matching basis.

Some planners are reluctant to recommend that you take full advantage of this option: It takes money away from them that they can otherwise manage on a fee basis and/or convince you to use to purchase commission-laden investment products.

Ignoring debts

Sometimes paying off outstanding loans — such as credit card, auto, or even mortgage debts — is your best investment option. But most financial planners don't recommend this strategy, because paying down debts depletes the capital with which you can otherwise buy investments — the investments that the broker may be trying to sell you to earn a commission or that the planner would like to manage for an ongoing fee.

Not recommending real estate and small-business investments

Investing in real estate and small business, like paying off debts, takes money away from your investing elsewhere. Most planners won't help with these choices. They may even tell you tales of real-estate and small-business investing disasters to dissuade you.

The value of real estate can go down just like any other investment. But over the long haul, owning real estate makes good financial sense for most people. With small business, the risks are higher, but so, too, are the potential returns. Don't let a financial planner convince you that these options are foolish — in fact, if you do your homework and know what you're doing, you can make higher rates of return investing in real estate and small business than you can in traditional securities such as stocks and bonds.

That said, certain real-estate and small-business investments can be risky, inefficient, and illiquid — so caution by a planner informed in these fields (and who is objective) may be helpful. See Part 3 to read more about your real-estate and small-business investment options.

Selling ongoing money-management services

The vast majority of financial planners who don't work on commission make their money by managing your money for an ongoing fee percentage (typically 1 percent to 2 percent of your investment annually). Although this fee removes the incentive to *churn* your account (frequently trade your investments) in order to ring up more commissions, the service is something that you're unlikely to need. (As we explain in Part 3, you can hire professional money managers for less.)

An ongoing fee percentage still creates a conflict of interest: The financial planner may tend to steer you away from beneficial financial strategies that reduce the asset pool from which he derives his compensation, which is based on a percentage. Financial strategies such as maximizing contributions to your employer's retirement savings plan, paying off debts like your mortgage, investing in real estate or small business, and so on, may make the most sense for you. Planners who work on a percentage-of-assets-under-management basis may be biased against such strategies.

Selling legal services

Some planners are in the business of drawing up trusts and providing other estate-planning services for their clients. Although these and other legal documents may be right for you, legal matters are complex enough that the competence of someone who isn't a full-time legal specialist should be carefully scrutinized. And lower-cost options may be available if your situation is not complicated.

TIP

If you need help determining whether you need these legal documents, do some additional reading or consult a planner who won't actually perform the work. If you do ultimately hire someone to perform estate-planning services for you, make sure you hire someone who specializes in estate planning and works at it full time. See Chapter 18 to find out more about estate planning.

Scaring you unnecessarily

Some planners put together nifty computer-generated projections that show you that you're going to need millions of dollars by the time you retire to maintain your standard of living or that university will cost hundreds of thousands of dollars by the time your 2-year-old is ready to enroll.

Waking up a client to the realities of his financial situation is an important and difficult job for good financial planners. But some planners take this task to an extreme, deliberately scaring you into buying what they're selling. They paint a bleak picture and imply that you can fix your problems only if you do what they say. Don't let them scare you; read this book and get your financial life in order.

Creating dependency

WARNING

Many financial planners create dependency by making things seem so complicated that their clients feel as though they can never manage their finances on their own. If your planner is reluctant to tell you how you can educate yourself about personal money management, you probably have a self-perpetuating consultant. Financial planning is hardly the only occupation guilty of this. As author George Bernard Shaw said, "All professions are conspiracies against the laity."

Finding a Good Financial Planner

Locating a good financial planner who is willing to work with the not-yet-rich-and-famous and who doesn't have conflicts of interest can feel like trying to find a needle in a haystack. Personal referrals and associations are two methods that can serve as good starting points.

Soliciting personal referrals

Getting a personal referral from a satisfied customer you trust is one of the best ways to find a good financial planner. Obtaining a referral from an accountant or lawyer whose judgment you've tested can help as well. (Beware that such professionals in other fields may also do some financial planning and recommend themselves.)

The best financial planners continue to build their practises through word of mouth. Satisfied customers are a professional's best and least costly marketers. However, you should *never* take a recommendation from anyone as gospel. We don't care *who* is making the referral — even if it's your mother or the pope. You must do your homework. Ask the planner the questions we list in the upcoming section "Interviewing Financial Planners: Asking the Right Questions." We've seen people get into real trouble because they blindly accepted someone else's recommendations. Remember that the person making the recommendation is (probably) not a financial expert and may be financially clueless.

You may get referred to a planner or broker who returns the favour by sending business to the tax, legal, or real-estate person who referred you. Hire professionals who make referrals to others based on their competence and ethics.

Seeking planners through associations

Associations of financial planners are more than happy to refer you to planners in your area. But as we discuss earlier in this chapter, the major trade associations are composed of planners who sell products and work on commission.

TIP

Here are two solid places to start searching for good financial planners:

>> **Institute of Advanced Financial Planners (IAFP; 888-298-3292;** www.iafp.ca**):** IAFP was founded in 2002 by Registered Financial Planners (RFPs) after their existing association — the Canadian Association of Financial Planners — merged with the Canadian Association of Insurance and Financial Advisors to form Advocis (see the next bullet). (In French, the designation is Planificateur Financier Certifié [PFC].) In addition to letting you find RFPs in your area, the IAFP website lets you search for planners that meet a number of different criteria. In particular, you can narrow your search by specifying the type of compensation — commission only, fee only, fee and commission, or salary. Put another way, this lets you come up with a short list of planners according to how you want to pay for their services.

>> **Advocis: The Financial Advisors Association of Canada (800-563-5822;** www.advocis.ca**):** Like the IAFP site, the Advocis site has a feature that allows you to search for financial planners. Be sure to scroll down on the search page so you can specify the credentials.

Interviewing Financial Planners: Asking the Right Questions

Don't consider hiring a financial planner until you read the rest of this book. If you're not educated about personal finance, how can you possibly evaluate the competence of someone you may hire to help you make important financial decisions?

We firmly believe that you are your own best financial planner. However, we know that some people don't want to make financial decisions without getting assistance. Perhaps you're busy or you simply can't stand making money decisions.

You need to recognize that you have a lot at stake when you hire a financial planner. Besides the cost of her services, which generally don't come cheap, you're placing a lot of trust in her recommendations. The more you know, the better the planner you can hire and the fewer services you need to buy.

The following questions will help you get to the core of a financial planner's competence and professional integrity. Get answers to these questions *before* you decide to hire a financial planner:

>> **What percentage of your income comes from clients' fees versus commissions?** Asking this question first may save you the trouble and time of asking the next nine questions. The right answer is "100 percent of my income comes from fees paid by clients." Anything less than 100 percent means that the person you're speaking to is a salesperson with a vested interest in recommending certain strategies and products.

Sadly, more than a few financial planners don't tell the truth. In one undercover investigation, about one-third of self-proclaimed fee-only planners turned out to be brokers who also sold investment and insurance products on a commission basis.

TIP

How can you ferret out these people? The simplest way is to have them put down in writing exactly how they're compensated. To check out if a financial planner or an financial-planning firm is registered and what they're licenced to sell, start off with the website of the Canadian Securities Administrators (www. securities-administrators.ca). The Registration tab at the top will take you to the National Registration Search page where you can look up both individuals and companies. The Enforcement tab takes you to a list of disciplinary actions and sanctions against both individuals and companies.

The provinces and territories also have securities and financial-services regulators. You can find your local department by searching the web using the name of your province or territory and "securities regulator" or "securities commission." (If you live in Quebec, the regulators' website is www. lautorite.qc.ca.) You can also find a list of all the provincial and territorial authorities on the "Local Securities Regulator" page of the CSA website.

>> **What portion of client fees is for money management versus hourly planning?** The answer to how the planner is paid fees provides clues to whether she has an agenda to persuade you to hire her to manage your money. If you want objective and specific financial-planning recommendations, give preference to planners who derive their income from hourly fees. Many financial planners call themselves "fee-based," which usually means that they make their living managing money for a percentage.

If you want a money manager, you can hire the best quite inexpensively through a mutual fund. Or, if you have substantial assets, you can hire an established money manager (see Chapter 10).

>> **What is your hourly fee?** The rates for financial planners range from as low as $75 per hour up to several hundred dollars per hour. If you shop around, you can find fine planners who charge around $125 to $225 per hour. As you compare planners, remember that what matters is the total cost that you can expect to pay for the services you're seeking.

>> **Do you also perform tax or legal services?** Be wary of someone who claims to be an expert beyond one area. The tax, legal, and financial fields are vast in and of themselves, and they're difficult for even the best and brightest planner to cover well simultaneously.

One exception is the accountant who also performs some basic financial planning by the hour. Likewise, a good financial planner should have a solid grounding in the basic tax and legal issues that relate to your personal finances. Large firms may have specialists available in different areas.

>> **What work and educational experience qualifies you to be a financial planner?** This question doesn't have one right answer. Ideally, a planner should have experience in the business or financial services field. Some say to look for planners with at least five or ten years of experience. (We've always wondered how planners earn a living their first five or ten years if folks won't hire them until they reach these benchmarks!) A planner should also be good with numbers, speak in plain English, and have good interpersonal skills.

REMEMBER

Education is sort of like food. Too little leaves you hungry. Too much can leave you feeling stuffed and uncomfortable. And a small amount of high quality is better than a lot of low quality.

Because investment decisions are a critical part of financial planning, take note of the fact that the most common designations of educational training among professional money managers are Master of Business Administration (MBA) and Chartered Financial Analyst (CFA).

>> **Have you ever sold limited partnerships? Options? Futures? Commodities? Invested with Madoff?** The correct answers here are *no, no, no, no,* and *no.* If you don't know what these disasters are, refer to Chapter 9. (Bernie Madoff ran a hedge fund that was a huge Ponzi scheme.) You also need to be wary of any financial planner who used to deal in these areas but now claims to have seen the light and reformed her ways. (Some sophisticated planners may use some of these instruments to hedge or reduce risk, but be sure you understand what they're doing and that you and the planner fully understand all costs and potential risks.)

Professionals with poor judgment may not repeat the same mistakes, but they're more likely to make some new ones at your expense. Our experience is that even planners who have been "reformed" are unlikely to be working by the hour. Most of them either work on commission or want to manage your money for a hefty fee.

» **Do you carry liability (errors and omissions) insurance?** Some planners may be surprised by this question or think that you're a problem customer looking for a lawsuit. On the other hand, accidents happen; that's why insurance exists. So, if the planner doesn't have liability insurance, she has missed one of the fundamental concepts of planning: Insure against risk. Don't make the mistake of hiring her.

You wouldn't (and shouldn't) let contractors into your home to do work without knowing that they have insurance to cover any mistakes they make. Likewise, you should insist on hiring a planner who carries protection in case she makes a major mistake for which she's liable. Make sure that she carries enough coverage given what she's helping you with.

» **Can you provide references from clients with needs similar to mine?** Don't just get references and feel assured because you've been given a list of clients. Take the time to actually talk to other people who have used the planner. And get specific. Ask what the planner did for them, and find out what her greatest strengths and weaknesses are. You can find out a bit about the planner's track record and style. And because you want to have as productive a relationship as possible with your planner, the more you find out about her, the easier it'll be for you to hit the ground running if you hire her.

Some financial planners offer a "complimentary" introductory consultation. If a planner offers a free consultation to allow you to check her out and it makes you feel more comfortable about hiring her, fair enough. But be careful: Most free consultations end up being a big sales pitch for certain products or services the planner offers.

The fact that a planner *doesn't* offer a free consultation may be a good sign. Planners who are busy and who work strictly by the hour can't afford to burn an hour of their time for an in-person free session. They also need to be careful of folks seeking free advice. Such planners usually are willing to spend some time on the phone answering background questions. They should also be able to send background materials by mail and provide references.

» **Will you provide specific strategies and product recommendations that I can implement on my own if I choose?** This is an important question. Some planners may indicate that you can hire them by the hour. But then they provide only generic advice without specifics. Some planners even *double-dip* — they charge an hourly fee initially to make you feel like you're not working with a salesperson, and then they try selling commission-based products. Also, be aware of planners who say that you can choose to implement their recommendations on your own and then recommend financial products that carry commissions.

>> **How is implementation handled?** Ideally, you should find a planner who lets you choose whether you want to hire her to help with implementation after the recommendations have been presented to you. If you know that you're going to follow through on the advice and you can do so without further discussions and questions, don't pay the planner to help you implement her recommendations.

On the other hand, if you hire the planner because you lack the time, desire, and/or expertise to manage your financial life in the first place, building implementation into the planning work makes good sense.

Learning from Others' Mistakes

WARNING

Over the many years that we've worked in the personal-finance world, we've heard too many stories of problems that people have encountered from hiring incompetent and unethical financial planners. To avoid repeating others' mistakes, remember the following:

>> **You absolutely must do your homework before hiring any financial planner.** Despite recommendations from others about a particular financial planner, you can end up with bad advice from biased planners.

>> **Avoid or minimize conflicts of interest.** The financial-planning and brokerage fields are minefields for consumers. The fundamental problem is the enormous conflict of interest that is created when "planners" sell products that earn them sales commissions. Selling ongoing money-management services creates a conflict of interest as well.

>> **You are your own best advocate.** The more you know, and the more you understand that investing and other financial decisions don't have to be complicated, the more you realize that you don't need to spend gobs of money (or any money at all) on financial planners. When you look in the mirror, you see the person who has your best interests at heart and is your best financial planner.

Chapter **20**

Using Technology to Manage Your Money

A lthough a computer and, to a lesser extent, a smartphone may be able to assist you with your personal finances, they simply represent two of many tools. Computers are best for performing routine tasks (such as processing lots of bills or performing many calculations) quickly and for aiding you with research.

This chapter gives you an overview of how to use technology, software, apps, and cyberspace with your finances. We tell you how to use this technology to pay your bills, focus on your spending, prepare taxes, research investments, plan for retirement, trade and invest, buy insurance, and plan your estate, and we suggest the best software, websites, and apps.

Surveying Software, Apps, and Websites

You can access major repositories of personal-finance information through your computer. Although the lines are blurring among these categories, they're roughly defined as follows:

>> **Software:** Computer programs that are either packaged in a box or DVD case or are available to be downloaded online. Most of the mass-marketed financial

software packages sell for less than $100. If you've ever used a word-processing program such as Microsoft Word or a spreadsheet program such as Microsoft Excel, you've used software.

>> **Apps:** Programs you download onto a smartphone or tablet. Apps are kind of like software. They run on your mobile device and tend to be less costly (albeit generally less sophisticated) than computer software.

>> **Websites:** Pages on the Internet that provide information and services to help you manage your financial life, including online bill paying. Most of the financial stuff on the Internet is supplied by companies marketing their wares and, hence, is available for free. Some sites sell their content for a fee.

Adding up financial software benefits

Although the number of personal-finance software packages, apps, and websites is large and growing, quality is lagging behind quantity, especially among the free websites. The best programs can

>> Guide you to better organization and management of your personal finances

>> Help you complete mundane tasks or complex calculations quickly and easily and provide basic advice in unfamiliar territory

>> Make you feel in control of your financial life

Mediocre and bad software, on the other hand, can make you feel stupid or, at the very least, make you want to scream. Lousy packages usually end up in the software graveyard.

Having reviewed many of the packages available, we can assure you that if you're having a hard time with some of the programs out there (and sometimes even with the more useful programs), it's not you that's the problem — it's the poorly put-together and ill-thought-out programs. Too many packages assume that you already know things such as your tax rate, your mortgage options, and the difference between stock and bond mutual funds. Much of what's out there is too technically oriented and decidedly not user-friendly. Some of it is even flawed in its financial accuracy.

A good software package, like a good tax or financial advisor, helps you better manage your finances. It simply and concisely explains financial terminology. And it helps you make decisions by offering choices and recommendations, allowing you to "play" with alternatives before following a particular course of action. With increasing regularity, financial software packages are being designed to perform more than one task or to address more than one area of personal finances.

But remember that no software package covers the whole range of issues in your financial life. Later in this chapter, we recommend some of our favourite financial software and apps.

Understanding how apps can benefit and harm your bottom line

At the risk of starting with the very basics, apps are to mobile devices what software is to personal computers. As we spend more time on smartphones and tablets, more programs — known as *apps* (short for *applications*) — are being developed to run on our phones.

Most apps are offered by large companies as another option for their customers to be in touch with and interact with what they offer. The financial institutions that you do business with — banks, mutual-fund companies, brokerage firms, and so on — are a common example. Here's what to be aware of in order to get the most out of apps without getting hurt:

>> **Use apps to solve problems and perform financial tasks more efficiently.** You can use apps to do more and more tasks that you previously had to do online and through a regular computer. The dizzying pace of technological change continues as many smartphones function as mini-computers in your hand. The best apps can help you to solve common challenges such as getting better value when shopping for a specific product or service, tracking where you're spending money, checking your bank account balances, doing basic investment research, and so on. Some apps are provided free of charge by companies that are seeking to promote their own services; others charge modest fees (like a software company does) because the app is all they're "selling."

>> **Beware the downside to "free" apps.** Though they haven't gotten the attention that computer viruses, computer malware, and computer ransomware attacks have garnered, similar problems have arisen with smartphone apps. Some will end up tracking and spying on you. The worst are a scam and/or some sort of virus or malware. In addition to those issues, you should also check out the background and agenda of any company offering a financial app, and how the company may be making money from the app. Most apps are nothing more than glorified advertising from the company behind the app. Sure, they may dangle something seemingly helpful (for example, offering a free credit score, stock quotes, and so on), but you should uncover what their actual agenda is and what kind of reputation they have. Many free-credit-score apps, for example, make money from affiliate fees from credit cards they pitch you.

>> **Use apps only from legitimate companies with lengthy track records.**
Most of the companies recommended in this chapter are fairly large companies with lengthy track records of success. For sure, technology is disrupting
and changing many industries and companies. But that doesn't mean that you
should only do business with firms that exist solely online, in the cloud, and so
on. Research the history of companies that you're considering doing business
with. When seeking the link for a mobile app, get that link and download the
app from the company's website so you're sure you're getting the actual app
rather than a knockoff or a fraudulent one. Do your homework and research
an app before downloading and beginning to use it. Check with more than
one independent source and read independent reviews, especially those that
are critical and less than flattering. And stay far away from the apps that claim
that they can show you how to make big bucks doing very little from the
comfort of your own home.

Consider the alternatives to an app. Before downloading and using an app, you
should question the need for it and consider the alternatives. Remember that the
company behind the app wants to tie you to it so you'll buy more and spend more
with them. Is that your goal? You likely have your phone with you all the time. Do
you really want this app running and in your face all the time? Maybe, maybe
not — think about it and examine the alternatives.

Surfing hazards online

Like the information you receive from any medium, you have to sift out the good
from the bad when you surf the Internet. If you navigate the Internet and naively
think that what's out there is useful "information," "research," or "objective
advice," you're in for a rude awakening.

Most personal-finance websites are free, which — guess what? — means that
these sites are basically advertising or are dominated and driven by advertising. If
you're looking for material written by unbiased experts or writers, finding it on
the web may seem like searching for the proverbial needle in the haystack because
the vast majority of what's online is biased and uninformed.

Considering the source so you can recognize bias

A report on the Internet published by a leading investment-banking firm provides
a list of the "coolest" finance sites. On the list is the website of a major bank.
Because it has been a long time since we were in high school, we're not quite sure
what "cool" means anymore. If cool can be used to describe a well-organized and
graphically pleasing website, then we guess we can say that the bank's website
is cool.

However, if you're looking for sound information and advice, then the bank's site is decidedly "uncool." It steers you in a financial direction that benefits (not surprisingly) not you, but the bank. For example, in the real-estate section, users are asked to plug in their gross monthly income and down payment. The information is then used to spit out the supposed amount that users can "afford" to spend on a home. No mention is made of the other financial goals and concerns — such as saving for retirement — that affect your ability to spend a particular amount of money on a home.

Consider this advice in the lending area of the site: "When you don't have the cash on hand for important purchases, we can help you borrow what you need. From a new car, to that vacation you've been longing for, to new kitchen appliances, you can make these dreams real now." Click a button at the bottom of this screen, and — presto! — you're on your way to racking up credit-card and auto debt. Why bother practicing delayed gratification, living within your means, or buying something used if getting a loan is "easy" and comes with "special privileges"?

Watching out for sponsored content

Sponsored content, a euphemism for advertising under the guise of editorial content (known in the print media as *advertorials*), is another big problem to watch out for on websites. You may find a disclaimer or note, which is often buried in fine print in an obscure part of the website, saying that an article is sponsored by (in other words, paid advertising by) the "author."

A mutual-fund "education" site, for example, states that its "primary purpose is to provide viewers with an independent guide that contains information and articles they can't get anywhere else." The content of the site suggests otherwise. In the "Expert's Corner" section of the site, material is reprinted from a newsletter that advocates frequent trading in and out of mutual funds to try to guess and time market moves. Turns out that the article is "sponsored by the featured expert." In other words, it's a paid advertisement. (The track record of the newsletter's past recommendations, which isn't discussed on the site, is poor.)

WARNING

Even more troubling are the large number of websites that fail to disclose (even cryptically) that their "content" comes from advertisers. Print publications generally have a tradition of disclosing when an article is paid advertising, but in the Wild West online, many sites fail to make this simple and vital disclosure. Mind you, we're not saying that disclosure makes paid-for content okay — we're simply stating that a lack of disclosure makes an already bad situation even worse.

Also, beware of websites, especially those that are "free," that are making money in a clandestine way from two sources: companies whose products they praise, and affiliates to whom they direct web traffic. In perusing the web, we noticed, for example, that many "free" financial websites were singing the praises of a particular brand of budgeting software. We test-drove the product (which is like a slimmed-down version of Quicken or Microsoft Money), and it's a decent but far from exceptional product. Our research uncovered the fact that the makers of this software paid a whopping 35 percent commission to website affiliates who pitch and direct users to buy the product. With the software selling for $60, a website flogging it for them pockets $21 for each copy it sells. Does that taint a site's decision as to whether to recommend the software? Of course, it does.

Increasingly, companies are paying websites outright to simply mention and praise their products; doing so is incredibly sleazy even if it's disclosed, but to do so without disclosure is unethical. Also, beware of links to recommended product and service providers to do business with — more often than not, the referring website gets paid an affiliate fee. Look for sites that post policies against receiving such referral fees from companies whose products and services they recommend.

Steering clear of biased financial-planning advice

We also suggest skipping the financial-planning advice offered by financial-service companies that are out to sell you something. Such companies can't take the necessary objective, holistic view required to render useful advice.

For example, on one major mutual-fund company's website, you find a good deal of material on the company's mutual funds. The site's financial-planning advice is, unfortunately, off the mark: It urges readers to think of investing as putting money into financial instruments, and quickly moves on to — you guessed it — the benefits of mutual funds. It makes no mention of the fact that paying off high-cost consumer debt usually offers the best return, and that real estate and even small businesses are also worth considering. If you did that, though, you would put less money into mutual funds, which this area of the site prods you to do.

Shunning short-term thinking

WARNING

Many financial websites provide real-time stock quotes as a hook to a site that is cluttered with advertising. Our experience with individual investors is that the more short-term they think, the worse they do. And checking your portfolio during the trading day certainly promotes short-term thinking.

Another way that sites create an addictive environment for you to return to, preferably — for them — multiple times a day, is to constantly provide news and other rapidly changing content. Do you really need "breaking news" updates that gasoline prices jumped 4 cents per litre over the past two weeks or that yet another cable-show personality is having a contest with a Hollywood celebrity to see who can sign up more Twitter followers in the next week?

Also, beware of tips offered around the electronic water cooler — comment sections. As in the real world, chatting with strangers and exchanging ideas are sometimes fine. However, if you don't know the identity and competence of commentators, why would you follow their financial advice or stock tips? Getting ideas from various sources is okay, but educate yourself and do your homework before making personal financial decisions.

TIP

If you want to best manage your personal finances and find out more, remember that the old expression "You get what you pay for" contains a grain of truth. Free information on the Internet, especially information provided by companies in the financial-services industry, is largely self-serving. Stick with information providers who have proven themselves offline or who don't have anything to sell except objective information and advice.

Accomplishing Money Tasks on Your Computer, Tablet, or Smartphone

In this section, we detail important personal financial tasks that your computer or mobile device can assist you with. We also provide our recommendations for the best software and websites to help you accomplish these chores.

Paying your bills and tracking your money

Plenty of folks have trouble saving money and reducing their spending. Thus, it's no surprise that in the increasingly crowded universe of free websites, plenty are devoted to supposedly helping you to reduce your spending. More of these websites and apps keep springing up, but among those you may have heard of and stumbled upon are Geezeo, Mint, Mvelopes, Wally, and Yodlee. As you can already see, attracting attention online starts with having a quirky name!

We've kicked the tires and checked out these sites and frankly have mixed to negative feelings about them. The biggest problems we have with these sites are that they're loaded with advertising and/or have affiliate relationships with companies. What does this mean? The site gets paid if you click a link to one of its recommended service providers and buy what it's selling.

We will give credit to Mint for at least admitting in black and white that it's soliciting and receiving affiliate payments when it states on its site:

> How can Mint be free? We give you personalized ideas on how to save money by showing you the best way to save among thousands of financial products. If you decide to make a change that saves you some cash, we sometimes earn a small fee from the bank or company you switch to.

This, of course, creates an enormous conflict of interest and thoroughly taints any recommendation made by Mint and similar sites that profit from affiliate referrals. For starters, they have no incentive or reason to recommend companies that won't pay them an affiliate fee. And, there's little — if any — screening of companies for quality service levels that are important to you as a consumer.

Also, be forewarned that after registering you as a site user, the first thing most of these sites want you to do is connect directly to your financial institutions (banks, brokerages, investment companies) and download your personal investment account and spending data. If your instincts tell you this might not be a good idea, guess what? You should trust your instincts. Yes, there are security concerns, but those pale in comparison to privacy concerns and concerns about the endless pitching to you of products and services.

Another problem that we have with these websites is the incredibly simplistic calculators they offer. One that purported to help with retirement planning didn't allow users to choose a retirement age younger than 62 and had no provisions for factoring in part-time work. When it asked about your assets, it made no distinction between equity in your home and financial assets (stocks, bonds, mutual funds, and so on). Finally, if you encounter a problem using these sites, they generally offer no phone support, so you're relegated to ping-ponging emails in the hopes of getting your questions answered.

TIP

We like the Goodbudget app for its simplicity and practicality. The basic version provides you with up to one year of expense-tracking history in ten main categories (envelopes). There is also a paid or premium version ($50 per year), which provides up to five years of expense tracking with unlimited categories, as well as email support. We suggest starting with the free version and then deciding down the road whether an upgrade is worth your while.

Some apps are simply designed to save you money. GasBuddy, for example, will show you the price for gasoline at various service stations in a local area. It's free for consumers to use.

Especially when going on lengthy car trips, car tolls can add up quickly. Tollsmart Toll Calculator is a low-cost app that enables you to compare toll costs for alternative routes.

Camelcamelcamel is a price tracker that scans items on Amazon, shows you their price history, and sends you alerts when a product you're interested in drops in price. PriceGrabber scans items everywhere online, although its website is much easier to use than its app.

TIP

Quicken is a good software program that helps with expense tracking and bill paying. In addition to offering printed cheques and electronic bill payment, Quicken is a financial organizer. The program allows you to list your investments and other assets, along with your loans and other financial liabilities. Quicken automates the process of paying your bills, and it can track your cheque-writing and prepare reports that detail your spending by category so you can find the fat in your budget. (For a complete discussion on how to track your spending, see Chapter 3.)

TIP

You can avoid dealing with paper cheques — written or printed — by signing up for online bill payment. With such services, you save on checks, stamps, and envelopes. These services are available to anyone with a chequing account through an increasing number of banks, credit unions, and brokerage firms, as well as through Quicken.

Planning for retirement

Good retirement-planning software and online tools can help you plan for retirement by crunching the numbers for you. But they can also teach you how particular changes — such as your investment returns, the rate of inflation, or your savings rate — can affect when and in what style you can retire. The biggest time-saving aspect of retirement-planning software and websites is that they let you more quickly play with and see the consequences of changing the assumptions.

Some of the major investment companies we profile in Part 3 of this book are sources for some high-quality, low-cost retirement-planning tools. Here are some good ones to consider:

>> Service Canada's website (www.canada.ca/en/employment-social-development/corporate/portfolio/service-canada.html) has all the detailed information you need about Canada Pension Plan (CPP) or Quebec Pension Plan (QPP) eligibility and payouts, as well as Old Age Security (OAS) and the Guaranteed Income Supplement (GIS). The site also has a good retirement-planning tool, and a useful list of questions to ask your employer about your pension plan.

>> The Ontario Securities Commission educational website (www.getsmarteraboutmoney.ca) can help with budgeting, developing a long-term financial plan, tracking your progress, and figuring savings goals to reach retirement objectives.

>> Tony's website (www.moneygrower.ca) has some helpful, easy-to-use tools, including a Registered Retirement Income Fund (RRIF) income calculator and a tool that lets you compare the income from different fixed-income investments. There is also a tool that lets you see the returns from a Registered Retirement Savings Plan (RRSP) compared to a Tax-Free Savings Account (TFSA). In addition, there are other calculators for everything from determining annuity income to a life expectancy calculator, which, if you can face it, will give you a sense of your longevity! You'll also find a number of useful worksheets, along with some helpful articles on RRSPs and RRIFs, the CPP and QPP, company pension plans, and estate planning.

Preparing your taxes

Good, properly used tax-preparation software can save you time and money. The best programs "interview" you to gather the necessary information and select the appropriate forms based on your responses. Of course, you're still the one responsible for locating all the information needed to complete your return. More-experienced taxpayers can bypass the interview and jump directly to the forms they know they need to complete. These programs also help flag overlooked deductions and identify other tax-reducing strategies.

TIP

StudioTax (www.studiotax.com) can easily handle everything but the most complicated returns. What's really surprising is that regardless of your income level, using the program is absolutely free. (The Ottawa-based developers do ask for a donation to help them maintain and improve the program.) TurboTax and H&R Block Tax Software are also good picks.

TIP

If you're mainly looking for tax forms, you can get them at no charge in tax-preparation books or through the CRA's website (www.cra-arc.gc.ca).

Researching investments

Gone are the days of schlepping off to the library to look at investing reference manuals, buying print versions for your own use, or slogging through voicemail hell when you call government agencies. Today you can access these and other investing resources on your computer. You can also often pay for just what you need:

>> **Globe Advisor:** The business and investing site run by *The Globe and Mail* (www.globeadvisor.com) lets you read many of the business stories published in the paper. You'll also find articles from the *Globe*'s helpful personal-finance section. Globe Advisor offers excellent stock data, as

well as information on the past performance, management, and top holdings of hundreds of different funds. You can also use the site's filters to get a list of funds that meet your criteria, such as low-cost, low-fee index funds that mirror the return of the major stock markets.

>> **Morningstar:** You can access Morningstar's mutual fund reports, as well as reports on U.S. stocks, at www.morningstar.ca. The basic reports are free, but they're watered-down versions of the company's comprehensive software and paper products. If you want to buy Morningstar's unabridged fund reports online, you can do so for a fee.

>> **SEDAR:** The System for Electronic Document Analysis and Retrieval (SEDAR) website at www.sedar.com is run for the Canadian Securities Administrators (CSA). It provides free access to the various documents that publicly traded Canadian companies and mutual funds must file with the regulators. You'll find everything from annual reports and financial statements to news releases. This website is a good place to start when you already have particular stocks in mind and want to find out more about the companies' businesses and financials. The site is also loaded with promotion-free material on mutual funds.

>> **U.S. Securities and Exchange Commission (SEC):** The SEC allows unlimited, free access to its documents at www.sec.gov. All public corporations, as well as mutual funds, file their reports with the agency. Be aware, however, that navigating this site takes patience.

Trading online

If you do your investing homework, trading securities online may save you money and perhaps some time. For years, discount brokers (see Chapter 8) were heralded as the low-cost source for trading. Then online brokers set a lower-cost standard. The major mutual-fund companies also offer competitive online services.

A number of discount brokers have built their securities brokerage business around online trading. By eliminating the overhead of branch offices and by accepting and processing trades by computer, online brokers keep their costs and brokerage charges to a minimum. Cut-rate electronic brokerage firms are for people who want to direct their own financial affairs and don't want or need to work with a personal broker. However, some of these brokers have limited products and services. For example, some don't offer many of the best mutual funds. And our own experience with reaching live people at some online brokers has been trying — we've had to wait on hold for more than ten minutes before a customer service representative answered the call.

REMEMBER

Although online trading may save you on transaction costs, it can also encourage you to trade more than you should, resulting in higher total trading costs, lower investment returns, and higher income-tax bills. Following investments on a daily basis encourages you to think short-term. Remember that the best investments are bought and held for the long haul (see Part 3 for more information).

Reading and searching periodicals

Many business and financial publications are online, offering investors news and financial market data. *The Globe and Mail*'s Globe2Go offers a digital version of the actual paper, along with the ability to look at articles up to seven days back at `www.theglobeandmail.com/globe-products`. The cost in 2018 was $26.99 for four weeks.

The Globe Unlimited service lets you read Globe articles — current and historical — and gives you full access to `www.globeinvestor.com`, which, beyond additional articles and columns, offers a range of market and investment data and tools. The cost is regularly $5.99 a week, but special offers are sometimes available. At the time of writing, a discounted price of just $1.50 a week for the first 52 weeks was being offered. You can find out more at `http://subscribe.theglobeandmail.com`.

Leading business publications such as *Profit* magazine and *Canadian Business* (both found at `www.canadianbusiness.com`) and *BusinessWeek* (`www.bloomberg.com/businessweek`) put some or all of the content of their latest issues on the Internet. Some publications charge for archived articles and for some current content for nonsubscribers to their print magazine.

WARNING

Be careful to take what you read and hear in the mass media with many grains of salt (see Chapter 21). Much of the content revolves around tweaking people's anxieties and dwelling on the latest crises and fads.

Investing through automated investment managers: Robo advisors

Increasing numbers of websites offer an automated investing service. These sites purport to help you choose an overall investment mix (asset allocation) and then divvy that money up, typically among exchange-traded funds (ETFs). Over time, the allocations can be tweaked or adjusted based on some predetermined formulas.

For this largely automated service, so-called robo advisors like Betterment and Wealthfront generally charge around 0.25 percent to 0.5 percent per year of the assets they're managing. We believe that you can educate yourself enough about investing in funds that paying an ongoing fee for such services isn't worth it.

Buying life insurance

If loved ones are financially dependent on you, you probably know you need life insurance. But add together the dread of life-insurance salespeople and a fear of death, and you have a recipe for procrastination. Although your computer can't stave off the Grim Reaper, it can help you find a quality, low-cost policy that can be more than 80 percent less costly than the most expensive options, all without your having to deal with high-pressure sales tactics.

TIP

The best way to shop for term life insurance online is through one of the quotation services we discuss in Chapter 17. At each of these sites, you fill in your date of birth, whether you smoke, how much coverage you'd like, and for how long you'd like to lock in the initial premium. When you're done filling in this information, a new web page pops up with a list of low-cost quotes (based on assumed good health) from highly rated (for financial stability) insurance companies.

Invariably, the quotes are ranked by how cheap they are. Although cost is certainly an important factor, many of these services don't do as good of a job explaining other important factors to consider when doing your comparison shopping. For example, the services sometimes don't cover the projected and maximum rates after the initial term has expired. Be sure to ask about these other future rates before you agree to a specific policy.

If you decide to buy a policy from one of the online agencies, you can fill out an online application form. The quotation agency will then mail you a detailed description of the policy and insurer, along with your completed application. In addition to having to deal with snail mail, you'll also have to deal with a *medical technician*, who will drop by your home to check on your health status . . . at least until some computer genius figures out a way for you to give blood and urine samples online!

Preparing legal documents

Just as you can prepare a tax return with the advice of a software program, you can also prepare common legal documents. This type of software may save you from the often difficult task of finding a competent and affordable lawyer.

Using legal software is generally preferable to using fill-in-the-blank documents. Software has the built-in virtues of directing and limiting your choices and preventing you from making common mistakes. Quality software also incorporates the knowledge and insights of the legal eagles who developed the software. And it can save you money.

If your situation isn't unusual, legal software may work well for you. As to the legality of documents that you create with legal software, remember that a will, for example, is made legal and valid by your witnesses; the fact that a lawyer prepares the document is *not* what makes it legal.

TIP

A good package for preparing your own will is the *Complete Canadian Wills Kit on CD*, by Alison Sawyer (Self-Counsel). The CD is loaded with all the worksheets and forms you'll need. In addition to allowing you to prepare wills, the *Complete Canadian Wills Kit* can also help you prepare a living will and a medical power of attorney document.

WARNING

Although wills and powers of attorney are all fairly standard legal documents that you can properly create with the guidance of a top-notch software package, it often makes sense to also seek professional guidance. If legal software has a failing, it's that it's designed for the average person and sometimes overlooks the specifics that should be addressed in particular situations, especially for a will. A wise strategy is to prepare your documents yourself, but then have them looked at — and reworked where necessary — by a lawyer. It will cost you much less than having a lawyer do everything from scratch. Plus, you'll learn some useful information — and perhaps gain some insights — along the way.

Chapter **21**

Online, On Air, and in Print

We have too many options for finding radio and TV news, websites, newspapers, magazines, and books that talk about money and purport to help you get rich. Tuning out poor resources and focusing on the best ones are the real challenges.

Because you probably don't consider yourself a financial expert, more often than not you won't know who to believe and listen to. We help you solve that problem in this chapter.

Observing the Mass Media

For better *and* for worse, the mass media has a major influence on our culture. On the good side, news is widely disseminated these days. So, if a product is recalled or a dangerous virus breaks out in your area, you'll probably hear about it, perhaps more than you want to, through the media or from tuned-in family members! The downsides of the mass media are plenty, though.

Alarming or informing?

In case you didn't already know, you've relatively recently lived through the second Great Depression. During the "financial crisis" of 2008–2009, we heard over and over and over again how it was the worst economy and worst economic crisis since the Great Depression. Endless parallels were drawn between the Great Depression of the 1930s and the recently slumping economy.

For sure, we suffered a significant *recession* (economic downturn). But some in the news media (and pundit class) went overboard in suggesting we were in the midst of another depression. During the Great Depression of the 1930s, the unemployment rate hit 25 percent and remained in double digits for years on end. Half of all homes ended up in foreclosure during that period. Although job losses and home foreclosures mounted during the recent recession, they were nowhere near Great Depression levels. The recessions of the late 1970s and early 1980s were actually worse because of the pain and hardship caused by the 10+ percent inflation rate and interest rates of that period. The unemployment rate was also above 10 percent in the early 1980s recession.

Stock markets suffered a steep decline during the 2008 financial crisis and recession and, in fact, the percentage decline in the widely followed S&P/TSX Composite and the Dow Jones Industrial Average were the worst since the 1930s. Interestingly, the severity of the 2008–2009 stock market decline was likely exacerbated by all the talk and fear of another Depression. Various research polls taken during late 2008 found that more than 60 percent of people believed we were about to enter another Great Depression. Those who panicked and bailed out when the Dow sagged below 6,500 in early 2009 learned another hard lesson when the market surged back, as it always inevitably does after a significant sell-off. (To date, the Dow has approximately quadrupled in value since that market bottom in 2009.)

WARNING

Some news producers, in their quest for ratings and advertising dollars, try to be alarming to keep you tuned in and coming back for their "breaking news" updates. The more you watch, the more unnerved you get over short-term, especially negative, events.

Teaching questionable values

Daily doses of mass media, including all the advertising that comes with them, essentially communicate the following messages:

>> Your worth as a person is directly related to your physical appearance (including the quality of clothing and jewellery you wear) and your material possessions — cars, homes, electronics, and other gadgets.

- » The more money you make, the more "successful" you clearly are.

- » The more famous you are (especially as a movie or sports star), the more you're worth listening to and admiring.

- » Don't bother concerning yourself with the consequences before engaging in negative behaviour.

- » Delaying gratification and making sacrifices are for boring losers.

WARNING

Continually inundating yourself with poor messages can cause you to behave in a way that undermines your long-term happiness and financial success. Don't support (by watching, listening, or reading) forms of media that don't reflect your values and morals.

Worshipping prognosticating pundits

Quoting and interviewing experts are perhaps the only things that the media loves more than hyping short-term news events. What's the economy going to do next quarter? What's stock XYZ going to do next month? What's the stock market going to do in the next few hours? No, we're not kidding about that last one — stock-market cable channels regularly interview traders during the trading day to get their opinions about what the market will do in the hours just before closing!

WARNING

Prognosticating pundits keep many people tuned in because their advice is constantly changing (and is, therefore, entertaining and anxiety producing), and they lead investors to believe that investments can be manoeuvred in advance in order to outfox future financial market moves. Common sense suggests, though, that no one has a working crystal ball, and if he did, he certainly wouldn't share such insights with the mass media for free. (For more on experts who purport to predict the future, see Chapter 8.)

Rating Radio and TV Financial Programs

Over the years, money issues have received increased coverage through the major media of TV and radio. Some topics gain more coverage on radio and TV because they help draw more advertising dollars (which follow what people are watching). When you turn on the radio or TV, you don't pay a fee to tune in to a particular channel (with pay cable channels being an exception). Advertising doesn't necessarily prevent a medium from delivering coverage that is objective and in your best interests, but it sure doesn't help foster this type of coverage either.

For example, can you imagine a financial radio or TV correspondent saying the following?

> We've decided to stop providing financial-market updates every five minutes because we've found it causes some investors to become addicted to tracking the short-term movements in the markets and to lose sight of the bigger picture. We don't want to encourage people to make knee-jerk reactions to short-term events.

Sound-bite-itis is another problem with both of these media. Producers and network executives believe that if you go into too much detail, viewers and listeners will change the channel.

Finding the Best Websites

Yes, the Internet has changed the world, but certainly not always for the better and not always in such a big way. Consider the way we shop. You can buy things online that you couldn't in the past. Purchasing items online broadens the avenues through which you can spend money. We see a big downside here: Overspending is easier to do when you surf the Internet a lot.

WARNING

Some of the best websites allow you to more efficiently access information that may help you make important investing decisions. However, this doesn't mean that your computer allows you to compete at the same level as professional money managers. The best pros work at their craft full-time and have far more expertise and experience than the rest of us. Some nonprofessionals have been fooled into believing that investing online makes them better investors. Our experience has been that people who spend time online every day dealing with investments tend to trade and react more to short-term events and have a harder time keeping the bigger picture and their long-term goals and needs in focus.

If you know where to look, you can more easily access some types of information. However, you often find a lot of garbage online — just as you do on other advertiser-dominated media like TV and radio. In Chapters 20 and 21, we explain how to safely navigate online to find the best of what's out there.

Navigating Newspapers and Magazines

Compared with radio and TV, print publications generally offer lengthier discussions of topics. And in the more financially focused publications, the editors who work on articles generally have more background in the topics they write about.

Even within the better publications, we find a wide variety of quality. So don't instantly believe what you read, even if you read a piece in a publication you like.

TIP

Here's how to get the most from financial periodicals:

>> **Read some back issues.** Go to your local library (or visit the publication's website) and peruse some issues that are at least one to two years old. Although reading old issues may seem silly and pointless, it actually can be *very* enlightening. You can begin to get a taste of a publication's style, priorities, and philosophies, as well as how its prior advice has worked out . . . or not!

>> **Look for solid information and perspective.** Headlines reveal a lot about how a publication perceives its role. Publications with cover stories such as "Ten hot stocks to buy now!" and "Funds that will double your money in the next three years!" are probably best avoided. Look for articles that seek to educate with accuracy, not pave your way to overnight riches with predictions.

>> **Note bylines.** As you read a given publication over time, you should begin to make note of the different writers. After you get to know who the better writers are, you can skip over the ones you don't care for and spend your limited free time reading the best.

>> **Don't react without planning.** Here's a common example of how *not* to use information and advice you glean from publications: A would-be investor had some cash he wanted to invest. He would read an article about investing in real estate investment trusts (REITs) and then go out the next week and buy several of them. Then he'd see a mention of some technology-stock funds and invest in some of those. Eventually, his portfolio was a mess of investments that reflected the history of what he had read rather than an orchestrated, well-thought-out investment portfolio.

Betting on Books

Reading a good book is one of our favourite ways to get a crash course on a given financial topic. Good books can go into depth on a topic in a way that simply isn't possible with other resources. Books also aren't cluttered with advertising and the conflicts inherent therein.

REMEMBER

As with the other types of resources we discuss in this chapter, you definitely have to choose carefully — plenty of mediocrity and garbage is out there. Book publishers are businesses first. And like most businesses, their business practises vary. Some have a reputation for care and quality; others just want to push a product out the door with maximum hype and minimum effort.

For instance, you may think that book publishers check out an author before they sign him to write an entire book. Well, you may be surprised to find out that some publishers don't do their homework. What most publishers care about first is the marketability of a particular book and author. Some authors are marketable because of their well-earned reputation for sound advice. Others are marketable because of stellar promotional campaigns built on smoke and mirrors. Even more troubling is that few publishers require advice books to be technically reviewed for accuracy by an expert in the field other than the author, who sometimes is *not* an expert. You, the reader, are expected to be your own technical reviewer. But do you have the expertise to do that? (Don't worry — this book has been checked for accuracy by an objective third party.)

As financial authors with business degrees, we know that financial ideas and strategies can differ considerably. Different is not necessarily wrong. When a technical reviewer looks at our text and makes a comment or suggestion, we take a second look. We may even see things in a new way. If we were the only experts to see our books before publication, we wouldn't benefit from this second expert opinion. How do you know whether a book has been technically reviewed? Check the credits page or the author's acknowledgments.

Authors write books for many reasons other than to teach and educate. The most common reason people write financial books is to further their own business interests. That's not the best thing for you when you're trying to educate yourself and better manage your own finances. For example, some investment newsletter sellers write investment books. Rather than teach you how to make good investments, the authors make the investment world sound so complicated that you feel the need to subscribe to their ongoing newsletters.

TIP

In addition to books that we recommend throughout this book, here's a list of some of our other favourite financial titles:

>> *Built to Last: Successful Habits of Visionary Companies,* by Jim Collins and Jerry I. Porras (HarperCollins)

>> *Good to Great: Why Some Companies Make the Leap . . . and Others Don't,* by Jim Collins (HarperCollins)

>> *Investing For Canadians For Dummies,* 4th Edition, by Tony Martin and Eric Tyson, MBA (Wiley)

>> *A Random Walk Down Wall Street: The Time-Tested Strategy for Successful Investing,* by Burton G. Malkiel (Norton)

>> Self-Counsel Press's Canadian legal and small-business titles (www. self-counsel.com)

>> *Tax Planning for You and Your Family,* produced by KPMG (Carswell)

6

The Part of Tens

Get advice on how to deal with major life changes.

Discover how to minimize and prevent identity theft.

Chapter **22**

Survival Guide for Ten Life Changes

Some of life's changes come unexpectedly, like earthquakes. Others you can see coming when they're still far off, like the birth of a child or a big storm moving in off the horizon. Whether a life change is predictable or not, your ability to navigate successfully through its challenges and adjust to new circumstances depends largely on your degree of preparedness.

Perhaps you find our comparison of life changes to natural disasters to be a bit negative. After all, some of the changes we discuss in this chapter should be occasions for joy. But understand that what you define as a "disaster" has a lot to do with preparedness. To the person who has stored no emergency rations in her basement, the big snowstorm that traps her in her home can lead to problems. But to the prepared person with plenty of food and water, that same storm may mean a vacation from work and some relaxing time off in the midst of a winter wonderland.

TIP

First, here are some general tips that apply to all types of life changes:

» **Stay in financial shape.** An athlete is best able to withstand physical adversities during competition by prior training and eating well. Likewise, the more sound your finances are to begin with, the better you'll be able to deal with life changes.

>> **Changes require change.** Even if your financial house is in order, a major life change — starting a family, buying a home, starting a business, divorcing, retiring — should prompt you to review your personal financial strategies. Life changes affect your income, spending, insurance needs, and ability to take financial risk.

>> **Don't procrastinate.** With a major life change on the horizon, procrastination can be costly. You (and your family) may overspend and accumulate high-cost debts, lack proper insurance coverage, or take other unnecessary risks. Early preparation can save you from these pitfalls.

>> **Manage stress and your emotions.** Life changes often are accompanied by stress and other emotional upheavals. Don't make snap decisions during these changes. Take the time to become fully informed and recognize and acknowledge your feelings. Educating yourself is key. You may want to hire experts to help (see Chapter 19), but don't abdicate decisions and responsibilities to advisors — the advisors may not have your best interests at heart or fully appreciate your needs.

Here, then, are the major changes you may have to deal with at some point in your life. We wish you more of the good changes than the bad!

Starting Out: Your First Job

If you just graduated from university, college, or some other program, or you're otherwise entering the workforce, your increased income and reduction in educational expenses are probably a welcome relief. You'd think, then, that more young adults would be able to avoid financial trouble and challenges. But they face these challenges largely because of poor financial habits picked up at home or from the world at large. Here's how to get on the path to financial success:

>> **Don't use consumer credit.** The use and abuse of consumer credit can cause long-term financial pain and hardship. To get off on the right financial foot, young workers need to shun the habit of making purchases on credit cards that they can't pay for in full when the bill arrives.

REMEMBER

Here's the simple solution for the problem of running up outstanding credit-card balances: Don't carry a credit card. Stick with your debit card (see Chapter 5). If you do keep a credit card, make sure you'll be able to pay each monthly bill in full and on time. Setting it up to have your monthly bill paid automatically out of your bank account can help you accomplish that.

>> **Get in the habit of saving and investing.** Ideally, your savings should be directed into a Registered Retirement Savings Plan (RRSP) or another savings plan that offers tax benefits. *Remember:* Even if you want to accumulate down payment money for a home or small-business purchase (see Chapter 4), you can withdraw up to $25,000 from your RRSP to help you buy a home without getting hit by a tax bill, as long as you pay it back over no more than 15 years at the required rate.

TIP

Thinking about a home purchase or retirement is usually not in the active thought patterns of first-time job seekers. We're often asked, "At what age should a person start saving?" To us, that's similar to asking at what age you should start brushing your teeth. Well, when you have teeth to brush! So, we say you should start saving and investing money from your first paycheque. Try saving 5 percent of every paycheque and then eventually increase your saving to 10 percent. If you're having trouble saving money, track your spending and make cutbacks as needed (refer to Chapters 3 and 6).

>> **Get insured.** When you're young and healthy, imagining yourself feeling otherwise is hard. But because accidents and unexpected illnesses can strike at any age, forgoing coverage can be financially devastating. When you're in your first full-time job with more limited benefits, buying disability coverage, which replaces income lost due to a long-term disability, is also wise. And as you begin to build your assets, consider making out a will so that your assets go where you want them to in the event of your untimely passing.

>> **Continue your education.** If you're like lots of people, after you get out in the workforce, you may realize how little you learned in formal schooling that can actually be used in the real world and, conversely, how much you need to learn that school never taught you. Read, learn, and continue to grow! Continuing education can help you advance in your career and enjoy the world around you.

Changing Jobs or Careers

During your adult life, you'll almost surely change jobs — perhaps several times a decade. We hope that most of the time you'll be changing by your own choice. But let's face it: Job security is not what it used to be. Downsizing has impacted even the most talented workers, and more industries are subjected to global competition.

TIP

Always be prepared for a job change. No matter how happy you are in your current job, knowing that your world won't fall apart if you're not working tomorrow can give you an added sense of security and encourage openness to possibility. Whether you're changing your job by choice or necessity, the following financial manoeuvres can help ease the transition:

» **Structure your finances to afford an income dip.** Spending less than you earn always makes good financial sense, but if you're approaching a possible job change, spending less is even more important, particularly if you're entering a new field or starting your own company and you expect a short-term income dip. Many people view a lifestyle of thriftiness as restrictive, but ultimately those thrifty habits can give you more freedom to do what you want to do. Be sure to keep an emergency reserve fund (see Chapter 8).

If you lose your job, batten down the hatches. You normally get little advance warning when you lose your job through no choice of your own. It doesn't mean, however, that you can't do anything financially. Evaluating and slashing your current level of spending may be necessary. Everything should be fair game, from how much you spend on housing to how often you eat out to where you do your grocery shopping. Avoid at all costs the temptation to maintain your level of spending by accumulating consumer debt.

» **Evaluate the total financial picture when relocating.** At some point in your career, you may have the option of relocating. But don't call the moving company until you understand the financial consequences of such a move. You can't simply compare salaries and benefits between the two jobs. You also need to compare the cost of living between the two areas: housing, commuting, provincial income and local property taxes, food, utilities, and all the other major expenditure categories that we discuss in Chapter 3.

Getting Married

Ready to tie the knot with the one you love? Congratulations! We hope that you'll have a long, healthy, and happy life together. In addition to the emotional and moral commitments that you and your spouse will make to one another, you're probably going to be merging many of your financial decisions and resources. Even if you're largely in agreement about your financial goals and strategies, managing as two is far different than managing as one. Here's how to prepare:

» **Take a compatibility test.** Many couples never talk about their goals and plans before marriage, and failing to do so breaks up many marriages. Finances are just one of numerous issues you should discuss. Ensuring that you know what you're getting yourself into is a good way to minimize your chances for heartache. Ministers, priests, and rabbis sometimes offer premarital counselling to help bring issues and differences to the surface.

» **Discuss and set joint goals.** After you're married, you and your spouse should set aside time at least once a year to discuss personal and financial goals for the years ahead. When you talk about where you want to go, you help ensure that you're both rowing your financial boat in unison.

» **Decide whether to keep finances separate or manage them jointly.** Philosophically, we like the idea of pooling your finances better. After all, marriage is a partnership. In some marriages, however, spouses may choose to keep some money separate so they don't feel the scrutiny of a spouse with different spending preferences. Spouses who have been through divorce may choose to keep the assets they bring into the new marriage separate in order to protect their money in the event of another divorce.

WARNING

As long as you're jointly accomplishing what you need to financially, some separation of money is okay. But for the health of your marriage, don't hide money, transactions (unless it's a gift for your spouse), or debts from one another, and if you're the higher-income spouse, don't assume power and control over your joint income.

» **Coordinate and maximize employee benefits.** If one or both of you have access to a package of employee benefits through an employer, understand how best to make use of those benefits. Coordinating and using the best that each package has to offer is like getting a pay raise. If you both have access to health insurance, compare which of you has better benefits. Likewise, one of you may have a better company pension plan — one that matches and offers superior investment options. Unless you can afford to save the maximum through both your plans, saving more in the better plan will increase your combined assets. (**Note:** If you're concerned about what will happen if you save more in one of your retirement plans and then you divorce, in most provinces, the money is considered part of your joint assets to be divided equally.)

» **Discuss life and disability insurance needs.** If you and your spouse can make do without each other's income, you may not need any income-protecting insurance. However, if you both depend on each other's incomes, or if one of you depends fully or partly on the other's income, you may each need long-term disability and term life-insurance policies (refer to Chapter 17).

» **Update your wills.** When you marry, you should make or update your wills. Having a will is potentially more valuable when you're married, especially if you want to leave money to others in addition to your spouse, or if you have children for whom you need to name a guardian. See Chapter 18 for more on wills.

>> **Reconsider your beneficiaries on investments and life insurance.** With registered retirement plans, funds, and life-insurance policies, you name beneficiaries to whom the money or value in those accounts will go in the event of your passing. When you marry, you'll probably want to designate your spouse as your beneficiary.

Buying a Home

Most Canadians eventually buy a home. You don't need to own a home to be a financial success, but home ownership certainly offers financial rewards. Over the course of your adult life, the real estate you own is likely going to appreciate in value. Additionally, you'll pay off your mortgage someday, which will greatly reduce your housing costs.

TIP

If you're thinking about buying a home, take these steps:

>> **Get your overall finances in order.** Before buying, analyze your current budget, your ability to afford debt, and your future financial goals. Make sure your expected housing expenses allow you to save properly for retirement and other long- or short-term goals. Don't buy a home based on the maximum amount lenders are willing to lend you.

>> **Determine whether now's the time.** Buying a house when you don't see yourself staying put three to five years rarely makes financial sense. Buying and selling a home gobbles up a good deal of money in transaction costs — you'll be lucky to recoup all those costs even within a five-year period. Also, if your income is likely to drop or you have other pressing goals, such as starting a business, you may want to wait to buy.

For more about buying a home, be sure to read Chapter 15.

Having Children

If you think that being a responsible adult, holding down a job, paying your bills on time, and preparing for your financial future are tough, wait 'til you add kids to the mix. Most parents find that with children in the family, their already precious free time and money become much scarcer. The sooner you discover how to manage your time and money, the better able you'll be to have a sane, happy, and financially successful life as a parent.

Here are some key things to do both before and after you begin your family:

» **Set your priorities.** As with many other financial decisions, starting or expanding a family requires that you plan ahead. Set your priorities and structure your finances and living situation accordingly. Is having a bigger home in a particular community important, or would you rather feel less pressure to work hard, giving you more time to spend with your family? Keep in mind that a less hectic work life not only gives you more free time, but also often reduces your cost of living by decreasing meals out, dry-cleaning costs, day-care expenses, and so on.

» **Take a hard look at your budget.** Having kids requires you to increase your spending. At a minimum, expenditures for food and clothing will increase. But you're also likely to spend more on housing, insurance, day care, and education. On top of that, if you want to play an active role in raising your children, some full-time jobs, given the demands and expectations, may not be feasible. So, while you consider the added expenses, you may also need to factor in a decrease in income.

TIP

No simple rules exist for estimating how kids will affect your household's income and expenses. On the income side, figure out how much you want to cut back on work. On the expense side, statistics show that the average household with school-age children spends about 20 percent more than a household without children. Going through your budget category by category and estimating how kids will change your spending is a more scientific approach. (You can use the worksheets in Chapter 3.)

» **Boost insurance coverage** *before* **getting pregnant.** With disability insurance, pregnancy is considered a pre-existing condition, so women should secure this coverage before getting pregnant. This means that if you don't already have coverage in place and you get pregnant, a disability that is the result of your pregnancy will generally not enable you to receive benefits. And most families-to-be should buy life insurance. Buying life insurance after the bundle of joy comes home from the hospital is a risky proposition — if one of the parents develops a health problem, she may be denied coverage. You should also consider buying life insurance for a stay-at-home parent. Even though the stay-at-home parent is not bringing in income, if she were to pass away, hiring assistance can cripple the family budget.

» **Check maternity and paternity leave with your employers.** Many larger employers offer to top-up government Employment Insurance benefits. Some may also allow for additional (unpaid) time off. Understand the options and the financial ramifications before you consider the leave and, ideally, before you get pregnant. Also, check laws within your province for mandated maternity and paternity leave.

>> **Update your will.** If you have a will, update it; if you don't have a will, make one now. With children in the picture, you need to name a guardian who will be responsible for raising your children if you and your spouse both pass away.

>> **Understand the Canada Child Benefit (CCB).** If you have children under the age of 18, you may be eligible for the CCB. (The CCB replaced its predecessor, the Canada Child Tax Benefit [CCTB], as well as the Universal Child Care Benefit [UCCB], in 2016.)You should apply for the CCB as soon as possible after your child is born. The payment period for CCB runs from July to the following June. The amount you'll receive is based on the previous year's tax return. So, for example, your 2018 tax return would determine the amount you would receive for the 12 months running from July 2019 to June 2020.

For the 2017 to 2018 period, the maximum for each child under the age of 6 was $6,400, or $533.33 per month. For children ages 6 to 17, the maximum was $5,400, or $450 per month. (You can get an estimate of how much you would receive by searching for the Child and Family Benefits calculator, found on the CRA's website, www.canada.ca/en/revenue-agency.)

However, the CCB is decreased if your family's income (technically, your *adjusted family net income* [AFNI]) exceeds a set amount. For the 2017–2018 period, that amount was $30,000. If you had one child, your benefit would be decreased by 7 percent of the amount your AFNI exceeded $30,000, up to $65,000. Your CCB would be further reduced by 3.2 percent of any AFNI above $65,000.

The more children you have, the higher the percentage reductions, up to four children. If you have four or more children, your benefit would have been decreased by 23 percent of the amount your AFNI exceeded $30,000, up to $65,000. Your benefit would be further reduced by 9.5 percent of your family income over $65,000.

>> **Understand childcare tax benefits.** You can claim childcare expenses as a deduction if they're incurred in order for you or your spouse to earn an income. You can also claim childcare expenses if you're paying someone to look after your children while you run a business, attend school, or carry out research for which you've received a grant. In addition to caregivers and day-care centres, childcare expenses also include payments to day camps and day sports schools where the primary focus is caring for the child, as well as boarding schools and overnight camps or sports schools (excluding the portion of the fees that relate to education costs).

In a two-parent family, the deduction must usually be claimed by the lower-earning spouse. For the 2018 tax year, you can claim up to $8,000 in expenses for each child under the age of 7, and $5,000 for children ages 7 to 16. (Some provinces also provide an additional childcare tax credit for lower-income families.)

However, the total you can claim is limited to two-thirds of your earned income. Plus, regardless of the actual cost, there are set weekly maximum amounts you can claim for expenses that relate to a stay in a boarding school (other than the education-cost portion), an overnight camp, or an overnight sports school.

>> **Plan ahead for postsecondary education costs (see Chapter 14).** Investigate the valuable benefits of saving for your child's university or college education in a Registered Education Savings Plan (RESP). Your contributions don't earn you a tax deduction (which contributions to an RRSP do), but money inside an RESP is allowed to grow tax-free. In addition, your contributions earn you a 20 percent grant (the Canada Education Savings Grant [CESG]), up to a set maximum per individual. And, if the money inside the plan is used to pay for qualifying educational expenses, it's taxed as if it were the income of the student. Given that the typical student barely scrapes by financially due to a low income and high qualifying expenses, they generally end up paying little, if any, tax on RESP payments.

>> **Don't indulge the children.** Toys, art classes, music lessons, sports and associated lessons, smartphones, field trips, and the like can rack up big bills, especially if you don't control your spending. Some parents fail to set guidelines or limits when spending on children's programs. Others mindlessly follow the examples set by the families of their children's peers. Introspective parents have told us that they often feel some insecurity — not to mention stress — about providing the best for their children. But remember that the parents (and kids) who seem the happiest and most financially successful are the ones who clearly distinguish between material luxuries and family necessities.

TIP

As children get older and become indoctrinated into the world of shopping, all sorts of other purchases come into play. Consider giving your kids a weekly allowance and letting them discover how to spend and manage it. When they're old enough, having your kids get a part-time job can help teach financial responsibility.

Starting a Small Business

Many people aspire to be their own bosses, but far fewer people actually leave their jobs in order to achieve that dream. Giving up the apparent security of a job with benefits and a built-in network of coworkers is difficult for most people, both psychologically and financially. Starting a small business is not for everyone, but don't let inertia stand in your way.

TIP

Here are some tips to help get you started and increase your chances for long-term success:

>> **Prepare to ditch your job.** To maximize your ability to save money, live as spartan a lifestyle as you can while you're employed. You'll develop thrifty habits that'll help you weather the reduced income and increased expenditure period that comes with most small-business start-ups. You may also want to consider easing into your small business by working at it part-time in the beginning, with or without cutting back on your normal job.

>> **Develop a business plan.** If you research and think through your business idea, not only will you reduce the likelihood of your business's failing and increase its success if it thrives, but you'll also feel more comfortable taking the entrepreneurial plunge. A good business plan describes in detail the business idea, the marketplace you'll compete in, your marketing plans, and expected revenue and expenses.

>> **Replace your insurance coverage.** Before you finally leave your job, get proper insurance. With disability insurance, secure coverage before you leave your job so you have income to qualify for coverage. If you have life insurance through your employer, obtain new individual coverage as soon as you know you're going to leave your job. (See Chapter 17 for details.)

>> **Establish a retirement savings plan.** After your business starts making a profit, consider establishing an RRSP, which allows you to shelter a good chunk of your income from tax. We explain everything you need to know about RRSPs in Chapter 11.

Caring for Aging Parents

For many people, there comes a time when they reverse roles with their parents and become the caregivers. As your parents age, they may need help with a variety of issues and living tasks. Although you probably won't have the time or ability to perform all these functions yourself, you may end up coordinating some service providers who will.

Here are key issues to consider when caring for aging parents:

>> **Get help where possible.** In most communities, a variety of nonprofit organizations offer information and counselling to families who are caring for elderly parents. Numerous government agencies, and for-profit companies can help with everything from simple cleaning and cooking, to health checks and medication monitoring, to assisted living and health advocacy. You may

be able to find your way to such resources through your province's ministry of health, as well as through recommendations from local hospitals and doctors. You'll especially want to get assistance and information if your parents need some sort of home care, nursing home care, or assisted living arrangement.

» **Get involved in their healthcare.** Your aging parents may already have a lot on their minds, or they simply may not be able to coordinate and manage all the healthcare providers who are giving them medications and advice. Try, as best you can, to be their advocate. Speak with their doctors so you can understand their current medical conditions, the need for various medications, and how to help coordinate caregivers. Visit home-healthcare providers and nursing homes, and speak with prospective care providers.

TIP

When you attend appointments with your parents, consider recording any discussions. (If you have a smartphone, it likely has an easy-to-use built-in voice recorder app.) Typically, you'll be overloaded with information — and probably jargon — and being able to review it later can help you understand what you've been told.

» **Understand tax breaks.** If you're financially supporting your parents, you may be eligible for both federal and provincial tax credits. Be aware that there have been some major changes to who — and how — these are made available.

The *Canada caregiver credit* came into being in 2017. It consolidated — and replaced — three long-standing credits: the infirm dependant credit, the caregiver credit (for in-home care of a relative), and the family caregiver credit. The credit is nonrefundable, meaning it can reduce your taxes, but it won't earn you a return.

TIP

To claim the Canada caregiver credit, your dependent parent must have a physical or mental impairment. Obtain a Disability Tax Certificate from a doctor or nurse practitioner.

One notable change is that your parent doesn't have to live with you for you to be eligible, but your parent does have to be dependent upon you for "support." This includes basic necessities including food, shelter, and clothing. (Previously, you were generally eligible for the credit for supporting a parent who lived with you and was at least 65, but who did not have a medical condition.) The maximum credit amount for 2017 was $6,883. However, it may be less, depending on your infirm parent's net income. For 2017, the credit was reduced dollar-for-dollar for the parent's income above $16,163, and was reduced to zero if the parent's net income was $23,046 or higher.

Alternatively, if you're single, widowed, divorced, or separated, and you support a parent in your home, you can claim the eligible dependent credit. This gives you the same credit as if that person were your spouse. The base amount in 2017 was $11,635. You can then also claim the Canada caregiver credit, but the maximum in this situation is lower. For 2017, it was capped at $2,150. Note that if this alternative credit provides you with less tax savings than if you had gone with the higher credit, you receive a top-up for the difference.

British Columbia, Ontario, and Yukon have corresponding credits. The other provinces, however, have stuck with the older caregiver amount, which provides a credit if your parent lives with you and is 65 or older, or if you're caring for an infirm adult relative.

>> **Discuss getting the estate in order.** Parents don't like thinking about their demise, and they may feel awkward discussing this issue with their adult children. But opening a dialogue between you and your folks about such issues can be healthy in many ways. Not only does discussing wills, living wills, living trusts, and estate-planning strategies (see Chapter 18) make you aware of your parents' situation, but it can also improve their plans to both their benefit and yours.

>> **Take some time off.** Caring for an aging parent, particularly one who is having health problems, can be time-consuming and emotionally draining. Do your parents and yourself a favour by using some personal/vacation time to help get things in order.

Divorcing

In most marriages that are destined to split up, both parties recognize early warning signs. Sometimes, however, one spouse may surprise the other with an unexpected request for divorce. Whether the separation is planned or unexpected, here are some important considerations when getting a divorce:

>> **Question the divorce.** Some say that divorcing is too easy, and we tend to agree. Although some couples are indeed better off parting ways, others give up too easily, thinking that the grass is greener elsewhere, only to later discover that all lawns have weeds and crabgrass. Just as with lawns that aren't watered and fertilized, relationships can wither without nurturing.

Money and disagreements over money are certainly major contributing factors in marital unhappiness. Try talking things over, perhaps with a marriage counsellor.

>> **Separate your emotions from the financial issues.** 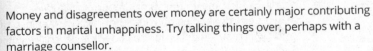 Feelings of revenge may be common in some divorces, but they'll probably only help ensure that the lawyers get rich while you and your spouse butt heads. If you really want a divorce, work at doing it efficiently and harmoniously so you can get on with your lives and have more of your money to work with.

- » **Detail resources and priorities.** Draw up a list of all the assets and liabilities that you and your spouse have. Make sure you list all the financial facts, including investment account records and statements. After you know the whole picture, begin to think about what is and isn't important to you financially and otherwise.

- » **Educate yourself about personal finance and legal issues.** Divorce some-times forces nonfinancially oriented spouses to get a crash course in personal finance at a difficult emotional time. This book can help educate you financially. Peruse a bookstore and buy a good legal guide or two about divorce.

- » **Choose advisors carefully.** Odds are, you'll retain the services of one or more specialists to assist you with the myriad issues, negotiations, and concerns of your divorce. Legal, tax, and financial advisors can help, but make sure you recognize their limitations and conflicts of interest. The more complicated things become and the more you haggle with your spouse, the more lawyers, unfortunately, benefit financially.

REMEMBER

Don't use your divorce lawyer for financial or tax advice — your lawyer probably knows no more than you do in these areas. Also, realize that you don't need a lawyer to get divorced. A variety of books and kits can help you. As for choosing tax and financial advisors, if you think you need that type of help, see Chapters 7 and 19 for advice on how to find good advisors.

- » **Analyze your spending.** Some divorcees find themselves financially squeezed in the early years following a divorce because two people living together in the same property can typically do so less expensively than two people living separately. Analyzing your spending needs predivorce can help you adjust to a new budget and negotiate a fairer settlement with your spouse.

- » **Review needed changes to your insurance.** If you're covered under your spouse's employer's insurance plan, make sure you get this coverage replaced (see Chapter 17). If you or your children will still be financially dependent on your spouse post-divorce, make sure the divorce agreement mandates life insurance coverage. You should also revise your will (see Chapter 18).

- » **Revamp your retirement plan.** With changes to your income, expenses, assets, liabilities, and future needs, your retirement plan will surely need a post-divorce overhaul. Refer to Chapter 4 for a reorientation.

Receiving a Windfall

Whether through inheritance, stock options, small–business success, or lottery winnings, you may receive a financial windfall at some point in your life. Like many people who are totally unprepared psychologically and organizationally for their sudden good fortune, you may find that a flood of money can create more problems than it solves.

Here are a few tips to help you make the most of your financial windfall:

>> **Educate yourself.** If you've never had to deal with significant wealth, we don't expect you to know how to handle it. Don't pressure yourself to invest it as soon as possible. Leaving the money where it is or stashing it in one of the high-yield savings accounts or higher-yielding money-market funds we recommend in Chapter 13 is far better than jumping into investments that you don't understand and haven't researched.

>> **Beware of the sharks.** You may begin to wonder whether someone has posted your net worth, address, and phone number in the local newspaper and on the Internet. Brokers and financial advisors may flood you with marketing materials, phone solicitations, and lunch-date requests. These folks pursue you for a reason: They want to convert your money into their income either by selling you investments and other financial products or by managing your money. Stay away from the sharks, educate yourself, and take charge of your own financial moves. Decide on your own terms whom to hire, and then seek them out.

>> **Recognize the emotional side of coming into a lot of money.** One of the side effects of accumulating wealth quickly is that you may have feelings of guilt or otherwise be unhappy, especially if you expected money to solve your problems. If you didn't invest in your relationship with your parents and, after their passing, you regret how you interacted with them, getting a big inheritance from your folks may make you feel bad. If you poured endless hours into a business venture that finally paid off, all that money in your investment accounts may leave you with a hollow feeling if you're divorced and you lost friends by neglecting your relationships.

>> **Pay down debts.** People generally borrow money to buy things that they otherwise can't buy in one fell swoop. Paying off your debts is one of the simplest and best investments you can make when you come into wealth.

>> **Diversify.** If you want to protect your wealth, don't keep it all in one pot. Mutual funds and exchange-traded funds (ETFs) are diversified, professionally managed investment vehicles worth considering (see Chapter 10). And if you want your money to continue growing, consider the wealth-building investments — stocks, real estate, and small-business options — that we discuss in Part 3 of this book.

>> **Make use of the opportunity.** Most people work for a paycheque for many decades so they can pay a never-ending stream of monthly bills. Although we're not advocating a hedonistic lifestyle, why not take some extra time to travel, spend time with your family, and enjoy the hobbies you've long been putting off? How about trying a new career that you may find more fulfilling and that may make the world a better place? What about donating to your favourite charities?

Retiring

If you've spent the bulk of your adult life working, retiring can be a challenging transition. Most Canadians have an idealized vision of how wonderful retirement will be — no more irritating bosses and pressure of work deadlines; unlimited time to travel, play, and lead the good life. Sounds good, huh? Well, the reality for most Canadians is different, especially for those who don't plan ahead (financially and otherwise).

Here are some tips to help you through retirement:

>> **Plan both financially and personally.** Planning your activities is even more important than planning financially. If the focus during your working years is solely on your career and saving money, you may lack interests, friends, and the ability to know how to spend money when you retire.

>> **Take stock of your resources.** Many people worry and wonder whether they have enough money to cut back on work or retire completely, yet they don't crunch any numbers to see where they stand. Ignorance may cause you to misunderstand how little or how much you really have for retirement when compared to what you need. See Chapters 4 and 12 for help with retirement planning and investing.

>> **Re-evaluate your insurance needs.** When you have enough money to retire, you don't need to retain insurance to protect your employment income any longer. On the other hand, as your assets grow over the years, you may be underinsured with regards to liability insurance (refer to Chapter 18).

>> **Evaluate healthcare/living options.** Medical expenses in your retirement years (particularly the cost of nursing-home care) can be daunting. Which course of action you take — supplemental insurance, buying into a retirement community, or not doing anything — depends on your financial and personal situation. Early preparation increases your options; if you wait until you have major health problems, it may be too late to choose specific paths. (See Chapter 17 for more details on healthcare options.)

>> **Decide what to do with your RRSP.** When you're set to retire, you may have to elect what to do with your RRSP funds. Making the right choice is similar to choosing a good investment — different features carry different risks, benefits, and tax consequences. Read Chapter 11 for information on how to assess your different options for taking money out of your RRSP. Read Part 3 of this book to learn about investing.

>> **Pick a pension option.** Selecting a *pension option* (a plan that pays a monthly benefit during retirement) is similar to choosing a good investment — each pension option carries different risks, benefits, and tax consequences. Pensions are structured by actuaries, who base pension options on reasonable life expectancies. The younger you are when you start collecting your company pension and Canada Pension Plan (CPP) or Quebec Pension Plan (QPP) benefits, the less you get per month. Check to see whether the amount of your monthly pension stops increasing past a certain age. You obviously don't want to delay access to your pension benefits past that age, because you won't receive a reward for waiting any longer and you'll collect the benefit for fewer months.

If you know you have a health problem that shortens your life expectancy, you may benefit from drawing your company pension and CPP or QPP benefits sooner. If you plan to continue working in some capacity and earning a decent income after retiring, waiting for higher pension benefits when you're in a lower tax bracket is probably wise.

You'll also need to make a choice as to what amount your surviving spouse receives from your employer's pension plan if you die first. At one end of the spectrum, you have the risky *single-life option,* which pays benefits until you pass away and then provides no benefits for your spouse thereafter. This option maximizes your monthly take while you're alive. Consider this option only if your spouse can do without this income. The least risky option, and thus least financially rewarding while the pensioner is still living, is the *100 percent joint and survivor option,* which pays your survivor the same amount that you received while still alive. The other joint and survivor options fall somewhere between these two extremes and generally make sense for most couples who want decent pensions early in retirement but want a reasonable amount to continue in the event that the pensioner dies first.

The 75 percent joint and survivor option is a popular choice, because it closely matches the lower expense needs of the lone surviving spouse at 75 percent of the expenses of the couple, and it provides higher payments than the 100 percent joint and survivor option while both spouses are alive.

>> **Get your estate in order.** Confronting your mortality is never fun, but when you're considering retirement or you're already retired, getting your estate in order makes all the more sense. Find out about wills and trusts that may benefit you and your heirs. You may also want to consider giving monetary gifts now if you have more than you need. This enables you to enjoy and see how others will utilize your funds.

Chapter **23**

Ten Tactics to Thwart Identity Theft and Fraud

Hucksters and thieves are often several steps ahead of law enforcement. Eventually, some of the bad guys get caught, but many don't, and those who do get nabbed often go back to their unsavoury ways after penalties and perhaps some jail time. They may even be in your neighbourhood or on the board of your local theatre. (For an enlightening read, check out Dr. Martha Stout's book *The Sociopath Next Door* [Three Rivers Press].)

Years ago, when Eric lived on the West Coast, he got a call from his bank informing him that it had just discovered "concerning activity" on the joint chequing account he held with his wife. Specifically, what had happened was that a man with a bogus ID in Eric's name had gone into five different bank branches on the same day and withdrawn $80 from his chequing account at each one. After some detective work, Eric discovered that someone had pilfered his personal banking information at his wife's employer's payroll office. Fortunately, the bank made good on the money that it had allowed to be withdrawn by his impostor.

Eric had been the victim of identity theft. In his situation, the crook had accessed one of his accounts; in other cases, the criminal activity may develop with someone opening an account (such as a credit card) using someone's stolen personal information. Victims of identity theft can suffer trashed credit reports, reduced ability to qualify for loans and even jobs (with employers who check credit reports), out-of-pocket costs and losses, and the stressful dozens of hours of time to clean up the mess and clear their credit records and names.

Unfortunately, identity theft is hardly the only way to be taken to the cleaners by crooks. All sorts of scamsters hatch schemes to separate you from your money. Follow the ten tips in this chapter to keep yourself from falling prey and unnecessarily losing money.

Save Phone Discussions for Friends Only

WARNING

Never, ever give out personal information over the phone, especially when you aren't the one who initiated the call. Suppose you get a call and the person on the other end of the line claims to be with a company you conduct business with (such as your credit-card company or bank). Ask for the caller's name and number and call back the company's main number (on the back of your credit card or on your bank statement) to be sure the caller is, indeed, with that company and has a legitimate business reason for contacting you.

Sometimes, you have to push back a little, too! Tony was once called by his bank because they had spotted a strange charge going through on his credit card. After explaining the potential problem, the bank representative asked Tony to provide some personal information to verify his identity. Tony responded by saying it should be the other way around, because he had no way to know if the caller actually worked for the bank or was, in fact, a scammer looking to steal his identity. The representative was taken aback by the response, reiterating that he had been the one who called Tony. Tony, of course, repeated the simple point that that was exactly his concern. "Hang on a minute!" said the representative, "I'll get my supervisor!" And, yup, the supervisor came on the line to *reassure* Tony the caller was indeed a legitimate bank employee. After all, the supervisor's logic went, he was the representative's boss, and he should know. Tony once again went over the concept that the caller can keep putting on different people with the same declaration, but it still provided him with zero evidence that this was not a scam — and not even a particularly sophisticated one. What's more, Tony quoted the bank's own consumer newsletters that regularly warned its customers to never, ever offer up personal information to callers or emailers requesting personal information. Tony ended the call and did what we advise you to do in such situations, which is to initiate communication so you know you're dealing with a legitimate person at the other end. In Tony's situation, all it took was phoning the toll-free number on the back of his credit card to find out what the mysterious charge was, which it turned out had been a normal purchase he himself had made.

With caller ID on your phone line, you may be able to see what number a call is originating from, but more often than not, calls from business-registered phone numbers come up as "unavailable." And, crooks have gotten more advanced and can "spoof" real phone numbers that aren't actually the numbers they're calling from. A major red flag: calling back the number that comes through on caller ID and discovering that the number is bogus (a nonworking number) or that it always goes to voicemail.

Never Respond to Emails Soliciting Information

You may have seen or heard about official-looking emails sent from companies you know of and may do business with asking you to promptly visit their website to correct some sort of billing or account problem. Crooks can generate a return/sender email address that looks like it comes from a known institution but really does not.

This unscrupulous practise is known as *phishing*, and if you bite at the bait, visit the site, and provide the requested personal information, your reward is likely to be some sort of future identity-theft problem and possibly a computer virus. Tony has received just such scam emails purporting to be from a number of the big banks, as well as Canada Post, complete with authentic-looking logos and letterhead!

TIP

To find out more about how to protect yourself from phishing scams, visit the website of APWG at www.antiphishing.org.

Review Your Monthly Financial Statements

Although financial institutions such as banks may call you if they notice unusual activity on one of your accounts, some people discover problematic account activity simply by reviewing their monthly credit-card and bank statements.

REMEMBER

Do you need to balance bank-account statements to the penny? No, you don't. Neither of us has for years (decades, actually!), and we don't have the time or patience for such minutiae. The key is to review the line items on your statement to be sure that all the transactions were yours and are correct.

Secure All Receipts

When you make a purchase, be sure to keep track of and secure receipts, especially those that contain your personal financial or account information. You can keep these in an envelope in your home, for example. Then cross-check them against your monthly statement.

REMEMBER

When you no longer need to retain your receipts, be sure to dispose of them in a way that prevents a thief, who may get into your garbage, from being able to decipher the information on them. Rip up the receipts or, better yet, buy a small paper shredder for your home and/or small business. Consider it good insurance — the small outlay will go a long way toward helping ensure your data doesn't get into the wrong hands and cause you all sorts of financial and bureaucratic headaches.

Close Unnecessary Credit Accounts

Open your wallet and remove all the pieces of plastic within it that enable you to charge purchases. The more credit cards and credit lines you have, the more likely you are to have problems with identity theft and fraud and the more likely you are to overspend and carry debt balances.

Reduce credit-card offers by contacting the Canadian Marketing Association and signing up for the Do Not Contact Service. You can register online at `www.the-cma.org/consumers/do-not-mail`.

You can also reduce unwanted telemarketing calls by registering your phone number with the National Do Not Call List operated by the Canadian government. For more information, visit `www.lnnte-dncl.gc.ca` or call 866-580-3625.

REMEMBER

Unless you maintain a card for small-business transactions, you really "need" only one piece of plastic with a Visa or MasterCard logo. Use a debit card for your purchases if you have a history of carrying a balance on your credit card.

Regularly Review Your Credit Reports

You may also be tipped off to shenanigans going on in your name when you review your credit report. Some identity-theft victims have found out about credit accounts opened in their names by reviewing their credit reports.

TIP

Because you're entitled to a free credit report from each of the three major credit agencies every year, we recommend reviewing your reports at least that often. The reports generally contain the same information, so you can request and review one agency report every four months, which enables you to keep a closer eye on your reports and still obtain them without cost.

We don't generally recommend spending the $100 or so annually for a so-called credit-monitoring service that updates you when something happens on your credit reports.

Keep Personal Info Off Your Cheques

Don't place personal information on cheques. Information that is useful to identity thieves — and that you should not put on your checks — includes your credit card number, driver's licence number, Social Insurance Number (SIN), and so on. We also encourage you to leave your home address off your preprinted cheques when you order them. Otherwise, every Tom, Dick, and Jane whose hands your cheque passes through knows exactly where you live.

When writing a cheque to a merchant, question the need for adding personal information to the cheque (in fact, in numerous areas, requesting and placing credit-card numbers on cheques is against the law). Remember that your credit card doesn't advertise your home address and other financial account data, so there's no need to publicize it to the world on your cheques.

Protect Your Computer and Files

Especially if you keep personal and financial data on your computer, consider the following safeguards to protect your computer and the confidential information on it:

>> Install a firewall.

>> Use virus protection software.

>> Password-protect access to your programs and files.

Protect Your Mail

Some identity thieves have collected personal information by simply helping themselves to mail in home mailboxes. Stealing mail is easy, especially if your mail is delivered to a curbside box.

Consider using a locked mailbox or a post-office box to protect your incoming mail from theft. Consider having your investment and other important statements sent to you only by email, or simply access them online, and eliminate mail delivery of the paper copies.

REMEMBER

Be careful with your outgoing mail as well, such as bills with cheques attached. Minimize your outgoing mail and save yourself hassles by signing up for automatic bill payment for as many bills as possible. Drop the rest of your outgoing mail in a secure Canada Post box, such as those you find at the post office.

Clean Out Your Wallet

Minimize the number of items in your wallet that carry personal information. Take all the cards, licences, and memberships out of your wallet, and only put back those that you absolutely need to have with you on a regular basis. For example, for most of your daily life, you don't need your SIN card or your passport.

TIP

Take photocopies of both sides of all the cards, licences, and other pieces of identification that you do need to carry with you. That way, if your wallet or purse is ever lost or stolen, you'll have a list of all the different accounts you need to cancel, along with the phone numbers to call.

Glossary

adjusted cost basis: For capital-gains tax purposes, the adjusted cost basis is how the Canada Revenue Agency determines your profit or loss when you sell an asset such as a home or a security. For an investment such as a mutual fund or stock, your cost basis is what you originally invested plus any reinvested money. For real estate, you arrive at the adjusted cost basis by adding the original purchase price to the cost of any *capital improvements* (expenditures that increase your property's value and life expectancy).

alternative minimum tax (AMT): The name given to a sort of shadow tax system that may cause you to pay a higher amount in income taxes than you otherwise would. The AMT was designed to prevent higher-income earners from lowering their tax bills too much through large deductions.

AMT: *See* alternative minimum tax (AMT).

annual percentage rate (APR): The figure that states the total yearly cost of a loan as expressed by the actual rate of interest paid. The APR includes the base interest rate and any other add-on loan fees and costs. The APR is inevitably higher than the rate of interest that the lender quotes.

annuity: An investment that is a contract backed by an insurance company. An annuity is frequently purchased for retirement purposes. Its main benefit is that it allows your money to compound and grow without taxation until withdrawal. Selling annuities can be lucrative source of income for insurance agents and financial planners who work on commission, so don't buy an annuity unless you're sure it makes sense for your situation.

APR: *See* annual percentage rate (APR).

asset allocation: When you invest your money, you need to decide how to proportion (allocate) it between risky, growth-oriented investments (such as stocks), whose values fluctuate, and more stable, income-producing investments (like bonds). How soon you'll need the money and how tolerant you are of risk are two important determinants when deciding how to allocate your money.

audit: A Canada Revenue Agency examination of your financial records to substantiate your tax return. Audits are among life's worst experiences.

bank prime rate: *See* prime rate.

bankruptcy: Legal action that puts a halt to creditors' attempts to collect unpaid debts from you. If you have a high proportion of consumer debt to annual income, filing for bankruptcy may be your best option.

bear market: A period (such as the early 2000s and late 2000s) when the stock market experiences a strong downward swing. A bear market is often accompanied by (and sometimes precedes) an economic recession. Imagine a bear in hibernation, because this is what happens in a bear market: Investors hibernate, and the market falters. During a bear market, the value of stocks can decrease significantly. The market usually has to drop at least 20 percent from its peak before it's considered a bear market.

beneficiary: The person to whom you want to leave your assets (or in the case of life insurance or a pension plan, benefits) in the event of your death. You denote beneficiaries for each of your registered retirement plans.

blue-chip stock: The stock of the largest and most consistently profitable corporations. This term comes from poker, where the most valuable chips are blue. This list is unofficial and changes.

bond: A loan that investors make to a corporation or government. Bonds generally pay a set amount of interest on a regular basis. They're an appropriate investment vehicle for conservative investors who don't feel comfortable with the risk involved in investing in stocks and who want to receive a steady income. All bonds have a maturity date when the bond issuer must pay back the bond at *par* (full) value to the bondholders (lenders). Bonds should not be your primary long-term investment vehicle, because they produce little real growth on your original investment after inflation is factored in.

bond rating: *See* Standard & Poor's (S&P) ratings *and* Moody's ratings.

bond yield: A yield is quoted as an annual percentage rate of return that a bond will produce based on its current value if it makes its promised interest payments. How much a bond will yield to an investor depends on three important factors: the stated interest rate paid by the bond, changes in the creditworthiness of the bond's issuer, and the maturity date of the bond. The better the rating a bond receives, the less risk involved and, thus, the lower the yield. As far as the maturity date is concerned, the longer you loan your money, the higher the risk (because it's more likely that rates will fluctuate) and the higher your yield generally will be.

broker: A person who acts as an intermediary for the purchase or sale of investments. When you buy a house, insurance, or stock, you're most likely to do so through a broker. Most brokers are paid on commission, which creates a conflict of interest with their clients: The more the broker sells, the more he makes. Some insurance companies let you buy their policies directly, and many mutual-fund families bypass stockbrokers. If you're going to work with a broker, a discount broker can help you save on commissions.

bull market: A period (such as most of the 1990s and mid-2000s) when the stock market moves higher, usually accompanied and driven by a growing economy and increasing corporate profits.

callable bond: A bond for which the lender can decide to pay the holder earlier than the previously agreed-upon final maturity date. If interest rates are relatively high when a bond is issued, lenders may prefer to issue callable bonds because they have the flexibility to call back these bonds and issue new, lower-interest-rate bonds if interest rates decline. Callable bonds are risky for investors, because if interest rates decrease, the bondholder will get his investment money returned early and may have to reinvest his money at a lower interest rate.

Canada Disability Savings Grant (CDSG): A government grant earned by contributing money to a Registered Disability Savings Plan (RDSP).

capital gain: The profit from selling your stock at a higher price than the price for which it was purchased. For example, if you buy 50 shares of Rocky and Bullwinkle stock at $20 per share and two years later you sell your shares when the price rises to $25 per share, your profit or capital gain is $5 per share, or $250. If you hold this stock outside of a tax-sheltered retirement plan, you'll owe capital-gains tax on this profit when you sell the stock.

capital-gains distribution: Distribution by a mutual fund or real-estate investment trust (REIT) created by securities that are sold within the fund or REIT at a profit.

cash-value insurance: A type of life insurance that's extremely popular with insurance salespeople because it commands a high commission. In a cash-value policy, you buy life-insurance coverage but also get a savings-type account. Unless you're looking for ways to limit your taxable estate (if you're extremely wealthy, for example), avoid cash-value insurance. The investment returns tend to be mediocre, and your contributions aren't tax-deductible.

CD: *See* certificate of deposit (CD).

CDSG: *See* Canada Disability Savings Grant.

certificate of deposit (CD): A specific-term loan that you make to your banker. The maturity date for CDs ranges from a month up to several years. The interest paid on CDs is fully taxable, making CDs inappropriate for higher-tax-bracket investors investing outside tax-sheltered retirement plans.

closed-end mutual fund: A mutual fund for which the exact number of shares that are going to be issued to investors is decided upfront. After all the shares are sold, an investor seeking to invest in a closed-end fund can only do so by purchasing shares from an existing investor. Shares of closed-end funds trade on the major stock exchanges and, therefore, sell at either a discount (if the sellers exceed the buyers) or a premium (if demand exceeds supply).

CMA: *See* comparable market analysis (CMA).

commercial paper: A short-term debt or IOU issued by larger, stable companies to help make their businesses grow and prosper. Creditworthy companies can sell this debt security directly to large investors and, thus, bypass borrowing money from bankers. Money-market funds invest in soon-to-mature commercial paper.

commission: The percentage of the selling price of a house, stock, bond, or other investment that's paid to agents and brokers. Because most agents and brokers are paid by commission, understanding how the commission can influence their behaviour and recommendations is important for investors and home buyers. Agents and brokers make money only when you make a purchase, and they make more money when you make a bigger purchase. Choose an agent carefully and take your agent's advice with a grain of salt, because this conflict of interest can often set an agent's visions and goals at odds with your own.

commodity: A raw material (gold, wheat, sugar, or gasoline, for example) traded on the futures market.

common stock: Shares in a company that don't offer a guaranteed amount of dividend to investors; the amount of dividend distributions, if any, is at the discretion of company management. Although investors in common stock may or may not make money through dividends, they hope that the stock price will appreciate as the company expands its operations and increases its profits. Common stock tends to offer you a better return (profit) than other investments, such as bonds or preferred stock. However, if the company falters, you may lose some or all your original investment.

comparable market analysis (CMA): A written analysis of similar houses currently being offered for sale and those that have recently sold. Real-estate agents usually complete CMAs.

consumer debt: Debt on consumer items that depreciate in value over time. Credit-card balances and auto loans are examples of consumer debt. This type of debt is bad for your financial health because it carries a high interest rate and encourages you to live beyond your means.

Consumer Price Index (CPI): The Consumer Price Index reports price changes, on a monthly basis, in the cost of living for such items as food, housing, transportation, healthcare, entertainment, clothing, and other miscellaneous expenses. The CPI is used to adjust government benefits and is used by many employers to determine cost-of-living increases in wages and pensions. An increase in prices is also known as *inflation.*

CPI: *See* Consumer Price Index (CPI).

credit report: A report that details your credit history. It's the main report that a lender uses to determine whether to give you a loan. You may obtain free copies of your credit reports annually.

DCA: *See* dollar cost averaging (DCA).

debit card: Although they may look like credit cards, debit cards are different in one important way: When you use a debit card, the amount of the purchase is deducted from your bank account, all but immediately. Thus, a debit card gives you the convenience of a credit card without the danger of building up a mountain of consumer debt.

deductible: With insurance, the deductible is the amount you pay when you file a claim. For example, say that your car sustains $800 of damage. If your deductible is $500, the insurance covers $300, and you pay $500 out of your own pocket for the repairs. The higher the deductible, the lower your insurance premiums and the less paperwork you expose yourself to when filing claims (because small losses that are less than the deductible don't require filing a claim). Choose the highest deductible that you can afford when selecting insurance.

deduction: An expense you may subtract from your income to lower your taxable income. Examples include childcare expenses, business losses, and most registered retirement plan contributions.

derivative: An investment instrument whose value is derived from other securities. For example, the value of an option to buy Disney stock is derived from the price of Disney's stock.

disability insurance: Disability insurance replaces a portion of your employment income in the unlikely event that you suffer a disability that keeps you from working.

discount broker: Unlike a full-service broker, a discount broker generally offers no investment advice and has employees who work on salary rather than on commission. In addition to trading individual securities, most discount brokerage firms also offer no-load (commission-free) mutual-fund-trading networks.

diversification: If you put all your money into one type of investment, you're potentially setting yourself up for a big shock. If that investment collapses, so does your investment world. By spreading (diversifying) your money among different investments — bonds, Canadian stocks, international stocks, real estate, and so on — you ensure yourself a better chance of investing success and fewer sleepless nights.

dividend: The dividend is the income paid to investors holding an investment. With stock, the dividend is a portion of a company's profits paid to its shareholders. For example, if a company has an annual dividend of $2 per share and you own 100 shares, your total dividend is $200. Usually, established and slower-growing companies pay dividends, while smaller and faster-growing companies reinvest their profits for growth. For assets held outside registered retirement plans, dividends are taxed at a lower rate than interest and, depending on your tax bracket, capital gains.

DJIA: *See* Dow Jones Industrial Average (DJIA).

dollar cost averaging (DCA): The process of regularly investing money. You can do it with a lump sum of money you may have awaiting investment or through regular payroll earnings.

Dow Jones Industrial Average (DJIA): A widely followed stock market index composed of 30 large, actively traded U.S. company stocks. Senior editors at *The Wall Street Journal* select the stocks in the DJIA.

down payment: The part of the purchase price for a house that the buyer pays in cash upfront and does not finance with a mortgage. The larger the down payment, the smaller the mortgage amount and often the lower the interest rate. You can usually get access to the best mortgage programs with a down payment of at least 25 percent of the home's purchase price.

earthquake insurance: Although the West Coast is often associated with earthquakes, other areas are also quake prone. An earthquake insurance rider (which usually comes with a deductible of 5 percent to 15 percent of the cost to rebuild the home) on a homeowner's policy pays to repair or rebuild your home if it's damaged in an earthquake. If you live in an area with earthquake risk, consider earthquake insurance coverage.

Emerging Markets Index: The Emerging Markets Index, which is published by Morgan Stanley, tracks stock markets in developing countries. The main reason for investing in emerging markets is that these economies typically experience a higher rate of economic growth than developed markets. However, the potential for higher returns is coupled with greater risk.

equity: In the real-estate world, this term refers to the difference between the market value of your home and what you owe on it. For example, if your home is worth $400,000, and you have an outstanding mortgage of $150,000, your equity is $250,000. *Equity* is also a synonym for *stock.*

estate: The value, at the time of your death, of your assets minus your loans and liabilities.

estate planning: The process of deciding where and how your assets will be transferred when you die and structuring your assets during your lifetime so as to minimize taxes due upon your death.

exchange-traded fund (ETF): These funds are similar to mutual funds, except that they trade on a major stock exchange and thus can be bought and sold throughout the trading day.

ETF: *See* exchange-traded fund (ETF).

financial advisors: *See* financial planners.

financial assets: A property or investment (such as investment real estate or a stock, mutual fund, or bond) that is held primarily as an investment to generate a positive return over time.

financial liabilities: Your outstanding loans and debts. To determine your net worth, subtract your financial liabilities from your financial assets.

financial planners: A sometimes-motley crew that professes an ability to direct your financial future. Financial planners come with varying backgrounds and degrees — Master of Business Administration (MBA), Chartered Professional Accountant (CPA), and so on. A useful way to distinguish among this mixed bag of nuts is to determine whether the planners are paid by commission, a flat fee, or by the hour. *Also known as* financial advisors.

fixed-rate mortgage: The granddaddy of all mortgages. You lock into an interest rate (for example, 5 percent), and it never changes during the life (term) of your mortgage. Your mortgage payment and interest rate will be the same amount each and every month. If you become a cursing, frothing maniac when you miss your morning coffee or someone is five minutes late, then this mortgage may be for you!

flood insurance: If there's a remote chance that your area may flood, having flood insurance, which reimburses rebuilding your home and replacing its contents in the event of a flood, is wise.

full-service broker: A broker who gives advice and charges a high commission relative to discount brokers. Because the brokers work on commission, they have a significant conflict of interest: namely, to advocate strategies that will benefit them financially.

futures: An obligation to buy or sell a commodity or security on a specific day for a preset price. When used by most individual investors, futures represent a short-term gamble on the short-term direction of the price of a commodity. Companies and farmers use futures contracts to hedge their risks of changing prices.

GIC: *See* guaranteed investment certificate (GIC).

guaranteed investment certificate (GIC): Offered by most financial institutions, a GIC is an investment that appeals to skittish investors. A GIC generally tells you in advance what your interest rate will be for the term of the GIC, which generally can range from one to ten years. Thus, you don't have to worry about fluctuations and losses in your investment value. On the other hand, GICs offer you little upside, because the interest rate is comparable to what you may get on a high-interest savings account.

home equity: *See* equity.

home-equity loan: Technical jargon for what used to be called a *second mortgage*. With this type of loan, you borrow against the equity in your house. If used wisely, a home-equity loan can help pay off high-interest consumer debt or be tapped for other short-term needs (such as a remodelling project). In contrast with consumer debt, mortgage debt usually has a much lower interest rate.

homeowner's insurance: Dwelling coverage that covers the cost of rebuilding your house in the event of fire or other calamity. The liability-insurance portion of this policy protects you against lawsuits associated with your property. Another essential element of homeowner's insurance is the personal property coverage, which pays to replace your damaged or stolen worldly possessions.

index: A security market index, such as the S&P/TSX or Standard & Poor's 500 Index, is a statistical composite that tracks the price level and performance of a basket of many securities, typically within a specific investment asset class. Indexes exist for various stock and bond markets and are typically set at a round number, such as 100, at a particular point in time. *See also* S&P/TSX Composite Index, Dow Jones Industrial Average (DJIA), *and* Russell 2000.

inflation: The technical term for a general rise in prices in the economy. Inflation usually occurs when too much money is in circulation and not enough goods and services are available to spend it on. As a result of this excess money, prices rise. A link is present between inflation and interest rates: If interest rates don't keep up with inflation, no one will invest in bonds issued by the government or corporations. When the interest rates on bonds are high, it usually reflects a high rate of expected inflation that will eat away at your return.

initial public offering (IPO): The first time a company offers stock to the investing public. An IPO typically occurs when a company wants to expand more rapidly and seeks additional money to support its growth. A number of studies have demonstrated that buying into IPOs in which the general public can participate produces subpar investment returns. A high level of IPO activity may indicate a cresting stock market, as companies and their investment bankers rush to cash in on a "pricey" marketplace. (IPO can stand for *it's probably overpriced.*)

interest rate: The rate lenders charge you to use their money. The higher the interest rate, the higher the risk entailed in the loan. With bonds of a given maturity, a higher rate of interest means a lower quality of bond — one that's less likely to return your money.

international stock markets: Stock markets outside of Canada account for the great majority of the world stock market capitalization (value). Some specific stock indices (such as the MSCI EAFE Index and the Emerging Markets Index) track international markets. International investing offers one way for you to diversify your portfolio and reduce your risk. In addition to the United States, some of the foreign countries with major stock exchanges include Britain, France, Germany, and Japan.

IPO: *See* initial public offering (IPO).

junk bond: A bond rated B (Moody's) or BB (Standard & Poor's) or lower. Historically, these bonds have had a 1 percent to 2 percent chance of default, which is not exactly "junky." Of course, the higher risk is accompanied by a higher interest rate.

leverage: Financial leverage affords its users a disproportionate amount of financial power relative to the amount of their own cash invested. In some circumstances, you can borrow up to 50 percent of a stock price and use all funds (both yours and those that you borrow) to make a purchase. You repay this so-called *margin loan* when you sell the stock. If the stock price rises, you make money on what you invested plus what you borrowed. Although this money sounds attractive, remember that leverage cuts both ways — when prices decline, you lose money not only on your investment but also on the money you borrowed.

limited partnership (LP): A private partnership, which is designed to limit the legal liability of the investors who participate, is often promoted in a way that promises high returns, but it generally limits one thing: your investment return. Why? Because it's burdened with high commissions and management fees. Another problem is that it's typically not liquid for many years.

load mutual fund: A mutual fund that includes a *sales load,* which is the commission paid to brokers who sell commission-based mutual funds. The commission can range up to 6 percent. This commission is deducted from your investment money, so it reduces your returns.

LP: *See* limited partnership (LP).

marginal tax rate: The rate of income tax you pay on the last dollars you earn over the course of a year. Why the complicated distinction? Because not all income is treated equally: You pay less tax on your first dollars of your annual earnings and more tax on the last dollars of your annual income. Knowing your marginal tax rate is helpful because it can help you analyze the tax implications of important personal financial decisions.

market capitalization: The value of all the outstanding stock of a company. Market capitalization is the quoted price per share of a stock multiplied by the number of shares outstanding. Thus, if Rocky and Bullwinkle Corporation has 100 million shares of outstanding stock and the quoted price per share is $20, the company has a market capitalization of $2 billion (100 million × $20).

Moody's ratings: Moody's rating service measures and rates the credit (default) risks of various bonds. Moody's investigates the financial condition of a bond issuer. Its ratings use the following grading system, which is expressed from highest to lowest: Aaa, Aa, A, Baa, Ba, B, Caa, Ca, and C. Higher ratings imply a lower risk but also mean that the interest rate will be lower. *See also* Standard & Poor's (S&P) ratings.

mortgage broker: Mortgage brokers shop for mortgages wholesale from lenders and then mark up the mortgages (typically from 0.5 percent to 1 percent) and sell them to borrowers. A good mortgage broker is most helpful for people who don't want to shop around on their own for a mortgage or people who have blemishes on their credit reports.

mortgage life insurance: Mortgage life insurance guarantees that the lender will receive its money in the event that you meet an untimely demise. Many people may try to convince you that you need this insurance to protect your dependents and loved ones. Mortgage life insurance is relatively expensive given the cost of the coverage provided. If you need life insurance, buy low-cost, high-quality term life insurance instead.

MSCI EAFE Index: The MSCI EAFE Index tracks the performance of the more established countries' stock markets in Europe and Asia. (*EAFE* stands for *Europe, Australia, Far East.*) This index is important for international-minded investors who want to follow the performance of overseas stock investments.

mutual fund: A portfolio of stocks, bonds, or other securities that is owned by numerous investors and managed by an investment company. *See also* no-load mutual fund.

NASDAQ system: *See* National Association of Securities Dealers Automated Quotation (NASDAQ) system.

National Association of Securities Dealers Automated Quotation (NASDAQ) system: An electronic network that allows brokers to trade from their offices all over the country. With NASDAQ, brokers buy and sell shares using constantly updated prices that appear on their computer screens.

NAVPS: *See* net asset value per share (NAVPS).

negative amortization: Negative amortization occurs when your outstanding mortgage balance increases despite the fact that you're making the required monthly payments. Negative amortization occurs with adjustable-rate mortgages that cap the increase in your monthly payment but do not cap the interest rate. Therefore, your monthly payments don't cover all the interest that you actually owe. Avoid loans with this "feature."

net asset value per share (NAVPS): The dollar value of one share of a mutual fund. For a no-load fund, the market price is its NAVPS. For a load fund, the NAVPS is the "buy" price minus the commission.

New York Stock Exchange (NYSE): The largest stock exchange in the world in terms of total volume and value of shares traded. It lists companies that tend to be among the oldest, largest, and best known.

no-load mutual fund: A mutual fund that doesn't come with a commission payment attached to it. Some funds claim to be no-load but simply hide their sales commissions as an ongoing sales charge; you can avoid these funds by educating yourself and reading the prospectuses carefully.

NYSE: *See* New York Stock Exchange (NYSE).

open-end mutual fund: A mutual fund that issues as many shares as investors demand. These open-end funds do not generally limit the number of investors or amount of money in the fund. Some open-end funds have been known to close to new investors, but investors with existing shares can often still buy more shares from the company.

option: The right to buy or sell a specific security (such as a stock) for a preset price during a specified period of time. Options differ from futures in that with an option, you pay a premium fee upfront and you can either exercise the option or let it expire. If the option expires worthless, you lose 100 percent of your original investment. The use of options is best left to companies as hedging tools. Investment managers may use options to reduce the risk in their investment portfolio. As with futures, when most individual investors buy an option, they're doing so as a short-term gamble, not as an investment.

P/E ratio: *See* price/earnings (P/E) ratio.

pension: A benefit offered by some employers. Assuming they're defined-benefit plans, they generally pay you a monthly retirement income based on your years of service and former pay with the employer. In contrast, a defined-contribution plan pays a monthly retirement income based on how much money you (and often your employer) contrib-uted to the plan, and how well the investments in which the money was invested did over the years. *Also known as* Registered Pension Plans (RPPs).

performance: You traditionally judge an investment's performance by looking at the historic rate of return. The longer the period over which these numbers are tallied, the more useful they are. Considered alone, these numbers are practically meaningless. You must also note how well a fund has performed in comparison to competitors with the same investment objectives. Beware of advertisements that tout the high returns of a mutual fund, because they may not be looking at risk-adjusted performance, or they may be promoting performance over a short time period. Keep in mind that high-return statistics are usually coupled with high risk and that this year's star may turn out to be next year's crashing meteor.

preferred stock: Preferred stock dividends must be paid before any dividends are paid to the common-stock shareholders. Although preferred stock reduces your risk as an investor (because of the more secure dividend and greater likelihood of getting your money back if the company fails), it also often limits your reward if the company expands and increases its profits.

price/earnings (P/E) ratio: The current price of a stock divided by the current (or sometimes the projected) earnings per share of the issuing company. This ratio is a widely used stock analysis statistic that helps an investor get an idea of how cheap or expensive a stock price is. In general, a relatively high P/E ratio indicates that investors feel that the company's earnings are likely to grow quickly.

prime rate: The rate of interest that major banks charge their most creditworthy corporate customers. Why should you care? Well, because the interest rates on various loans you may be interested in are often based on the prime rate. And, guess what — you pay a higher interest rate than those big corporations!

principal: No, we're not talking about the big boss from elementary school who struck fear into the hearts of most 8-year-olds. The principal is the amount you borrow for a loan. If you borrow $100,000, your principal is $100,000. Principal can also refer to the amount you originally placed in an investment.

prospectus: Individual companies and mutual funds are required by securities regulators to issue a prospectus. For a company, the prospectus is a legal document presenting a detailed analysis of that company's financial history, its products and services, its management's background and experience, and the risks of investing in the company. A mutual-fund prospectus tells you about the fund's investment objectives, costs, risk, and performance history.

RDSP: *See* Registered Disability Savings Plan (RDSP).

real estate investment trust (REIT): Real estate investment trusts are like a mutual fund of real estate investments. Such trusts invest in a collection of properties (from shopping centers to apartment buildings). REITs trade on the major stock exchanges. If you want to invest in real estate while avoiding the hassles inherent in owning property, REITs may be the right choice for you.

refinance: Refinance, or refi, is a fancy word for taking out a new mortgage loan (usually at a lower interest rate) to pay off an existing mortgage (generally at a higher interest rate). Refinancing is not automatic, nor is it guaranteed. Refinancing can also be a hassle and expensive. Weigh the costs and benefits of refinancing carefully before proceeding.

Registered Disability Savings Plan (RDSP): A special savings plan for individuals with disabilities. In order to be the beneficiary of an RDSP, the individual must be eligible for the disability tax credit by having a severe and prolonged impairment. Anyone can make contributions to the plan, but they are not tax-deductible. Contributions may earn a grant called the Canada Disability Savings Grant, which is deposited into the plan. Withdrawals are taxed as income of the beneficiary of the plan.

Registered Education Savings Plan (RESP): A special account in which you can save money to pay for a postsecondary education. The money you put in does not earn you a tax deduction. The money inside the plan, however, can grow tax-free. The profits are taxed when the money is withdrawn to pay for education costs, but it's taxed as income to the student. Because students' overall income is likely to be very low, they'll generally have to pay little if any tax on the proceeds.

Registered Retirement Income Fund (RRIF): A type of retirement savings account that allows your investments to grow tax-free. Unlike a Registered Retirement Savings Plan, you cannot make annual contributions to an RRIF. Instead, you're required to withdraw at least a certain minimum amount each year, which is taxed as regular income.

Registered Retirement Savings Plan (RRSP): A type of retirement savings plan available to almost everybody who has earned some money either through a job or by being self-employed. Your contributions are usually exempt (yes!) from federal and provincial income taxes and compound without taxation over time. The money, however, is taxed as income when you withdraw it from the plan.

REIT: *See* real estate investment trust (REIT).

RESP: *See* Registered Education Savings Plan (RESP).

return on investment: The percentage of profit you make on an investment. If you put $1,000 into an investment, and then one year later it's worth $1,100, you've made a profit of $100. Your return on investment is the profit ($100) divided by the initial investment ($1,000) — in this case, 10 percent.

reverse mortgage: A reverse mortgage enables elderly homeowners, typically those who are low on cash, to tap into their homes' equity without selling their homes or moving out of them. Specifically, a lending institution makes a cheque out to you each month, and you can use the money as you want. This money is really a loan against the value of your home, so it's tax-free when you receive it. The downside of these loans is that they deplete your equity in your estate, the fees and interest rates tend to be on the high side, and some require repayment within a certain number of years.

RRIF: *See* Registered Retirement Income Fund (RRIF).

RRSP: *See* Registered Retirement Savings Plan (RRSP).

Russell 2000: An index that tracks the returns of 2,000 small-company U.S. stocks. Small-company stocks tend to be more volatile than large-company stocks. If you invest in U.S. small-company stocks or stock funds, this index is an appropriate benchmark to compare your stock's performance to.

S&P/TSX Composite Index: This index measures the broad performance of the Toronto Stock Exchange. If you invest in larger-company Canadian stock or stock funds, this is a good benchmark to compare the performance of your investments to.

S&P/TSX Venture Composite Index: This index measures the broad performance of the TSX Venture Exchange, where the shares of many smaller and emerging Canadian companies trade.

SEC: *See* Securities and Exchange Commission (SEC).

Securities and Exchange Commission (SEC): The U.S. federal agency that administers U.S. securities laws and regulates and monitors investment companies, brokers, and financial advisors.

Standard & Poor's 500 Index: An index that measures the performance of 500 large-company U.S. stocks that account for about 80 percent of the total market value of all stocks traded in the United States. If you invest in larger-company stocks or stock funds, the S&P 500 Index is an appropriate benchmark to compare the performance of your investments to.

Standard & Poor's (S&P) ratings: Standard & Poor's rating service is one of two services that measure and rate the risks in buying a bond. The S&P ratings use the following grading system, listed from highest to lowest: AAA, AA, A, BBB, BB, B, CCC, CC, and C. *See also* Moody's ratings.

stock: Shares of ownership in a company. When a company goes public, it issues shares of stock to the public in an initial public offering. Many, but not all, stocks pay dividends — a distribution of a portion of the company's profits. In addition to dividends, you make money investing in stock via appreciation in the price of the stock, which normally results from growth in revenues and corporate profits. You can invest in stock by purchasing individual shares or by investing in a stock mutual fund that offers a diversified package of stocks.

stripped (strip) bond: A bond that doesn't pay explicit interest during the term of the loan. Such bonds are purchased at a discounted price relative to the principal value paid at maturity. The interest-bearing coupons have been removed or stripped off. Thus, the interest is implicit in the discount.

Tax-Free Savings Account (TFSA): A special type of savings account that allows cash and investments held inside the account to grow tax-free. Contributions to these accounts are not tax-deductible (unlike contributions to a Registered Retirement Savings Plan, which are tax-deductible). Money can be withdrawn from a TFSA at any time. No tax is payable on withdrawals, regardless of whether principal or gains earned inside the account are withdrawn.

T-bills: *See* Treasury bills (T-bills).

term life insurance: If people are dependent on your income for their living expenses, you may need this insurance. Term life insurance functions simply: You determine how much protection you would like and then pay an annual premium based on that amount. Premium rates vary by age, health, and whether you smoke. Although much less touted by insurance salespeople than cash-value insurance, it's the best life insurance out there for the vast majority of people.

TFSA: *See* Tax-Free Savings Account (TFSA).

Treasury bills (T-bills): IOUs from the federal government that mature within a year.

underwriting: The process an insurance company uses to evaluate a person's likelihood of filing a claim on a particular type of insurance policy. If significant problems are discovered, an insurer will often propose much higher rates or refuse to sell the insurance coverage.

will: A legal document that ensures that your wishes regarding your assets and the care of your minor children are heeded when you die.

zero-coupon bond: A bond that doesn't pay explicit interest during the term of the loan. Zero-coupon bonds are purchased at a discounted price relative to the principal value paid at maturity. Thus, the interest is implicit in the discount. These bonds do not offer a tax break, because the investor must pay taxes on the implicit interest that is paid when the bond matures.

Index

About the Authors

Eric Tyson: Eric first became interested in money more than three decades ago. After his father was laid off during a recession and received some retirement money from his employer, Eric worked with his dad to make investing decisions with the money. A couple of years later, Eric won his high school's science fair with a project on what influences the stock market. Dr. Martin Zweig, who provided some guidance, awarded Eric a one-year subscription to the *Zweig Forecast*, a famous investment newsletter. Of course, Eric's mom and dad share some credit with Martin for Eric's victory.

After toiling away for a number of years as a management consultant to Fortune 500 financial-service firms, Eric finally figured out how to pursue his dream. He took his inside knowledge of the banking, investment, and insurance industries and committed himself to making personal financial management accessible to all.

Today, Eric is an internationally acclaimed and best-selling personal finance book author, syndicated columnist, and speaker. He has worked with and taught people from all financial situations, so he knows the financial concerns and questions of real folks just like you. Despite being handicapped by an MBA from the Stanford Graduate School of Business and a BS in Economics and Biology from Yale University, Eric remains a master of "keeping it simple."

An accomplished personal finance writer, his "Investor's Guide" syndicated column, distributed by King Features, is read by millions nationally, and he is an award-winning columnist. He is the author of five national best-selling financial books in the *For Dummies* series, on personal finance, investing, mutual funds, home buying (coauthor), and small business (coauthor). A prior edition of this book was awarded the Benjamin Franklin Award for best business book of the year.

Eric's work has been featured and quoted in hundreds of local and national publications, including *Newsweek, The Wall Street Journal,* the *Los Angeles Times,* the *Chicago Tribune, Forbes, Kiplinger's Personal Finance* magazine, *Parenting, Money, Family Money,* and *Bottom Line/Personal;* on NBC's *Today Show,* ABC, CNBC, Fox News, PBS *Nightly Business Report,* CNN; and on CBS national radio, NPR's *Sound Money,* Bloomberg Business Radio, and Business Radio Network.

Eric's website is www.erictyson.com.

Tony Martin: Tony Martin has always had an innate understanding of money. Instead of getting his (tiny) allowance paid out to him weekly in shiny coins like his brothers did, he asked him mom to keep track of how much he was owed.

After emerging from Queen's University business school with a B. Comm — despite a transcript that listed courses such as "Electronic Music" and "The Philosophy of Religion," Tony set off to see the world. On his return, he joined CBC radio, and ever since he has been helping people understand the world of money.

Noticing there was an absence of sound, easy-to-read financial guides for Canadians that were also easy to implement, Tony approached the publishers of the *For Dummies* series with the idea of writing a Canadian-centric version of *Personal Finance For Dummies*. And thus, the first non-U.S. *For Dummies* title was born, with Tony becoming the first Canadian — and first ever non-American period — *For Dummies* author. In addition to coauthoring the national Canadian best-seller *Personal Finance For Canadians For Dummies*, Tony and Eric also worked together to write the best-selling *Investing For Canadians For Dummies*.

For over a decade, Tony's widely read column "Me and My Money" appeared in the *Globe and Mail*'s weekend personal finance section. He was also the investing columnist for *Report on Business Magazine.* His work has been featured in many leading publications, including MoneySense, IE Money, *Profit, Reader's Digest,* and *Canadian Business.* Tony is a frequent commentator and speaker on personal finance and investing and regularly appears on television and radio, including BNN CBC Radio, CBC Television, BCC, and TVOntario.

Tony has been instrumental in the design and development of many leading online resources, including an interactive investor-training program using simulated stock-market transactions. He also was editorial head for i|money.com, Canada's first financial website, which later became the content for Canoe.ca. He has worked extensively as a communications consultant, editorial advisor, and educator. His clients include Bank of America, Barrick, BMO, Business Development Bank of Canada, Fidelity, Geico, IBM, Integra, Manulife, The Principal Group, Scotiabank, Sun Life Financial, TD Bank, and VISA Canada.

Tony is also an accomplished and engaging teacher, lecturer, and management trainer. He leads courses across the country on finance and accounting, as well as speaking and presenting, business writing, writing for the web, public speaking and presenting, negotiating, and conflict resolution for national management training leaders, as well as many major companies and organizations, including Shoppers Drug Mart, Siemens, the Ontario Government, and Ontario Power Corp.

Tony's website is www.moneygrower.ca.

Dedication

This book is hereby and irrevocably dedicated to our family and friends, as well as to our counselling clients and customers, who ultimately have taught us everything that we know about how to explain financial terms and strategies so that all of us may benefit.

Authors' Acknowledgments

Eric: Being an entrepreneur involves endless challenges, and without the support and input of my good friends and mentors Peter Mazonson, Jim Collins, and my best friend and wife, Judy, I couldn't have accomplished what I have.

I hold many people accountable for my perverse and maniacal interest in figuring out the financial services industry and money matters, but most of the blame falls on my loving parents, Charles and Paulina, who taught me most of what I know that's been of use in the real world.

I'd also like to thank Michael Bloom, Chris Dominguez, Maggie McCall, David Ish, Paul Kozak, Chris Treadway, Sally St. Lawrence, K.T. Rabin, Will Hearst III, Ray Brown, Susan Wolf, Rich Caramella, Lisa Baker, Renn Vera, Maureen Taylor, Jerry Jacob, Robert Crum, Duc Nguyen, Maria Carmicino, and all the good folks at King Features for believing in and supporting my writing and teaching.

Many thanks to all the people who provided insightful comments on this edition and previous editions of this book, especially Bill Urban, Barton Francis, Mike van den Akker, Gretchen Morgenson, Craig Litman, Gerri Detweiler, Mark White, Alan Bush, Nancy Coolidge, and Chris Jensen.

And thanks to all the wonderful people at my publisher on the front line and behind the scenes, especially Tracy Boggier and Elizabeth Kuball.

Tony: The support, good humour, and advice of many are essential to my success. There is no such thing as succeeding on one's own.

I owe special thanks to my good friend and colleague since our days writing for *The Ottawa Clarion*, Geoff Rockburn, who has been endlessly supportive and helpful over the years. I'm grateful as always to my parents, Ruth and John, for teaching me so much about what really matters.

Many people in the personal finance industry have kindly offered me their assistance in penetrating, understanding, and explaining money matters. Many thanks to everybody who has generously shared insights and expertise, including Peter Volpe, Gena Katz, Sandra McLeod, Anthony Layton, Paul Hickey, Jim Bullock, Alisa Dunbar, Alan Silverstein, and Janet Freedman. In addition, I'd like to thank Karen Benzing, David Chilton, Patricia Davies, Dorothy Engleman, Dave Pyette, Jack Fleischmann, Peggy Wente, and Richard Quinlan for their support and encouragement over the years.

Many thanks as well to all the people who have provided insightful comments on this book over the years, especially tax and financial planner extraordinaire Barton Francis and Warren Baldwin, as well as Mike van den Akker, Gretchen Morgensen, Craig Litman, Gerri Detweiler, Mark White, Alan Bush, Nancy Coolidge, and Chris Jensen. Special thanks to Becky Wong for her detailed, eagle-eyed, and helpful technical review of this book.

Publisher's Acknowledgments

Acquisitions Editor: Tracy Boggier
Project Editor: Elizabeth Kuball
Copy Editor: Elizabeth Kuball
Technical Editor: Becky Wong
Sr. Editorial Assistant: Cherie Case

Production Editor: Vasanth Koilraj
Cover Image: © shapecharge/Getty Images;
Canadian flag © alexsl/iStock.com